Thinking in Psychological Science

Thinking in Psychological Science

Ideas and Their Makers

Jaan Valsiner
editor

Transaction Publishers
New Brunswick (U.S.A.) and London (U.K.)

Copyright © 2007 by Transaction Publishers, New Brunswick, New Jersey.

All rights reserved under International and Pan-American Copyright Conventions. No part of this book may be reproduced or transmitted in any form or by any means, electronic or mechanical, including photocopy, recording, or any information storage and retrieval system, without prior permission in writing from the publisher. All inquiries should be addressed to Transaction Publishers, Rutgers—The State University, 35 Berrue Circle, Piscataway, New Jersey 08854-8042. www.transactionpub.com

This book is printed on acid-free paper that meets the American National Standard for Permanence of Paper for Printed Library Materials.

Library of Congress Catalog Number: 2006040463
ISBN: 978-07658-0348-1
Printed in the United States of America

Library of Congress Cataloging-in-Publication Data

Thinking in psychological science : ideas and their makers / editor, Jaan Valsiner.
   p. cm.
   Includes bibliographical references.
   ISBN 0-7658-0348-8 (alk. paper)
     1. Psychology—History. 2. Psychologists—Biography. I. Valsiner, Jaan.

BF81.T473 2006
150.9—dc22
                                               2006040463

Contents

List of Tables

List of Figures

Introduction—How our Future can be Observed in   xi
Our Past: Mental Bases for Scientific Inquiry
Jaan Valsiner

Part I. Roots of Cognitive Science: Karl Duncker

1. Karl Duncker and Cognitive Science   3
   Herbert A. Simon

2. Life as the Problem: Karl Duncker's Context   17
   Simone Schnall

3. Duncker's Account of Productive Thinking: 39
   Exegesis and Application of a Problem-Solving Theory
   Jeanette A. Lawrence and Agnes E. Dodds

4. Duncker's Analysis of Problem-Solving as Microdevelopment   59
   Kurt Fischer and Jeffrey Stewart

Part II. Abstractive Generalization through Language: The Legacy of Karl Bühler

5. The Pleasure of Thinking: A Glimpse into Karl Bühler's Life   69
   Jaan Valsiner

6. Remembering Karl Bühler: Discovering Unanticipated   97
   Resemblances with My Distancing–Representational Model
   Irving E. Sigel

7. Bühler's Legacy: Full Circle and Ahead   115
   Nancy Budwig

Part III. Thinking and Speaking: Development through Thinking, Acting, and Speaking

8. Arnold Gesell and the Maturation Controversy   135
   Thomas C. Dalton

9. Alexander F. Chamberlain: A Life's Work   163
   Julia Berkman

10. The Fate of the Forgotten: Chamberlain's Work Reconsidered   179
    Jaan Valsiner

Part IV. The Dynamic Whole: Gestalt Ideas and Social Practices

11. Tamara Dembo's European Years   213
    René van der Veer

12. Between Scylla and Charybdis: Tamara Dembo and Rehabilitation Psychology   235
    Simone de Lima

13. Tamara Dembo's Socio-Emotional Relationships   265
    Joseph de Rivera

Part V. Dissecting Methodology and Thinking of Development

14. The Legacy of Adolf Meyer's Comparative Approach: Worcester Rats and the Strange Birth of the Animal Model   283
    Cheryl A. Logan

15. Zing-Yang Kuo: Personal Recollections and Intimations of Developmental Science   299
    Gilbert Gottlieb

16. Kuo's Epigenetic Vision for Psychological Sciences: Dynamic Developmental Systems Theory   315
    Robert Lickliter

Index   331

List of Tables

Table 1.1: Frequency of Citation in Woodworth

Table 13.1: Socio-Emotional Relations Chosen by Students

Table 13.2: Dembo's Categorization of Socio-Emotional Relations

Table 13.3: Interrelations of Socio-Emotional Relationships

List of Figures

Introduction Figure 1: Freud in his current presence on Clark University Campus
Figure 1.1: European and American Influences on Early Cognitive Simulation by Carnegie-Rand Group
Figure 2.1: *"Psychologische Forschung*: Populäre Sondernummer"
Figure 4.1: Duncker's Analysis of a Case of Problem-solving
Figure 4.2: Phases in Microdevelopment of Solving a Problem
Figure 5.1: The Organon Model
Figure 7.1: Three Dimensions of Communicative Practice. (Hanks, 1996a, p. 230)
Figure 8.1: G. Stanley Hall. Photo courtesy of Clark University Archives, Special Collections, Goddard Library, Worcester, Massachusetts.
Figure 8.2: Arnold Gesell in the 1930s. Photo courtesy of Yale University, Harvey Cushing/John Hay Whitney Medical Library.
Figure 8.3: George E. Coghill in the 1930s. Photo courtesy of Dr. Robert Williamson.
Figure 8.4: Myrtle McGraw assisting Johnny Woods on a step slide, when he was twenty-two months old in 1932. Photo courtesy of Mitzi Wertheim.
Figure 8.5: Gesell's Spiral Organization of Reciprocally Woven Behavior: Prehension. Adapted from (Gesell, 1945, p. 174).
Figure 8.6: McGraw's Neurobehavioral Theory of Development and Consciousness.
Figure 10.1: Drawing of a Kootenay "medicine man" (pure case) (from Chamberlain, 1901d, p. 97).
Figure 10.2: Drawing of a Kootenay "medicine man" (interference from Christian traditions) (from Chamberlain, 1901d, p. 97).
Figure 10.3: Kootenay picture of a war dance (from Chamberlain, 1901c, p. 253)
Figure 11.1: The Topology of the Experimental Situation (after Dembo, 1931b).

Figure 11.2:	Spacious Maze Allowing for Free Behavior (after Dembo, 1930).
Figure 11.3:	Bird Cage for the Study of Food Searching (after Dembo, 1929).
Figure 15.1:	Kuo hosted a dinner at the Peking Restaurant in Washington, DC, in August, 1963.
Figure 15.2:	Kuo as an academic in China in his younger years.
Figure 15.3:	To make an observation window in the side of the egg, it is necessary to make a puncture in the shell over the air space.
Figure 15.4:	To make a Kuo observation window, one cuts away the shell and outer shell membrane over the air space of the egg.
Figure 15.5:	Two types of embryonic observation windows.
Figure 15.6:	Kuo in Hong Kong in the late 1960s.

Introduction
How Our Future can be Observed in Our Past: Mental Bases for Scientific Inquiry

Jaan Valsiner

This book is about the future of something we have nicely labeled "the cognitive science." Labels are often confusing—and so this one. As the movements within the cognitive science reveal over the past few decades, the reliance on new technologies is not automatically giving us a head start on new ideas. Thus, the legacy of Vladimir Bekhterev's associative reflexes is transparent in our contemporary neural network modeling attempts, and much of contemporary problem solving themata were anticipated by Otto Selz and Karl Duncker (Simon, chapter 1 in this book).

Yet scientists usually dump their own history, considering it to be a graveyard of failures. Of course in terms of the *post factum* successes in a given area they may be right—if 99 percent of suggested solutions turn out to be wrong, the glory of the remaining one would be seriously undermined to show that scientific breakthroughs are outlayers in the normal distribution of efforts within the normal science. The demonstration of the actual slow and inefficient movement in ideas is far from the need of creating a hero image of the scientists for the lay public. Such hero images are undoubtedly on demand for granting research funding in democratically controlled governmental funding agencies. Hence the revelation of the failures of the past ideas may be detrimental for the future.

However, aside from the granting of money and prestige to new generations of scientists, the reality of science operates on the transformation of basic ideas. Some of such transitions are very slow—it took chemistry around two centuries to move from alchemy to science. Psychology—since the nineteenth century—may be seen to be undergoing a similar transformation—without a clear image of the end point in mind. In the process of such creative search for new solutions, a look back into the history of the given discipline can provide two kinds of guidelines for the future. First, it can show the futility of some directions of thought that were tried out in the past and failed to provide productive solutions. However, these failures may have been caused by circumstances external to science—the lack of resources, or illness or demise of the scientists right before they were about to arrive at a solution. Thus, secondly, a scrutiny of history allows us to find the potentially productive—yet dismissed or unfinished—directions of our thought. For example, a careful scrutiny of the thinking that went into the construction of introspection experiments in the "Würzburg School" could have relieved our contemporary cognitive science from unproductive discussions about "the method."

History of sciences as I conceive it here is thus useful for the future of these sciences. Hence the creation of the From Past to Future project in 1998. At my arrival at Clark I decided it is a place where a careful re-look at psychology's history can be appropriate. The American Psychological Association was founded at Clark in 1892, and the whole University lives under the totemic symbol of the 1909 visit to Clark by Sigmund Freud. The latter's contribution is presented locally as a revolutionary challenge to conformity—rather than the basis for an alternative conforming community (see figure 1). Thus, the tensions present in psychology at large have had their local counterparts within that tiny private university in New England. Psychology has had its "ups" and "downs" at Clark since 1889, with the times of G. Stanley Hall and Heinz Werner clearly marking the unique productive periods

The From Past to Future project was initially born as a small-scale "technical reports" series that brought together a small set of historically oriented scholars who enjoyed contributing to the series. However, their contributions remained inaccessible to the wider world—the series was known only to few enthusiasts. Yet our work was productive—over seven years (1998-2005) we published ten issues on a number of topics. Its aim was

> ... to chart out a new role for the study of psychology's history for contemporary and potential future research in the discipline. Many of the empirical research problems in contemporary psychology could benefit from a fresh look at how similar issues were approached in the past of the discipline. Therefore, we seek to analyze different ideas from the past through the prism of their potential usefulness for the future.

Psychology, similarly to many other disciplines, has been trying to forget its history. Or, when history is unavoidable, it has been rewritten so as to glorify the heroes of the past and overlook their tedious fight with themselves, their peers, their surrounding society, and—last but not least—for mere physical survival during hard economic times. The heroes of our past are usually depicted as able problem-solvers who rarely moved in unproductive directions in their thinking, but if they did, corrected themselves immediately. If that were true, then psychology should have solved its major problems a long time ago, thanks to all of our heroes. Yet this is obviously not the case. Psychology in our time is caught in the web of conceptual confusions and phenomenological oversights that often seem to resemble some of the issues with which the major psychologists of the past attempted to wrestle. Therefore, it may be useful for contemporary psychology to trace the efforts of the past, precisely because we need that for our present efforts to solve our still unsolved basic science problems. Thus, analysis of the past can become productive for the construction of the future. Sure, taking this position amounts to creating yet another version of history of psychology.

Thanks to the initiative of Transaction Publishers (and Irving Horowitz who, after seeing some of the issues we had published, was fascinated by our intellectual efforts), the present book brings to the wider audience a selection relevant for the investigation into cognitive processes. A second book (Diriwächter and Valsiner, 2007) will also build on the results of this project. And—last but not least—From Past to Future becomes a new international annual series published by Transaction Aldine in 2007. Our local history of studying psychology's history at Clark thus becomes an international framework for such study on a wider scale.

References

Diriwächter, R. and Valsiner, J. (eds.). (2007). *Striving for the Whole: Creating Theoretical Synthesis*. New Brunswick N.J.: AldineTransaction.

Introduction Figure 1
Freud in his current presence on Clark University Campus

attempted to wrestle. Therefore, it may be useful for contemporary psychology to trace the efforts of the past, precisely because we need that for our present efforts to solve our still unsolved basic science problems. Thus, analysis of the past can become productive for the construction of the future. Sure, taking this position amounts to creating yet another version of history of psychology.

Thanks to the initiative of Transaction Publishers (and Irving Horowitz who, after seeing some of the issues we had published, was fascinated by our intellectual efforts), the present book brings to the wider audience a selection relevant for the investigation into cognitive processes. A second book (Diriwächter and Valsiner, 2007) will also build on the results of this project. And—last but not least—From Past to Future becomes a new international annual series published by Transaction Aldine in 2007. Our local history of studying psychology's history at Clark thus becomes an international framework for such study on a wider scale.

References

Diriwächter, R. and Valsiner, J. (eds.). (2007). *Striving for the Whole: Creating Theoretical Synthesis*. New Brunswick N.J.: AldineTransaction.

Introduction Figure 1
Freud in his current presence on Clark University Campus

Part I

Roots of Cognitive Science: Karl Duncker

1

Karl Duncker and Cognitive Science

Herbert A. Simon[1]

This is a paper about Karl Duncker and his significance for American psychology. But, as Newton and others have pointed out, you can't talk long about scientists' discoveries without mentioning those on whose shoulders they stood, or those who stood on their shoulders. Nor need the shoulders belong to giants, for as there is a whole succession of shoulders, any desired altitude can be reached by conjoining persons of normal height. So I shall discuss Duncker as standing on shoulders of predecessors who extend back to the beginnings of modern psychology in Germany, and offering shoulders that connect these origins with the present—actually only four or five generations in all. Moreover, the story concerns the transmission as well as discovery of knowledge, and is complicated at many points by multiple independent inventions of the same ideas.

Accordingly, at least three different topics arise in assessing the significance of Karl Duncker's research on problem solving. The first topic is the direct influence of Duncker's publications upon the various strands of research that formed the "cognitive revolution." The second is the specific relation of Duncker's theory of problem solving to the information processing theories produced by the revolution. The third is the relation between the ideas that originated with Duncker and the ideas that were transmitted by Duncker but originated with other German psychologists, especially those of Leipzig, Munich, Berlin, Würzburg and Mannheim, during the first four decades of the twentieth century. The three inquiries lead to different, complementary pictures of Duncker's impact.

I will say something about each of these topics, not from the standpoint of someone who has made a professional study of the whole history, although I have examined most of the source materials, but from the standpoint of a researcher who participated in the cognitive revolution and has had occasion to think and write about it and its origins (Newell and Simon, 1972-, Historical Addendum, pp. 873-889; Simon, 1981). After a prelude describing how the events appeared to our own research group, it will be convenient to continue with the second question about Duncker posed above, then take up the first, and finally address the third. In dealing with the second question, I will draw upon a paper by Allen Newell (1981) that used Duncker as a prototype of German research on problem solving during the first half of the twentieth century.

Prelude: A View of the Cognitive Revolution from Pittsburgh

The cognitive revolution[2] that took place in American psychology beginning in the 1950s, gradually reconstituting and replacing the then-dominant behaviorism with an information-processing formulation, has sometimes also been referred to as a counter-revolution, for it rebuilt ties to European psychology, notably to Gestalt psychology and Denkpsychologie, that had been greatly weakened during the behaviorist era. Whether revolution or counter-revolution, it is of considerable interest to see how psychology on the two continents became reconnected.

The new psychology involved not only conceptual innovations but new or rejuvenated methodologies as well. One wholly novel component in the information processing approach to cognition was to model human behavior by computer simulation. Only a minority of those constructing the new psychology used computer models, but they were central to the work at Carnegie Mellon. A rejuvenated method was to use verbal think-aloud protocols of subjects as data, to test the validity of the theories incorporated in the computer programs. Both of these procedures were viewed by behaviorists with great suspicion and skepticism.[3] Verbal protocols were usually considered a throwback to turn-of-the-century introspection, which had been almost wholly rejected as a valid source of empirical data. The computer programs were at first only admitted as "metaphors," rather than, as claimed by their proponents, theories in the form of systems of difference equations.

Both protocols and computer models of psychological processes occurring inside the brain were widely regarded as inadmissible manifestations of "mentalism." Even Edward Tolman, almost the sole American psychologist of that time whose views were close to those of *Denkpsychologie* (whether by direct influence or independent invention I cannot say), strove very hard to cast his writing in behaviorist terms. He evidently thought that this concession was a precondition to his remaining in conversation with his peers and thereby having his work taken seriously.

Experimentation also had an increasingly strict discipline, especially with the introduction of the new statistical hypothesis testing theories before World War II. Within this discipline, the purpose of experimentation was to verify or reject theories by testing whether the data could not be equally well explained by a "null hypothesis." There was little understanding of how theories could be generated in the first place, or of the role of observation and experimentation in theory generation. No concept of exploratory experimentation was abroad; such experiments were dismissed as "counting the bricks in a wall."

When Allen Newell, Cliff Shaw, and I began research using computer simulation, around 1954, none of us had done graduate study in psychology, or had psychologists as mentors or as a principal reference group. Therefore, we did not need the courage that genuine psychologists would have had to muster (and that psychologists like George A. Miller and Carl Hovland did soon muster) to experiment with the new methods. The papers that grew out of our first efforts—the Logic Theorist (LT), the NSS chess program, the General Problem Solver—and the laboratory experiments associated with them, were all published in computer science journals, that had their own newly formed conceptions and standards of what constituted publishable research. These standards, mainly influenced by the physical sciences and mathematics, differed substantially from those prevalent in experimental psychology and were easier than the latter to reconcile with the new practices. In particular, they did not limit experiment to hypothesis testing, with "controls" and "null hypotheses," and were thoroughly comfortable with exploratory research.

When the time arrived, however, to publish in psychological journals, we had to be concerned with the legitimacy of our methods in the eyes of psychologists. For the initial plunge we choose *Psychological Review*, believing that a theoretical journal encompassing social as well as experimental psychology would be least bound by behaviorist scruples. I also knew the editor, Ted Newcomb, well. He was a sociologist as well as a social psychologist of distinction, and I was aware that he had a broad tolerance for diversity. Our first psychological paper, "Elements of a Theory of Human Problem Solving," was mostly devoted to describing the Logic Theorist program and its implications for human problem solving, but we devoted several pages to what we titled "Comparisons with Other Theories."

With respect to "associationism," we declared our adherence to the associationist belief that "the highest mental functions can be performed by mechanisms" but proposed "a theory of the information processes involved in problem solving and not a theory of neural . . . mechanisms for information processing." We suggested that the computer provided psychology "with a much profounder idea than we have hitherto had of the characteristics a mechanism must possess if it is to carry out complex information processing tasks."

Next we turned to "Gestalt" theories, saying, "The theory we have presented resembles the associationist theories largely in its acceptance of the premise of mechanism, and in few other respects. It resembles much more closely some of the Gestalt theories of problem solving and perhaps most closely the theories of 'directed thinking' of Otto Selz and Adriaan de Groot."[4] We then proceeded to enumerate and discuss seven specific respects in which the Logic Theorist could be mapped onto the problem solving theory of Selz, focusing on the relation between LT's processes and Selz's "schematic anticipation."

It cannot be said that either behaviorists or Gestaltists embraced the new theory or its methodology with enthusiasm, and several decades passed before it became a major current in the psychology of thinking and problem solving. To reach that status, behaviorists had to become reconciled with the use of theoretical terms that referred to events within the head (goals, strategies, discrimination nets, and so on) and to the "subjectivism" of verbal protocols and the frequent absence of the null hypothesis, while Gestaltists had to become reconciled with the idea of assembling Gestalts and thought processes from components realizable by mechanism. It would be an exaggeration to say that the reconciliation with either view is complete today, but information processing psychology has acquired a large following, to the point where it is the mainstream, at least in the domain of cognition and much of perception.

Meanwhile, publication remained a problem, which we solved through the decade of the 1960s mainly by publishing in computer journals (at least eight major papers), the annual Spring Symposium that we initiated at Carnegie Mellon University (four papers), *Psychological Review*, which continued its tolerance (three papers), *Verbal Learning and Verbal Behavior* (two papers), *Journal of Math Psychology* (one paper), *British Journal of Psychology* (one paper), and invited papers for symposium volumes (at least fifteen papers). Invitations to symposia of psychologists began to arrive about 1962. The publication problem was further eased by the creation of *Cognitive Psychology* in 1969 and *Cognitive Science* in 1977, which, at least to some extent, were open to papers containing computer models and verbal protocols. Notice that none of the standard American experimental journals appear on this list. Nevertheless one cannot argue that the work went unnoticed, and by 1970, it was beginning to appear in the textbooks.

Duncker's Theory and Information Processing Psychology

Allen Newell (1981), in a paper prepared for the American Psychological Association's celebration of the centennial of the establishment of Wundt's laboratory in Leipzig, and using Duncker as a prototype of German research on problem solving before World War II, compared the central ideas of Duncker's monograph, *On Problem Solving*, with the new information processing ideas and methods that were introduced by the cognitive revolution. He summarized what he found in the following paragraph:

> Duncker interpreted everything through Gestalt spectacles. To first order what he says is familiar: task demands, functions, blind solving, understanding, insight. Yet, as an acute observer of the actual problem solving behavior of his subjects, in his understanding of process he moved beyond anything to be found in the other Gestaltists.[5] He understood much that we now see in modern information processing terms: the structure of general heuristic methods, means-ends analysis, search. He was even reaching for how to characterize the underlying processing structure—the architecture.

Newell also describes what is missing from Duncker and the other European psychologists, and had to be supplied by the cognitive revolution. These missing pieces include: 1) the demonstration of a process theory that was sufficient to account for successful problem solving; 2) the need for an underlying symbol system to carry out the processes; 3) a precise notion of how means-ends analysis works, by the use of operators to reduce differences between current situation and goal; and 4) recognition that selective (heuristic) search is at the core of all problem solving and is not to be equated with blind trial and error.

Newell then goes on to examine Duncker's notion of insight, concluding that "[it] was for [Duncker] a special computational device where, having encoded the knowledge, the computation could be made by recognition"—a view of insight that sounds entirely modern.

For the analysis that led Newell to these conclusions, I refer the reader to his article. With respect to Duncker's influence on American psychology, a point I will discuss more generally in a moment, Newell argues, and I think correctly, that the ideas just described had relatively little impact: that Duncker's main influence in this country was to focus a great deal of attention and experimental energy on a specific issue, the phenomena of functional fixity as a source of problem difficulty.

My own view is that, in finding many of the ideas of information processing psychology clearly embedded in Duncker's theories, Allen Newell was writing a slightly Whiggish history. It is reasonably easy, given the hindsight of operational computer simulations of human thought processes, including means-ends analysis, verbal learning, recognition, understanding and reorganization, and at least one form of intuition, to interpret the much less precise and process-oriented Gestalt language as embodying these concepts. It was much less easy before the appearance of computers, lacking the actual simulations and therefore working in the forward direction, to generate the modern concepts *de novo* from the Gestalt language that was used to describe the experimental findings.

In reaching this conclusion, I do not rely only on my own distant memories of how foggy and undefined the Gestalt and *Denkpsychologie* theories, with their "concretization" and "reorganization," appeared to me before we undertook our computer simulations. In Humphrey (1951), we have someone thoroughly sympathetic with the Würzburg and Gestalt theories but unfamiliar with modern information processing formulations. Yet in his final assessment of Selz's theory, he concludes:

> Selz's diagrams [of a schematically anticipated complex] really do no more than state the problem. They do not give any basis for understanding the psychology of its solution. . . . As an analysis, in general terms, of the form assumed by the process of thought at a certain stage, it is valuable. As a schema showing the working of particular acts of thought, it is as valueless as was the general statement of the problem of medicine—*given the disease, problem, to find the remedy*— . . . in showing the manner by which a particular disease is healed (Humphrey, 1951, p. 144).

In a similar vein, Humphrey says of the Gestalt theory of thinking, in which he includes Duncker's theory:

> At the present time, the Gestalt theory of thinking constitutes a program rather than a fulfillment. Nevertheless, the program is sufficiently suggestive, sufficiently developed, and, in part at least, insufficiently clear outline to merit somewhat detailed consideration (Humphrey, 1951, p. 150).

Among the major problems Humphrey regards as "left unanswered" are the distinction between productive and reproductive thought, and the fact that certain problems seem clearly to be motivated "from without" rather than "from the dynamics of the perceived-situation." He observes further that "the Gestalt theory of thinking has developed over a period of years . . . the contributors to the theory have stressed different things both in their theoretical statements and in their experiments. The accounts have not yet hardened into a coherent doctrine" (pp. 182-183.).

So, without having already available a set of mechanisms and a language for describing them with some precision, it was not at all easy, even for a sympathetic analyst, to extract a viable theory of problem solving from Selz's account, or from Duncker's, however informative and suggestive their experimental findings. This asymmetry between interpretation by hindsight (Newell) and by foresight (Humphrey) is familiar to every historian of ideas.

The Routes of Transmission

German psychology was by no means unknown to American psychologists prior to World War II. Indeed many of the most prominent "first-generation" American psychologists had studied in Germany—especially, during the early years of the century, with Wundt at Leipzig—and several of the Germans, notably Duncker himself, had made shorter or longer visits to the United States even before Nazism forced many of them to immigrate. In fact, Duncker earned his Master's degree at Clark University in 1925, and, after further study in Berlin leading to a doctorate under Köhler, returned to the United States about 1938, where he taught at Colgate during the last two years of his life.

We can obtain some information on these matters by looking at frequency of mention of some prominent psychologists in the first edition of Woodworth's Experimental Psychology, published in 1938. Table 1.1 includes most of the German psychologists frequently cited by Woodworth, and, for calibration, some among the important American psychologists who were more or less contemporary with them. The German psychologists who played a major role in establishing modern psychology and many of its key experimental paradigms in sensory, perceptual (including form perception), motor, and learning psychology dominate the list. Müller, Wundt, Fechner, Weber, Helmholtz and Titchener, along with one Gestaltist, Köhler, a Russian, Pavlov, and two Americans, Thorn-

Table 1.1
Frequency of Citation in Woodworth

Müller	30	Helmholtz	20	James	9
Wundt	29	Titchener	20	Duncker†	8
Köhler†	27	Wertheimer†	14	Gibson	8
Fechner	26	Hull	13	Külpe ‡	7
Thorndike	24	Lashley	13	Selz‡	7
Pavlov	22	Koffka†	12	Ach‡	5
Woodworth	21	Bühler	10	Katona†	4
Weber	21	Brunswick†	9	Maier†	4

This is a partial list of German (and some American) psychologists cited by Woodworth in his Experimental Psychology, 1938. The numbers following the names are the total numbers of citations.
†Gestaltists ("Berliners")
‡Members of the Würzberg School

dike and Woodworth, constitute the top ten. Four more Gestaltists, Wertheimer, Koffka, Brunswik, and Duncker, are included in the next ten, along with the Würzburger Külpe. Selz (whom we can associate with the Würzburg school), Ach, also a Würzburger, and Katona and Maier, younger Gestaltists who both migrated to the University of Michigan, follow.

It is evident from the table, and confirmed by Woodworth's text, that the German psychology that lay within the mainline experimental tradition (whatever its exact theoretical orientation) was well-known in America and was part of the standard corpus. But while the psychologists who are associated with Gestalt theory and Würzburg ideas are cited by Woodworth, they are not, except for Köhler, cited with anything like the frequency of the pioneers in sensory, perceptual or motor psychology. Moreover, nearly half of the citations to Köhler are for work on sensory and perceptual phenomena not directly related to form perception or thinking.

All the citations of Duncker, Selz, and Külpe, and a majority of those of Ach occur in Woodworth's chapters on problem solving and thinking (only eighty pages in an 800 page book)[6], and all the citations of Wertheimer occur either in those two chapters or the one on form perception. Throughout, more emphasis is placed upon the experimental phenomena, then upon the associated theories. Some attention is paid to intuition, directed association, set and "constellation theory," but much more to Köhler's experiments with apes, Thorndike's with cats, and other problem solving experiments with humans. Woodworth discusses briefly, and not unsympathetically, the use of thinking aloud as a source of data, and contrasts it with introspection.

One might say that Woodworth was extracting from this research its empirical content and was not principally concerned with drawing out the theoretical implications of the experiments for behaviorism, "thought psychology," or his own functionalism. His emphasis is not inappropriate for a textbook titled "Experimental Psychology," but students who depended on Woodworth or similar books for their knowledge of theory would have only an exceedingly sketchy picture of the conceptual frameworks within which Ach, or Selz, or Wertheimer, or Duncker were working, or the hypotheses they were seeking to test. However, we must also recall that Köhler's Mentality of Apes had appeared in English translation in 1924 his Gestalt Psychology in 1929, and Koffka's Principles of Gestalt Psychology in 1935, prior to the time we are considering, so that Americans had excellent access to Gestalt theory if not to the problem solving theories of Duncker or Selz.[7]

The main problem was not access but the difficulty of providing an interpretation of the Gestalt and *Denkpsychologie* findings and concepts that would be consistent with the dominant behaviorism. With rare exceptions, mostly in developmental and social psychology and in form perception, the European theoretical ideas about thinking and problem solving, were largely ignored prior to World War II as unintelligible within the behaviorist framework and as violating its rules for both method and theory. What was not ignored were some of the experimental paradigms, particularly those concerned with "complex" behaviors, of which the "insight" problems of Maier, whose publications on these topics (in English) began about 1930, and Dunker's famous x-ray experiment are examples.

With the arrival in America of European refugees from Nazism, and with the beginnings of new interpretations and translations of European psychology just after World War II, new connections began to form. For example, the three principal Gestaltists, Koffka, Wertheimer and Köhler, assumed academic positions in American universities in 1928, 1933, and 1934, respectively, and Duncker spent time here in the middle-1920s. Figure 1.1 displays, in highly simplified form, some major routes of communication for problem solving research and theories before and after the war. A number of critically important European sources are shown above the horizontal line and two important potential bridges to our own (Newell-Shaw-Simon) work, Woodworth (1938), and Humphrey (1951), just below the line. Wertheimer's *Productive Thinking* (1945) is represented by a direct path across the ocean; as is de Groot's, *Het Denken van den Schaker*, (1946; English translation, 1965). Paths emanating from the names of Polya and Tolman and from a range of topics outside psychology represent major American in-fluences on our work that are not traceable to the German sources mentioned.

In his paper on Duncker, Allen Newell states that he first became acquainted with *On Problem Solving* shortly after we completed our work on the Logic Theorist and published our early papers on information processing psychology.

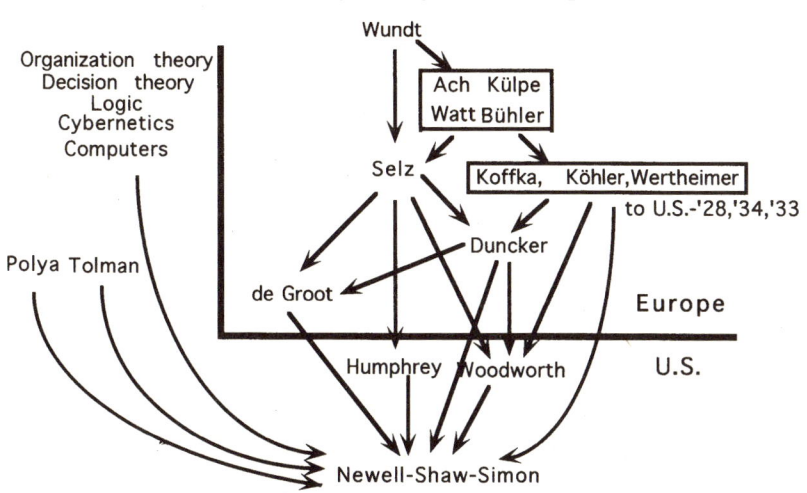

Figure 1.1
European and American Influences on Early Cognitive Simulation by Carnegie-Rand Group

```
                           Wundt
  Organization theory        │
  Decision theory         ┌──┴──────────┐
       Logic              │ Ach   Külpe │
    Cybernetics           │ Watt Bühler │
    Computers             └──┬───┬──────┘
                             ↓   ↓
                        Selz ←──┌────────────────────────┐
                             ╲  │ Koffka, Köhler,Wertheimer│
                              ╲ └────────────────────────┘
                               ╲         │  to U.S.-'28,'34,'33
                                ↓ Duncker│
  Polya Tolman                  │   │    │
            ╲            de Groot←──┤    │
             ╲                      │    │      Europe
              ╲                     ↓    ↓   ─────────
               ╲            Humphrey  Woodworth    U.S.
                ╲                  │    │
                 ╲                 ↓    ↓
                  ╲→ Newell-Shaw-Simon
```

My own recollections of my first encounter with Duncker are less clear than Allen's, but our two dates could not be far apart, for we were working very closely together, and whoever found it first would have immediately called it to the attention of the other. As I am rather compulsive about referencing relevant papers, even if first encountered when I am revising a paper for final publication, I find confirmation of his recollection in the fact that Duncker is not cited in two papers on decision and problem-solving processes that I published in 1955 and 1956, respectively. The second of these papers, however, has the following footnote on p. 21:

> Since writing [the 1955 paper], I have found confirmation for a number of its hypotheses in the interesting and significant study by A. de Groot (1946), of the thought processes of chess players.

This footnote indicates that *Denkpsychologie's* influence on us came from de Groot (and indirectly Selz) rather than Duncker, and that its main importance was in providing us with supporting evidence for our approach to cognition, based on heuristic search and simulation, which was already formulated by 1954. Hence we were now able to read and interpret Selz and Duncker with hindsight and without requiring foresight. I received de Groot's book and began reading it (in Dutch) in August 1954. It may be that it was acquaintance with the book that led us to acquire Duncker's monograph, but I have no evidence on that point.

So as far as the evidence goes, then, it does not appear that Duncker's work directly influenced the initial formulation of information processing psychology or the implementation of the first computer programs, the Logic Theory Machine and the General Problem Solver that embodied the theories. In the historical appendix to *Human Problem Solving* (published sixteen years later), our description of the actual influences has mostly to do with: 1) the psychology of William James and E. C. Tolman, 2) the ideas of Polya about the role of heuristics in mathematical problem solving, 3) developments in logic, 4) the congeries of "cybernetic" ideas emanating from the recently invented digital computer, information theory, and feedback control theory, and 5) decision making theories in economics and statistics.

On the other hand, de Groot's book, which we first encountered in 1954, guided us into the extensive use of think-aloud protocols; and de Groot, in his book, credits Duncker with developing the think-aloud methodology well beyond the state in which the Würzburgers left it, and relies largely on Duncker's monograph for his discussion of protocols. De Groot, however, derives his substantive theoretical framework directly from Selz, and only makes occasional reference to Duncker on substantive points.

But much was going on during this period in other groups than ours. A number of experimental psychologists who were now moving into the domain of human problem solving came into contact with such immigrant Gestalt theorists as Wertheimer, and Katona, and with Maier, so that Duncker's work was only one communication channel among many. These Americans were encouraged by the writings of the whole group of Gestaltists to experiment on such phenomena as insight, functional fixity, and set, and to employ methods in their experiments that challenged behaviorist restrictions on what counted as data. They were much less influenced by the structuralist ideas of Selz, whether transmitted through de Groot, Humphrey, or Duncker.

Thus, comparing Newell's analysis of Duncker's theories, with this account of their impact in the United States, we come to the conclusion that although Duncker had, prior to the cognitive revolution, come a considerable way along its path toward a process theory of problem solving, his writings played only a limited role in bringing the revolution about. Here priority and influence must be distinguished.

Duncker and Selz

There remains one important chapter of the story. It is clear that de Groot's book on the thought processes of chess players did play an important role in the new developments in our group (and among other American psychologists after the translation became available in 1965), although mainly on the side of empirical methods for testing the new theories than upon the substance of the computer simulations themselves. Is this another route along which Duncker exerted substantial influence? De Groot is quite explicit in attributing the foundations of his theory of chess playing to Otto Selz. What, then, is the relation between Selz's theory of problem solving and that of Duncker?

Otto Selz is a tragic figure who died at Auschwitz in the Autumn of 1943, aged sixty-one. He received a Ph.D. in philosophy in Munich, then went to Bonn for his Habilitation and to work with Külpe. He was much influenced, also, by the theories of Bühler (1907/1908), Watt (1905), and Ach (1905), hence was a thorough "Würzburger," although he spent the main part of his career, a decade, in Mannheim. He published his major work, *On the Laws of Ordered Thinking*, in two parts, in 1913 and 1922, the interruption being caused by his military service in World War I.

Selz was a lonely person who never married and had only a few serious students, notably Julius Bahle and Adriaan de Groot (neither of whom were actually his doctoral students, but both of whom were strongly influenced by him). Having been removed from his professorship in Mannheim by the Nazis in 1933, he became even more isolated from the world than before.

Shortly after its publication, Selz read Duncker's *Zur Psychologie des Produktiven Denkens*, and wrote on April 4, 1935, to Bahle:

> You must read Duncker's book on the psychology of productive thinking. His terms are often confessedly translations of mine. He sticks close to me even when he claims to diverge. So apparently my whole Work, parts of it somewhat watered down, is now taken over by the Berliners. On the whole, he has behaved fairly, but did not send the book to me.

This has the familiar ring of "he stole my ideas," and this was not the first time that Selz had shown sensitivity on that score (a trait that does not distinguish him from many, perhaps most, other scientists). It is likely that his sensitivity had been acerbated by his having been declared a non-person by the Nazi government; his last defense against oblivion was being taken from him. But there is more to the matter than that. Selz acknowledges that Duncker behaved fairly, and generally he had: He acknowledged his debt to Selz in nine references, more than were given to any other psychologist except Köhler, and many of them accompanied by substantial discussions. This even required a measure of courage on Duncker's part in 1935, for references to Jewish scientists were not encouraged by the authorities, if not yet quite banned by law.

The crucial additional fact is that Duncker touched a spot in Selz that was already sore.[8] In 1925, in the *Manual of Philosophy*, Koffka had written a hundred-page article on psychology that was so biased from a Gestaltist's viewpoint that he was strongly reproved for having borrowed Selz's ideas without citing him. Bühler, in a review of Koffka's article, uses strong language: "How can Koffka venture, in his manual, to describe the whole theory as a product of 'Gestaltpsychology,' without mentioning the name of Selz except to criticize him on insignificant points?" Two years later, Koffka replied with the claim that there was no need to cite Selz, as the Berlin "structure theory" and the Würzburg "process theory" were completely different! With this exchange still in recent memory, Selz had good reason to be sensitive to the intellectual imperialism of the "Berliners."

By Duncker's own account in *Zur Psychologie des Produktiven Denkens*, his theory was based squarely on Selz's, although developed further in several respects and supported by substantial new evidence gathered by means of innovative experimental designs and methods. Without insisting on an either-or decision, we have to regard the contributions of de Groot and Duncker, apart from the empirical evidence they provided (an important qualification), as primarily acts of transmission rather than innovation in theory. Their contributions do not thereby become any less significant or original. In contemporary views of science we are all too prone to idolize theory and describe empirical contributions as "mere fact-finding," or at best, simply confirming (or refuting) what the theorist has wrought. That is a bad reading of the history of science, where important theories have as often emerged from imaginative (or even lucky) experiments that revealed new phenomena, as have "crucial" experiments from theory.

The central advance that Selz made in our understanding of problem solving involved the concept of "schematic anticipation," which he diagrammed with the relational structure, aR?b, where a is a given concept, ?b a desired concept and R a relation (*Aufgabe*). Given a and R, the problem is to produce an appropriate b: e.g., given "cat" and "coordinate," to produce "dog" or "tiger." In its simplest form, this is simply the "directed association" of Watt and Ach. What Selz does is to show how problems in general may be solved by replacing an initial schematic anticipation with successive new ones, derived from a and R, that approach closer and closer to the desired b. What a logician might say (exercising a little of the hindsight that I complained about earlier in Newell's account of Duncker) is that Selz had rediscovered the great power of simple two-argument relational structures and their applicability to problem solving. What a computer specialist might say is that he had anticipated the "description lists" or "property lists" of list processing languages. What an information processing psychologist might say is that he had found the underlying structure of means-ends analysis and thereby of heuristic search. This is the basic structure that Duncker learned from Selz and applied in his own important research.

So we come to the end of our examination of Duncker's work on problem solving, with findings much more complex than a simple enumeration of "innovations" and "influences." Duncker was an excellent and innovative experimentalist; he understood Selz's theory and its basic importance, and he extended it in its application to the processes of problem solving. He was an important channel of communication of the European ideas of problem solving to the American psychologists who were questioning behaviorism. The early instigators of the cognitive revolution came to understand clearly how Duncker's experiments and concepts fit their theories; they would have found it much harder to generate the theories from his formulation of them.

We have seen Karl Duncker standing on shoulders, and we have seen others standing on his shoulders. At each level as we ascend the pyramid, both our factual knowledge and our understanding become richer. Nor is there just a single pyramid, but rather many parallel paths, and a considerable redundancy of rediscovery and reinvention. It would be a pity if it were otherwise, if everything were neatness and efficiency. For then far fewer of us would have the opportunity to enjoy the adventure of lives in science, the opportunity to contribute to the building of its fantastic structure.

Notes

1. Previously published in: *From Past to Future, Vol. 1*(2), *The Drama of Karl Duncker*, pp. 1–11. ©1999 Frances L. Hiatt School of Psychology, Clark University. Author: Herbert A. Simon, late of Department of Psychology, Carnegie Mellon University, Pittsburgh, PA.
2. I will use this term throughout as a convenient and conventional label for the changes in American cognitive psychology that began in the two decades following World War II. The revolution is sometimes dated from the Dartmouth Conference of 1956, sometimes from the publication of Neisser's textbook, titled *Cognitive Psychology* (1967). I adopt the earlier date as corresponding more closely with the critical initial events.
3. However, J.B. Watson himself accepted thinking aloud as a legitimate source of data, contrasting it with introspection. "The present writer has often felt that a good deal more can be learned about the psychology of thinking by making subjects think aloud about definite problems than by trusting to the unscientific method of introspection" (Watson, 1919, p. 91).
4. Notice that we refer to Selz as a "Gestalt" theorist, indicating how broadly that term was then used by American psychologists to embrace virtually all German non-behaviorist psychological theory, including the Gestalt psychology (in the narrower sense) of Berlin, the Denkpsychologie of Würzburg and its offshoots, and a number of other schools. Selz himself drew a clear distinction between his own theories and those of the Gestaltists, whom he referred to as "the Berliners." The Würzburgers, by and large, were reductionists who sought explanations in the form of mechanisms and thought of themselves as biologists; the Berliners were much more holistic in their outlook and often anti-mechanistic in their language.
5. Here, we must interpret "Gestaltists" in its narrower historical sense: essentially the group around Koffka, Köhler, and Wertheimer, for, as we shall see, this assertion surely does not apply to Selz.
6. Woodworth begins his Chapter 29 (wryly?) with the statement: "Two chapters will not be too many for the large topic of thinking . . . "
7. Köhler's books were on the reading list for my single psychology course at the University of Chicago in 1935, but I cannot reconstruct now how much of their content I assimilated.
8. I take this account from Seebohm (1970, pp. 271-272). The translation of the quotation from Bühler, like the earlier one of Selz's letter to Bahme, is mine.

References

Ach, N. (1905). *Über die Willenstätigkeit und das Denken*. Göttingen.
Bühler, K. (1907/1908). Tatsachen und problemen zu einer psychologie der denkvorgänge. *Archiv für die Gesamte Psychologie, 9*:297-365; 12:1-122.

De Groot, A. (1946). *Het Dencken van den Schaker*. Amsterdam: Noord-Hollandsche Uitgevers Maatschappij.
De Groot, A. (1965). *Thought and choice in chess*. The Hague: Mouton
Duncker, K. (1935). *Zur Psychologie des productiven Denkens*. Berlin: Springer.
Duncker, K. (1945). On problem solving. *Psychological Monographs* 58 (Whole No. 270). Washington, DC: American Psychological Association.
Frijda, N. H. and de Groot A. (Eds.) (1981). *Otto Selz: His contribution to psychology*. The Hague: Mouton Publisher.
Humphrey, G. (1951). *Thinking*. London: Methuen.
Katona, G. (1940). *Organizing and memorizing*. New York, NY: Columbia University Press.
Maier, N.R.F. (1930). Reasoning in humans I: On direction. *Journal of Comparative Psychology 10*:15-143.
Maier, N.R.F. (1931). Reasoning in humans II: The solution of a problem and its appearance in consciousness. *Journal of Comparative Psychology, 12*:181-194
Newell, A. (1981). Duncker on thinking: An inquiry into progress in cognition. In S. Koch and D. Leary (Eds.) *A Century of Psychology as Science: Retospections and Assessments*. New York, NY: McGraw-Hill.
Newell, A., Shaw, J.C. and Simon, H.A. (1958). Elements of a theory of human problem solving. *Psychological Review 65*:151-166.
Newell, A. and Simon, H.A. (1972). *Human Problem Solving*. Englewood Cliffs, NJ: Prentice-Hall.
Seebohm, H.-B. (1970). *Otto Selz: Ein Beitrag zur Geschichte der Psychologie*. Inauguraldissertation, Universität Heidelberg. Mannheim: Published by the author.
Selz, O. (1913). *Über der Gesetze des geordneten Denkverlaufs* Erster Teil: *Eine experimentelle Untersuchung*. Stuttgart: Speman.
Selz, O. (1922). *Über der Gesetze des geordneten Denkverlaufs* Zweiter Teil: *Zur Psychologie des productiven Denkens und des Irrtums*. Bonn: Cohen.
Simon, H.A. (1955). A behavioral theory of rational choice. *Quarterly Journal of Economics 69*: 99-118.
Simon, H.A. (1956). Rational choice and the structure of the environment. *Psychological Review 63*:129-138.
Simon, H.A. (1981). Otto Selz and information processing psychology. In N. H. Frijda, and A. de Groot (Eds.), *Otto Selz: His contribution to psychology*. The Hague: Mouton Publisher.
Watson, J.B. (1919). *Psychology from the standpoint of a behaviorist*. Philadelphia, PA: Lippincott.
Watt, H.J. (1905). Experimentelle Beiträge zu einer Theorie des Denkens. *Archiv für die Gesamte Psychologie, 4*:289-436.
Wertheimer, M. (1945). *Productive Thinking*. New York, NY: Harpers
Woodworth, R.S. (1938). *Experimental Psychology*. New York, NY: Henry Holt.

2

Life as the Problem: Karl Duncker's Context

Simone Schnall[1]

Among the people who left their mark on cognitive psychology, Karl Duncker's intellectual legacy is certainly outstanding (Newell, 1985; Zimmer, 1989). Some of the tasks on problem solving that he designed as part of his M.A. thesis when he was a twenty-three-year-old graduate student at Clark University in 1926 are still discussed now—more than seventy years later—in basic psychology textbooks. Most students of introductory psychology are probably quite familiar with the "candle problem," or the "radiation problem," but probably most of them (and most of us) only know very little about the background of the extraordinarily promising scholar, Karl Duncker, whose life took such a tragic course and ended in suicide when he was only thirty-seven years old. In this paper I will focus on the context in which Karl Duncker's life and work were situated, ranging from the context of Berlin in the 1920s and 1930s, to Clark University in 1925-1926, as well as his depression and forced emigration from Germany.

Karl Duncker's Life

Karl Duncker was born on February 2, 1903, the son of Hermann and Käthe Duncker, in Leipzig. Both his parents were active Marxists, a fact that would become central to Karl Duncker's life later on. From 1923 to 1928, Duncker was a student at the Friedrich-Wilhelms-University in Berlin, where he worked with Wolfgang Köhler and Max Wertheimer, among others. When Köhler was appointed to spend a year as visiting professor at Clark University in Worcester, Massachusetts, in 1925-1926, he selected Karl Duncker to join him there and Duncker was awarded a Clark University Fellowship. Duncker received an M.A. from Clark in 1926 with his thesis on "An Experimental and Theoretical Study of Productive Thinking (Solving of Comprehensible Problems)," which was published the same year under a slightly modified title in *Pedagogical Seminary* (Duncker, 1926).

In spring 1927, Köhler selected his "best student" (Wendelborn, 1996) to temporarily replace his University Assistant Kurt Gottschaldt. Both Köhler and Wertheimer were very impressed with Duncker's exceptional abilities, as can be gathered from an undated letter of recommendation in which Wertheimer described Karl Duncker as his and Köhler's favorite student, and one of the best younger psychologists (Wertheimer, n.d., cited in King, Cox and Wertheimer, 1998). Köhler predicted a splendid university career for him (Wendelborn, 1996), and a former fellow student of his recalled that he was undoubtedly the brightest and most versatile of the students (Metzger, 1976).

After completing his dissertation on induced motion in 1929, Duncker became University Assistant in 1930, a position that he held until he was dismissed from the university for political reasons in 1935.

In 1933, the year of the "Machtergreifung" of the National Socialists, Duncker had applied to the university for his "Habilitation." In Germany, the Habilitation is a substantial thesis that is required to apply for professorship and to be allowed to teach at a university, after having completed a doctoral dissertation. Duncker's application for his habilitation thesis on problem solving [Zur Psychologie des Denkens beim Lösen von Problemen] was not accepted. A look into his personal file reveals that the reason for this decision was Duncker's communist connections, and the fact that he had been married to a Jewish woman, although, by that time, he had already gotten a divorce (Wendelborn, 1996). A re-application for his habilitation in 1935 was rejected as well, making it impossible for him to move up on the ladder of academia in Germany. Furthermore, by September 1935, his contract as an assistant was terminated.

However, during that year, building on his Master's thesis, Duncker published his seminal book *Zur Psychologie des produktiven Denkens* [Psychology of productive thinking] (Duncker, 1935a), which later would be listed among one of the "key events in one hundred years of the study of cognition" (Newell, 1985, p. 394). The same year, he published an article on learning and insight in the service of goal attainment [Lernen und Einsicht im Dienst der Zielerreichung] (Duncker, 1935b).

After being expelled from the university, Duncker left for England, and started doing work on pain with Sir Frederick Bartlett in Cambridge in 1936. Duncker's mental health had been bad, probably for at least a decade (King et al., 1998) and was deteriorating, and by 1937, Duncker was treated for endogenous depression by the psychiatrist Ludwig Binswanger in Kreutzlingen, Switzerland, where he stayed for two months (King et al., 1998). Wertheimer and Köhler, who both had academic appointments in the U.S. by that time, were very concerned about Duncker's state, and tried to find work for him. In 1938, Köhler arranged for Duncker to follow him to Swarthmore College, where he himself had been a professor from 1935 onward. Duncker spent two years as instructor at Swarthmore. While there, he published an article together with Isadore Krechevsky "On solution-achievement" (Duncker and Krechevsky, 1939), as well as a paper on taste perception (Duncker, 1939a) and a paper on ethical relativity (Duncker, 1939b). Apparently, Duncker's mental health was getting worse, and following several "nervous breakdowns," the Köhlers tried to take care of Duncker, but alas, in vain (King et al., 1998). He took his own life shortly after his thirty-seventh birthday.

The Berlin Institute

What could it have been like for somebody like Karl Duncker to be a graduate student at the Berlin Institute in the 1920s and 1930s?

In order to better understand the circumstances of his life, consider the historical and political context of the time. After the painful defeat in World War I, the first democratic German republic, the "Weimar Republic" had been proclaimed by Social Democrat Philipp Scheidemann in November of 1918. The war had left the country with high debts, an extremely high inflation, unemployment and a shortage of food and goods. Because of the dissatisfaction with the concessions made in the Versailles treaty, the government stood on shaky grounds, with upheavals from both rightist and leftist extremists threatening the young democracy. The fact that the government had changed twenty-one times by the time Hitler came into power in 1933 serves as a good indicator of how unstable the general political situation was.

Things promised to get better with the introduction a new currency in 1923, and indeed, the economic situation consolidated and the living conditions for the majority of the German population improved considerably thereafter. The "Golden Twenties" swept the country, with technical and cultural innovations, such as mass production of cars and "Rundfunk für alle" [radio for everybody]. A new form of mass entertainment was born with the rise of the film industry, and movies became popular all over the country, and especially in the city, Berlin (Kracauer, 1995). By the end of the decade, the standard of living had reached its level from before the war (Thieme, 1994).

In the mid-1920s, according to Gay (1969), Berlin was the center of cultural, technological, and scientific life not only of Germany, but of Europe.

To go to Berlin was the aspiration of the composer, the journalist, the actor: with its superb orchestras, its 120 newspapers, its forty theaters, Berlin was the place for the ambitious, the energetic, the talented (Gay, 1969, p. 83).

Among "the talented," to name only a few, were Berthold Brecht, Erich Kästner, Alfred Döblin, and Robert Musil (who had in fact received a Ph.D. from the Berlin Psychology Institute) in literature, and Max Pechstein, as well as Max Liebermann in the visual arts. The Dada movement had its first international fair in Berlin in 1920, exhibiting works by Otto Dix, Max Ernst,

George Grosz, and others (Ferrier, 1988). In addition, many distinguished scientists and Nobel price laureates lived in Berlin, and Wolfgang Köhler himself maintained friendly relationships with the physicists Max Planck and Otto Hahn (Jaeger, 1992; Ash, 1995), as did Max Wertheimer with Albert Einstein (King and Wertheimer, 1995).

Gay (1969) captures the cultural atmosphere of Germany during the time of the Weimar Republic in the following way:

> The excitement that characterized Weimar culture stemmed in part from exuberant creativity and experimentation; but much of it was anxiety, fear, a rising sense of doom. ... [I]t was a precarious glory, a dance on the edge of a volcano. Weimar culture was the creation of outsiders, propelled by history into the inside, for a short, dizzying, fragile moment (Gay, 1969, p. 12).

Stumpf's Institute

During the Weimar period, the Berlin Institute was certainly the most influential psychology institution in Germany (Ash, 1985a). Carl Stumpf (1848-1936) had been appointed as chair of psychology within the three chairs of philosophy of the Friedrich-Wilhelms-University in Berlin in 1893. He had studied philosophy with Franz Bretano (1838-1917) and with Hermann Lotze (1817-1881), and had also attended lectures in physiology with Georg Meißner (1829-1905), and physics with Wilhelm Weber (1904-1891) (Sprung and Sprung, 1995).

At the time, working in psychology with a strong background in philosophy was not only common, but in fact mandatory. Although the foundation of Wilhelm Wundt's laboratory in Leipzig in 1879 is often mentioned in the context of the emergence of psychology as an empirical, "new" science, psychology as a discipline was by no means independent from other disciplines. On the contrary, at most German universities, psychology was approached as providing an innovative methodological tool for solving the problems of one more traditional science, namely philosophy (Ash, 1985a; Geuter, 1984a).

For instance, Carl Stumpf in Berlin, as well as Wundt in Leipzig, hoped to find answers to questions of epistemology by using experimental psychological methods (Ash, 1984b). Thus, in contrast to the U.S. where independent psychology departments already existed before World War I., in Germany, psychology was more of a sub-discipline, or "Propädeutik" (Ash, 1985a) to philosophy. In fact, the competition between philosophy and psychology was considerable, and professors of philosophy feared that experimental methods would contaminate the pursuit of "pure" philosophy, or, at the least, not contribute to any new insights. The conflict between members of the two science reached its peak in 1912 in a declaration of more than two thirds of the academics in philosophy who protested against hiring any more psychologists within any of the philosophy departments (Ash, 1984b; 1985b; 1995; Geuter, 1984a). Thus, psychology as a discipline was relatively weak, and had yet to free itself from philosophy, as well as to demonstrate the value of its practical applicability within society (Ash, 1984b; 1985b).

Grounded in a life-long fascination with music (Stumpf, 1924), Stumpf's research centered around auditory perception, especially musicology (Stumpf, 1883; 1890), but he also studied emotion (Stumpf, 1928), and he approached questions of the relationship of psychology and philosophy, especially questions of epistemology (Stumpf, 1939; 1940). Carl Stumpf shared a deep, cordial friendship with William James (1842-1910) (Stumpf, 1924; Sprung and Sprung, 1996), and although they disagreed on the topic of pragmatism, their theoretical positions were certainly closer to each other than either was to Wundt's, and both saw themselves in opposition to Wundt's views, as a letter from James to Stumpf in 1887 documents:

> He aims at being a sort of Napoleon of the intellectual world. Unfortunately he will never have a Waterloo, he is a Napoleon without genius and with no central idea ... (Perry, 1935, cited in Sprung and Sprung, 96, p. 338).

Sprung and Sprung (1995) point out that in addition to his scientific contributions, Stumpf's accomplishments for psychology as a discipline were considerable: He was instrumental not only in the establishment but also the expansion of the Berlin Institute. There he compiled, together with Erich Moritz von Hornbostel (1877-1935), the Phonogram Archives that became an extensive collection of ethnic music recordings. In addition, he was among the founders of the "Anthropoiden-Station" on Teneriffe which later on would become central to the work of his student Wolfgang Köhler and would make him known throughout the world.

Thanks to Stumpf's successful negotiations, in 1920 the Psychological Institute of the Friedrich-Wilhelm University of Berlin moved into the extremely spacious former Imperial Palace right in the center of the city. In addition to more than doubling its size, the budget of the institute increased by a phenomenal 600 percent, allowing for more staff and faculty to be hired. The structure of the institute changed as it was compartmentalized into a theoretical and an applied division. All these developments made the Institute one of the best equipped psychological laboratories of the time (Ash, 1985a; 1995). As such, of course, the Berlin Institute was in constant competition with Wilhelm Wundt's laboratory in Leipzig (Ash, 1995; King and Wertheimer, 1995).

Köhler's Institute

In 1922 Köhler was appointed to follow Stumpf's footsteps as director of the Institute. Although the number of doctoral students had increased, compared to Stumpf's time, a more stringent selection process ensured that the number of students was still low enough to provide them with marvelous resources and opportunities to do their own research as well as to collaborate with more senior faculty (Ash, 1985a; 1995; Jaeger, 1992). Many of its members recall that the atmosphere at the institute was not very hierarchical or authoritarian, and students were being treated by the faculty as being of equal status, rather than being subordinate (Ash, 1995). The ratio of women was remarkably high for the standards of the time, and some of them became quite influential as to their contribution to the field of psychology, such as Tamara Dembo, Bluma Zeigarnik, and Maria Ovsiankina (see van der Veer, 1999, for a discussion of Dembo's life within the Berlin context). A large number of students and visitors from other countries, for example from the Soviet Union, Japan, and the United States, contributed to the diverse and intellectually stimulating atmosphere of the Institute (Ash, 1995; Jaeger, 1992).

Since, as Ash (1985a) notes, doing research in psychology was not a profession to make a living, but rather, was a "luxury subject," and the only degree obtainable in the rather lengthy course of years and years of study (with an average of nine years; Ash, 1985b), was the doctorate, we can assume that the students at the Berlin Institute were really driven by a passion for the pursuit of theoretical knowledge. It was the Institute that offered them the support to do so, and it certainly also offered them a sense of belonging to an elitist scientific community.

It seems that, although an intellectual one, the atmosphere at the Institute was warm and friendly, as can be concluded from the humorous "Popular Special Issue" (Populäre Sondernummer) of the *Psychologische Forschung* that was jovially put together by the Institute's members upon the return of Herrn Professor Dr. Köhler, "aus Freude über seine Wiederkehr" from Clark University in March 1926 (figure 2.1). The issue contained brief stories and vignettes that alluded to central issues of Gestalt theory. For example, in a little love story, a lover says that she had a sudden Aha!-experience, after a process of re-structuring had taken place, and thought, "Him, or nobody!" and he replies coldly that, certainly, there had been an irresistible association between the piece of cake he ate and the taste of sweetness. Disappointedly, she asks, "But can't you see the Gestalt?" whereupon he leaves the field. Another vignette describes how Alfred Adler mediates as interpreter between Wertheimer and Freud, because the two have difficulties in communicating.

A short editorial at the end alludes to the fact that apparently, the standards for submission to (the real) *Psychologische Forschung* were quite high:

> Manuscripts may not be submitted before the fifth revision. Further changes will be made by the editor upon special request of the author. Recognition of the manuscript cannot be guaranteed. However, the editor reserves the right to print the original manuscript.

Figure 2.1
"Psychologische Forschung: Populäre Sondernummer"

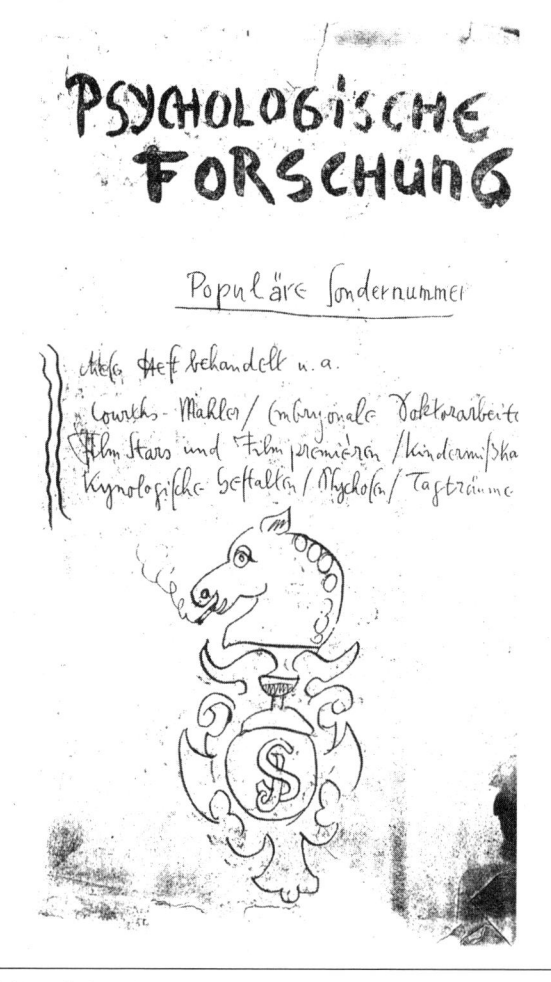

A "Popular Special Issue" of Psychological Research dedicated to Wolfgang Köhler upon his return from Clark University (1926). Translation (by I. Josephs): This issue is about—among other things —Courths-Mahler / Doctoral dissertations in embryonic form / Film stars and film premiers / Child abuse / Kynological Gestalts / Psychoses / Day dreams

Psychologische Forschung

In 1921 Max Wertheimer, Kurt Koffka, Wolfgang Köhler, Kurt Goldstein, and Hans Gruhle founded the journal *Psychologische Forschung* [Psychological Research], which became the forum for the publications of the Gestalt psychologists. For example, Duncker's dissertation on induced motion (Duncker, 1929) was published in the *Psychologische Forschung*, as well as dissertations and research report of other institute members. However, also high-quality work from researchers at other German universities, as well as foreign universities, for example, from Vienna, Prague, and the Soviet Union, was published and gave the *Psychologische Forschung* an internationally oriented character and a high profile (Ash, 1985a; van der Veer, 1999).

A New School: Gestalt Theory

In addition to paving the way for the successful development and expansion of the Institute, its first director Stumpf had also paved the way for a new school of thought: Gestalt psychology. As Sprung and Sprung (1995) point out, he can justifiably be called the "grandfather of Gestalt psychology," since many of his basic ideas were to be used and elaborated later on by his doctoral students Wertheimer, Köhler, Koffka, and Lewin.

The movement of Gestalt psychology was a reaction to the elementaristic views of psychology as proposed by Ernst Heinrich Weber (1795-1878) and Gustav Theodor Fechner (1801-1887), or Wilhelm Wundt (1832-1920) who were searching for structural components and laws of mental functioning. In addition to rejecting the associationist tradition, the Gestalt school argued strongly against behaviorism (e.g., Köhler, 1947) which was very influential at the time, especially in the U.S. For example, Duncker's writings reflect the critical attitude towards "the American psychology" (Duncker, 1927; 1932).

Sprung and Sprung (1993) summarize four main principles that guided the thinking of the Berlin school of Gestalt psychology. The central tenet, of course, was the holistic assumption based on Aristotle's well-known statement that "the whole is more than the sum of its parts." Further, the unit of analysis was the phenomenon, that is, the experience, rather than stimulus-response contingencies. In terms of methodology, the Gestalt psychologist prioritized experimental methods. Duncker's experiments on problem solving illustrate nicely how the focus of study was on how the person experienced the process of arriving at a solution. The phenomenology of the thought process was captured by instructing the person to "think aloud," that is, to verbalize all ideas related to the problem situation, thus providing insight on how "insight" occurs. Finally, another central principle of the "Berliner" was the principle of psychopysiological isomorphism, which stated that "actual consciousness resembles in each case the real structural properties of the corresponding psychophysiological process (Köhler, 1938, p. 38)."

Psychology Course Offerings 1920-1935

Jaeger (1994) demonstrated that in the period of 1920 to 1935, a main portion of the class offerings at the Berlin institute were devoted to applied psychology (28 percent), within the areas of "Psychotechnik" and "Wirtschaftspsychologie," very closely followed by courses in philosophy (25 percent), and by General Psychology (13 percent). The rest of the courses covered topics such as pedagogical psychology (9 percent), child psychology (8 percent), characterology (5 percent), thinking, (5 percent) perception (3 percent) and "will" (3 percent). In addition to lectures, the main type of courses were experimental exercises ("experimentelle Übungen," 37 percent), with an also relatively high number of supervised research ("Leitung wissenschaftlicher Arbeit," 31 percent) and colloquia (22 percent). According to Ash (1995), supervision for writing, especially on dissertation theses, was collaborative and very intense.

Only one course offered in 1925 dealt with methodology, and at that time, Duncker was probably at Clark University. Jaeger (1994) notes that a lot of the classes were taught collaboratively. Köhler taught together with Lewin, Wertheimer, or both. Of all the faculty members, Köhler had the highest number of students per semester attending his classes. Like Stumpf, Köhler tried to keep his courses to general interest, rather than lecture on topics within his specialty area. Even the term "Gestalt" occurs only in the title of one course. Lewin's classes were also very popular, probably due to the—at the time innovative—use of film material to demonstrate developmental concepts (Jaeger, 1994).

The Turning Point: 1933

Geuter (1984c) notes that before 1933, in addition to occupying a special position in the scientific landscape, the Berlin Institute had also a special position in political respects. At no other institute were as many leftist and antifascist researchers as at the Berlin Institute. For example, Lewin was a socialist, Gottschaldt was associated with the communist party, and von Lauenstein was close to the Social Democrat Party. Duncker was thought to be associated with Marxist ideology, because his father was known to be the leader of the "Marxist Arbeiterschulung," although Karl Duncker himself apparently later distanced himself from his father's ideological background (Geuter, 1984c; Wendelborn, 1996). Of all institute members, Wolfgang Köhler's political convictions would become the most problematic for the National Socialist regime.

In April of 1933, a special law, Gesetz zur Wiederherstellung des Deutschen Berufsbeamtentums [Law for the Re-establishment of the Professional Civil Service], was enforced that determined that persons who were of Jewish origin or whose past gave indications that they would not be "unconditionally supportive of the new political system" would no longer be employed by states or government. This law, of course, had serious consequences for German universities. In psychology, a third of the full professors were dismissed in 1933 because they were Jewish (Geuter, 1984b, 1984c).

Köhler, who was not Jewish himself, was one of the very few university professors who publicly spoke out against the National Socialist system in a widely read newspaper article published in the *Deutschen Allgemeinen Zeitung* on April 28, 1933, which was reprinted in the *Times* and in the *New York Times*. According to Henle (1978), Köhler's courageous act of writing the article entitled Gespräche in Deutschland [Conversations in Germany] was so politically charged, that in anticipation of being arrested the same night, Köhler and some of the institute members spent the evening playing chamber music. It is certainly an indicator of his extraordinary recognition and international reputation that nothing happened that night. However, by the end of the year, political searches of the institute and denunciations of its members Duncker, von Lauenstein, and Köhler took place, which were instigated by students of the university who stood close to the Nazi government (Ash, 1985a, Geuter, 1984c; Henle, 1978; Jaeger, 1992). When his assistant Otto von Lauenstein was dismissed in April 1934, Köhler was so infuriated by the intrusions on his autonomy as director of the institute that he threatened to resign from his position. Köhler's international reputation was probably the reason that von Lauenstein was re-instated in 1934 (Ash, 1985a), and a public statement by the Ministry of Science, Art and Public Education conceded that "Professor Köhler has the confidence of the Minister" (Henle, 1978). Even the denunciation of Duncker, whose father had been deported to a concentration camp because of his Marxist activities, had at first no consequences (Wendelborn, 1996). The president of the Berlin police department denied the denunciation in May, and in October 1933 the Minister noted that he saw no reason for Duncker's dismissal (Geuter, 1984c). However, both von Lauenstein and Duncker were reportedly involved in student demonstrations against the takeover of the National Socialist regime on the campus of the university (Ash, 1979; 1985a). In addition, foreign newspapers were found on Duncker's desk (King et al., 1998). As a result, Duncker's application for the "Habilitation" was rejected twice, and he was suspended from the university starting September 30, 1935.

Köhler's decision to leave became final when it was clear that his assistants Karl Duncker, Otto von Lauenstein, and Hedwig von Restorff would not be reinstated, and he accepted a position in the U.S. at Swarthmore College. Interestingly, as Ash's (1979) research showed, only a year later, a report from the Ministerium itself suggested that the dismissal of the assistants may have been unjustified, since it had been based on evidence from somebody who himself profited from the denunciation, namely Johann Baptist Rieffert, who became director of the Institute after Köhler resigned.

Generally, Geuter (1984c) points out that in many cases, it was not so much orders from "above" that resulted in dismissals of professors and other faculty members, but rather, opportunistic careerists who tried to get ahead were instrumental in denunciations and leave us with the impression that academic psychology was undermined from "below."

Apparently, from 1934-1936, Duncker had actively tried to find ways to stay and work in Germany, with no success (Wendelborn, 1996). For example, in 1936, he explicitly claimed in a letter (addressee unknown) that he had become very critical of communism and had turned way from it. Also, he had rejected university positions abroad, because he didn't want to leave Germany under any circumstances, and thought it would be possible to stay on in Germany:

> (...) denn ich wollte Deutschland um keinen Preis verlassen, wollte nicht unter die Emigranten gehn, und ich glaubte zuversichtlich, man würde mich weiter in Deutschland arbeiten lassen (Wendelborn, 1996, p. 267).

> [(...) because I did not want to leave Germany under any circumstances, did not want to be among the emigrants, and I was confident that I would be allowed to continue working in Germany (Wendelborn, 1996, p. 267)].

Those hopes were in vain. Duncker left Germany, along with many other eminent researchers.

Niedergang oder Neubeginn?: Emigration of the Gestalt Psychologists

The list of psychologists who had to leave Germany after 1933 is long; names such as Wolfgang Köhler, Max Wertheimer, Kurt Lewin, Kurt Goldstein, Adhémar Gelb, Rudolf Arnheim, Ernst Cassirer, and Heinz Werner leave the impression that not much of scientific psychology was left in Germany. However, as Geuter (1984a) shows in a quantitative analysis, for most psychology departments, when considering the number and status of professorships, the situation did not deteriorate in the time from 1932-1945. On the contrary, it was during that time that psychology managed to break free from philosophy and established itself as in independent discipline, with a degree of its own, the "Diplom," which was introduced in 1941. Because of its expansion into applied areas, psychology as a discipline was by no means threatened by extinction, but offered even more opportunities for employment than ever.

Nevertheless, qualitatively, when looking at the consequences regarding one of its most famous schools, by 1935, Gestalt psychology was practically wiped out from Germany (Geuter, 1984c; see Stadler, 1985; Ash, 1995, chap. 20-21, for an analysis of the few Gestalt psychologist remaining in Germany). Altogether, one-third of full professors were dismissed, including almost all of the internationally renown psychologists (Ash, 1984a).

An examination of the development of Gestalt theory after most of its representatives left Germany and its influence on psychology in Germany and in other countries, notably the in U.S., offers interesting insights. One view (Metzger, 1976; Wellek, 1964) claims that psychology as a discipline had been subject to the National Socialist persecution more than other disciplines, for both ideological and content reasons. Wellek (1964) and Metzger (1976) argue that psychology was viewed as a "Jewish science," and therefore subject to antisemitism. However, contrary to Wellek"s (1964) assertion that academic psychology—as a result of being a content area that was inherently incompatible with the National Socialist system—was more affected by dismissals than other disciplines, Ash (1984a; 1991) showed that the percentage of scientists who lost their positions and emigrated after 1933 corresponds to the figure for German academics as a group.

A second thesis put forward by Metzger, and even more strongly by Wellek, is that émigré psychologists, and most of all, the Gestalt psychologists, had a fundamental, impact on American psychology:

> Die amerikanische Psychologie der Gegenwart wäre nicht was sie ist und könnte nicht werden, was sie zu werden verspricht, ohne den Humus der deutschen Emigration (Wellek, 1964, p. 261).

> [Contemporary American psychology would not be what it is now, and would not be able to become what it promises to become, without the base provided by the German emigrants (Wellek, 1964, p. 261)].

This view is also challenged by Ash (1984a; 1996) who points out that despite adding features to the scientific landscape, Gestalt psychology did not fundamentally change it. Ash (1984a) offers an analysis of the various stages in the transfer of scientific knowledge from one country to another, consisting in reception, transfer and integration, and illustrates this process with the example of Gestalt psychology. First, a reception of the theory in the new country needs to take place, before any emigration occurs. For Gestalt psychology, in addition to maintaining written correspondence with researchers in the U.S., several representatives visited psychology departments in the U.S. (e.g., Köhler at Clark, 1925-1926; Koffka at Cornell, 1924-1925, and Wisconsin, 1926-1927) and gave lectures all over the country and thus made the theory available to other researchers. Ash (1984a; 1996) argues that although the open critique of behaviorism was welcomed by many, overall, the reception of Gestalt theory was rather ambivalent, mainly because it was so strongly tied to philosophical issues which were looked upon critically by theorists with a more empirical outlook.

The second phase, the transfer phase, describes the actual emigration of the Gestalt theorists, and makes them permanent residents of a new scientific community. Although one may think that arriving at the U.S. meant arriving at a safe haven, far away from denunciations and anti-Semitic sentiments and persecutions, anti-Semitism became increasingly explicit in the 1920s and 1930s in the U.S. For example, when writing letters of recommendation for a graduate student applying for an academic appointment, it was standard practice to point out whether the person was Jewish, and whether any "objectionable" traits "characteristic" for Jews were apparent in the candidate's personality (Winston, 1998).

Given the obstacles that American Jews, who had been living in the U.S. all their lives, had to face when seeking an academic position in psychology, the situation was, of course, exponentially worse for Jewish émigré psychologists, such as Kurt Lewin or Heinz Werner.

Heinz Werner, for example, who had been internationally renowned for the work in developmental psychology and who had been a full professor already in 1926 in Hamburg, had spent years with short-term appointments at various institutions before he was appointed professor at Clark University in 1947. Others, few however, found good positions immediately. Wertheimer, for example, found a new intellectual home at the New School of Social Research in New York. Both Koffka and Köhler accepted positions at colleges that offered them optimal research conditions. Koffka, who strictly speaking cannot be counted as an emigrant because he had moved to the U.S. already in 1927, accepted an extremely well-paid position at Smith College in Northampton, Massachusetts, where he was exempt from teaching for five years, and was given the opportunity to establish a brand new laboratory with two assistants of his choice. Similarly, Köhler found optimal working conditions at Swarthmore College near Philadelphia. But the biggest downside of their appointment at undergraduate institutions was that they did not work with doctoral students, which would have been crucial in educating a new generation of Gestalt psychologists. In fact, all three of Köhler's most outstanding assistants (Karl Duncker, Otto von Lauenstein, and Hedwig von Restorff) died young. Not having enough intellectual descendants was probably the reason why the legacy of Gestalt theory was not as influential as it could have been (Ash, 1995).

As a consequence, as far as the integration of Gestalt theory into psychology in the U.S. is concerned, Ash (1984a) argues that although aspects of Gestalt theory were incorporated into psychological theorizing, the approach as a whole was not adopted and advanced by the scientific community in the U.S. Or, as Luchins succinctly summarized: "The language, but not the assumptions nor the approach nor the spirit of Gestalt psychology, has been fully absorbed" (Luchins, 1975, p. 41).

Ironically, as the example of Köhler shows, by trying to adopt different experimental methods that were prevalent in the U.S., Köhler opened himself up to criticism and refutation on his own terms (Ash, 1996). Thus, trying to bridge the gap between fundamentally different basic assumptions, and integrating the "imported" holistic assumption on one hand, and the analysis of relatively independent parts on the other hand, failed.

Can we therefore conclude that the war was responsible for the decline of a very influential school of thought in psychology? Prinz (1985) asks the question whether the political situation led to the "end of a beginning," or, whether it merely facilitated the "beginning of the end." He argues that, independently from the political development in Germany, "Gestaltpsychologie" had reached its peak already around 1930. On theoretical grounds, it was problematic for Gestalt theory to be formulated in abstract "principles" (cf. Koffka's *Principles of Gestalt Psychology*, 1935), which were more descriptive than explanatory, and were not organized into a coherent theory. In addition, according to Prinz (1985), the strong nativist orientation of the Gestalt school left no room for learning and assigned a privileged status to phenomena, relative to theories. Thus, phenomena did not modify theory, and theory did not address the nature of phenomena adequately. Following Prinz's (1985) argument, it is probably justified to say that the end of the Gestalt school of thought was multifactorially caused, rather then being the consequence of the political context in Germany.

Visiting Clark University (1925-1926)

Having considered Duncker's life within the context of the Berlin Institute, a brief flashback will illuminate the different environment that he was exposed to when he came to the U.S. as a visiting student. Wolfgang Köhler had been invited by Carl Murchison to visit Clark University for a year, and when offered a fellowship for one of his graduate students, he selected Karl Duncker.

Of what kind was the intellectual atmosphere that Duncker encountered when he came to Clark University in 1925? Certainly, the theoretical climate at Clark was very different from what both Köhler and Duncker had been accustomed to in Berlin. While in Berlin Gestalt psychology was the leading school of thought, in the United States, research in psychology was strongly influenced by behaviorism.

Interestingly, in his sharp criticism of behaviorism (Duncker, 1927), Duncker draws a parallel between the behavioristic approach and the American way of life:

> Inwiefern ist der Behaviorismus etwas typisch Amerikanisches? Er ist es zunächst insofern, als ein solch konsequentes Drauflosgehen, unbehindert von jenem oft so heimtückischen Ballast tausendfacher Über lieferung und dadurch bewirkter Kompromißlerei, eigentlich nur in Amerika so erstaunliche Dimensionen annehmen konnte; wenigstens in Wissenschaften, die wie die Psychologie noch so sehr an den Rock schößen veralteter Philosopheme hängen. Diese Respektlosigkeit ist amerikanisch, und gerade in besagter Hinsicht ist sie, wie mir scheint, herzhaft zu begrüßen (Duncker, 1927, p. 699).

> [In what respect is behaviorism something typical American? In the sense that such a consistent heading for the goal, regardless of the often insidious ballast of thousands of traditions and its resulting compromises, could only have happened in America to such an extent; at least in the sciences such as psychology that still cling so strongly to ancient philosophies' coat-tails. This lack of respect is American, and in this context, it seems to me, it should be warmly welcomed (Duncker, 1927, p. 699)].

Duncker also notes that in no other country is capitalism as pervasive as in the East of America. He describes "the American" in the following way:

> Und wer Geld hat, hat alles. Wie charakteristisch steht der Amerikaner z. B. zur landschaftlichen Natur. Er wandert nicht—er fährt Auto (auch sein "hiking" ist nicht wandern); er schaut nicht—er photographiert und veranstaltet Picknicks (Duncker, 1927, p. 701).

[If you have money, you have everything. For example, how does the American characteristically relate to nature. He does not walk—he drives a car (even his "hiking" is no hiking); he does not look—he takes pictures and goes for picnics (Duncker, 1927, p. 701)].

How could one therefore be surprised that behaviorism is the school of thought in American psychology, Duncker wonders. We don't know what exactly prompted Duncker to get this impression of the United States, but given that the paper was published the year after he returned to Berlin, it was probably his stay at Clark University.

Duncker came to Clark at a time when the psychology was in the process of recovering from a serious crisis, which had culminated in the decision of the trustees to discontinue the Ph.D. program in psychology in 1923. A series of events led to this difficult situation, which almost meant the end of a program that had become one of the nation's leading institutions to produce Ph.D.s in psychology under the guidance of G. Stanley Hall (Koelsch, 1987). Clark University had changed its main commitment to graduate education and research by admitting undergraduate students, and in 1921, the Graduate School of Geography was founded, with Wallace W. Atwood, Clark's president, as director of the new program. Under Atwood's direction, the new focus of the university was shifting to geography and related fields, and away from psychology, on which the emphasis had been during Hall's presidency.

By 1922, several faculty members, such as E. G. Boring and his wife Lucy, Samuel W. Fernberger, L. R. Geissler, Karl J. Karlson, and James P. Porter had either left or resigned, leaving the psychology and education departments with only three faculty members: Sanford as chair of psychology, Burnham as chair of education, and Kimball Young, a social psychologist on leave from the University of Oregon (Koelsch, 1990).

Sanford had come to Clark together with Hall, under whom he received his Ph.D. from Johns Hopkins University. According to Goodwin (1987), Sanford never managed to step out of the omnipresent shadow of his mentor, and he neither developed a systematic program of research, nor a systematic theoretical position. The impending retirement of Sanford and Burnham led to the trustees' decision to stop accepting new Ph.D. candidates in 1923.

However, a number of factors prevented the department from becoming extinct. Most importantly, Clark alumni and other psychologists protested against the trustees' decision. In addition, the discontinuation of the Ph.D. programs in physics, sociology, and chemistry freed up funds that were invested into the psychology department. Additional funds became available when G. Stanley Hall, who had already retired in 1920, died in 1924 and left an endowment, "to be strictly and solely devoted to research in genetic psychology" (Ross, 1972, p. 437). A professorship in Hall's name was established, and in 1925, Walter S. Hunter of the University of Kansas was appointed the first G. Stanley Hall Professor of Genetic Psychology.

Carl A. Murchison

Carl Murchison (1887-1961), who had earned his Ph.D. from Johns Hopkins under Knight Dunlap, was appointed to be head of the psychology undergraduate department in 1923 (Thompson, 1996). Although his colleagues considered his research methods to be dubious, and he was notorious as a bad teacher (Koelsch, 1990), he managed to raise considerably Clark's profile in the scientific community by editing numerous journals and books and organizing lecture series. Muchinson was involved in editing an impressive list of journals, namely the *Pedagogical Seminary*, which he had taken over, and renamed in *Journal of Genetic Psychology*, he founded the *Genetic Psychology Monographs*, the *Journal of General Psychology* (together with E. B. Titchener), the *Journal of Social Psychology*, as well as the *Journal of Psychology*. He was also responsible for the "Powell Lectures in Psychological Theory" held at Clark from 1924 to 1926 (named after Muchison's father-in-law, Elmer Ellsworth Powell who contributed the financial means) which featured such outstanding scholars as J. B. Watson, W. S. Hunter, W. Köhler, K. Koffka, and W. McDougall, among others.

Walter S. Hunter

Hunter (1889-1954) was one of the prominent behaviorists of the time. He was first reluctant to accept the offer because he was very concerned about the problematic administrative situation at Clark, which had even prompted an investigation of the American Association of University Professors (Koelsch, 1987). Upon consultation with Angell, Warren, Boring and Watson, he decided to accept the offer, and, in his autobiography, recalls that he was certainly happy at Clark (Hunter, 1952). In the summer of 1925, he became editor of the *Psychological Index*, he founded the *Psychological Abstracts* in 1926, and he was president of the American Psychological Association in 1931. He also lectured at Harvard, where among his students was B. F. Skinner. Hunter was a very active and productive researcher, he published twenty-one experimental papers, five theoretical studies, four book chapters, and one textbook in the eleven years that he was at Clark (Hunter, 1952). Twenty-two more papers were published by his graduate students in the same period of time.

On a trip to Europe in 1926, when both Köhler and Duncker had already left Clark to go back to Berlin, Hunter visited Köhler and the other Gestaltists at the Berlin institute. Interestingly, Hunter considered establishing a primate behavior station at Clark, modeled after Köhler's "Antropoiden-Station" on Tenerife. However, the project did not get funded and was never carried out (Koelsch, 1990).

John Paul Nafe

Murchison's first appointment was John Paul Nafe (1888-1970) who had earned his Ph.D. at Cornell University (Thompson, 1996) and who came to Clark in 1924. Nafe was a follower of Titchener's structuralism (e.g., Nafe, 1930), and although he signed off on Duncker's M.A. thesis, it is unlikely that he influenced Duncker's thinking in any fundamental way, given that the thesis was fundamentally grounded in the Gestalt framework. Still, of the three available faculty members, Nafe's research and theoretical interest were certainly closest to Duncker's, and he was the person of choice to be the (at least formal) supervisor of Duncker's project. Nafe's research focused on sensation and perception, and according to reports of his students, he was an exceptionally good teacher (Koelsch, 1990).

Including the visiting scholar Köhler's, the mix of theoretical positions at Clark at the time Duncker was visiting represented behaviorism (Hunter), structuralism (Nafe), and Gestalt psychology (Köhler) and must have provided a quite stimulating atmosphere. In terms of the interpersonal context, on average, there were nine to twelve resident graduate students in the department each year (Koelsch, 1990). Interestingly, Duncker (1927) noted when talking about "Amerika," that the students "over there" were a bit too liberal for his taste, for example regarding "die Geschlechterfrage" [Women's rights] (Duncker, 1927, p. 702).

Problem Solving—Solving His Problems?

Although Karl Duncker was interested in a broad spectrum of research topics, ranging from induced motion (Duncker, 1929), to perception of pain (1937), taste perception (Duncker, 1939a), ethics (1939b), to motivation (1938), his main contribution to psychology, in particular to cognitive science, certainly lies in his work on problem solving (Duncker, 1926; 1935a; 1935b; Duncker and Krechevsky, 1939) (see Newell, 1985; Simon, this issue, for an account of Duncker's impact on the information-processing paradigm).

Problem solving, or "productive thinking," as Duncker, and before him, Wertheimer (1920) called it, is often discussed in the context of creativity (e.g., Langley, Simon, Bradshaw, and Zytkow, 1987; Weisberg, 1988). Most authors agree that creativity can be defined as the ability to come up with novel and appropriate solutions to a given problem (Amabile, 1983; Gardner, 1993; MacKinnon, 1978; Sternberg and Lubard, 1996). Interestingly, according to that definition, Duncker was certainly very creative himself, while laying the groundwork for creativity research. For example, he created a number of unique problem situations that he used in his experiments, such as the candle problem, the radiation problem, etc. Furthermore, his approach to thinking was quite innovative compared to other models of his time (Newell, 1985).

On a different level, it is noteworthy that one of the most controversial questions in the area of creativity is how emotional stability and mental health are related in the process of creative achievement. For example, in Maslow's humanistic view, (e.g., Maslow, 1959) self-actualizing creativeness is synonymous with health, as he sees creativity as epiphenomenon of self-acceptance and integration. In contrast to psychoanalytic views which try to explain creative achievement as a result of inner conflict, Maslow claims that only when conflicts have been resolved and a person reaches self-acceptance, time and energy is available for creative purposes. A different view suggests that extraordinary creativity might be accompanied by psycho-pathology: "Those who have become eminent in philosophy, politics, poetry, and the arts have all had a tendency toward melancholia" is attributed to Aristotle (Simonton, 1994, p. 284). Indeed, the list of eminent individuals with supposed affective disorders is long: C. Darwin, J. B. Watson, W. James, J. S. Mill, Michelangelo, F. Chopin, E. Hemingway, V. van Gogh, P. Tchaikovsky, to name only a few, and the last three of the list all committed suicide (Simonton, 1994). Of course, it is impossible to make any causal statement and conclude that either exceptional abilities lead to psychological problems, or that psychopathology leads to an overcompensation through creative achievement. However, Simonton (1994) speculates that creators often tend to exhibit a "little bit" of mental disturbances, more than "normal" individuals, but less than clinically diagnosed patients, suggesting that mental problems are often the price that outstandingly creative individuals have to pay.

Certainly, Karl Duncker's life was full of complexities and problems, only one of them being his depression (King et al., 1998), in addition to the hardships that he had to endure because of his political convictions, resulting in his emigration from a country that he apparently felt very attached to. It must have been extremely hard for him to accept that he could not continue his professional career in the way that he had hoped for while still in Germany. In that sense, Karl Duncker was facing problems (in his life) and working with problems (in his research) at the same time.

Those who suffer from mental disturbances often have an abundance of psychological problems to solve, or if they are not trying to solve them through their writing or art, may gain relief from their own problems by solving problems not particularly related to their personal histories. (Ludwig, 1995, p. 193.)

Perhaps that was the case for our protagonist Karl Duncker, and his theoretical focus was motivated by the attempt to address and solve problems of his own life.[2]

Notes

1. Previously published in *From Past to Future, Vol. 1(2), The Drama of Karl Duncker*, pp. 13–28. ©1999. Frances L. Hiatt School of Psychology, Clark University. Author: Simone Schnall, Department of Psychology, University of Plymouth (England).

2. The support of my work through the Gottlieb-Daimler und Karl-Benz-Stiftung is gratefully acknowledged. I am also very thankful to Mitchell G. Ash, Jaan Valsiner, and Hannlore Putz for valuable comments on an earlier version of this paper.

References

Amabile, T. M. (1983). *The social psychology of creativity*. New York: Springer.
Ash, M. (1979). The struggle against the Nazis. *American Psychologist, 34*, 363-364.
Ash, M. G. (1984a). Diziplinentwicklung und Wissenschaftstransfer—Deutschsprachige Psychologen in der Emigration. *Berichte zur Wissenschaftsgeschichte, 7*, 207-226.
Ash, M. G. (1984b). Psychologie in Deutschland bis 1933. In H. E. Lück, R. Miller, and W. Rechtien (Eds.), *Geschichte der Psychologie: Ein Handbuch in Schlüsselbegriffen*. (pp. 17-22). München: Urban und Schwarzenberg.
Ash, M. G. (1985a). Ein Institut und eine Zeitschrift. Zur Geschichte des Berliner Psychologischen Instituts und der Zeitschrift "Psychologische Forschung" vor und nach 1933. In C.-F. Graumann (Ed.), *Psychologie im Nationalsozialismus*. (pp. 113-137). Berlin: Springer.
Ash. M. G. (1985b). Die experimentelle Psychologie an den deutsch-sprachigen Universitäten von der Wilhelminischen Zeit bis zum Nationalsozialismus. In M. G. Ash, and U. Geuter (Eds.), *Geschichte der deutschen Psychologie im 20. Jahrhundert* (pp. 45-82). Opladen: Westdeutscher Verlag.
Ash, M. G. (1991). Thesen zur Emigration in der deutschsprachigen Psychologie nach 1933. In H. Lück, and R. Miller (Eds.), *Theorien und Methoden psychologiegeschichtlicher Forschung* (pp. 77-90). Göttingen: Hogrefe.
Ash, M. G. (1995). *Gestalt psychology in German culture, 1890-1967: Holism and the quest for objectivity*. Cambridge, MA: Cambridge University Press.
Ash, M. G. (1996). Emigré psychologists after 1933: The cultural coding of scientific and professional practices. In M. G. Ash, and A. Söllner (Eds.), *Forced migration and scientific change: Emigré German-speaking speaking scientists and scholars after 1933* (pp. 117-138). Cambridge: Cambridge University Press.
Duncker, K. (1926). A qualitative (experimental and theoretical) study of productive thinking (solving of comprehensible problems). *Pedagogical Seminary, 33*, 642-708.
Duncker, K. (1927). Der Behaviorismus—Die Amerikanische Psychologie. *Pädagogisches Zentralblatt, 7*, 690-702.
Duncker, K. (1929). Über induzierte Bewegung. (Ein Beitrag zur Theorie optisch wahrgenommener Bewegung.). *Psychologische Forschung, 12*, 180-259.
Duncker, K. (1932). Behaviorismus und Gestaltpsychologie (Kritische Bemerkungen zu Carnaps "Psychologie in physikalischer Sprache"). *Erkenntnis, 3*, 162-176.
Duncker, K. (1935a). *Zur Psychologie des produktiven Denkens*. Berlin: Springer.
Duncker, K. (1935b). Lernen und Einsicht im Dienst der Zielerreichung. *Acta Psychologica, 1*, 77-82.
Duncker, K. (1937). Some preliminary experiments on the mutual influence of pains. *Psychologische Forschung, 21*, 311-326.
Duncker, K. (1938). Experimental modification of children's food preferences through social suggestion. *Journal of Abnormal and Social Psychology, 33*, 489-507.
Duncker, K. (1939a). The influence of past experience upon perceptual properties. *American Journal of Psychology, 52*, 255-265.
Duncker, K. (1939b). Ethical relativity (An enquiry into the psychology of ethics). *Mind, 48*, 39-57.
Duncker, K., and Krechevsky, I. (1939). On solution-achievement. *Psychological Review, 46*, 176-185.

Ferrier, J.-L. (1988). *Art of our century: The chronicle of Western art, 1900 to the present* (W. D. Glanze, trans.). New York: Prentice Hall.
Gardner, H. (1993). *Creating minds.* New York: Basic Books.
Gay, P. (1969). Weimar culture: The outsider as insider. In D. Fleming, and B. Bailyn (Eds.), *The intellectual migration: Europe and America, 1930-1960* (pp. 11-93). Cambridge, MA: Harvard University Press.
Geuter, U. (1984a). *Die Professionalisierung der deutschen Psychologie im Nationalsozialismus.* Frankfurt: Suhrkamp.
Geuter, U. (1984b). Psychologie im Nationalsozialismus. In H. E. Lück, R. Miller, and W. Rechtien (Eds.), *Geschichte der Psychologie: Ein Handbuch in Schlüsselbegriffen* (pp. 22-28). München: Urban und Schwarzenberg.
Geuter, U. (1984c). "Gleichschaltung" von oben? Universitätspolitische Strategien und Verhaltensweisen in der Psychologie während des Nationalsozialismus. *Psychologische Rundschau, 35,* 198-213.
Goodwin, C. J. (1987). In Hall's shadow: Edmund Clark Sanford (1859-1924). *Journal of the History of the Behavioral Sciences, 23,* 153-168.
Henle, M. (1978). One man against the Nazis: Wolfgang Köhler. *American Psychologist, 33,* 939-944.
Hunter, W. S. (1952). Walter S. Hunter. In E. G. Boring, H. S. Langfeld, H. Werner, and R. M. Yerkes (Eds.), *A history of psychology in autobiography* (Vol. 4, pp. 163-187). Worcester, MA: Clark University Press.
Jaeger, S. (1992). Wolfgang Köhler in Berlin. In L. Sprung, and W. Schönpflug (Eds.), *Zur Geschichte der Psychologie in Berlin* (pp. 161-183). Frankfurt: Lang.
Jaeger, S. (1994). Entwicklung und Struktur des psychologierelevanten Lehrangebotes an der Berliner Universität 1900-1945. In H. Gundlach (Ed.), *Arbeiten zur Psychologiegeschichte.* Göttingen: Hogrefe.
King, D. B., Cox. M., and Wertheimer, M. (1998). Karl Duncker: Productive problems with beautiful solutions. In G. A. Kimble, and M. Wertheimer (Eds.), *Portraits of pioneers in psychology* (Vol. III, pp. 163-178). Mahwah, NJ: Erlbaum.
King, D. B., and Wertheimer, M. (1995). Max Wertheimer at the University of Berlin. In S. Jaeger, I. Staeuble, L. Sprung, and H.-P. Brauns (Eds.), *Psychologie im soziokulturellen Wandel—Kontinuitäten und Diskontinuitäten* (pp. 276-280). Frankfurt: Lang.
Koelsch, W. A. (1987). *Clark University 1887-1987: A narrative history.* Worcester: Clark University Press.
Koelsch, W. A. (1990). The "magic decade" revisited: Clark psychology in the twenties and thirties. *Journal of the History of the Behavioral Science, 26,* 151-175.
Koffka, K. (1935). *Principles of Gestalt psychology.* New York: Hartcourt.
Köhler, W. (1938). Physical Gestalten. In W. D. Ellis (Ed.), *A source book of Gestalt psychology* (pp. 17-54). London: Routledge.
Köhler, W. (1947). *Gestalt psychology.* New York: Liveright.
Kracauer, S. (1995). *The mass ornament: Weimar essays* (T. Y. Levin, trans). Cambridge, MA: Harvard University Press.
Langley, P., Simon, H. A., Bradshaw, G. L., and Zytkow, J. M. (1987). *Scientific discovery: Computational explorations of the creative process.* Cambridge, MA: MIT Press.
Luchins, A. S. (1975). The place of Gestalt theory in American psychology: A case study. In S. Ertel, L. Kemmler, and M. Stadler (Eds.), *Gestalttheorie in der modernen Psychologie* (pp. 21-44). Darmstadt: Steinkopf.
Ludwig, A. M. (1995). *The price of greatness: Resolving the creativity and madness controversy.* New York: Guilford.
MacKinnon, D. W. (1978). *In search of human effectiveness: Identifying and developing creativity.* New York: Creative Education Foundation.

Maslow, A. H. (1959). Creativity in self-actualizing people. In H. H. Anderson (Ed.), *Creativity and its cultivation* (pp. 83-95). New York: Harper.
Metzger, W. (1976). Gestalttheorie im Exil. In H. Balmer (Ed.), *Psychologie des 20. Jahrhunderts.I. Die Europäische Tradition* (pp. 659-683). Zürich: Kindler.
Nafe, J. P. (1930). Structural psychology. In C. Murchison (Ed.), *Psychologies of 1930* (pp. 128-140). Worcester, MA: Clark University Press.
Newell, A. (1985). Duncker on thinking: An inquiry into process in cognition. In S. Koch, and D. E. Leary (Eds.), *A century of psychology as science.* (pp. 392-419). New York: McGraw-Hill.
Prinz, W. (1985). Ganzheits- und Gestaltpsychologie im Nationalsozialismus. In C.-F. Graumann (Ed.), *Psychologie im Nationalsozialismus* (pp. 89-111). Berlin: Springer.
Ross, D. (1972). *G. Stanley Hall: The psychologist as prophet*. Chicago: University of Chicago Press.
Simon, H. A. (1999). Karl Duncker and cognitive science. *From Past to Future, 1*, 1-11.
Simonton, D. K. (1994). *Greatness: Who makes history and why*. New York: Guilford.
Sprung, L., and Sprung, H. (1993). Die Berliner Schule der Gestaltpsychologie. In H. Lück, and R. Miller (Eds.), *Illustrierte Geschichte der Psychologie.* (pp. 80-84). München: Quintessenz.
Sprung, H., and Sprung, L. (1995). Carl Stumpf (1848-1936) und die Anfänge der Gestaltpsycholgie an der Berliner Universität. In S. Jaeger, I. Staeuble, L. Sprung, and H.-P. Brauns (Eds.), *Psychologie im soziokulturellen Wandel—Kontinuitäten und Diskontinuitäten* (pp. 259-268). Frankfurt: Lang.
Sprung, H., and Sprung, L. (1996). Carl Stumpf (1848-1936), a general psychologist and methodologist, and a case study of a cross-cultural scientific transition process. In W. Battmann, and S. Dutke (Eds.), *Processes of the molar regulation of behavior* (pp. 327-342). Lengerich: Pabst.
Stadler, M. (1985). Das Schicksal der nichtemigrierten Gestaltpsychologen im Nationalsozialismus. In C.-F. Graumann (Ed.), *Psychologie im Nationalsozialismus* (pp. 139-164). Berlin: Springer.
Sternberg, R. J., and Lubard, T. I. (1996). Investing in creativity. *American Psychologist, 51*, 677-688.
Stumpf, C. (1883). *Tonpsychologie* (Vol. I). Leipzig: Hirzel.
Stumpf, C. (1890). *Tonpsychologie* (Vol. II). Leipzig: Hirzel.
Stumpf, C. (1924). Carl Stumpf. In R. Schmidt (Ed.), *Die Philosophie der Gegenwart in Selbstdarstellungen* (pp. 205-265). Leipzig: Meiner.
Stumpf, C. (1928). *Gefühl und Gefühlsempfindung*. Leipzig: Barth.
Stumpf, C. (1939). *Erkenntnislehre* (Vol I). Leipzig: Barth.
Stumpf, C. (1940). *Erkenntnislehre* (Vol II). Leipzig: Barth.
Thieme, H. (1994). Hitler's Weg zur Macht: Krise und Untergang der Weimarer Republik. In J. Hampel (Ed.), *Der Nationalsozialismus* (Vol. I., pp. 17-48). München: Bayerische Landeszentrale für politische Bildungsarbeit.
Thompson, D. (1996). Carl Murchison: Psychologist, editor, and entrepreneur. In G. A. Kimble, C. A. Boneau, and M. Wertheimer (Eds.), *Portraits of pioneers in psychology* (Vol. II, pp. 151-165). Mahwah, NJ: Erlbaum.
Van der Veer, R. (1999). Tamara Dembo's European years. *From Past to Future, 2*, 1.
Weisberg, R. W. (1988). Problem solving and creativity. In R. J. Sternberg (Ed.), *The nature of creativity: Contemporary psychological perspectives* (pp. 148-176). Cambridge, MA: Cambridge University Press.
Wellek, A. (1964). Der Einfluß der deutschen Emigration auf die Entwicklung der amerikanischen Psychologie. *Psychologische Rundschau, 15*, 239-262.

Wendelborn, S. (1996). Emigration aus Deutschland während der Zeit des Nationalsozialismus—Ein Beitrag zur Biographie Karl Dunckers. In H. Gundlach (Ed.), *Untersuchungen zur Geschichte der Psychologie und Psychotechnik* (pp. 263-272). München: Profil-Verlag.

Wertheimer, M. (1920). *Über Schlußprozesse im produktiven Denken*. Berlin: De Gruyter.

Winston, A. S. (1998). "The defects of his race": E. G. Boring and Antisemitism in American Psychology, 1923-1953. *History of Psychology, 1*, 27-51.

Zimmer, A. (1989). Gestaltpsychologische Texte—Lektüre für eine aktuelle Psychologie? *Gestalt Theory, 11*, 95-121.

3

Duncker's Account of Productive Thinking: Exegesis and Application of a Problem-Solving Theory

Jeanette A. Lawrence and Agnes E. Dodds[1]

Life is of course, among other things, a sum total of solution-processes which refer to innumerable problems, great and small.(Duncker, 1945, p. 13.)

This footnote in Duncker's (1945) monograph encapsulates his approach to the study of thinking. Treating problem solving as a defining human characteristic, he set out to analyze the processes by which people develop solutions for difficult problems: the activity he called "productive thinking." It is productive in terms of its outcome for resolving a difficult situation, and in terms of the processes by which the successful resolution is attained. In Duncker and Krechevsky (1939, p. 177), he clarified this notion of productivity as a "functional sense of problem-solving, not in the material sense of a special, e.g., imageless, kind of representation."

At the end of the millennium, many people need to think productively, as they are confronted with new technological things to manipulate, and new, complex social problems that affect life at the global and personal level. In the search for psychological analyses of problem solving, one may be skeptical that any advance could come from revisiting the experiments and theorizing of a researcher who admittedly has had little direct impact on mainstream psychology in sixty years. Newell (1985, p. 412), for instance, observed that Duncker had not successfully communicated his ideas, either to his own world, or to Newell's world of the cognitive revolution. Is it possible for his ideas to be useful to researchers today?

The question of Duncker's relevance is not new. It resembles the question Newell (1985) raised when he took up Duncker's research as a foil against which to gauge the achievements of the cognitive revolution. Our perspective is somewhat different, for we start with the working premise that Duncker's emphases are relevant to contemporary psychology's concerns about relations between the social and the cognitive, and with the premise that personal cognition can make a contribution to analyses of problem-solving in different settings, by virtue of the uniqueness of the situation-person connection.

In order to examine the lasting contribution of Duncker's approach, we first lay out and exegete his original (1926) theorizing, giving close attention to his perspective on the problem situation as a whole unit of activity, involving: the givens of the situation, the person's solution and the productive thinking processes by which they are bound together. We then address how Duncker's emphases are relevant to contemporary discussions of the contextualization and situatedness of cognition, and relevant to discussions about the effectiveness of individualized cognitive processes. We submit that Duncker provides an account of problem solving that can assist the psychological researcher (whether observationist, experimentalist, discourse analyst, or interventionist) to address some of the thorny problems that are encountered when the environment and the person are bound together in research and life settings. Finally, we suggest some ways that Duncker's ideas can extend and refine research on the processes of problem solving.

Despite the achievements of the cognitive revolution, problem-solving research has not become as mainstream in psychology as the work of Newell and Simon (1972) and their colleagues would have led one to expect (Norman, 1993a). Although it is unexceptional for research tasks to be described as problem solving, it is quite exceptional, outside the problem-solving paradigm, to find analyses of the cognitive processes by which these tasks are accomplished. It is even more exceptional to find analyses where the accomplishments are carefully shown to meet the demands of a domain of activity and the specifics of a given problem. Duncker's theory provides a way of bridging the gap between adherents of the problem-solving paradigm and a larger group of researchers who are seeking ways of explaining how people resolve problematic situations.

Starting with Duncker's footnote, he characterized people as problem solvers who encounter problems and resolve them with varied success, as measured against contextualized criteria. In search of Duncker's basic concepts we went behind the 1945 monograph (Lee's English translation of the 1935 book), to the 1926 paper where he reported the original experiments, together with the Clark University thesis of the same year that it substantially reports. We also went forward to Duncker's social application of his theorizing in the 1939 *Mind* paper on ethical relativity and his joint work on problem solving and learning with Krechevsky (1939).

Newell (1985, p. 398) noted that "Duncker was clear about what he wanted to know: 'How does the solution arise from the problem situation?'" This opening question of the 1945 monograph (Duncker, 1945, p.1) had been behind his experiments since 1926. The early work reveals how the basic account of problem-specific cognitive processing shaped the more frequently cited 1945 monograph. However, some clarification and extensions in the later works need to be incorporated in the theoretical critique, especially where they represent theoretical or expressive refinements of the fundamental ideas. Most notably, we refer to the concept of "restructuration" or re-organization of the psychological structure of the problem situation or its parts (1945, pp. 29ff; 102, 110) that is a clarification of the process of understanding and manipulating it in order to develop the problem and its solution. Similarly, in the Duncker and Krechevsky paper, some restatements of the basic concepts are less dense, and suggest that Duncker probably benefited from explaining his ideas to Krechevsky who was working from a different, learning, perspective. The 1939 paper on ethical relativism represents an example of how Duncker applied his concepts to a wider social issue, modeling the process of problem solving.

Characterizing Problem Solving

In the 1926 paper, after analyzing his experimental data, Duncker plainly laid out his theory of a problem situation-and-solution (1926, p. 696ff), demonstrating how a solution arises in the interpretive and re-organizing processes of the problem solver, working on a specific set of givens. Basically, each problem situation is cast as a setting or an event in which a conflict occurs that demands a cognitive response, such that, the response is made in order to resolve the conflict, while satisfying the conditions prevailing in the situation.

Duncker's Problems

The types of problem Duncker addressed were designed to present his research subjects with situations for which there was no immediate, direct or obvious solution. They were not exclusively "mathematical" or "physical" problems as often assumed (1926, p. 705), but their level of difficulty meant they could not be solved by associative or simple recognition responses. They required cognitive work. Although he presented them in the laboratory in paper form for convenience, Duncker saw them as a subset of real life problems.

By way of contrast to his problems, Duncker argued that in Humean and all associationist accounts, the connections between the problem situation and the human response were not intrinsically related, but could be "incidental relative to each other" (p. 699). Any attachment between the external conditions and the cognitive processing would be inferred post-hoc by virtue of the effect of the response.

In non-Humean situations, such as those he generated for his research subjects, and those that in real life present people with unknowns that must be discovered, situation-person connections have a different quality. Problematic features of the situation and problem-resolving thinking processes are bound together as parts of a unified whole. A solution cannot be immediately extracted from the problem situation, either from the observables or from direct application of past experience. The bridge across the gap between the problem and its appropriate solution arises within the person's cognitive activity, but only as that cognitive work is directed at, and directed right into the core (causal connections) of the situation. Neither the situation nor the thinking process stands alone: neither is sufficient in itself. They are bound together, such that, the situation does not yield the solution without the cognitive activity through which it is understood, worked over conceptually, and reorganized to yield a solution. In turn, that cognitive activity is only effective as it is applied to the specifics of the situation and the meaning that is discerned in the process.

From that perspective, effective cognitive activity is not a matter of abstract thought, but rather, thinking connected to, and under the demands of the specifics. In this sense, Duncker claimed that his theory differed significantly from that of Selz (to whom he was admittedly indebted, de Groot, 1965; Simon, this issue), but with whom he differed significantly in at least one fundamental way. He was not proposing the application of a general abstraction to the particular as a problem-solving strategy, as he claimed was the case for Selz. On the contrary, for Duncker, cognitive activity always worked within the actual, specific features of a problem, restructuring them, and simultaneously, restructuring the whole.

The significance of the features of the given situation was demonstrated in his belief that all his subjects needed should be given ("materially contained") in the problematic situation. He did not devise guessing problems, because he was interested in what people would do with what was available. Where the original problem specifications were not sufficiently clear to a subject, Duncker had no scruples about supplying relevant information along the way with hints and suggestions. He, as experimenter was another part of the total situation.

In sum, productive thinking as situation specific and problem oriented could be specified only in terms of the situation-person connection. It involved neither the application of a principle nor a connectionist association. In these terms, it does no violence to Duncker's account to infer that he was making the point that productive thinking is "situated" or "grounded" reasoning (cf., Brown, Collins, and Duguid, 1989; Norman, 1993b). For instance, he specifically drew on Wertheimer to strengthen his case, namely, that an appropriate response to the situation is brought about by dint, and presumably only by dint, of its "'definite formal relations within the situation as a whole (Wertheimer)" (Duncker, 1926, p. 702).

The Processes of Productive Thinking

Under the aegis of the specific problem situation, Duncker identified several different cognitive heuristics by which the problem solver works on the givens with the goal of a solution firmly in mind. As they are described in the 1926 theoretical statement (pp. 702-707), they could easily be read off as a set of sequenced steps, working from "comprehending" to resolving the problematic situation. The sense of sequentiality (e.g., "*After* the prob. Sit. as such has been fully comprehended," p. 703; and "the penetration *terminates* in the functional value," p. 704), arises because the activities, too, are connected parts of a whole, with, this time, the unit being the whole process of cognitive work on the problem. There is an inner logic to the whole work of understanding and restructuring the problem in the service of resolving it. Directly on this point of re-organizing, transforming cognitive processes, that was well developed by 1935, Duncker characterized the poor mathematician by an inability to do this very restructuring. S/he is "not able to restructure so easily, because his thought-material is relatively inelastic, rigid, and therefore not sufficiently plastic to be reshaped" (Duncker, 1945, p. 110). By 1939 in Duncker and Krechevsky, the connection was explained as a "hierarchy" involving the progressive refinement from "general to specific features of the sought-after solution" (1939, p178). The sequentiality belongs to the need to understand a problem situation prior to transforming it and resolving it.

These steps do not, however, represent a thorough process model in the sense now understood. The connections are rather loose, and the expression is informal (Newell, 1985). Furthermore, alternative heuristic methods could be used (e.g., learning from mistakes, analysis of goals or problem parts) within the phases, so that any formalized model would need to account for alternatives and to account for the fact that these alternatives are likely to emerge only once the processing work has begun.

The processes of productive thinking are described as two mediating phases of cognitive activity, that together, identify the development of the problem situation and simultaneously, the development of its solution. Actually, problem development and solution development merge into the same thing within the mediating process, "It is therefore meaningful to say that what is really done in any solution of problems consists in formulating the problem more productively" (Duncker, 1945, p. 9). The work of the person, expressed in everyday terms, is to understand what the situation involves and the solution (goal) that is needed, then to develop that solution using what is to hand, either externally or internally.

(1) Comprehending the situation as a whole ("to have it as a gestalt," p. 653), involves to "represent" it and to "grasp" it (p. 703) as a total situation (phenomenon or relationship) that contains a conflict. This conflict means the givens do not yield a solution. There is a "gap" and it is vexing and troublesome, and demands that the gap between the problem and the solution be bridged. For the problem solver that means first understanding that there is something wrong within the situation as given, that may be expressed in the form, "Something is not right, it doesn't work as it should, and I do not have a way of resolving the troublesome thing."

(II) *"Penetrating"* into the problem involves going into it and its features in order to search for and identify the underlying cause of the gap, then it involves re-organizing the parts of the problem situation in order to remove that cause. Duncker illustrated the two levels of processes of comprehension and penetration with a table of eight examples from his problem tasks (p. 704). The table illuminates the connections he was making, because it draws out the relationship between understanding that there is a gap and identifying the underlying or second-order cause of the gap.

In the classic x-ray problem, for example, the successful research subject was able to understand and comprehend that the situation was problematic because rays could not be used to destroy a tumor. The surrounding healthy tissue also would be damaged. Penetration into the problem involved understanding that "the bundle of rays was *too* concentrated, *too* united (or *too* thick, or working *too* long at the same spot" p. 704). Here the *"too ... "* expression denotes discerning the causal connection, for instance, between the concentration of the rays and the possibility of destroying the healthy tissue. For the problem solver, this means seeing that, "Whatever it is causing that something wrong, or whatever does not fit in this situation, must be changed. Only then can I remove the gap between what is there and how it ought to be."

The penetrating phase issues in *the functional value of the solution*, what the solution must do, what can be used to do it and how it (a tool of method) can be used. This involves seeing how the problem situation works, and what the solution will actually accomplish as it removes the offending, underlying cause. For Duncker, this activity of extracting the meaning of the problem situation was crucial. By taking that step, the person has fully entered into the problem situation, and "how-it-works" (1926, p 656).

Realization or execution of the functional value means making the "choice of what would do it." The problem situation will need to be reorganized, rearranged or reformulated in one or more of several ways, with Duncker making suggestions that the type of problem may dictate the form. For example, understanding that the rays are "too concentrated" may involve simultaneously seeing the necessity of getting around the concentration obstacle, by breaking up or dispersing that concentration. When that realization is closely linked to comprehension, it is an "Aha" situation, where minimal reorganization and transformation is needed. These are "moments in which such a sudden restructuring of the thought-material takes place, in which something 'tips over'" (Duncker, 1945, p. 29). This form of instantaneous realization does not come for all people or for all problems. Not all Duncker's student subjects made this connection, even when he gave them explicit prompts.

In other forms of realization, understanding how the situation works, with its obstacle and underlying cause does not suggest an immediate solution. In the case of Köhler's ape, for example, where the ape's arm is too short, the meaning lies in the need for elongation, and implies the need to lengthen it.

In relation to where realization requires further work, Duncker described two other effective heuristic methods drawn from his theory and experimental data. The person "glances around" (p. 705), searches through the problem situation or searches through memory, looking for something that can be applied to the conflict. This activity is the creative use of something (a tool or method) that is available. However, the tool or method that is picked up and used is not likely to be available in a form immediately seen as relevant to the conflict. Using it is a matter of "singling out the fitting particular aspect which need not have been singled out ever before" (p. 705). For the problem solver, it has the sense of, "That x can be used as a y here."

The search through personal memory involves looking for something that has been experienced that could be made to fit the task in hand. By this, Duncker does not mean making a direct association between memory and the situation, but the idea of something previously experienced that may "overlap" (p. 705) with the present problem: something that suggests it can be pressed into service for developing the presently needed solution. In addition to accessing experiential material, there is the work of fitting it to the current requirements. Duncker is referring to a search through knowledge, with re-organization of that material as much as he is referring to the re-organization of the situational givens. It is not an association or a matching process that he describes. In both the search through the situation and through memory, there is an element of making something different out of existing material in order to fit it to the situation criteria, along the lines of, "There's something I've used before, and it doesn't quite belong here, but I think I can make it do the job here." This experience is quite different from the "Aha" realization that can serve the same purpose when it automatically comes with the realization of how-it-must-work.

The solution itself is given little attention in the theoretical summary. Its suitability is dictated by situational criteria and constraints, and Duncker later gave the reason. He was more interested in the processes mediating between the difficulty and its solution than in the content of that resolution. In explaining the relationship between Duncker's problem-solving and Krechevsky's learning experiments, they observed:

> Further, both have been primarily interested in the "qualitative" aspects of problem solving, that is., the progressive modes and changes of the subject's procedure rather than in the efficiency of his response as expressed in terms of time, trial and error units (Duncker and Krechevsky, 1939, p. 178).

In the 1945 paper, however, Duncker paid more attention to the solution, and the approximations to it that are made in the mediating phase, "The final form of a solution is typically attained by way of mediating phases of the process, of which each one, in retrospect, possesses the character of a solution, and, in prospect, that of a problem." (Duncker, 1945, p. 9). This later formulation reiterates the dynamic and transformational nature of the processing work.

In summary, the two phases, with their various heuristics described a developmental activity in which the problem and the solution are transformed to come together.

Example Problem: Ethical Relativity

We refer now to Duncker's own intellectual processing of a different form of problem: the 1939 paper on ethical relativism. Here the significance of the situation-person connection is clear, together with the psychological meaning of the individual situation for understanding the meaning of an ethical concept.

Duncker worked on the meaning of situations where ethical problems were involved, and specifically, "the pattern of situated meanings" (p. 43) that linked the use of ethical concepts and judgments across incidents, historical periods and cultures. Further, he insisted that the fundamental meanings of ethical concepts were psychological meanings and that these meanings were situationally understood.

There is a widespread view that the sole invariants of morals is their sociological function to secure the preservation and welfare of a social group. This function, however, is external to the psychological situation. (Duncker, 1939, p. 39).

This statement and the whole argument is dependent on the close connections Duncker saw between the issue (situation) and the cognitive agent processing that issue (in this case, Duncker himself, in constructing an argument for his philosophical audience). In consequence, the process of reasoning by which he tackled social ethics was similar to that which he had formulated in relation to his observations of his student subjects' work on constrained laboratory problems (p. 705). His concept of productive thinking had wider applications than laboratory problems in his mind, and in fact, permeated his thinking. It is possible to trace the close parallels between Duncker's analysis of students' reasoning processes and his own development of an argument. The situatedness and the focus on cognitive meanings for situations emerge as major points in the ethical argument.

In confronting Locke's ethical formula, Duncker in the strongest terms took the argument away from abstract meanings and social trends and into psychological, contextually grounded meanings.

> Well if one leaves out "meanings," that is, if one fails to define the situation in psychological terms, how can one expect to meet with general consent? *For ethical evaluation is not concerned with acts as abstract events in space-time. The ethical essence of an act depends upon its concrete pattern of situational meanings.* The term "situational meanings" is meant to convey the notion of "relevant features of the actual psychological situation with reference to which the subject behaves" (Duncker, 1939, p. 43, 44, his emphases).

Thus, the ethicality of an issue was not due to any general ethical ideas whether those ethical ideas referred to the virtues of honesty and bravery, or whether they also denoted ethically-relevant concepts that were used differently in different situations, namely, usury, modesty and the practice of cultural killing in some societies. Ethically relevant situations, rather, receive their moral identification in relation to the specific circumstances in which they are used, with the over-rider that the meaning of these thoughts and emotions had to be firmly embedded in the specific features of the circumstance.

Taking usury as an illustration, he demonstrated how its meaning as "the taking of interest on money lent" in fact, carried different meanings according to its historical setting. Consequently, the same activity could be given positive or negative connotations and values in relation to the circumstances of use. In earlier civilizations, for instance, where loans were used for consumption, the meaning of taking interest on loans carried negative implications because of the customs and social values that saw it as exploitation. In capitalistic societies, however, where loans are for the purpose of increasing capital, usury carries positive meanings. The same acts of lending for interest, thus, find their morality within prevailing economic arrangements. It is easy to see here the second-order meanings by which Duncker made his distinctions between concepts and their situational use. The ethical value was applied in the patterns of meanings pertaining to a situation (p. 41), in this case, historically imbedded custom.

Following on from this point, Duncker argued that moral evaluation has three parts that make explicit how the connection between problem situation and thinking person lies specifically in the interpretive cognition brought to bear on the situation. The three parts of his case against Locke's ethical relativism took the form:

A morally valued act must function to satisfy the condition of promoting the social good in given circumstances; but the ethical valuing "depends upon the meanings involved according to certain basic invariable relationships" (p. 44), so that once the meaning of an activity is defined in a particular way in its relevant circumstances, its ethically laden follows, where those meanings, nevertheless, depend on the circumstances involved (e.g., when usury means sharing in the profits it carries a positive valence).

This represents a very clear application of the idea of the totality of the situation, along with a strong distinction of the meanings of the situation from the situation itself. Meanings belong to the realm of the psychological, neither to the physical nor to the sociological. Meanings are not all the same, but can be of different types, including the symbolic, the causal and the definitional. They are inferred (our term) from the situation with its primary and secondary features. They cannot be "grafted upon" the situation (Duncker's term, p. 46) by the process of rationalization. Directly in the sense of the 1926 theory, the meaning is inherent to the situation and at the same time, psychologically "subjective." Thus, its semiotic function is both concretized and psychologically realized, so that it is the meaning that a situation yields on search, and it is the meaning sought for and discovered by a particular searcher.

In a further application of the functional nature of meanings, Duncker took up cultural customs about nudity and modesty. It is not simply that different customs give nudity itself a meaning, but that these customs, as external circumstances, provide secondary meanings to the psychological make-up of a situation. Exhibitionism, for instance, may be equally associated with covering or with uncovering, according to custom and circumstance. Nudity gains its significance within the situation of occurrence. It does not, for instance, obtain an erotic or modesty-type meaning in the gynecologist's consulting room.

Indeed, it only gains a modesty-type interpretation for an arts model under specific conditions. Here Duncker quotes from Havelock Ellis the case of a female model quietly posing in the art class, "suddenly she screamed and ran to cover herself with her garments. She had seen a workman on the roof gazing inquisitively at her through a skylight" (p. 49). Within the semiotic meaning of the art class, her nudity has a particular functional value and meaning, unrelated to modesty. The intrusion of another meaning associated with the change in the circumstance, makes her cover herself. The workman peering through the skylight is interpreted psychologically by the model in terms of cultural mores and now relates her nudity to modesty. The experience changes the meaning of her nudity in the particular circumstances, at least for her.

This example, and in fact, the whole paper is a case of the theorist using his own productive thinking processes to address a social question. In doing so, his paper concretizes and illustrates the significance and general application of his theoretical concepts. It was not that he denied the variability of ethics, but that he moved away from arguments based on abstractness, to focus on the use of ethical concepts by interpretation of meanings in particular situations. He did not deny the intellectual work of the ethical thinker, nor the importance of cultural meanings, but demanded that they be shown to work in relation to the specifics. For our day, his treatise highlights a distinctive but topical set of issues about relations between the situation and the person interpreting it.

Duncker's Contemporary Relevance and Contribution

From this brief revisiting of Duncker's account of problem solving, the contemporary relevance of his insistence on situation specificity and the situation-person connection becomes patently obvious. Less obvious, is the relevance of his theorizing for understanding how people create novel problems by turning over accepted uses and interpretations, and then set about solving the problems they have generated. In relation to each of these applications of Duncker's concepts, interpretive, transforming cognitive processing has a special significance, precisely because of the way it is bound up with specific problems. It follows that, in order to assess problem solving in terms of its ability to satisfy the criteria of productive thinking, one needs to know the goal being pursued and also the problem for which that goal forms the solution. The quality of the mediational activity lies in how it works as a set of progressive transformations between the problem and the solution, by which these two are made into one: the problem developed into its solution.

We are not advocating a direct transposition of Duncker's theorizing and experiments into current research settings. Actually, that would represent a violation of his basic assumptions about specificity. Rather, we draw attention to the pertinence of his thinking to discussions of specificity, situatedness and cognitive processing.

Situation Specificity

Duncker's dual concerns with the specifics of the situation and their unity have direct relevance to two contemporary issues that revolve around the contexts of cognitive activity. In each case, Duncker's analyses help clarify how attention to the specifics of a problem situation are central to enlarging the unit of analysis, and central to bringing the focus of the analyses onto understanding the processes of transformation in relation to all other aspects of a problem situation.

Concerning contexts of cognitive activity, Western psychologists largely inspired by Soviet psychology, have persistently called for cognitive research to broaden the scope of its analyses to include environmental and social factors as they interact dynamically with individualized cognition (e.g., Cole, 1996; Goodnow, 1997; Perret-Clermont, Perret, and Bell, 1991). In moving away from exclusively cognitive analyses, and insisting on the admission of social context into theoretical models and analyses, it has been possible to redress some of the exclusions of the sixties and seventies, where the social context was frequently dealt with as distracting noise in the study of "disembodied intelligence" (Norman, 1993a, p. 3). Unfortunately, this move can also lead to dichotomizing the social and the personal in ways that make it relatively easy to remove the thinking of the person from the analyses altogether (Dodds, Lawrence, and Valsiner, 1997; Juckes and Barresi, 1993). In such cases, as Juckes and Barresi point out, one can only be left with Durkheim's type of world where the psychological is treated as irrelevant. Few psychologists would wish to go that far.

Duncker's concentration on inner, psychological meanings in no way eliminates the significance of the social. Social dimensions of a situation, in fact, may actually form the underlying, second-level factors contributing to the problem, as in, for example, the ways that social custom can turn a behavior into an ethical problem. For instance, to use Duncker's (1939) own example, when local custom can make the length of a skirt into an object of shame in one culture, when in another it is perfectly accepted. Alternatively, social factors may particularize the gap between the givens and the resolution, where something is "*too* ... (e.g., too socially defined, or too constrained by power relations)." In such cases, the person seeking to determine how the situation works must devise bridges for crossing those social inhibitors.

Personal responses to the social dimensions of problematic situations can find fresh relevance in this scheme, where the problem is specifically devised as a social task, or partly a social task (e.g., where the activity involves accomplishing something by the collaborative effort of a pair or group, or where the direct focus is on the social communication). There may be even deeper functional significance, where working with others is the only way a difficult task can be achieved, or be achieved more effectively. For example, Oliveira (1997) reports studies of how young children's communications facilitate the development of a common script for an activity. and, in the process, give each other a place in the total experience. By their gestures and comments (even when these appear to be negative and excluding), they allow another child to construct a personal role. Duncker's transcripts show how he himself entered into this kind of exchange with his subjects, sometimes prompting them to think of new ideas, sometimes interfering with an unproductive line of thought, all to bring the subject to focus on the functional value and meaning of the problem. His excerpt of a transcript of Subject 1's work on the X-ray problem, illustrates his progressive attempts to assist the student to focus. We reproduce it using Duncker's structure, adding italics of Duncker's comments and activities for emphasis.

The rays would destroy the good tissues.

Focus by lens. ("Suppose you had no lens"—I *drew a cross section to make the conditions more conspicuous*).

Move around the apparatus so the rays are all the time concentrated in the tumor, but do not dwell in other parts long enough to do harm. (*When he saw that I was not quite satisfied he said:* "or you may also rotate the body"—*I said: "Cut out that moving around." Hint: "Look at your method b"*).

(Long intermission—*Then I gave the solution which he at once understood.*) (Time: c.15 min.). (Duncker, 1926, p. 670).

Essentially what we have in this excerpt, is the extraordinarily frank intrusion of social exchange into the experimental situation, with that intrusion acknowledged as part of the total problem-solving episode. For Duncker, it was important to know if his subjects could use his social exchanges, as an integral part of the whole. This is not unlike some of Piaget's intrusions, in its intent, or the Vygotskyan inspired concept of scaffolding. The directness of the "cut out that moving around" type of comment is different, and may reflect Duncker's youthful enthusiasm as much as his determination to give his subject every possibility of reaching an appropriate solution. Overall, however, this example makes the place of the social an integral part of the total experimental situation.

Of course, problems are not only concretized socially. Physical objects also exert constraints on cognitive processing. Things can make people smart, as

Norman (1993b) demonstrated, but they can also make us stupid. Objects can deflect attention from the central task in hand, or they can make it extremely difficult for a person to accomplish precisely the goals for which that object has been designed. Because of faulty or person-unfriendly designs, effort is expended on non-essentials. In such circumstances, a Duncker-inspired investigation would search for the unpremeditated uses that problem solvers make of these problem objects, as they turn over their uses to some other purpose. Gardening programs, for instance, thrive on the abundance of unimagined uses of plastic milk containers.

Whether the features of a problematic situation are social or physical in nature, or as in most problem areas, a combination or both, they can contribute to the making of a problem, by causing or exacerbating the gap between it and its solution. Alternatively, they may contribute to the making of a solution by being taken up as a tool in the reformational phase. Further, any contribution they make is as an element of the configuration and pattern of features that encompasses all the other features. The appropriate unit of analysis in any investigation of problem resolution, therefore, is likely to be complex and multifaceted. Identifying the appropriate unit of analysis is one of the thorniest issues in psychology, and always has been (for a history of the concept of unit of analysis, see Zinchenko, 1985), and current interests in contexts make it only more difficult to pin down the features to include and exclude. The seeming peripheral or incidental feature may have potential significance that becomes realized in the interpretive and manipulative mediation by the problem solver. It becomes, then, not simply a matter of including more features in the analysis of a situation, but of being able to track their consciously searched for, or serendipitously taken up, incorporation into the solution development processes.

Focus on the situatedness of cognition has directed attention more closely onto the environment and the role of the environment in shaping personal cognitive activities in a given situation. It also has directed attention more critically onto specifying the role that cognitive activities actually contribute. Theories of "situativity" (Greeno and Moore, 1993, p. 49) are grounded in concepts of the inter-relatedness of context and cognition, and the specificity of any given situation or circumstances. These moves sustain a continuing debate about the locus, nature and relatedness of cognitive processing (cf., Vera and Simon, 1993, and situationalist responses in a special issue of *Cognitive Science* and Kirshner and Whitson, 1997 for a recent review). Concentration on the distribution of cognition over several persons in the same situation becomes an understandable progression of situativity. The focus in this approach is on complex situations, usually in the workplace, where no single agent can develop appropriate resolutions of problems or accomplish multi-skilled tasks (e.g., in operating airline cockpits, control rooms or nuclear plants, see Engeström and Middleton, 1996).

Essentially, each of the situated and distributed approaches advocates locating more (not necessarily all) of the activity outside the individual head.

The person's cognitive activity becomes one of an array of activities of other persons and things, with the different theoretical approaches giving it more or less relevance.

The Situation-Person Connection

In relation to the various forms of contextualization, situativity or distributed cognition, Duncker's person-situation connection challenges both sides of the situation/cognition controversy. It challenges those insisting on the contribution of the internal, cognitive dimension of problem solving to build strong reasons for asserting how the cognitive is distinctive and effective, and to build better ways of drawing links that give the external a place other than as the setting of cognitive work. It also challenges those insisting on the situativity of all human activity to build into their models and methods ways of accounting for the transforming and re-organizing processes by which the external is given personal meaning, and in many cases, is made into something quite different from that originally imagined. The novelty that emerges in productive thinking belongs to the situation no more than it belongs to an isolated intelligence. Here, Duncker's idea of the unity of problem and problem solver as s/he takes up the situation with its patterns and turns it into an unexpected means of solution finds echoes in the development of expertise.

Genuine, creative experts, as opposed to the reproductive kind, not only spend enormous amounts of time and effort on domain-specific tasks, but also could be said to incorporate the externals into their internal representations in special ways. They continually anchor their thinking in the patterns and problems that arise in their area of specialty. They become absorbed with their problems and with their tools, to the point of eccentricity. Zinchenko (1996), for instance, reports a comment of the famed cellist Rostropovich about his relation to his cello, and we include part of that direct quote as an example of the situation–person connection in the expert. Of course, in the development of expertise, the connection occurs and re-occurs over situations and over different problems so that the two effectively become one over time:

> In Glikman's portrait, however, there I was—and my cello became just a red spot at my belly, like a dissected peritoneum. And actually I feel it now in this manner, much like a singer seems to feel his vocal cords. I experience no difficulty in playing sounds. Indeed, I give no report to myself on how I speak. Just so, I play music, involuntarily.   The cello is my tool no more. Does it not feel itself offended at being so dissolved? Sure it does! But so be it (quoted from Chernov, 1994) (Zinchenko, 1996, pp. 295-296).

Now this may seem far from Duncker's laboratory, but the test of the expertise of a domain-specialist does not simply reside in the ability to solve one reoccurring problem. As Scardamalia and Bereiter (1991) argued persuasively, an ongoing dialectic occurs between the immediate cases (situations) on which an expert works, and the development and incorporation of domain-related knowledge as the basis of interpreting new situations as they arise. The ability to go beyond what is already known and already mastered requires the transformation of existing knowledge to fit novel problems and the transformation of those problems into novel solutions. This kind of situation-person connection continues across situations and time. In the case of the cellist, and other virtuosi, it has other ramifications. Situations blend, from musical piece to piece, so that he and his cello as a unity, enter into an ongoing dialogue with the music. The processes by which that unity of music-cello-cellist is formed and developed, would, for an analysis of Duncker's type, require psychological interpretation, similar to the one Rostropovich gave about the cello-person connection.

Creative Problem Solving

Decades ago, Vinache (1951) was able to recognize the relevance of Duncker's analyses to the problem situations of everyday life, arguing mainly that imaginative solutions to practical problems occur in a "recentering" process, that we, following Duncker's theoretical statement have called re-organization. It involves transformation of what is into what it can become in the process of re-organization. Nowhere is this turning over of accepted uses more prominent than in the problem-solving that begins with problem finding, or the search for the yet unknown issue. Csikszentmihalyi (1996) makes a similar point about creativity;

> Creative people are constantly surprised. They don't assume that they understand what is happening around them, and they don't assume that anybody else does either. They question the obvious—not out of contrariness but because they see the shortcomings of accepted explanations before the rest of us do (Csikszentmihalyi, 1996, p. 363).

Here we have a striking resonance with Duncker's concept of penetration into a situation and turning it over to create new arrangements. The problem is discovered in the existing configuration, there is a recognition that something is wrong, and this leads on to the development of unconventional outcomes. These outcomes (patterns, objects, perspectives) were not foreseen by others, as indeed, the problem that elicited them was not seen.

Csikszentmihalyi illustrates this latter point about uniqueness by the discovery of perspective by Renaissance artists. Art was conventionally two dimensional and hierarchical, along with other forms of human expression. The discovery of perspective by artists who worked at the problem allowed the flatness of Byzantine composition to be broken down in painting, and also facilitated the freedom of thought from the similarly static representations prevailing in philosophy and religion (p. 364).

Weisberg (1986) adds that such breaks with existing forms and uses are not confined to the great moments of discovery. Seeking to dispel the myth of scientific creativity, he argued that ordinary people are constantly using transformational creativity in ways that are similar to those of great scientists. Weisberg traced through the steps of Watson and Crick's discovery of the structure of DNA, observing that the important thing in such creative work is what the person knows about the problem, and how s/he restructures it, where "restructurings are not intuitive leaps into the unknown, but responses to changes in the problem" (p.41). Some changes occur precisely because of the interpretations and interventions made by the discoverer, and here again, we see the problem-person connection and concept of their continuing dialog once more. The point here is not that the process is unique, as much as that the problem and persons are unified. Duncker's contribution is in specifying that the situation-person oneness develops because of the transformational processes. It is there initially, as Weisberg argued, but it becomes another oneness as the problem is turned into the solution by the meanings and functions that are discovered and rediscovered cognitively.

Interpretive Cognitive Processing

Directing attention to the interdependence; the connectedness of task and person, then, is a basic requirement of being able to analyze and evaluate their joint and unique contributions to a productive, or alternatively, non-productive resolution of a problem. The researcher interested in the processes of problem development will seek to explain the external and internal in terms of the relation between them, whether it is causal, consequential or sequential (cf., Harré and Secord, 1973; Lawrence, 1992). Naturally, the focus and depth of analyses of these connections will differ according to theoretical interests and methodological preferences and constraints.

Lichtenberg and Heck (1986), for example, demonstrated several ways that the sequences of counselor and client utterances could be traced through interview transcripts as "speaking turns" (p. 187). The form of interactions is reduced to patterns that could describe the relative contribution of the client (A) and counselor (B), so that taking up their terms, a sequence—ABABAB-BABBABBBABBBABBB—could be used to infer a build up of counselor dominance. As Highlen (1986) observed in her perceptive critique of their paper, this form of analysis lacks the contextual richness and meaning of the therapeutic process. In Duncker's terms, the critical, interpretive activity is missing. In situations where the possibility of developing power dominance is an issue for the therapist, or even for the researcher, then analysis of the interactions would be incomplete without information about their psychological meanings for all parties. Whatever is happening in the situation, an analysis stripped of the cognitive could not appropriately describe its core problem.

The process of understanding how-it-works and how-it-can-be-made-to-work not only makes a solution possible, but also gives that solution meaning in its progressive development.

Almost unbeknown to psychology, this transformational idea of Duncker's has been available, but not well understood, because it was situated under a different topic label, "functional fixity." In this negative form, it denotes a failure to reorganize the input from the environment and a failure to transform "Imbedded Use A" to "Novel, Unembedded Use B." For decades, functional fixity, as part of the study of "set" was the most retrieved aspect of Duncker's work (see Newell, 1985; Norman, 1993b; Carnevale and Probst, 1998).

By turning this concept around, however, to emphasize not the negative fixity of mind, but the positive "non-fixity," or flexibility of thought, we confront situativity with the transformational nature of the cognitive contribution. The person's internalizing take-up of the external does not simply involve transmission and acceptance, but rather, it also involves transformation of the existing relations and patterns of relations and events, (cf. Lawrence and Valsiner, 1993). If transmission or simple, direct perception were a sufficient processing of the problem to yield its solution, the difficult problem situation would not be difficult, in psychological terms. It would not need a solution. Instead, it is the transformational processing that is distinctive and effective in the development of a solution.

Once this kind of cognitive processing of the situation is admitted, then we may return to the question of Duncker's unique and lasting contribution to the psychological analysis of problem-solving. It would be forcing his account beyond its intentions and context, for instance, to try make his two phase problem-solving theory function as a general, all-purpose problem-solving model. As Newell (1985) demonstrated, other general models, including means-ends analysis, have been formalized, refined and tested at different levels of application within different domains. Furthermore, we now know that descriptive models are likely to be most powerful when they are domain-specific as opposed to general, all-purpose models, a fact that Duncker himself seemed to realize in his experiments. He certainly moved in that direction, by using mathematically appropriate concepts to describe the processes of mathematics problem solving.

While other models can cover the progressive transformations of problem definitions and solutions, it is the progressive refinements of meaning that are a distinctive Duncker factor not easily paralleled elsewhere. That Duncker factor keeps the analyses close to the actual situation and all its interacting dimensions. Analyses of the cognitive work, therefore, need to be able to describe problem and solution development against the demands and features of the situation, as they are progressively interpreted and re-interpreted. While that criterion may not be impossible to fulfill, situation-person interdependence must be given due weight in determining the depth and extent of the analyses.

Concerning methods of analysis, it is reasonable to expect that descriptions of problem solving in progress will benefit from advances in audio and visual technology and the ability to trace people's processing and particularly their meaning-making in various ways. Duncker's "coarse-grained" descriptive analyses (cf., de Groot, 1965; Newell, 1985), made at the level of annotated dialog, may not capture the fineness of detail in problem-solution development with all its external and internal features and emerging patterns. His adventurous interpretation of the role of the researcher in the research setting, however, challenges us to rethink some of our sterile methodologies.

In conclusion, by making a case for the continuing relevance and significance of Duncker's theorizing, we are not advocating that his concepts and methods be grafted onto contemporary research activities in a piecemeal way. As we have shown, other researchers have understood the significance of situation-specificity and the transforming, restructuring nature of cognitive processing. Rather, in the process of revisiting and exaggerating his account, we have sought to present the whole scheme with its own integrity and its inner logic. Its relevance is not simply that Duncker saw the importance of the situation before we did, nor that he tracked the transformational processes of productive thinking. Its lasting value resides in the way that Duncker's scheme gives each of these aspects of problem-solving its functional meaning in relation to the other, and in relation to the whole of the situation-person connection. Consequently, when considered together in an integrated system, they each gain their full potential for enlarging any analysis of the ways people solve problems of various levels of difficulty in various types of situations. Given that humans are problem solvers who encounter problems and difficulties throughout life and across experiences, Duncker's account of productive thinking allows us to understand and trace more clearly the processes by which problems are turned into solutions.

Note

1. Previously published in *From Past to Future, Vol. 1*(2), *The Legacy of Karl Duncker*, pp. 29–43. ©1999. Frances L. Hiatt Scholl of Psychology, Clark University. Jeanette Lawrence and Agnes Dodds, Department of Psychology, University of Melbourne, Parkville, Victoria 3052.

References

Brown, J. S., Collins, A., and Duguid, P. (1989). Situated cognition and the culture of learning. *Educational Researcher, 18*, 32-42.

Carnevale, P. J., and Probst, T. M. (1998). Social values and social conflict in creative problem-solving and categorization. *Journal of Personality and Social Psychology, 74*(5), 1300-1309.

Cole, M. (1996). *Cultural psychology: A once and future discipline.* Cambridge, MA: The Belknap Press of Harvard University Press.

Csikszentmihalyi, M. (1996). *Creativity: Flow and the psychology of discovery and invention.* New York: Harper Collins.

De Groot, A. D. (1965), *Thought and choice in chess.* Mouton Publishers: The Hague.
Dodds, A. E., Lawrence, J. A., and Valsiner, J. (1997). The personal and the social: Mead's theory of the "Generalized Other." *Theory and Psychology, 7*(4), 483-503.
Duncker, K. (1926). A qualitative (experimental and theoretical) study of productive thinking (solving of comprehensible problems). *Pedagogical Seminary, 33,* 642-708.
Duncker, K. (1939). Ethical relativity? (An enquiry into the psychology of ethics). *Mind, XLVIII,* 39-57.
Duncker, K. (1945). On problem-solving. *Psychological Monographs, 58* (Whole No. 270). Washington, DC: American Psychological Association.
Duncker, K. and Krechevsky, I. (1939). On solution-achievement. *Psychological Review, 46,* 176-185.
Engeström, Y., and Middleton, D. (Eds.). (1996). *Cognition and communication at work.* Cambridge: Cambridge University Press.
Goodnow, J. J. (1997). The interpersonal and social aspects of planning. In S. L. Friedman, and E. K. Scholnick (Eds.). *The developmental psychology of planning: Why, how, and when do we plan?* (pp. 339-357). Mahwah, NJ: Erlbaum.
Greeno, J. G., and Moore, J. L. (1993). Situativity and symbols: Response to Vera and Simon. *Cognitive Science, 17*(1), 49-59.
Harré, R. and Secord, P. F. (1973). *The explanation of social behavior.* Totowa, NJ: Littlefield Adams.
Heath, C. and Luff, P. (1996). Convergent activities: Line control and passenger information on the London Underground. In Y. Engeström and D. Middleton (Eds.). *Cognition and communication at work.* Cambridge: Cambridge University Press.
Highlen, P. S. (1986). Analyzing patterns and sequence in counseling: Reactions of a counseling process research. *Journal of Counseling Psychology, 33*(2), 186-189.
Juckes, T. J., and Barresi, J. (1993). The subjective-objective dimension in the individual-society connection: A duality model. *Journal for the Theory of Social Behavior, 23*(2) 197–216.
Kirshner, D., and Whitson, J. A. (1997). *Situated cognition: Social semiotic and psychological perspectives.* Mahwah, NJ: Erlbaum.
Lawrence, J. A. (1992). What if the how is a why? In J. B. Asendorpf and J. Valsiner (Eds.). *Stability and change in development* (pp. 240-248). Newbury Park, CA: Sage.
Lawrence, J. A. (1995). Sentencing processes and decisions: Influences and interpretations. In G. Hanlon, J. Jackson, and A. Atkinson (Eds.). *Judging and Decision Making, Proceedings of Second Annual Conference* (pp. 54-76). Sheffield: The Institute for the Study of the Legal Profession.
Lawrence, J. A., and Valsiner, J. (1993). Conceptual roots of internalization: From transmission to transformation. *Human Development, 36,* 150-167.
Lichtenberg, J. W., and Heck, E. J. (1986). Analysis of sequence and pattern in process research. *Journal of Counseling Psychology, 33*(2), 170-181.
Newell, A. (1985). Duncker on thinking: An inquiry into progress on thinking. In S. Koch and D. E. Leary (Eds.). *A century of psychology as science,* (pp. 392-419). New York: McGraw-Hill.
Newell, A. and Simon, H. A. (1972). *Human Problem Solving.* Englewood Cliffs, NJ: Prentice-Hall.
Norman, D. N. (1993a). Cognition in the head and in the world: An introduction to the special issue on situated action. *Cognitive Science, 17*(1), 1-6.
Norman, D. N. (1993b). *Things that make us smart: Defending human attributes in the age of the machine.* New York: Addison-Wesley.

Oliveira, Z. M. R. (1997). The concept of role and the discussion of the internalization process. In B. D. Cox and C. Lightfoot (Eds.). *Sociogenetic perspectives on internalization* (pp. 105-118). Mahwah, NJ: Erlbaum.

Perret-Clermont, A-N., Perret, J-F., and Bell, N. (1991). The social construction of meaning and cognitive activity in elementary school children. In L. B. Resnick, J. M. Levine and S. D. Teasley (Eds.). *Perspectives on socially shared cognition*, (pp. 41-62). Washington: American Psychological Association.

Scardamalia, M. and Bereiter, C. (1991). Literate expertise. In K. A. Anders and J. Smith (Eds.). *Toward a general theory of expertise* (172-194). New York: Cambridge University Press.

Simon, H. A. (1999). Karl Duncker and cognitive science. This volume.

Vera, A. H., and Simon, H. A. (1993). Situated action: A symbolic interpretation. *Cognitive Science, 17*(1), 7-48.

Vinache, W. E. (1951). *The psychology of thinking.* New York: McGraw-Hill.

Weisberg, R. (1986). Creativity, genius and other myths. New York: Freeman

Zinchenko, V. P. (1996). Developing activity theory. In B. A. Nardi (Ed.). *Context and consciousness: Activity theory and human-computer interaction* (pp. 283-324). Cambridge, MA: The MIT Press.

4

Duncker's Analysis of Problem Solving as Microdevelopment[1,2]

Kurt W. Fischer and Jeffrey Stewart

The search for an understanding of the organization of human problem solving runs through most of this century in psychology (Fischer, 1975; Fischer and Granott, 1995). The founder of the Gestalt School in Germany, Max Wertheimer (1945), and his colleague Wolfgang Köhler (1925) examined problem solving during the 1910s and 1920s. Building upon their work, Karl Duncker (1945) produced some of the most exciting and seminal work in problem solving. Today, cognitive psychologists are still using Duncker's ideas and learning from his work, even when some of them are unaware of these roots. While fitting firmly within the traditions of problem-solving research of his time, Duncker's research also pointed beyond those traditions in important directions, anticipating subsequent work on both analysis by synthesis and microdevelopment. Current researchers still have much to learn from his concepts and methods for analysis of the processes of problem solving.

Explanation of Problem Solving

Two traditional concepts in cognitive psychology are especially relevant to Duncker's work. First, much of learning is understood as a process of solving a problem. A person begins with a goal, then thinks about ways of accomplishing the goal, and finally implements those plans—while paying attention to whether the plans actually move him or her in the direction of accomplishing the goal. Second, cognitive psychologists see behavior as organized or patterned, often in hierarchical components, with higher levels integrating or coordinating lower levels. Given these two assumptions, the scientific objective is to describe how the many components of a person's thought and action become coordinated over time, often as a result of processes of problem solving.

Heinz Werner (1948; 1957) suggested that processes of short-term change, such as problem solving and learning, can be understood best as involving short-term development, termed microgenesis or microdevelopment. Duncker's classic research on problem solving provides some of the best examples to support this argument, although modern researchers sometimes fail to appreciate the insight and power of this research as a model of microdevelopmental analysis. In Duncker's work, people solved difficult problems by gradually working out different approaches until they settled on one that seemed to provide an effective solution.

The requirements of problem solving face all of us every day. Some problems are relatively simple, like finding our car keys. Other problems, like learning to ride a bicycle, seem to require more from our body than from our mind, and may require repeated efforts. The problems that Duncker studied were complex cognitively, requiring long-term planning, attention to many details, and organization of diverse means or strategies. An example is the now famous problem of finding a way to destroy a tumor in the stomach without destroying the person's other tissue:

> A person has an inoperable stomach tumor. He can be treated with radiation, but radiation of sufficient intensity will destroy healthy tissue as well as the tumor. How can radiation be used to eliminate the tumor without destroying the healthy tissue surrounding it?

One part of Duncker's framework for analyzing solutions of such problems is the classic concept of hypothesis testing—that people approach problems by formulating a hypothesis about how a goal might be reached (Krech, 1932; Tolman, 1948). Even rats negotiating a maze appear to use strategies like choosing all left-hand pathways for several trials before changing to another strategy when that no longer works. In describing how hypotheses were chosen and elaborated and how different hypotheses interact in complex tasks, Duncker took a microdevelopmental approach and also foreshadowed what came to be called analysis by synthesis (Lindsay and Norman, 1972).

In analysis by synthesis, the way a person conceptualizes a problem—their synthesis of the elements into a workable unit—determines the interpretation of those components, the analysis of the pattern. In 1935, Karl Duncker suggested a similar explanation for how problems are initially conceived and described. In his research, a complex problem such as the one about removing a tumor was read to a person, who was asked to "think out loud" while working on the problem. Duncker observed that people working on such problems typically began their analysis with relatively complex "hypotheses" that were really general outlines of possible solutions. Gradually people analyzed these outlines or syntheses further into distinct means of solution. Finally, specific solutions were rejected until the "best solution" remained. In other words, conceptualizations from an upper level of general synthesis led to a series of analyses containing more specific detail at the next lower level, and this process continued until a solution was found.

For the tumor problem, figure 4.1 illustrates Duncker's analysis of the phases or steps in problem solving. We have organized the figure to highlight both the process of analysis by synthesis and the microdevelopmental phases of solution. In moving from one row to the next down the diagram, the person uses his general conceptualization from one row or phase as a synthesis from which to analyze the problem into the conceptualizations at the next row or phase. First, the experimenter provided a general conception of the problem to the participant (top row of figure), such as that the tumor could be destroyed somehow by rays without destroying healthy tissue. Then, starting from this "synthesis," the person began a process of gradually constructing increasingly specific outlines for solution, which can be divided into phases two, three, and four.

In the second phase, he or she analyzed the problem by constructing several possible outlines for solutions, shown in the second row. Perhaps the rays could be prevented from contacting healthy tissue, or perhaps the tissue could be made insensitive to the rays, or perhaps the intensity of the rays passing through the healthy tissue could somehow be lowered. Third, each of these outlines was analyzed into several possible means for solving the problem, diagramed in the third row. Many possible means were generated through these outlines and evaluated. Two examples are finding some open path to the tumor, such as through the stomach, and removing the healthy tissue out of the path of the rays. Fourth, after considering these various means, the person chose some to construct specific solutions, as demonstrated in the bottom row. Some solutions were rejected as they were elaborated and analyzed, such as in this case sending the rays through the esophagus and operating to open the healthy tissue and expose the tumor. Eventually the person settled upon the best solution, which in the present case is shown in the bottom right-hand corner: By starting with the rays diffused over a wide area and using a lens to gradually focus them, the rays could pass through healthy tissue at low intensity and focus on the tumor with high intensity to destroy it.

Duncker's approach raised questions about a number of issues central to understanding problem solving and pointed in directions for answers to them as well. A number of those questions and directions center on the microdevelopmental framework implied in figure 4.1. What is the nature of the earliest phase in problem solving—the recognition that there is a problem? How are the early phases of analysis different from the later phases? How are new elements brought into the process in proceeding through the phases? How are elements combined and reorganized to form a new pattern of behavior or solution to the problem?

Figure 4.1
Duncker's Analysis of a Case of Problem Solving

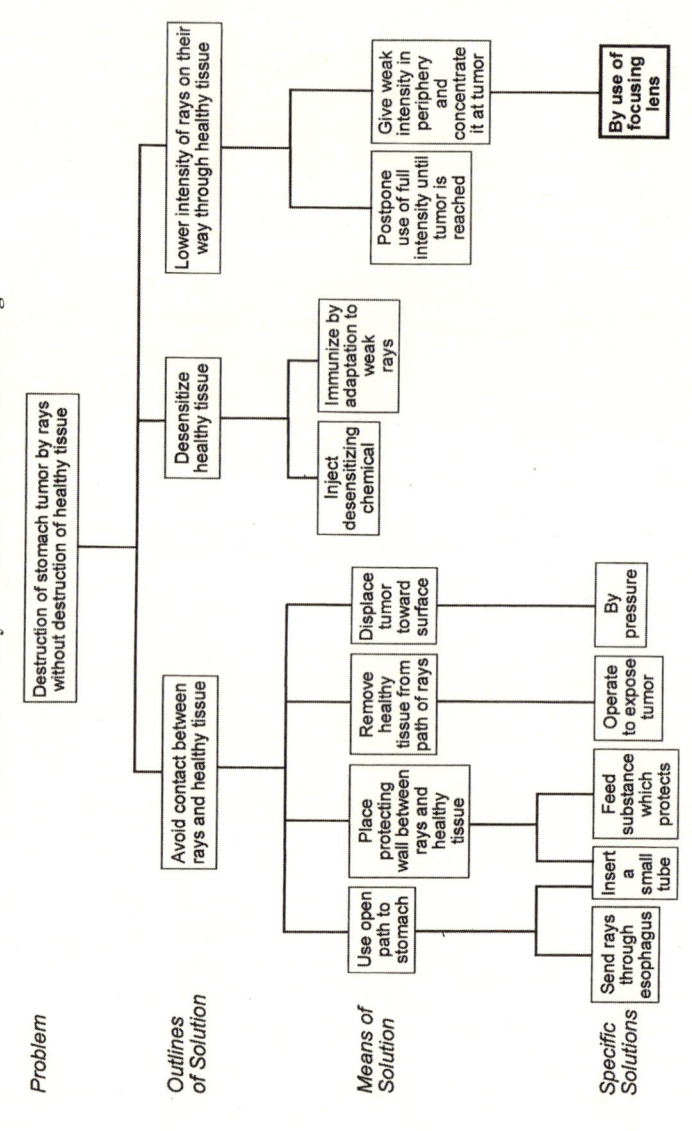

Problem

Destruction of stomach tumor by rays without destruction of healthy tissue

Outlines of Solution

- Avoid contact between rays and healthy tissue
- Desensitize healthy tissue
- Lower intensity of rays on their way through healthy tissue

Means of Solution

- Use open path to stomach
- Place protecting wall between rays and healthy tissue
- Remove healthy tissue from path of rays
- Displace tumor toward surface
- Inject desensitizing chemical
- Immunize by adaptation to weak rays
- Postpone use of full intensity until tumor is reached
- Give weak intensity in periphery and concentrate it at tumor

Specific Solutions

- Send rays through esophagus
- Insert a small tube
- Feed substance which protects
- Operate to expose tumor
- By pressure
- **By use of focusing lens**

Adapted from Duncker (1935/1945)

Phases of Microdevelopment in Problem Solving

The structure in figure 4.1 highlights the microdevelopmental nature of Duncker's analysis, falling into four phases. A person formulates the general properties of a solution early in the process and over time develops more specific properties out of the general ones. The problem solver thus moves through phases in which he or she gradually constructs a solution, much as a child moves gradually through levels or stages in long-term development, except that the phases occur in minutes or hours instead of months or years.

This approach has clear parallels to recent work in developmental psychology, where several independent investigators have suggested that microdevelopment involves progression through a series of phases much like those in figure 4.1 and approximating the more explicit formulation of phases in figure 4.2 (Berman, 1986; Karmiloff-Smith, 1979; MacWhinney, 1978; Palmer, 1996). We will use Fischer's (1975; 1980a) formula to portray the general nature of the four phases and the microdevelopmental transformations that lead from one to the next.

Fischer describes four phases of problem solving, as well as a zero beginning state, as shown in figure 4.2. From no understanding (Phase 0), a person moves through a vague, diffuse conception of the problem (Phase 1). This general conception facilitates formulation of one or more general directions for solution, which include some sketches of key components (Phase 2). The person then uses these sketches to articulate the necessary components for a solution (Phase 3) and gradually tries out combinations of those components until he or she finds a pattern that produces a solution (Phase 4). Note that there is a different organization of behavior at each phase, and mechanisms of transition accompany the movement from one phase to another, as shown in figure 4.2.

This phase theory, or something similar to it, seems to apply in many different domains, from solving Piagetian tasks to learning language rules and even to learning and problem solving in animals. The similarities across these diverse domains are remarkable. Even rats running an S-shaped maze appear to follow a similar phase order to Duncker's problem-solvers (Fischer, 1980a): 0) At first the rats meander with no understanding that there is food at the end. 1) Then they realize that there is food somewhere in the maze but do not know where. 2) Soon they realize that there is food to be found at the end and use that general conception to motivate action. 3) Gradually distinguish the separate components of running through the maze. 4) Eventually they integrate the components for running from beginning to end, as if they form a mental representation of the spatial relationships of the parts of the maze.

A natural question to ask is why there would be four microdevelopmental phases of problem solving, as opposed to some other number—three, six, or twenty-seven. Indeed, developmental changes in the organization of behavior for a problem or task can show many different numbers of phases, levels, or steps (see, for example, Case, 1991; Fischer, 1980b; Fischer and Granott, 1995). Yet

Figure 4.2
Phases in Microdevelopment of Solving a Problem

Phase	Level of Understanding	Temporal Organization	Transition
0	No understanding of problem	Activity shows no systematic organization with respect to problem to be solved.	
			Recognition of a problem to be solved
1	Vague, diffuse conception of problem	Parts of activity show clear goal direction and are performed energetically. Much activity remains relatively disconnected and irregular.	
			General outline of solution
2	General direction for solution	Activity shows long goal-directed sequences performed energetically, along with periods of hesitation, delay, and confusion, especially at start of goal-directed sequences and during shifts between sequences.	
			Differentiation of components of solution
3	All components needed for solution	Most activity is goal-directed and smooth, with occasional spontaneous pauses scattered throughout performance.	
			Coordination of components into an integrated whole
4	Full conception of solution	Activity pattern is similar to Phase 3, but even more regular. Skill becomes a new unit or chunk, which can be manipulated and recombined with others.	

Adapted from Fischer (1980) and Bidell (1990)

it appears that four is an unusually common number in microdevelopmental and developmental patterns. Even Piaget's main stages are four in number (sensorimotor, pre-operational, concrete operational, and formal operational periods), although people sometimes distinguish only three, combining pre-operational and concrete operational. Also, independently of the four Piagetian stages, several neo-Piagetian theorists have argued that cognitive development moves through four successive substages, tiers, or levels as schemes are reorganized to become more complex, although the exact formulations of those four-step sequences differ (Biggs and Collis, 1982; Case, 1991; Fischer, 1980b; Halford, 1987).

Analysis of Dynamic Structures in Problem Solving and Development

A good place to look for a grounded answer to this question is dynamic systems analysis of development and learning, in which growth processes are specified mathematically and the properties of growth functions are studied systematically. A beginning of an explanation is suggested by van Geert (1998) dynamic growth model based on Piaget's and Vygotsky's constructivist conceptions of growth. The model is based on broad Piagetian and Vygotskian principles of development, involving a dynamic interaction between person and environment. Surprisingly, for a wide range of values of parameters, development progressed not continuously but discontinuously: Most changes involved small increments, but activities tended to cluster in four (or sometimes three or five) different levels. This pattern also exhibited a fractal structure: When the changes in one of the clusters were analyzed in finer detail, they again showed a clustering of growth in four (plus or minus one) different sublevels.

More important than the question of the number of phases, however, is providing better descriptions of how microdevelopment occurs. Duncker's protocols provide a good sense of how to proceed. Researchers need to combine two levels of analysis: Based on richly detailed individual protocols about what people actually do in problem-solving in real time, we need to build models that capture the dynamic structures for action and understanding that people are constructing, as Duncker began to do in his model in figure 4.1. Realizing this goal requires building methods for analyzing structure and relating it to individual people's variable activities (Fischer and Bidell, 1998; Granott, 1998). Much has been learned since the days of Wertheimer, Köhler, and Duncker, but building theoretical and methodological tools to solve the problem of problem solving is sure to keep investigators engaged well into the future.

Notes

1. Portions of this article are adapted from Fischer (1975). Preparation of the manuscript was supported by grants from Mr. and Mrs. Frederick P. Rose, NICHD, and Harvard University.

2. Previously published in *From Past to Future, Vol. 1*(2), *The Drama of Karl Duncker*, pp. 45–50. ©1999 Frances L. Hiatt School of Psychology, Clark University. Author: Kurt W. Fischer, Harvard School of Education, Harvard Graduate School of Education, Appian Way, Cambridge, MA.

References

Berman, R. A. (1986). A step-by-step model of language acquisition. In I. Levin (Ed.), *Stage and structure: Reopening the debate* (pp. 191-219). New York: Plenum.

Biggs, J., and Collis, K. (1982). *Evaluating the quality of learning: The SOLO taxonomy (structure of the observed learning outcome)*. New York: Academic Press.

Case, R. (Ed.) (1991). *The mind's staircase: Exploring the conceptual underpinnings of children's thought and knowledge*. Hillsdale: Erlbaum.

Duncker, K. (1945). On problem solving. *Psychological Monographs, 58* (Whole no. 270).

Fischer, K. W. (1975). Thinking and problem solving: Cognitive psychology. In K. W. Fischer, P. R. Shaver, and A. Lazerson (Eds.), *Psychology today: An Introduction* (3rd ed., pp. 120-143). New York: CRM/Random House.

Fischer, K. W. (1980a). Learning and problem solving as the development of organized behavior. *Journal of Structural Learning*, 6, 253-267.

Fischer, K. W. (1980b). A theory of cognitive development: The control and construction of hierarchies of skills. *Psychological Review, 87*, 477-531.

Fischer, K. W., and Bidell, T. R. (1998). Dynamic development of psychological structures in action and thought. In R. M. Lerner (Ed.), and W. Damon (Series Ed.), *Handbook of child psychology: Vol. 1. Theoretical models of human development* (5th ed., pp. 467-561). New York: Wiley.

Fischer, K. W., and Granott, N. (1995). Beyond one-dimensional change: Parallel, concurrent, socially distributed processes in learning and development. *Human Development, 38*, 302-314.

Granott, N. (1998). Units of analysis in transit: From the individual's knowledge to the ensemble process. *Mind, Culture, and Activity, 5*, 42-66.

Halford, G. S. (1987). A structure-mapping approach to cognitive development. *International Journal of Psychology, 22*, 609-642.

Karmiloff-Smith, A. (1979). Micro and macrodevelopmental changes in language acquisition and other representational systems. *Cognitive Science, 3*, 91-118.

Köhler, W. (1925). *The mentality of apes*. New York: Harcourt, Brace.

Krech, D. (1932). The genesis of "hypotheses" in rats. *University of California Publications in Psychology, 6*, 45-64.

Lindsay, P. H., and Norman, D. A. (1972). *Human information processing*. New York: Academic Press.

MacWhinney, B. (1978). *The acquisition of morphophonology. Monographs of the Society for Research in Child Development, 43*(1-2, Serial No. 174).

Palmer, G. (1996). *Toward a theory of cultural linguistics*. Austin, TX: University of Texas Press.

Tolman, E. C. (1948). Cognitive maps in rats and men. *Psychological Review, 55*, 189-208.

van Geert, P. (1998). A dynamic systems model of basic developmental mechanisms: Piaget, Vygotsky, and beyond. *Psychological Review, 105*, 634-677.

Werner, H. (1948). *Comparative psychology of mental development*. New York: Science Editions.

Werner, H. (1957). The concept of development from a comparative and organismic point of view. In D. B. Harris (Ed.), *The concept of development*). Minneapolis: University of Minnesota Press.

Wertheimer, M. (1945). *Productive thinking*. New York: Harper.

Part II

Abstractive Generalization through Language: The Legacy of Karl Bühler

5

The Pleasure of Thinking: A Glimpse into Karl Bühler's Life

Jaan Valsiner[1]

Karl Bühler (1879–1963) can be seen as one of the thinkers in psychology whose work was of profound programmatic value for other disciplines—linguistics and philosophy of language in his case (Eschbach, 1987, 1989; Sebeok, 1983; Wetterstein, 1988). It was relevant for the "speech act" theory (Smith, 1988), as well as for the role of language in human mental processes (Cassirer, 1942). Furthermore, Bühler created a model of communication (the *Organonmodell*), and made notable contributions to semiotics—which he himself labeled sematology (Innis, 1983). He benefited from the liaisons with Husserl's phenomenology, the holistic thought of *Gestalt-* and *Ganzheitspsychologie* of the beginning of the twentieth century. He became (together with Charlotte Malachowski) a substantial contributor to developmental psychology. He certainly belongs to the top of German theoreticians of psychology of this century, alongside of Ernst Cassirer, William Stern, and Max Wertheimer. Yet Bühler is probably more consistent than the others in his linking of philosophical, theoretical, and empirical domains in his version of psychology.

Disciplinary History Writing: Effects of "-ist"-ing

Histories of psychology are accounts that function in the present—and bring about a future. Hence psychologists have been eager to write their history in terms of "schools" or orientations. We usually operate with general categories of "introspectionism," "behaviorism," "cognitivism," etc., looking at particular persons who were trying to solve some intellectual problems as if they primarily belonged to the roaming gangs of "*-ists*" of some category. Yet such writing of history has two limitations. First, the individual person's specificity becomes lost behind category labels. For instance, John B. Watson and Edward C. Tolman may both be labeled "behaviorists," and even George Herbert Mead may be described by that label (with an interesting qualification—"a *sophisticated* behaviorist"—see Glock, 1986, p. 142). Second, persons who are not easily classifiable into the consensual categories would easily remain out of focus for history writers. Unless the label of an "*-ist*" is attached to a person, he or she has good chances for being overlooked in the social discourse about history *in the present*.

Karl Bühler can be seen as a scientist to whom the attachment of an "*-ist*" categorization is difficult. It is only easy to point out which category does not apply to him—Bühler certainly would not be considered a "behaviorist" (even a "sophisticated" one)—yet there were moments of interest in behavior in his work. He was "introspectionist," "gestaltist," "cognitivist," "holist," "socio-culturalist"—yet application of any (or all) of these labels provides no further help in understanding Bühler's intellectual contributions. His role in the history of psychology is certainly recognized. Yet this recognition proceeds along the lines of disciplinary (rather than interdisciplinary) history. He (together with Charlotte Bühler[2]) is known as one of the classic authors in child psychology, and his speech theory or analysis of crisis in psychology may be mentioned. Yet his linkages with the Prague Linguistics Circle—which were very important for semiotics (Eschbach, 1990a; Innis, 1983)—have been overlooked. Furthermore, his direct role in the introspectionist research on thinking has been glossed over—not surprisingly, as the methodological credo of introspectionism was socially discredited in psychology. Bühler's speech theory has its roots in his Würzburg-time experiments on thinking processes (e.g., Bühler, 1912).

Undoubtedly Karl Bühler belongs to the group of psychologists who advanced the discipline in major ways in the twentieth century. By gaining his historical place, Bühler becomes an intellectual skeleton in a closet of a history museum of an otherwise hyper-empiricist contemporary enterprise of psychology. The latter at times borrows historical personages to use them as *guru*-type figureheads (e.g., Piaget or Vygotsky—Van der Veer and Valsiner, 1991). This may be sufficient for the immediate pragmatic needs of the empirical enterprise, but is surely counterproductive for advancement of knowledge.

Parallels in Personal Quests: Bühler and Vygotsky

Bühler was continuously concerned with issues of meaning construction, from his early work (Bühler, 1907, 1908a) to the end of his life. As the question of meaning is the cornerstone of most of intellectual crises in psychology, Bühler addressed directly issues of methodology. He moved in parallel with Lev Vygotsky to outline the crisis in psychology (Bühler, 1926, 1927; Vygotsky, 1927/1982; see also Innis, 1988; Pléh, 1988). There are similarities in the directions taken by Vygotsky and Bühler on making sense of the crisis and finding ways to overcome it. This is not too surprising, since from the perspective of both relative outsiders to psychology, the problems of psychology and solutions were self-evident. Bühler was a medical doctor interested in philosophy, and through that entered psychology. Vygotsky was a literary scholar interested in philosophy and medicine, arriving at psychology.

More interesting, there is even an almost perfect parallelism between them in timing. Both proceeded in parallel to publish their main collections of ideas on how to overcome the crisis by a focus on semiotic mediation in the same year 1934 (Bühler, 1934/1965; Vygotsky, 1934). Last, but not least, there were similarities in their rhetorical styles. Both Bühler and Vygotsky could be critical of others' ideas—without extending that criticism to the persons, and both borrowed constructively from the ideas they criticized. Both strove toward unity of psychology—in ways that maintain the centrality of phenomena rather than glorify any particular set of methods or theoretical perspectives.

Karl Bühler's *Lebenslauf*

Bühler's life course has been described in detail in German by Lebzeltern (1969), as well as by Eschbach (1990b) and Sebeok (1983) in English. Karl Bühler was born on May 27, 1879, in Merkesheim (near Heidelberg) to the family of a railwayman, Ludwig B. Bühler (1852–1926) and Berta Bühler (Emmerich, 1852–1916). The parents came from Swiss heritage (Basel and Zürich regions). Karl had one younger brother and two sisters. His parents were of different religious backgrounds—his father a Protestant, his mother a Catholic. His studies in Matthias-Grünewald-Gymnasium led (in 1898) the young nineteen-year-old to the wide world after secondary education, divided in interests between theology and mathematics. Yet he continued in neither—he entered the University of Freiburg to study medicine (and graduated in 1903 with a dissertation on physiology of color vision, under the advisorship of Johannes von Kries). He began to work in medical practice in Strassburg, continuing his studies in philosophy. A year later—in 1904—he received his second doctorate (in philosophy) from University of Strassburg (on the psychology in the thought of eighteenth century Scottish philosopher Henry Home). The work in medicine was not of great intellectual pleasure for Bühler; he gravitated toward psychology. He studied in Berlin with Benno Erdmann for a brief time (to which period his contacts with Edmund Husserl's phenomenology can be dated) and was assistant to von Kries in Freiburg. In 1906 he became an assistant to Oswald Külpe in Würzburg. It is precisely in the context of the "Würzburg School" that Bühler arrived at the beginnings of his most relevant ideas of the presentational functions in language.

The Würzburg Intellectual Climate

Probably there could be no better match for Bühler's interests around 1905/6 in Germany than the intellectual orientation of the "Würzburg School" of psychology. That label became attached to the group of psychologists who worked with Oswald Külpe in Würzburg in the period 1894 to 1909. Külpe (or his coworkers) did not use that label (Ogden, 1951).

Külpe was a kind person[3], and a very intelligent thinker (see Marbe, 1961, pp. 192-193). His move away from Wundt's ideas led to the establishment of a process-oriented look at complex human intra-psychological functions. The introspectively available psychological phenomena needed appropriate—systematic—methodology, which was careful, experimentally triggered externalization of the introspective process. In that process, phenomena—which we now recognize as semiotic—dominated the flow of reasoning (Eschbach, 1990a; Wetterstein, 1988).

Külpe considered the centrality of volitional processes as integrating forces of human personality:

> Circumstances do not rule us, but we confront circumstances—choosing, arranging, and directing. Our mind is not the sport of incalculable accident; but according to the measure of the strength that is in us, the strength that manifests itself in attention, we can transcend the limits of our organism and help to move the universe, propounding and realizing ideal ends. We do not stand in the mere course of events, indifferent transmitters of mechanical processes; we prove our independence and our freedom by rational test and consideration of the impressions that pour in upon us, and by consistent devotion to the plans and tasks that our conscience has approved (Külpe, 1903, p. 68).

The focus on holistic integrative processes of the psychological (internal) and the external worlds emerged from Külpe's earlier work (e.g., the "joint region" of self and external world—Külpe, 1892). Through the act of abstraction it is possible for consciousness to grasp reality.

The focus on *processes* of human reasoning, which at times resurfaces in contemporary cognitive psychology, can be traced back to the work of Külpe and his colleagues. Yet Külpe had to argue forcefully—and in the end unsuccessfully—in favor of finding his perspective a place in the consensually accepted scientific psychology (Wetterstein, 1988). Attempting to study both *processual* and *intentional* aspects of psychological processes in combination was (and remains) a difficult task for any psychologist.

The volitional side of these processes got coverage in the work of Narziss Ach (1905), who worked at Würzburg somewhat separately from Külpe (Ogden, 1951, p. 10). The psychologists who worked with Külpe were united around basic issues which were empirically addressed—those of the role of the task (*Aufgabe*), the importance of the will, and the nature of thought—both imageless and image-based (Lindenfeld, 1978). The focus on the investigation of higher psychological functions (which later were a prominent focus for Vygotsky's and Luria's cultural-historical theory) found its beginning in Würzburg (Mack, 1993).

Külpe's group of coworkers at the time included a group of young and active psychologists—August Messer, August Mayer, Ernst Dürr, Henry Watt,

Johannes Orth, Klaus Marbe, Johannes Lindworsky, Robert Ogden, and others. Messer and Watt worked on thinking processes before Bühler started in 1906 (Messer, 1906; Watt, 1905).

Külpe had numerous short-term visitors working with him, among whom Kurt Koffka (who worked toward his *Habilitation* with Külpe), Max Wertheimer (whose dissertation was done with Külpe—Wertheimer, 1905), Charles Spearman, and Albert Michotte could be noted. Much empirical work, performed mostly in the years 1901 through 1908, was guided by Külpe and produced by him as he was also performing the role of the subject (in those times subjects were called "observers").

When Bühler joined Külpe in 1906, he "worked on the psychology of thought afresh, entirely under Külpe" (Marbe, 1961, p. 197). He was immediately recognized by Külpe's co-workers as an intellect of excellent quality[4]. Bühler was the first in the history of psychology to document the presence of insight (*Aha-Erlebnis*) in psychological experiments in thinking (Bühler, 1908a, p. 13; in English: Bühler, 1951, p. 49). His subject/observer in this description was Külpe himself. Külpe never published experimental research of his own, but his participation was central in the work of his coworkers, and he insisted upon the establishment or improvement of psychology laboratories in each place he accepted appointment (Würzburg, Bonn, Munich).

The core of epistemological thought characteristic of the Külpe group was the focus on realization—the dynamics of becoming real. Külpe's main lifework of three volumes was called *Die Realisierung* (Külpe, 1912, 1920, 1923). For him, reality was "the occasion for the phenomena presented to a knowing subject" (Ogden, 1951, p. 19). This is fully in line with the experiments that were conducted by the Külpe group. These experiments were oriented toward giving the introspecting person a specific task for comprehension that was to be marked by a brief response. This amounts to creating conditions for the occasion under which the phenomena can become realized. The task often entailed a sentence or saying, with the goal of getting a yes/no answer to the direction, "Do you understand: <saying>?" The yes or no answer was not meant to be data per se, but merely a transition point for the observer to move to immediate reporting of how the answer was arrived at. This moment tapped into the processes that the knowing subject could report. For example:

> Experimenter (Karl Bühler): "Do you understand: *when the minds begin to moralize, the devils are set loose?*" [Erst wenn der Geist in die Moral fährt, geht der Teufel los].

> Observer (Ernst Dürr): <9 seconds> "Yes"— "… comprehension came with the word: Nietzsche. This stood for the thought: Nietzsche is an example that if one wants both to be witty and treat of ethics, one is shadow-boxing […wenn man geistreich sein will und Ethik treibt, man die Geister hintereinander jagt …] (Bühler, 1908, p. 15, and in Bühler, 1951, p. 50).

The format of the introspective experiments where the subject-observer plays a central role—while the experimenter communicates the task—already includes the basic structure of the *Organonmodell* that Bühler developed later, in his Vienna years. The similarity of the method to that of the "clinical interview" used later by Jean Piaget in Geneva has been noted (Murphy, 1966). In Külpe's time, the priority claim for the methodology used was made by Alfred Binet, who argued that the "Würzburg methodology" should actually be called "Paris methodology." The time (early 1900s) may have been ripe for addressing the issue of higher psychological functions as time-based processes, with different investigators working in a similar direction. This was the time of radical breakthroughs in developmental science (Baldwin, 1902) and in understanding the role of language in organizing human psychological processes (Bergson, 1907). Music was a widespread target phenomenon for many psychologists of that time (Ehrenfels, 1890/1967; Stumpf and von Hornbostel, 1911). Aside from being a favorite pastime of the more affluent classes, it constituted a puzzle for psychology—how can a sequence of sounds, unfolding over time, result in a person's subjective perception of a musical tune? Surely the person creates holistic patterns that unfold over time through the acoustic perception system. Likewise, the person creates a flow of ideas through speaking, which is perceived in terms of holistic sequences (word, sentence, utterance). But how can one study such complex processes?

The "Würzburg method" entailed a major role being transferred to the subject who was called "observer"[5] (a person who observes the experimental stimuli—either given externally or evoked internally—and reports the observations). The observer (or "person of the experiment"— *Versuchsperson*) was recognized as an active co-constructor of the data—the latter are available only to him, and the experimenter (the "experiment leader" or *Versuchsleiter*) is fully dependent upon the observer's communicative messages about whatever had taken place in the inner world of the observer immediately before the decision was made. Of course this dependency led to the dispute about the authenticity of the personal communicated messages relative to the posited "true happening" in the mind (Aster, 1908; Dürr, 1908; Wundt, 1907, 1908). Bühler's defense of the procedure is noteworthy in a number of ways. First, in response to criticisms that the *Ausfrage*-experiment elicits non-true constructions, Bühler (referring to his best subject—Külpe) emphasized that all experiences triggered by new situations are based on the previously lived-through personal events (Bühler, 1908b, p. 94; Bühler, 1909). Second, the criticisms that the tasks given to the introspecting subject produce surprise (and therefore lead to unreal responses) were answered through the contrast between verifying what *is in* the mind (not claimed by Bühler to be elicited) and what the mind *works through*—once it is given a "surprise" (=new input). This distinction has plagued methodological discourse in all of psychology—the ontological (*as is*) and constructionist (*as is being made to be*) *foci* set up very different demands upon methodology.

Külpe's (and Bühler's) lack of success in persuading their colleagues of the ontological persuasion to accept the alternative standpoint as appropriate to the issues they addressed can be seen as the failure of the others—psychology's mainstream—to accept an axiom without which human psychological phenomena cannot be investigated.

Third, Bühler—largely based on Ach's (1905) focus on the determining tendency—accepted the goal-oriented nature of human thought processes. In an introspectionist experiment, the goal had to be externally given. For example (see above), the "yes/no" answer format suggests to an observer a desired end point of the introspection process. Whether "yes" or "no" is answered is by itself irrelevant, yet the act of reaching the suggested goal allows for immediate reflection on how the outcome was reached. *It is **the process that leads to the outcome** that is in the focus of analysis.* The outcome itself is merely an anchor point for allowing for access to the process. This orientation became lost from psychological methods later. Consider the majority of questionnaires that require subjects to give "yes" or "no" (or "true" or "false") answers to questions worded vaguely and in common-sense terminology. The "data" from these questionnaires are assumed to be exactly the outcomes (i.e., whether a subject answered "yes" or "no"), with the process through which the particular answer was generated left out of such data. From the perspective of Külpe, Bühler, and their colleagues such data were of no value, if the research question was set to be the process of reasoning.

Of course Külpe and Bühler were not building their empirical approach on an empty ground. Discourse about the qualities of the whole (*Gestaltqualitäten*) had been around in German psychology since the end of the nineteenth century (Cornelius, 1897; Ehrenfels, 1890; Meinong, 1902/1983). It is only by way of later reconstructions of history of psychology that the "birth date" of Gestalt psychology is given as 1912 (and connected with Wertheimer's demonstration of the phenomenon of stroboscopic movement). In reality, scientific discourse in German-speaking areas from 1880s onwards (to say the least) was filled with holistic ideas, which in their different versions operated around the notion of the whole having primacy over its parts. The phenomena of music and general discourse of aesthetics were leading psychology toward adopting a holistic stance.

The holistic ethos was likewise part of phenomenological orientations in philosophy and psychology. Edmund Husserl's phenomenological philosophy was one of the sources for Bühler's thought (C. Bühler, 1965; Eschbach, 1987; Smith, 1988). All through his professional life, a phenomenological focus was of relevance to Bühler. This became particularly clear in the Vienna (and *Sprachtheorie*, e.g., Bühler, 1990, pp. 10-13) period, but was already in present before Bühler joined Külpe in Würzburg.

The Würzburg School continued in a smaller version in Bonn, where Külpe and Bühler moved in 1909. It was here that Bühler carried out a series of empirical investigations on perception that led to his first major book (Bühler, 1913). Theoretically, his interest was linked with the discourse about holistic qualities. Bühler demonstrates here—as well as in his later work—his non-reductionistic basis that is simultaneously open to ideas of development and abstraction. The latter two notions became central for him in the most productive period of his life, in Vienna. Bühler can be characterized as a thinker who tried to unite the relevant aspects of phenomenology, holistic thinking, and the dynamic nature of the processes of psychological synthesis.

The Munich Interlude

In 1913 Oswald Külpe received the call to a professorship in Munich, and Bühler went with him. They re-established the role of the Psychological Institute of University of Munich—well-known before for its philosophical and aesthetic traditions of Theodor Lipps and Hans Cornelius—as an experimental research center. The First World War soon interfered—Bühler went to the war as a medical doctor (and served on the Western front); Külpe continued at the University of Munich until his sudden death (on December 30, 1915). Bühler was invited back from the front to continue Külpe's work at the university. Three days later, on the day of Külpe's funeral, he got to know a twenty-two-year-old woman by the name of Charlotte Malachowski, with whom he got married on April 4, 1916. Bühler was thirty-seven at that time. The couple became reproductively successful soon after that—their first child (Ingeborg) was born April 2, 1917). The topic of observations over child development entered thus into the intellectual field of both Bühlers. Charlotte Bühler's diary of child development began in the private realm—similarly to the recordings of development of their own children by psychologists Clara and William Stern, James Mark Baldwin, Jean Piaget, William Preyer, and others.

Karl Bühler was not released from the military service once back in Munich. He had to continue to serve as a doctor in a military hospital in Munich (in the mornings), while working on the maintenance and development of the Psychological Institute, as well as continuing Külpe's lecture course (on logic) in the afternoons. Charlotte Bühler finished her doctorate in 1918, and in the same year Karl Bühler published the first edition of his to-be-classic book on child development (K. Bühler, 1918).

As World War I ended, the Bühlers moved to Dresden (in 1918), where Karl Bühler was appointed professor ordinarius at the Technische Hochschule. They had their second child (Rolf, born June 2, 1919) while in Dresden. The post-war times in Germany were economically difficult (the Bühlers remained grateful to food packages sent to them by American Quakers). Professionally, the teaching duties in the Technische Hochschule Dresden were less than stimulating for Karl Bühler, so it was an appropriately good result for both of them when Karl got the call for professorship in Vienna in 1922.[6]

The Hightime: Years in Vienna

Both Bühlers were lucky to move to Vienna. The old Austro-Hungarian monarchy had collapsed, and the Austrian social system was in a creative flux. The University of Vienna was a wide open place for new developments in early 1920s. The professorship (on philosophy, with orientation toward psychology and experimental pedagogics) was contended for by a number of leading scholars of the German-speaking areas. The final two candidates were Karl Bühler and Erich Jaensch. Finally, Bühler was invited (on March 20, 1922) on the basis of his demonstrated capacity to address complex problems experimentally (see Lebzeltern, 1969, p. 26; and Ash, 1988, for full account). At the same time, Moritz Schlick was invited to take a professorship in philosophy in Vienna. The new republic of Austria was aiming toward a positive future under the political dominance of the social democratic party. The Bühlers' arrival in Vienna, and the development of their work over the following decade, was closely tied to the supportive role of the Social Democrats (Ash, 1988). Their status changed after 1934 (when the social democrats lost power) and of course came to a dramatic end in 1938 as a result of Hitler's takeover of Austria.

Karl Bühler literally created the popularity for psychology as a study area in the university. By his own claim, when he arrived in Vienna in 1922 his lectures attracted only about twenty listeners, but ten years later that number was over 1000. Thus it is not surprising that encountering only a few students at Clark in 1941 (see Sigel, this issue) must have reminded him of the beginning of his days in Vienna. Perhaps his reference to the "intellectual zeal" that could compensate for the small numbers was a reference to his early times in Vienna.

Indeed, the 1920s and early 1930s (at least until 1934) were a period of rapid intellectual development in philosophy and psychology in Vienna. By 1937, Bühler had attracted to Vienna doctoral student candidates from eighteen countries. The salon of the Bühlers was an intellectual hub in Vienna, with foreign visitors coming for serious intellectual encounters. The seminars at the Institute (on Wednesdays) involved junior researchers in constructive discussions, which regularly ended in joint merrymaking in a local hotel restaurant and dance floor. Life was filled with intellectual yet physiognomically lived-through experiences for the participants—a far cry from narrowly defined "doing research" situated activity settings of contemporary psychology. In the social accessibility and role in the Viennese intellectual community, it is probable that the relevance of the role of both Bühlers surpassed that of Freud—a point the followers of Freud would surely actively contest. There was no contact between Bühler and Freud—despite the fact that a number of Bühler's students at the time were involved in psychoanalytic training (Ekstein, 1966). Bühler was critical of psychoanalytic constructions, yet did not overlook the phenomena that were highlighted by psychoanalysts.

The Psychological Institute

The Psychological Institute worked in three thematic areas. The *experimental psychology* direction was oriented towards investigation of perception, building upon Karl Bühler's earlier work on perception (Bühler, 1913)—yet in new ways. The work of assistants Egon Brunswik (who began as Bühler's assistant in 1927) and Lajos Kardos is notable here. Brunswik developed his "lens model" subsequently, and made major contributions to the issues of "representative research design" in psychology (Brunswik, 1947).

Secondly, there was a research group of *economic psychology and sociology*, led by Paul Lazarsfeld from 1927 onwards. It included, among others, Marie Jahoda. It was closely connected with the Marxist economic social reforms movement (see Ash, 1988, pp. 314-315). It undertook investigation of the effects of unemployment in a working-class suburb of Vienna (Marienthal).

Finally—but most importantly—Charlotte Bühler developed her own institutional framework of child and youth psychology. She spent a year (1914–1915) at Yale University as a Rockefeller Fellow, getting to know the work of Arnold Gesell in his Child Study Center.[7] The result of the stay was that the Rockefeller Foundation support to different child study centers (at Yale, Minnesota, Iowa, Berkeley, etc.) was extended to Charlotte Bühler's work group in Vienna. Charlotte—who had been in the role of assistant to Karl—became autonomous as a professor in 1929. There was active support by the City of Vienna for the study of children. The city established its own Pedagogical Institute, which served as a basis for the Bühlers' child study efforts.

In 1925, the Psychological Institute moved into larger space, and gained financial support (for a ten-year period) from the Rockefeller Foundation for the research direction of child study. This led to a productive research program on child and adolescent development in the late 1920s (C. Bühler, 1928), and to the establishment of life-course developmental psychology in the 1930s (C. Bühler, 1933). A series of monographs emanating from the Institute (*Quellen und Studien zur Jugendkunde*, 1925-31) reported empirical materials collected in the 1920s. Charlotte Bühler attracted numerous researchers who were interested in child development, among them Hildegard Hetzer (e.g., C. Bühler, Hetzer, and Tudor-Hart, 1927; see Rauh, 1990), Lotte Schenk-Danzinger, Else Frenkel, Beatrix Tudor-Hart. The City of Vienna—under the social-democratic leadership—established a special institution (*Kinderüber-namestelle*) which created conditions for unlimited observations over children's actions in their ordinary habitats.

Among the students whom Karl Bühler advised in Vienna were Lajos Kardos (later professor of psychology in Budapest), followed by Egon Brunswik (who left for the U.S. in the mid-1930s). Konrad Lorenz, and Paul Lazarsfeld (1959) did their work with Bühler. Also, Karl Popper finished his Ph.D. on the problems of method in the psychology of thinking (Kurtz, 1996, p. 174) at University of

Vienna with Karl Bühler and Moritz Schlick, and left psychology (not to speak of social work) forever, opting for a career that ended up on an aristocratic note. He credited Bühler's ideas of the three levels of the function of language (see the analysis of the *Darstellungsfeld*, below) as crucial for his later work (Popper, 1976, p. 74). Numerous international visitors passed through Vienna in the hightime of the Bühlers' Institute, and there were offers to Karl Bühler of more professorships in the U.S.[8] The Bühlers declined—the context in Vienna was far more productive intellectually than these lucrative offers could entail.

Major Themes of Inquiry in the Vienna Period

Based on the interest in child development that had started already in Munich (C. Bühler, 1918; K. Bühler, 1918, chap. 6), the Bühlers were interested in the ways in which fairy tales guide human development as a good explanation of how the communication process works. Communication entails the fantasy-world, exaggeration, and disconnected lines of reasoning—all characteristics of fairy tales. Bühler claimed that some achievements of imagination are encouraged by the fairy tale, while others are called into play by it only very slightly, or not at all. Thus, fairy tales create some domains of actively promoted imagination, while bypassing other possible domains of thought. As an example—rapid and varied changes in the image content are highly exaggerated in the fairy tales, whereas the simultaneous combination of ideas is usually ignored. The fairy tale avoids all thinking that is in any way complicated, and replaces complications by exaggerations of temporal transformations of events, often creating unexplained yet plausible sequences of happenings. This description would fit in our contemporary world with most of television programs—so perhaps the Bühlers were ahead of their time in recognizing the power of advertising.

Critical Evaluation of Psychology: Die Krise der Psychologie

Bühler wrote the book on crisis in psychology first in the form of a long article (Bühler, 1926), which then became a book (Bühler, 1927/1978). The book includes Bühler's analyses of the state of affairs in different schools of psychology (associationistic psychology, "thinking psychology"—*Denkpsychologie*; behaviorism, and "soul"—psychology—psychoanalysis). Bühler analyzes these directions, critically, yet without complete dismissal. All of them have their place—albeit a differential one—within the general construction of psychology. Yet—more importantly—the book contains a systematic exposure of Bühler's speech theory in the making, emphasizing the sign-constructor's and sign-user's complementarity, the notion of cultural psychology, and the notion of *Funktionslust* (Bühler, 1927/1978, chapter 4).

The notion of function-pleasure emerged in Bühler's work in conjunction with his look at child development—particularly in conjunction with issues of child's play (Bühler, 1918, p. 209), but was not recorded as a notable concept in the index of the book. By its third edition (in 1922) it appears in the index. Aside from the pleasure of function, one could get pleasure from satisfaction of need (satiation pleasure, or *Geniessen*) and from creative work (*Schaffenslust*).

Bühler liked to create triadic conceptual structures. Not only did his Institute include three sub-parts, but all of his major theoretical suggestions (see *Organonmodell*, below) tended to include three different—yet interdependent—parts. Thus, the pleasure of functioning can be seen as leading into the pleasure of satiation, and further into a new version of functioning—that of creative processes. The latter were amply demonstrated in observational studies of children (Hetzer, 1931).

On the topic of functioning pleasure, Bühler elaborated his main discrepancy from Freud (who was considered to be a *Stoffdenker*—unable to think in terms of form, Gestalt, and productivity—Allport, 1966), on the issues of the role of pleasure in human functioning. Freud was oriented to go beyond the "pleasure principle." In contrast, Bühler so to speak, stayed *within* the pleasure *as* a principle—he emphasized the pleasurable nature of human movements *per se* (Bühler, 1928a, p. 197). Locating the pleasure in the process of acting itself made it possible to see the world of children's play and adult lives going beyond the pleasure *principle*, towards the enjoyment of non-principled process of living.

The relevance of the child development materials that were collected in Vienna is visible in the book. The primacy of the social ("mutual guidance" of communication partners) in the psychological domain was made evident here. The notion of steering (*Steuerung*)—guidance of one person's actions by another—was relevant for Bühler in a number of ways. First, it maintained a focus on future objectives. Secondly, it entailed the sociogenetic side in Bühler's psychological system. Needless to say, this notion fits with the systematic introspection experiments of his Würzburg period. Still, Bühler was not ready in his Vienna period to study the process of interpersonal communication. The steering principle has also been viewed as antedating cybernetics (Allport, 1966, p. 202).

Yet Bühler denied that one human being can enter into the psychological field of another directly. Instead, all efforts of interpretations of others are possible through mediation of signs. In fact, the impossibility of direct contact between persons makes the duality of signs and experiences necessary. Hence the crucial contribution to science—at which he arrived at the height of his Vienna period, early 1930s, is his theory of the act of speaking. The act of speaking is necessarily bounded by the inter-personal situation (opportunity) and by intra-individual conditions (personal need). Obviously these ideas per se were not Bühler's creation; he borrowed them, but united them in an innovative way. In his communication theory, Bühler combined the principles of struggle for individual existence with that of mutual support. Both notions existed in biology (the first emphasized by Darwin, the other by Kropotkin). Bühler transposed then to the realm of higher psychological function and its medium—speech.

The Creation of Sprachtheorie

Bühler's main contribution emerged over the Vienna years in a step-by-step fashion. In parallel, three related components of Bühler's theoretical scheme— that of *expression* (*Ausdruck*), *appeal* (of speech), and *representation*—were integrated into his wider picture of theory. Roots of the building of his theory can be discovered in creative linkages with Alexius Meinong's treatise on emotional presentation (Meinong, 1917/1972—for specific links with Bühler see Krug, 1929). Bühler was an active participant in the Prague Linguistic Circle (e.g., Bühler, 1931; Koerner, 1988), and the work towards his integrative general framework was influenced by that connection. Bühler's interests in language date back to his Würzburg/Bonn years, but got their full extension in the 1920s. Last (but not least), Bühler's experiments on the thinking process involved communicating sentences to the observers that were to be understood.

The basic components of *Sprachtheorie*—the triad of *Auslösung* (later re-labelled *Appell*– "appeal"), *Kundgabe* (expression), and *Darstellung* (representation)—were already in place in 1919 (Bühler, 1919b; Krug, 1929, p. 225). The expression in speech involves affective value (*Gefühls-wert*—Bühler, 1923, p. 284). The difference of communication systems of humans—in contrast to animals—entails mutual social guidance in shared perceived situations (Bühler, 1927b). Thus, the *Kundgabe* needed to be seen to have a parallel in *Kundnahme*—the communication process necessarily involves a difference of perspectives between the communicator and the recipient. Furthermore, the feedback-nature of speaking (the speaker hears his own speech while speaking) creates a situation within the person that is similar to that of shared perceptual field. What in mutual social guidance (steering) occurs between persons can in the act of speaking occur between person and the speaking output. This similarity guarantees the central relevance of the act of speaking (Bühler, 1928). Bühler's central concern in building the theory of speaking remained with the sentence as unit. Note that already in his early, Würzburg-period experiments, the use of sentences was eminent. A sentence in the communication process is the unit that both the speaker and the hearer can experience as a holistic unit—both during the act of speaking, and after (Sonneck, 1935, p. 446). The data on the emergence of phoneme complexes in children's speech (Mandell and Sonneck, 1935) were of relevance for the analysis of emergence of such units. The Vienna group around the Bühlers was involved in a careful analysis of all of the Bühlers' research on children's concept formation (e.g., Bühler and Hetzer, 1929; Köhler, 1929). The concentration on the study of children's development (with the leadership role here in the hands of Charlotte Bühler) provided the theory of speaking activity with rich empirical and interdisciplinary background. Again, parallels with Vygotsky's self-identification with the paedology movement (and its redefinition into an interdisciplinary science of development) in the Soviet Union during precisely the same years is notable here (see Van der Veer and Valsiner, 1991, chapter 12). In both cases, the "child study" ideas became a basis for a general science of development of higher psychological functions, mediated by speech.

Bühler's focus was certainly wider than the speech act in and by itself implied. Within the speech theory, analysis of heraldic symbols as both systems of personal and attributive representations (Klanfer, 1935), and analyses of reconstruction of personality through speech characteristics (Bonaventura, 1935; Herzog, 1933) served as themes that moved Bühler's theoretical ideas toward a general theory of signs. That goal was never accomplished, as the Vienna highpoint of the Bühlers' work ended in a crash.

The Devastation

The beginning of the end of the Bühlers' Institute in Vienna can be traced to political changes in Austria in 1934. After the loss of power by the Social Democrats, the Institute—which had clearly benefited from them—became a target of institutional attacks (budget cuts, see Ash, 1988). Members of the Institute continued their left-wing activities, including those of the underground. Marie Jahoda—after Paul Lazarsfeld's departure for the U.S. the main researcher in the Economic Psychology Section—was arrested in summer 1937 and imprisoned for three months. She managed to get into exile in England after release. Yet the Institute was clearly not in favor with the new rulers of the country. Thus it is not surprising that, soon after Germany took over Austria, Karl Bühler was arrested (on March 23, 1938), and later released (on May 7). It needs to be added that most of the Austrian intellectual elite were detained at that time—imprisonment was a scare tactic the Nazis used to force the intellectual leaders out of their power positions. In conjunction with detention, Bühler was "sent into vacation" from his university job, followed by full dismissal (called "pensioning," i.e., enforced retirement) from his academic posts. The whole intellectual realm of the Institute was changed by political power. Bühler's course offerings were replaced by topics that fitted with the Nazi regime ideologically (e.g., "psychology of race"). Forcing Bühler to leave his Institute was thus a part of a major takeover by the Nazis of the intellectual world of Vienna. Within a short time, the most central figure of Viennese psychology of the previous two decades was turned into a *persona non grata* in his own Institute. It need not be added that the impact of such treatment on Bühler's feelings was traumatic.

That Bühler managed to obtain permission to emigrate—albeit losing all his library and research materials—fits the scenario of political takeover of the intellectual domain in Austria. The authorities had everything to gain from getting the deposed intellectual leader out of sight. In September 1938, Karl Bühler traveled to exile in Norway. The period before leaving Vienna was naturally nervous—Bühler was afraid of another arrest (as described by his daughter in Lebzeltern, 1969, p. 50), while packing his belongings for indeterminate storage. He left Vienna with minimal luggage. After a brief stay in Norway (Oslo), Karl Bühler traveled to the U.S. to Scholastica College in Duluth, Minnesota, for his first U.S. temporary position as an immigrant. From there he moved to St. Thomas College in St. Paul, Minnesota, where he continued teaching until 1945. It is from there that he came to Clark as G. Stanley Hall Visiting Professor—where Irv Sigel, as a young student, met him.

The Bühlers had to struggle for income through accepting temporary teaching duties, which for Karl was clearly a task below his intellectual role as it had developed in Vienna. Charlotte Bühler adjusted better—thanks to her linkages with practical issues and skills in psychotherapy. Both Bühlers settled down in Los Angeles in 1945, where Charlotte entered into a successful clinical practice, while Karl obtained a nominal position at a medical school. In 1945 there were efforts in Austria to invite Karl Bühler back to Vienna to his former professorship. Yet now—in 1947—the Bühlers refused to go. Charlotte Bühler was not offered a position back in Vienna, and certainly the post-war Austria would have been a far cry from the context that had vanished in 1938.

Bühler continued with his intellectual interests, returning to issues of psychological mechanisms of navigation (by map and by immediate perceptual signs—Bühler, 1951/52, 1954). His last book, *The Gestalt Principle in the Life of Humans and Animals* (Bühler, 1960), demonstrates how Bühler maintained intellectual dialogue with thought systems popular in the 1950s, while elaborating the ideas he had worked through half a century before. Even if a psychologically shattered person (after the execution of his intellectual and social context in 1938), as documented by many people who knew him, he maintained an astute scholarly dialogue in his own mind about issues of concern.

Karl Bühler visited Europe only twice in the post-war years. He went back shortly to Vienna in 1956, and in 1960 as the honorary president of the International Psychological Congress in Bonn. He died in Los Angeles on October 24, 1963, at eighty-four years of age.

Bühler's Major Contributions

Karl Bühler was an encyclopedist whose work defies simple classification. He moved from psychology of thinking to child psychology, performed basic studies in the area of perception and expression, and issues of animal navigation. Yet his main contribution, in retrospect, could belong to the theory of communication.

84 Thinking in Psychological Science

The Organonmodell

Bühler's organon model (see figure 5.1) is the central concept of all of his language philosophy (Bühler, 1934/1965, pp. 24-33; 1990, pp. 34-39; see also Graumann, 1988). Alluding to Plato (for the idea that language is the "*organum* for the one to inform the other of something about things"—Bühler, 1990, p. 30), Bühler situates the act of speaking in the center of human life:

> The speech event has many causes (or motives) and locations in human life. Neither in the solitude of the desert nor in the dreams of sleep does it abandon one completely. But now and then it does fall silent, both at unimportant and important decisive moments. It does this not only when one is engaged in solitary reflection or wordless activity, but sometimes in the midst of communicative contact between people (Bühler, 1990, p. 30).

The *Organonmodell* grew out of Bühler's interest in human development (Bühler, 1918) and was prepared by the book on *Crisis*. It entails a three-part structure, which in and by itself is not original—a person perceives something, and creates a sign for another reflecting upon some aspect of that something. The other—while also having perceptual access to the stimulus—actively interprets the sign. The sign has thus a central, yet al.ways open-ended, nature in the communication process. In Bühler's own words (referring to figure 5.1):

> The circle in the middle symbolizes the concrete acoustic phenomenon [*Schallphänomen*]. Three variable factors in it go to give it the rank of a sign in three different manners. The sides of the inscribed triangle symbolize these three factors. In one way the triangle encloses less than the circle (thus illustrating the principle of abstractive relevance [*Prinzip der abstraktiver Relevanz*]). In another way it goes beyond the circle to indicate that what is given to the senses always receives an apperceptive complement [*apperzeptive Ergänzung*]. The parallel lines symbolize the semantic functions of the (complex) language sign. It is a *symbol* by virtue of its coordination to objects and states of affairs, a *symptom* (*Anzeichen*, *indicium*: index) by virtue of its dependence on the sender, whose inner states it expresses, and a *signal* by virtue of its appeal to the hearer, whose inner or outer behavior it directs as do other communicative signs [*Verkehrszeichen*] (Bühler, 1990, pp. 34-35; 1934/1965, p. 28).

The Organon model is based on the idea of the three functions that language use accomplishes:

(1) *Expression*: of sender's subjective understanding (*Kundgabe* or *Ausdruck*). The sender constructs the message through expressing oneself, thus the starting point for communication is expression of personal subjectivity, and the result—a constructed message.
(2) *Appeal*: the impact of the message to the receiver (*Auslösung* or *Appell*—the label appeal was for Bühler a nice extension from the American talk of "sex-appeal" to that of "speech-appeal," see Bühler, 1932, p. 106). The receiver

cannot avoid the message, encoded in signs. It is there to be received, yet by a process that entails active reconstruction.

(3) *Representation*: of the state of affairs of what is being reflected by language (*Darstellung*). The sender refers to some external world, which can also be perceived by the receiver. However, given the non-sameness of these two positions (sender, receiver), the same objective world can never the same from two different personal standpoints.

Bühler introduced both the *abstracting* and *apperceptive* moments into the center of his model. Yet in the graphic depiction in figure 5.1, both of these are poorly represented. In the tension between the versions of the message—as those are constructed by the sender and the receiver from the standpoint of their ego-perspectives—the meanings of the signs can grow in the direction of novel abstractness.

In fact, Bühler's figure needs complementing into the third dimension—it is at the intersection of the triangle and circle in figure 5.1 where new meanings of increasingly abstract kind are being constructed. The central question of how far (in the third, i.e., vertical, dimension) the sematological[9] process of abstraction and generalization might proceed remains open. Bühler pointed to its relevance, and illustrated it by his notions of representational fields (see below), but the full extent of the theory of sematological regulation of human meaning construction under uncertainty of communicative contexts remains to be created. After publishing the *Sprachtheorie*, at the very end of his Vienna stay, he thought of writing a treatise on general theory of signs (Eschbach, 1990b, p. xl).

**Figure 5.1
The Organon Model**

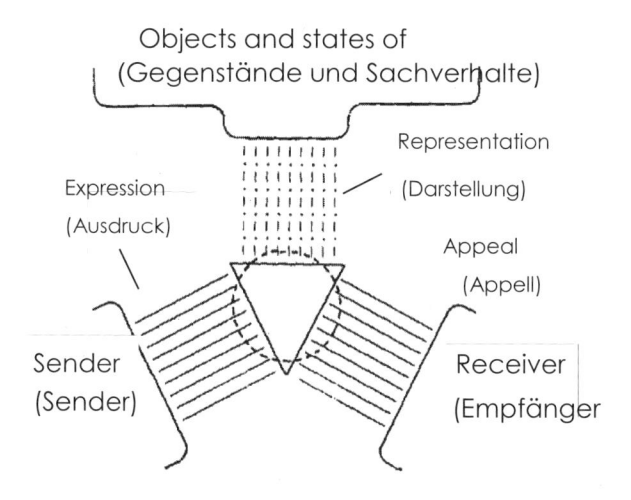

Relevance of Abstraction, and Its Nature

The problem of abstraction was seen by Bühler to take a key position in his sematology (Bühler, 1990, pp. 52-54). The principle of abstractive relevance (*Prinzip der abstraktiven Relevanz*) was necessary to set up a possible dominance relation in the coordination of different fields. By arbitrary consensus, obvious differences within one sign-field can be purposefully overlooked, under the control of an abstracted aspect. In Bühler's terms, " ... the perceptible here and now need not enter the semantic function. Rather, it may be only that this or that abstract factor is relevant for its calling to function as a sign" (Bühler, 1990, p. 52). The abstract convention can be set up to overrule the emergence of complex nuances of understanding.

In Bühler's scheme, construction of abstract concepts is not well represented—yet the principle of abstraction is of central relevance. The sign is constantly under tension of the discrepancies of expression and interpretation, which of course are guided by social constraints upon the communicative process. These include the assumption of intersubjectivity. It is embedded in the overlap between the triangle and the circle in figure 5.1. Yet it is not specified *how*—from the tension between the "circle" and "triangle" kinds of interpretation of the message—abstraction *emerges*. Bühler emphasized the reality-nearness (and interconnection) of the signs ("Whenever something is a sign, it is only abstract factors by virtue of which the concrete thing functions 'as' a sign"—Bühler, 1990, p. 48). But what these "abstract factors" (beyond the label of an "abstract") entail remains unclear. Despite the fact that Bühler declared the notion of abstraction to be of key relevance for sematology (see Bühler, 1990, pp. 52-54), his coverage of the issue provides little insight into it. His example for the functioning of the principle of abstractive relevance entails reliance on inter-personal convention (Bühler, 1990, pp. 50-51). On the basis of perceivable properties of the sign-material (be it speech sounds, or cloth colors), by way of convention new abstracted meaning of signs appears. Yet what that emergence process is like is not explicated by Bühler. How do people arrive at conventions that lead to consideration of different physical forms of the sign carrier (e.g., sound) as having the same meaning? In other words, convention between the communicator and the recipient regarding what the "circular triangle" of the message (figure 5.1) means requires a look at the process of abstracting, rather than a principle of abstraction as a given. Even the focus on language work (p. 63) with the emphasis on the process of speaking does not elaborate the making of abstraction.

Language as structured instrument sets clear constraints upon the process of communication. Furthermore, the realities of the act of speaking—production of a vocal gestalt over time—is constrained by the phonemic system afforded by the human motor system. Nevertheless Bühler successfully avoided the trap of assuming a unidirectional determinist stance, as he stated that:

... we claim only that the receiver's own constructive thought *cannot be eliminated* and that it is *innocuous* within wide limits, indeed that it is highly *conducive* to most goals of language (Bühler, 1990, p. 195; original Bühler, 1934/1965, p. 172).

The constructionist focus on the actions of the person in speech contexts complements that of general social guidance. The person transcends the immediate suggestions by the appealing sign through constructing his understanding that transcends the here-and-now nature of the concrete speech act.

The roots of that notion in the thought and practices of the Würzburg School is evident here. The act of communication leads to emergence of new reality—that of abstraction, mediated by signs. The act of speaking entails emergence of vocal forms, guided by language, yet produced in the context where the communicator is intentionally oriented towards some objective.

Bühler's Organon model can be interpreted—possibly here going beyond Bühler's own interpretation—as a model that could lead to co-constructionist thinking, if extended to include time. His model emphasized varied fields (with their specifiable boundaries) that guide all the three functions of speech, which may function concurrently in ongoing interaction. The field of possible sounds allows for phonemic patterns or relations with specific limits, within which different languages organize their phonemic structures differently. Given the high variability of possible combinations of speech-sign elements—phonemes—the level of semantic relevance of signs can further constrain the speech forms (Bühler, 1931). On the side of the speaker, the spheres of meaning carried by a specific range of linguistic structures are based on the experiencing of (what has seemed to be) successful communication. Yet the basic question—what successful-communication actually is—is not covered by Bühler's model. Bühler mentioned the "apperceptive component" of the sign, but that needs to be complemented by the expectations of the speaker and listener as to their ego-positions in the process of communication (see Rommetveit, 1992). The friction between two different constructions of the sign (triangle and circle in figure 5.1) can be based on the different goal-orientations of the participants, which would orient the apperceptive components of the signs. The different kinds of representational fields may be put to use by specific intentions of the participants in communication. The ways in which abstraction emerges from the sign processes in the middle of figure 5.1 can be interpersonally guided (for empirical examples, see Danet, 1980; Leis, 1982).

The remarkable freedom of personal expression via signs is—according to Bühler—outwardly constrained by pre-existing sentence structures with "empty lots" (*Leerstellen*) for expansion (Innis, 1988, p. 82). Physiological factors play their constraining role in the determination of the range of possible sound forms upon which meaningful communication in all its richness can be built.

Ego-Centeredness of Communication

The only anchor point in human communication is the self's perspective, which can never be *exactly* the same as that of another person. The "here-and-now" system (Bühler, 1990, p. 117) is the experiential basis for any sign construction. This uniquely individual-specific positioning creates the inevitable negotiation of intersubjectivity and the potential for construction of abstract signs. Furthermore, the speaker can constantly modulate the boundaries of inclusion/exclusion of specific meaning fields. Even as the inevitable anchor point of reference in the human case is the center of the ego, it can be mediated by signs to include domains extended far beyond that center. Thus, even as a speaker's only vantage point while speaking is "I," he or she can revert to the use of "we."

In a similar vein, the speaker (operating from his or her "here-and-now I" standpoint) can transcend the deictic field of the "here-and-now," and refer to past and future. The latter partly overlaps with what Bühler labeled imagination-oriented deixis. The I-centered, anaphoric, and imagination-oriented versions of deixis work in unison, yet carry different functions. Bühler made use of the widely popular field notion in his making sense of the work of language (see Budwig, Chapter 7).

Sematological Removal

The language work takes place in the middle of human phenomenological fields—yet it distances (or removes) the act of communication from the given context. This is achieved—according to Bühler—through syntax. All uttered "independent sentences" *are acts of removal* of the speaker from the given situation (Bühler, 1990, p. 190). The social context for speaking makes abstracting from that context possible, and abstracted nature of signs makes it possible to modify the social context.

Signs in Intentional Action: Fieldability

Bühler could not accept the usual linguistic talk about "arbitrary encoding" of the language signs in relation to their referents (Bühler, 1990, p. 210). This should not be surprising given his interest in the pragmatics of the communicative process, where signs are instruments in the texture of accomplishing some objects, rather than entities in themselves. Thus all signs must be "fieldable" (*feldfähig*—Bühler, 1934/1965, p. 187) in order to be usable in the given field. Surely there are limits to such "fieldability"—for instance, musical note symbols are not "fieldable" upon a geographical map (nor vice versa: geographical symbols are not "fieldable" upon music paper). Formal logical symbols are "fieldable" only within the narrowly defined field of the logician, and their function for the purposes of logic is exactly in such narrow evocation of the field.

Bühler (1928b) separated three levels of representational fields (*Darstellungsfeld*) for speech signs. These three fields can be seen as interdependent, in the sense of phenomena that are "fielded" within one setting up constraints for the other fields.

The *primary representational field* is the field, or the place, that the speech sign "brings with itself"—so to speak—when it is actualized. The sign, given its form, evokes a particular field of relations within which its meaningfulness can be further constructed by the interpreter. Bühler's example is that of a geographical map—a reference to some city or route evokes (as its necessary context) the whole reference system of the map (with all of its representational parts). Any answer to a geographical specific question can be given only within this reference system. Likewise, speech signs evoke a rich conglomerate of experiences.

The *secondary representational field* entails the field of personal memories and productive fantasies that the speech act evokes in the co-constructive hearer. This representational field frees the construction of the hearer's understanding from the immediate here-and-now, and leads to the development of the internalized control functions of the speech signs in the personal world of the hearer. This focus brings in Bühler's emphasis on the role of history (Bühler, 1990, pp. 65-66). The person brings her past experiences to the personal senses that are fielded within the secondary field.

Finally, *the tertiary representational field* entails the syntactic schemata that are evoked by a specific speech act. The speaker is intentional and encodes a particular message within a field of goal-oriented set of possible meanings.

Bühler's three fields can be illustrated by the stock example of speech act theory, the utterance "Can you pass me the salt?" Obviously, in its context of the tertiary field, that utterance is a goal-directed request, and if treated as such, leads to the utterer's receiving of the desired object from the other person. However, if we consider the same utterance fielded within the secondary field, we may observe rather anxious reactions from the other person (e.g., "why are you always laughing at me!?"—as the request is fielded within some personal life history episode of the past, interpreted in terms of "laughing at"). Furthermore, if fielded within the primary field, the response (without action) could be "yes, I can" (the receiver interprets the utterance as if it was a question about his or her abilities). If the request is interpreted simultaneously within the framework of the three hierarchical fields, it depends which version of "fielding" becomes dominant in this interpretation.

Conclusions

Bühler's role in the formation of psychological thought in the twentieth century is seminal. He attempted to overcome psychology's narrow focus on either mental phenomena, or behavior, by a focus on the third component—the sign—that stands between both (in the inner-psychological sphere) and which mediates inter-personal regulation of conduct. It is worth emphasizing that he was not a psychologist, in the narrow sense—his formative work was in medicine and philosophy. He took an active interest in very many topical areas—from the navigation of bees to processes of thinking, and—most important—in the act of speaking. His contribution of was of such kind that nowadays we are apt to label those "interdisciplinary." Yet such labels mean nothing—usually these just cover up the inability of the label-user to create a synthesis between disciplines. Bühler did not use labels, he created bridges between ideas from different disciplines. His ideas were well rooted in the work of his predecessors—from Aristotle and Plato to the holistic traditions in European psychology (Husserl, Meinong, et al..). The richness of human speaking was the source for the richness in Bühler's thinking. Thinking was sheer intellectual pleasure, the traces of which in Bühler's work are sources for further advancement of our contemporary ideas.[10]

Notes

1. Previously published in *From Past to Future, Vol. 1*(1), 15-34 *The Legacy of Karl Bühler.* ©1999. Frances L. Hiatt School of Psychology, Clark University. Author: Jaan Valsiner, Department of Psychology, Clark University, 950 Main Street, Worcester, MA.
2. Curiously—in line with intra-discipline boundaries within psychology—the work of the two Bühlers tends to be recognized separately, while the origins of the work of both were mutually intertwined. Thus, developmental or child psychologists may recognize Charlotte Bühler's work (and not link it with Karl's theoretical context for her work), while Karl Bühler's work has been known without recognition of the empirical basis for it in which Charlotte played an important part.
3. Already from the times when Külpe worked in Wundt's world he was described by F. Kiesow as "the kind mother of Wundt's Institute"(Kiesow, 1930, p. 167).
4. As Henry Watt wrote to Robert Ogden in 1907, "The 'movement' of the Würzburgers has been blown full and we will now have to conquer completely or die. ... If you want to be really up to date you should make yourself familiar with it. Bühler leaves all us minor prophets behind" (Ogden, 1951, p. 10).
5. The use of the term "observer" in American psychology became obsolete by late 1920s in conjunction with the prevalence of experiments on animal behavior, where the participants in the experiments—now called "subjects"—were not expected to observe anything, but rather rush to push appropriate levers. The colloquial phrase "running subjects" reminds one of the experimenters' full fate control over the rats and other animals who were parts of the laboratory study. In our present time, "subjects" are re-named "research participants"—who thus are assumed to have increased control over what happens with them in psychological studies.
6. In the same year, he almost got a professorship in Berlin, ranked second among appropriate candidates. It would be an interesting—yet useless—speculation effort to think what the life course of the Bühlers could have been had they spent the 1920s–1930s in Berlin, instead of Vienna.
7. Arnold Gesell received his doctorate from Clark University in 1906.
8. Harvard made an offer for a McDougall Professorship to Karl Bühler in 1930, in parallel with a professorship for Charlotte Bühler at its Radcliffe College. This of course followed Karl Bühler's shorter academic stays in the U.S.: He was visiting

professor at Stanford, Johns Hopkins and Harvard Universities in 1927/28, and at University of Chicago in 1929. In 1937 both Karl and Charlotte were offered professorships at Fordham University, yet the offers were withdrawn because of the "not sufficiently Catholic" status of the Bühlers (see C. Bühler, 1965, p. 188). Aside from the obvious economic difficulties in U.S. academia due to the Great Depression, there were clear extra-scientific testing criteria used to evaluate "suitability" of immigrant scholars to U.S. universities' psychology departments (see Winston, 1998).

9. Sematology was Bühler's name for a science of signs and their use. As was often the case with Bühler, he borrowed terms from past thinkers. Sematology can be traced back to Benjamin H. Smart's book *Outline of sematology* (published in 1831)—see Sebeok, 1983, pp. 359-360.

10. Critical comments by Nancy Budwig and Ingrid E. Josephs upon an earlier draft of this paper are gratefully acknowledged.

References

Ach, N. (1905). *Über die Willenstätigkeit und das Denken*. Göttingen: Vandenhoeck and Ruprecht

Allport, G. (1966). An appreciation of *Die Krise der Psychologie* by Karl Bühler. *Journal of General Psychology, 75*, 201-204.

Ash, M. (1988). Die Entwicklung des Wiener Psychologischen Instituts 1922-1938. In A. Eschbach (Ed.), *Karl Bühler's theory of language* (pp. 303-325). Amsterdam: John Benjamins.

Aster, E. von (1908). Die psychologische Beobachtung und experimentelle Untersuchung von Denkvorgängen. *Zeitschrift für Psychologie, 49*, 56-107.

Baldwin, J. M. (1902). *Development and evolution*. New York: Macmillan.

Bergson, H (1907/1945). *L'Evolution créatrice*. Genève: Éditions Albert Skira.

Bonaventura, M. (1935). Ausdruck der Persönlichkeit in der Sprechstimme und in Photogramm. *Archiv für die gesamte Psychologie, 94*, 501-568.

Brunswick, E. (1947). *Systematic and representative design of psychological experiments, with results in physical and social perception*. Berkeley, CA: University of California Press.

Bühler, C. M. (1918). Das Märchen und die Phantasie des Kindes. *Beihefte zur Zeitschrift für angewandte Psychologie, 17*, 1-82.

Bühler, C. M. (1928). *Kindheit und Jugend*. Leipzig: S. Hirzel.

Bühler, C. M. (1933). *Der menschliche Lebenslauf als psychologisches Problem*. Leipzig: S. Hirzel.

Bühler, C. M. (1965). Die Wiener Psychologische Schule in der Emigration. *Psychologische Rundschau, 16*, 187-196.

Bühler, C. M., Hetzer, H., Tudor-Hart, B. (1927). Soziologische und psychologische Studien über das erste Lebensjahr. *Quellen und Studien zur Jugendkunde*. Vol. 5. Jena: G. Fischer.

Bühler, C.M., and Hetzer, H. (1929). Zur Geschichte der Kinderpsychologie. In E. Brunswick et al. (Eds.), *Beiträge zur Problemgeschichte der Psychologie: Festschrift zu Karl Bühler's 50. Geburtstag* (pp. 204-224). Jena: G. Fischer.

Bühler, K. (1907). Tatsachen und Probleme zu eine Psychologie der Denkvorgänge. I. *Archiv für die gesamte Psychologie, 9*, 297-365.

Bühler, K. (1908a). Tatsachen und Probleme zu eine Psychologie der Denkvorgänge. II, III *Archiv für die gesamte Psychologie, 12*, 1-92.

Bühler, K. (1908b). Antwort auf die von W. Wundt erhobenen Einwände gegen die Methode der Selbstbeobachtung an experimentell erzeugten Erlebnissen. *Archiv für die gesamte Psychologie, 12*, 93-122.

Bühler, K. (1909). Zur Kritik der Denkexperimente. *Zeitschrift für Psychologie, 51*, 108-118.
Bühler, K. (1912). Denken. In E. Korschelt et al.. (Eds.), *Handwörterbuch der Naturwissenschaften*. Vol. 1 (pp. 889-896). Jena: G. Fischer.
Bühler, K. (1913). *Die Gestaltwahrnehmungen*. Stuttgart: W. Spemann.
Bühler, K. (1918) *Die geistige Entwicklung des Kindes*. Jena: G. Fischer.
Bühler, K. (1919a). Eine Bemerkung zu der Diskussion über die Psychologie des Denkens. *Zeitschrift für Psychologie, 82*, 97-101.
Bühler, K. (1919b). Kritische Musterung der neueren Theorien des Satzes. *Indogermanisches Jahrbuch*, 6. 1-20.
Bühler, K. (1926). Die Krise der Psychologie. *Kant-Studien, 31*, 455-526.
Bühler, K. (1927a/1978). *Die Krise der Psychologie*. Frankfurt-am-Main: Ullstein.
Bühler, K. (1927b). Zur grundlegung der Sprachpsychologie. *Proceedings of the 8th International Congress of Psychology, Groningen, 1926* (pp. 243-245). Groningen: P. Noordhoff.
Bühler, K. (1928a). Displeasure and pleasure in relation to activity. In M. L. Reymert (Ed.), *Feelings and emotions: The Wittenberg Symposium* (pp. 195-199). Worcester, MA.: Clark University Press.
Bühler, K. (1928b). Die Symbolik der Sprache. *Kant-Studien, 33*, 405-409.
Bühler, K. (1930). *The mental development of the child*. New York: Harcourt, Brace and Co.,
Bühler, K. (1931). Phonetik und Phonologie. *Travaux du Cercle Linguistique de Prague, 4*, 22-53.
Bühler, K. (1932). Das Ganze der Sprachtheorie, ihr Aufbau und ihre Teile. In G. Kafka (Ed.), *Bericht über den XII Kongreß der Deutschen Gesellschaft für Psychologie* (pp. 95-122). Jena: Gustav Fischer.
Bühler, K (1933a). *Ausdruckstheorie*. Jena: Gustav Fischer.
Bühler, K. (1933b). Die Axiomatik der Sprachwissenschaften. *Kant-Studien, 38*, 19-90.
Bühler, K. (1934/1965). *Sprachtheorie*. Jena-Stuttgart: Gustav Fischer.
Bühler, K (1935). Forschung zur Sprachtheorie: Einleitung. *Archiv für die gesamte Psychologie, 94*, 401-412.
Bühler, K (1938). Der dritte Hauptsatz der Sprachtheorie. In H. Piéron and I. Meyerson (Eds.), *Rapports et comptes rendus*, 11th International Congress of Psychology. Agen: Impremerie Moderne.
Bühler, K. (1951). On thought connections. In D. Rapaport (Ed.), *Organization and pathology of thought* (pp. 39-57). New York: Columbia University Press. [partial translation of Bühler, 1908a]
Bühler, K. (1951/52). The skywise and neighborwise navigation of ants and bees. *Acta Psychologica, 8*, 225-263.
Bühler, K. (1954). The essentials of contact navigation. *Acta Psychologica, 10*, 278-316.
Bühler, K. (1960). *Das Gestaltprinzip im Leben des Menschen und der Tiere*. Bern: Hans Huber.
Bühler, K. (1990). *Theory of language: The representational function of language*. Amsterdam: John Benjamins.
Cornelius, H. (1897). Psychologie als Erfahrungswissenschaft. Leipzig: B. G. Teubner.
Danet, B. (1980). "Baby" or "fetus"?: Language and the construction of reality in a manslaughter trial. *Semiotica, 32*, 3-4, 187-219.
Dürr, E. (1908). Über die experimentelle Untersuchung der Denkvorgänge. *Zeitschrift für Psychologie, 49*, 313-340.

Ehrenfels, C. von (1890/1967). Über "Gestaltqualitäten." In F. Weinhandl (Ed.), Gestalthaftes sehen: Ergebnisse und aufgaben der Morphologie (pp. 11-43). Darmstadt: Wissenschaftliche Buchgesellschaft [originally in Vierterjahreschrift für wissenschaftliche Philosophie, 14, 242-292].
Ekstein, R. (1966). Karl Bühler and psychoanalysis. *Journal of General Psychology, 75*, 204-212.
Eschbach, A. (1987). Edmund Husserl (1859-1938) und Karl Bühler (1879-1963). *Kodikas, 10*, 3/4, 301-315.
Eschbach, A. (1988). The characteristics of Karl Bühler's pragmatically integrated theory of signs. In G. Deledalle (Ed.), *Semiotics and pragmatics: Proceedings of the Perpignan symposium* (pp. 117-129). Amsterdam: John Benjamins.
Eschbach, A. (1990a). Denken: Der semiotische Ansatz der Würzburger Schule. *Kodikas, 13*, 1/2, 119-130.
Eschbach, A. (1990b). Editor's introduction—Karl Bühler: sematologist. In K. Bühler, *Theory of Language* (pp. xii-xlii). Amsterdam: John Benjamins.
Glock, H.-J. (1986). Vygotsky and Mead on the self, meaning and internalisation. *Studies in Soviet Thought, 31*, 131-148.
Herzog, H. (1933). Stimme und Persönlichkeit. *Zeitschrift für Psychologie, 130*, 300-369.
Hetzer, H. (1931). Kind und Schaffen: Experimente über konstruktive Bestätigungen im Kleinkinder. *Quellen und Studien zur Jugendkunde, 7*, 1-104.
Kiesow, F. (1930). F. Kiesow. In C. Murchison (Ed.), *A history of psychology in autobiography*. Vol. 1(pp. 163-190). Worcester, MA: Clark University Press.
Krug, J. (1929). Zur Sprachtheorie. In E. Brunswick et al. (Eds.), *Beiträge zur Problemgeschichte der Psychologie: Festschrift zu Karl Bühler's 50. Geburtstag* (pp. 225-258). Jena: G. Fischer.
Köhler, E. (1929). Kinderspache und Begriffsbildung. In E. Brunswick et al. (Eds.), *Beiträge zur Problemgeschichte der Psychologie: Festschrift zu Karl Bühler's 50. Geburtstag* (pp. 173-203). Jena: G. Fischer.
Külpe, O. (1892). Das Ich und die Aussenwelt. *Philosophische Studien, 7*, 394-413.
Külpe, O. (1903). The problem of attention. *The Monist, 13*, 38-68.
Külpe, O. (1912-23). *Die Realisierung: Ein Beiträg zur grundlegung der Realwissenschaften*. Vol. 1(1912), Vol. 2 (1920), Vol. 3 (1923). Leipzig: S. Hirzel.
Lazarsfeld, P. F. (1959). Amerikanische Beobachtungen eines Bühler-Schülers. *Zeitschrift für experimentelle und angewandte Psychologie, 6*, 69-76.
Leis, N. (1982). The not-so-supernatural power of Ijaw children. In S. Ottenberg (Ed.), *African religious groups and beliefs* (pp. 151-169). Meerut: Folklore Institute.
Lindenfeld, D. (1978). Oswald Külpe and the Würzburg School. *Journal of the History of the Behavioral Sciences, 14*, 132-141.
Mack, W. (1993). Die Würzburger Schule. In H. E. Lück and R. Miller (Eds.), *Illustrierte Geschichte der Psychologie* (pp. 50-53). München: Quintessenz.
Marbe, K. (1961). Karl Marbe. In C. Murchison (Ed.), *A history of psychology in autobiography*. Vol. 3 (pp. 181-213). New York: Russell and Russell.
Meinong, A. (1902/1983). *On assumptions*. Berkeley, CA: University of California Press.
Meinong, A. (1917/1972). *On emotional presentation*. Evanston, Il.: Northwestern University Press.
Murphy, G. (1966). Karl Bühler and the psychology of thought. *Journal of General Psychology, 75*, 188-195.
Messer, A. (1906). Experimentell-psychologische Untersuchungen über das Denken. *Archiv für die gesamte Psychologie, 8*, 1-224.

Graumann, C. - F. (1988). Aspektmodell und Organonmodell: Die Problematik des Verhältnisses zwischen Sprachwissenschaft und Psychologie bei Karl Bühler. In A. Eschbach (Ed.), *Karl Bühler's theory of language* (pp. 107-124). Amsterdam: John Benjamins.

Innis, R. E. (1983). The semiotic relevance of Bühler's Sprachtheorie. In T. Borbé (Ed.), *Semiotics unfolding.* Vol. 1 (pp. 143-149). Berlin: Mouton.

Innis, R. E. (1988). The thread of subjectivity: philosophical remarks on Bühler's language theory. In A. Eschbach (Ed.), *Karl Bühler's theory of language* (pp. 77-106). Amsterdam: John Benjamins.

Klanfer, J. (1935). Theorie der heraldischen Zeichen. *Archiv für die gesamte Psychologie, 94*, 413-445.

Koerner, K. (1988). *Saussurean studies/ Etudes Saussuriennes.* Genève: Editions Slatkine.

Kurtz, E. M. (1996). Marginalizing discovery: Karl Popper's intellectual roots in psychology; or, how the study of discovery was banned from science studies. *Creativity Research Journal, 9*, 2-3, 173-187.

Lebzeltern, G. (1969). Karl Bühler—Leben und Werk. *Österreichische Akademie der Wissenschaften, Philosophisch-historische Klasse Sitzungberichte, 265*, Bd. 3, 7-70.

Mandell, S. and Sonneck, B. (1935). Phonographische Aufnahme und Analyse der ersten Sprächhäusserungen von Kindern. *Archiv für die gesamte Psychologie, 94*, 478-500

Ogden, R. M. (1951). Oswald Külpe and the Würzburg School. *American Journal of Psychology, 64*, 1, 4-19.

Pléh, C. (1988). Two conceptions on the crisis of psychology: Vygotsky and Bühler. In A. Eschbach (Ed.), *Karl Bühler's theory of language* (pp. 407-413). Amsterdam: John Benjamins.

Popper, K. (1976). *Unended quest: an intellectual autobiography.* LaSalle, Il.: Open Court.

Rauh, H. (1990). Hildegard Hetzer und eine Psychologie, die dem Menschen nützt. *Zeitschrift für Entwicklungspsychologie und Pädagogische Psychologie, 22*, 3, 247-260.

Rommetveit, R. (1992). Outlines of a dialogically based social-cognitive approach to human cognition and communication. In A. H. Wold (Ed.), *The dialogical alternative: Towards a theory of language and mind* (pp. 19-44). Oslo: Scandinavian University Press.

Smith, B. (1988). Materials towards a history of speech act theory. In A. Eschbach (Ed.), *Karl Bühler's theory of language* (pp. 125-152). Amsterdam: John Benjamins.

Sonneck, B. (1935). Der Satz als Einheit und die Satzarten. *Archiv für die gesamte Psychologie, 94*, 446-477.

Stumpf, C., Hornbostel, E. von (1911). Über die Bedeutung ethnologischer Untersuchungen für die Psychologie und Ästhetik der Tonkunst. *Beiträge zur Akustik und Musikwissenschaft, 6*, 102-115.

Van der Veer, R., and Valsiner, J. (1991). *Understanding Vygotsky: A quest for synthesis.* Oxford: Basil Blackwell.

Vygotsky, L. S. (1926/1982). Istoricheskii smysl psikhologicheskogo krizisa. In L. S. Vygotsky, *Sobranie sochinenii.* Vol. 1. *Voprosy teorii i istorii psikhologii* (pp. 291-346). Moscow: Pedagogika.

Vygotsky, L. S. (1934). *Myshlenie i rec'* . Moscow-Leningrad: Gosudarstvennoe Sotsialno-eknomicheskoe Izdatel'stvo. (in Russian)

Watt, H. J. (1905). Experimentelle Beiträge zur einer Theorie des Denkens. *Archiv für die gesamte Psychologie, 4*, 289-436.

Wertheimer, M. (1905). Experimentelle Untersuchungen zur Tatbestandsdiagnistik. *Archiv für die gesamte Psychologie, 6,* 50-131.
Wetterstein, J. (1988). Külpe, Bühler, Popper. In A. Eschbach (Ed.), *Karl Bühler's theory of language* (pp. 327-347). Amsterdam: John Benjamins.
Winston, A. S. (1998). "The defects of his race": E. G. Boring and antisemitism in American psychology, 1923-1953. *History of Psychology, 1,* 1, 27-51.
Wundt, W. (1907). Über Ausfrageexperimente und über die Methoden zur Psychologie des Denkens. *Psychologische Studien, 3,* 301-306.
Wundt, W. (1908). Kritische Nachlese zur Ausfragemethode. *Archiv für die gesamte Psychologie, 11,* 445-459.

Wertheimer, M. (1905). Experimentelle Untersuchungen zur Tatbestandsdiagnistik. *Archiv für die gesamte Psychologie, 6,* 50-131.
Wetterstein, J. (1988). Külpe, Bühler, Popper. In A. Eschbach (Ed.), *Karl Bühler's theory of language* (pp. 327-347). Amsterdam: John Benjamins.
Winston, A. S. (1998). "The defects of his race": E. G. Boring and antisemitism in American psychology, 1923-1953. *History of Psychology, 1,* 1, 27-51.
Wundt, W. (1907). Über Ausfrageexperimente und über die Methoden zur Psychologie des Denkens. *Psychologische Studien, 3,* 301-306.
Wundt, W. (1908). Kritische Nachlese zur Ausfragemethode. *Archiv für die gesamte Psychologie, 11,* 445-459.

6

Remembering Karl Bühler: Discovering Unanticipated Resemblances with My Distancing-Representational Model

Irving E. Sigel[1]

Karl Bühler, the eminent Viennese psychiatrist and developmental psychologist, was at Clark University as the G. Stanley Hall Professor of Psychology from 1941 to 1942. I was an undergraduate student at Clark University at the time and consider myself fortunate to have been a student in his seminar. Last year I was asked by the editor of FPTF to describe my recollections of Professor Bühler and to reflect on the impact his ideas might have had on my subsequent work. I am delighted to undertake this twofold task: To offer my personal recollections and to reflect on the similarities between some of Bühler's work and my own.

Of course, recollections and autobiographies by their very nature constitute an individual's biased constructions of his or her life history, whose validity may be questioned. It is also important to emphasize that many of my recollections are, no doubt, refracted through the lenses of an undergraduate student (I was a sophomore then). Yet from my point of view as I begin to reconstruct these events, I discover a sense of a compatibility with Bühler's thoughts of which I was unaware until just recently. I am offering them here to illustrate how my career may have been shaped consistently within the Bühler perspective even though I was unaware of its influence.

My account will be in the form of a chronology, starting with Karl Bühler's arrival at Clark University and ending with a discussion of the uncanny resemblance of my work on representation and his theory of semiotics. However, the inter-relationship of these two occurrences becomes clearer if I anchor them within the educational environment of Clark University during the 1940s—how it may have affected Bühler, and how it shaped, and hence prepared me for, my career as a developmental psychologist.

I will begin this story with the arrival of Karl Bühler, then sixty-one, and his wife Charlotte, forty-three, at Clark University from St. Olaf's College in Minnesota. They had arrived in the United States quite penniless after being forced to leave Austria after its annexation to Nazi Germany in 1938. They had taught at various American institutions in addition to St. Olaf's before coming to Clark (Coser, 1984). The students knew little about them other than that they had been famous in Austria where they had headed the Institute of Psychology, centering on studies of children. Both were renowned in Europe for their research on the intellectual and social development of children. Karl Bühler's semiotic foundations of language theory had generated considerable influence among European scholars of language, while Charlotte was known for her research with infants and young children. Their reputation in Vienna rivaled that of Sigmund Freud and his group of psychoanalysts. In spite of their illustrious European reputation and even though a number of American psychologists had visited the Bühler's Psychological Institute during the 1920 and 1930s, Karl's major work was virtually unknown to the mainstream of non-German-reading American psychologists since his work was not available in English. By contrast, Charlotte's work with infants was known and cited in the American literature. Nevertheless, the news of their joining the Clark psychology department (Charlotte Bühler came as a visiting professor) generated some excitement and much curiosity among the students. We wondered how these eminent urban Europeans would fit into Clark, a small but well-regarded university.

To get the sense of the Clark University academic environment when the Bühlers arrived in 1941, let me describe the university as an undergraduate saw it, and how, as an alumnus, I construct those years. Clark University in the 1940s was a liberal arts university with a small faculty and a student body of about 400 undergraduate and graduate students. The departments of psychology and geography were the two graduate departments that enjoyed a national reputation. The psychology department at Clark had been one of the foremost departments in the country beginning with the founding of the university in 1887 by G. Stanley Hall, its first president, who had actively promoted the creation of an exceptionally strong psychology department. He retired in 1921, to be succeeded by Wallace W. Atwood, a geographer, who was far less interested in psychology and was disinclined to make long-term commitments to new faculty appointments. By the 1940s, when the Bühlers arrived, the university as a whole, and the psychology department in particular, were considerably smaller than they had been in the 1930s. Moreover, the university, along with the rest of the country, was just emerging from the Great Depression, and hence funds to develop any of the departments were exceedingly scarce. However, these financial constraints did not affect the quality of our undergraduate experience. Clark students were able to receive an excellent and especially rich education as well as crucial financial help. I felt fortunate then, as I do now, that there was a university of the caliber of Clark in my hometown and that it was open to me.

When I came to Clark in 1939, I enrolled with the idea of majoring in history. I had no idea what psychology was as a field of study. I elected psychology only in order to fulfill a science requirement and wondered how the study of human behavior could possibly be a science. The first course I took was a two-semester one titled "general psychology." The first semester had a strictly experimental focus, whereas the second semester featured a social and personality perspective. These two very different emphases probably reflected the interests of the faculty who taught the course rather than of any formal arrangements. During the first semester we studied Edward Boring's general text, *Introduction to Psychology*. The course emulated the methodology of physics, that is, the experimental mode, and focused on topics amenable to an experimental paradigm, such as vision and audition. I found this approach boring and fragmented because it decontextualized human experiences. The person was presented as a subject, reactive rather than proactive. Where was the mind in this kind of psychology? I could not figure out how psychologists could ever understand human nature.

After that first semester I might have been tempted not to enroll in the second one except that this was not an option if I wanted to meet the science requirement. This stricture proved to be a blessing in disguise because the second semester was taught by Raymond B. Cattell, a well-known social and personality psychologist. To my utter amazement and delight, Dr. Cattell's course was human-centered. We studied McDougall's *Energies of Man*, a text written from a purposive framework which held that behavior was purposeful and goal-directed. The task of the psychologist was to identify the goals of individuals and their sources (innate or acquired). We engaged in discussions of human nature, e.g., topics such as heredity versus environment and the nature of intelligence and its heritability. The course was so stimulating and so consistent with my interests that I decided to major in psychology. I had found my niche! It was a true conversion. I subsequently took other courses that enabled me to get a well-rounded major in psychology. I received an excellent introduction to the traditional fields of psychology, including: advanced experimental, educational, vocational, personality, and abnormal. Some courses were taught by regular Clark faculty members, and others by affiliates, such as Saul Rosenzweig. He was on the staff of the Worcester State Hospital—which was known at that time for the high quality of its clinical psychology program. Saul Rosenzweig taught personality theory, using Gordon Allport's *Personality* and Judson Brown's *Abnormal Psychology* as texts. These were excellent courses, intellectually stimulating and challenging. Issues such as definition and measurement of personality and concepts of normality were debated with considerable intensity inside and outside of class. Since Clark was a small university, with a small psychology faculty (four to five members, excluding the affiliates), the faculty was readily accessible to students. Upper-level courses were usually taught as seminars of ten students or fewer and were open to qualified undergraduates, so there was a mix of students at different experiential levels. This facilitated a high level of classroom discussion. I felt very fortunate to have had the opportunity to work with many of the faculty and to interact with some of the graduate students. Undergraduate psychology students were fortunate indeed. In fact, when I entered graduate school some years later, I discovered that the academic preparation in psychology that I had received at Clark University was equal to, and often superior to, that of students from other colleges and universities.

Among the courses that I still can recall because they affected the questions I was to investigate later was an advanced seminar taught by Raymond Cattell. It was in that seminar with Cattell that we were introduced to the social concept of the dysgenic trend. The dysgenic trend asserts that the intellectual level of populations depends on the differential birth rates of various segments of the population. If the less competent segments of the population consistently reproduce at higher rates than the more competent segments, the intellectual level of society will eventually decline. He also found that members of the upper-class and middle-class, as a collective, tended to score higher on standard intelligence tests. The question that remained to be answered was whether the lower classes scored lower on tests because they were really less competent intellectually or whether the standard intelligence measures were culturally biased, favoring the middle- and upper-middle-class groups. He proceeded to address this question by creating a test he believed to be culture-free. The seminar offered ample opportunity to discuss the issues he raised as well as related ones, such as questions dealing with measurement and with the social factors influencing tests of intelligence. The social and practical implications of these discussions came to mind years later when I had to work with illiterate adults in the U.S. Army. It is, of course, an issue that is still unresolved.

At this point my story turns to my experiences with Karl Bühler. He was scheduled to give a course in social psychology for upper level psychology majors, and I decided to enroll in it. With the enthusiasm of a psychology undergraduate major, I looked forward to a course with this famous Austrian professor. Since every seminar at Clark was small and informal and provided ample time for discussion, I expected some stimulating discussions from so eminent a figure and anticipated that he would give us a perspective on social psychology different from that of Cattell. Of course, all of these ideas were conjectures since, in spite of Karl Bühler's fame, we knew nothing of his approach to social psychology.

The class was held, as was customary, in the seminar room on the third floor of the Jonas G. Clark Building, with the pictures of all Clark Ph.D.s mounted on one wall of the room.[2] Students sat along three sides of a long rectangular table and the professor usually sat at the other end. This arrangement encouraged a certain amount of informality, but the morning we were scheduled to meet Dr. Bühler, we noticed that a lectern had been placed on the table. This was indeed an unexpected sight because lecterns were rarely used for classes in this room. Nevertheless, the seven or eight of us gathered expectantly about the table waiting for the moment he would make his entry. After a few moments, Karl Bühler did enter from the side door directly from his office. He wore a fashionable pearl-grey, double-breasted suit, and tie, which was a sharp contrast to the informal, conservative, and not elegant, attire of the rest of our faculty. I expected a younger man and was surprised to see someone much older. He walked briskly to the lectern and glanced around the room, perhaps wondering what we were like. He appeared old to me in spite of his elegant attire and firm stride. He immediately took his place at the lectern. He looked at us, all sitting there, quietly and expectantly, waiting for him to outline our work for the term, a usual procedure in our classes. We were accustomed to learn on the first day what reading and other requirements were expected from us during the term. Karl Bühler, however, did not produce a syllabus or a course outline, nor did he announce a textbook. He greeted us in a friendly but reserved manner. His first comment was something to the effect that he was unaccustomed to lecturing to such a small group because in Vienna his lectures were well-attended by large numbers of students. "But then," he said, "I assume your intellectual zeal and interest will compensate for the lack of numbers." To hear his comments about our intellectual zeal indicated some sensitivity to us but, nevertheless, I felt that he had said that for his sake as well as ours. I wondered if he had not realized what class sizes to expect, given the small size of the university. Somehow he conveyed a sense of an unhappy man who had seen better days of fame and recognition in his homeland.

After some introductory comments about the course, he announced that he was not going to use a text but instead would dictate the text of his lectures to us. Since we did not realize at the time that his own work was not available in English, we assumed this was the way European professors taught—formal and distant. He began his lecture by reading from his notes in a slow, modulated voice with a heavy German accent, and we attempted to record his lectures verbatim. He would pause periodically to peer down at us to make sure we were taking his dictation verbatim. If he saw one of us stopping for any reason, he would pause and ask if anything was wrong. He would then repeat the last few words to make sure we were on the same place in the text as he was. We were not expected to miss any words. Once reassured that we were all at the same place, he would continue. As he began the term, so he continued for the rest of the course. And so for the entire semester we recorded his lectures verbatim.

I have lost my notes from this course and cannot recall whether he integrated his theory of semiotics into the rest of the course. To the best of my recollection, the course was primarily a historically organized survey of what major Western thinkers had written and taught about human nature. His first lecture dealt with the Aristotelian concept of man as a socio-political creature. The names for the Aristotelian concepts were all dictated in the original Greek version, another new experience for me. I was much impressed with his many references to the classics. From Aristotle, he moved to St. Augustine's *City of God*, and then on to the work of notable social thinkers of the seventeenth, eighteenth, and nineteenth centuries, men like Locke, Hobbes, Comte, Spencer, Durkheim, and Levy-Bruhl, and coming to the twentieth century with a description of Terman's research on marital happiness. Somewhat to our surprise, his discussion of Terman's work was his most up-to-date reference to American research, and it seemed to us that he might be unfamiliar with recent American work. He revealed a thorough understanding of the development of psychological thought over the centuries and attempted to convey it to us. This was all new to most of us. We had little background in the history of intellectual thought and philosophy except for a minimal acquaintance with Descartes acquired in the introductory psychology course. I found the material interesting in its own right, but at the time I failed to see the connection between what Bühler was talking about and what we studied in our other courses. In addition, I also I wondered why he did not relate it to the problems raised in current social psychology. In retrospect, I have come to appreciate the excellent history of social thought with which he provided us, and I have come to recognize that such an historical perspective is essential for understanding the development of modern psychology in general.

His teaching method also came as a surprise. It was so unlike any of our experiences at Clark in which discussion and independent reading formed an integral part. Some of my fellow students found his lecture-only approach to classroom instruction frustrating, especially when compared to Cattell's courses in social psychology which were up-to-date, stimulating, controversial, and enlivened by class discussion in which students were encouraged to relate the findings from academic research to their own life experiences. Bühler, by contrast, did not invite class discussion, and when students raised questions, they were always answered very directly and didactically.

Maybe that was the reason why one day I asked Professor Bühler for a conference. I cannot recall the precise reason for my request, but I guess I wanted to hear from him in more detail a point that he had raised in class. In any event I asked, with some timorousness, whether I could meet him in order to talk about psychology. I had expected to go to his office at the university, but to my surprise he suggested I come to his hotel. I accepted this invitation, feeling very privileged that he would be willing to have me visit him in what was his home.

When I arrived at the hotel, he welcomed me graciously and warmly. I had a sense that he seldom had visitors and was lonely. I quickly surmised that the reason for meeting in his hotel suite instead of his office was for reasons of health. I did not get the impression that he was working on anything in particular at that time. He talked a good deal and was very interesting. I can still recall the excitement I felt while listening to him. What did we talk about? I know that I took notes, but unfortunately, all of my notes have been lost. There is little specific content that I remember now. Whatever I recall at this moment is pure conjecture. I suppose it may have had to do with his work and his life in Europe. All that I recall vividly was that I was in the presence of a sad and lonesome, perhaps even tragic, man who felt isolated socially and intellectually from his colleagues and even from his students. For example, I do not recall ever seeing him at any university functions or giving any public lectures. How much of the ennui and retreat from the academic community was of his own making is, of course, an open question. Whatever its basis, the loss of his professional stature apparently weighed heavily on him and for all intents and purposes paralyzed him intellectually and professionally. As a result his work remained unknown in the United States, at least during his lifetime.

My early impressions of Karl Bühler as being alienated from his environment and intellectually defeated was confirmed when I read an essay describing the experiences of both Bühlers in America. Coser (1984) refers to them as "casualties in exile" and documents Karl's failure to ever resume the productivity of his Viennese years, especially in contrast to Charlotte, who published over 200 papers after coming to the U.S.[3]

The haunting memory of him that I have to this day is that of a sad, lonesome, and defeated individual, overlooked by his colleagues, and immobilized, and almost frozen, in his pre-exile mode. His lifework, unlike that of Freud and his colleagues, had failed to become part of the American literature, even among developmental psychologists interested in language development. And now that his work is available and some attention is paid to him, I wonder if time has not passed him by and his work has lost its uniqueness.

The Bühlers left Clark University after only one semester except that Charlotte continued her teaching for one more term. The reason they left permanently, it is alleged, was that President Atwood did not want to make any long-term commitments to them or to the department of psychology (Koelsch, 1987). The failure to secure a permanent appointment at Clark, according to Coser (1984, p. 41), enhanced Karl Bühler's feeling of being rejected. After he left Clark University, it was as though he had never been there. He left no legacy and no faculty or student took cognizance of his work. Without his physical presence there was no reminder that he was ever there.

I made no effort to contact him after he left Clark. It was many years later that I learned that Charlotte had developed a humanistic orientation and had moved into clinical work, but she, too, never succeeded in obtaining a permanent academic appointment. Nothing further was heard from Karl. His stay in America continued to be nonproductive: "Karl Bühler did not produce any significant work either in Minnesota or Los Angeles. It might be argued that Karl Bühler's work, given his age, was largely done by the time he arrived in America. Both Bühlers became casualties of the American passage" (Coser, 1984, p. 41). Karl Bühler died in 1963 at the age of eighty-four.

The rest of my college years at Clark continued to be exciting and intellectually challenging, so I decided to pursue graduate work in psychology. But on December 7, 1941, Pearl Harbor was attacked, and the nation found itself at war. This forced my fellow students and myself to put career decisions on hold. It became most urgent that we get our degrees before entering military service. I graduated from Clark in January 1943 and entered the U.S. Army a few weeks later. I eventually was assigned as a psychologist to a minimum security military installation where the inmates were American soldiers incarcerated for violations of army rules and civilian laws, such as theft, burglary, drunkenness on duty, being absent without leave or overstaying their leave. Sometimes they were away for days or weeks, or even years. Many of these men came from isolated rural areas like Appalachia or the mining country of western Pennsylvania, Kentucky, or West Virginia. Most of them were illiterate and had never been out of their towns or hollows. Many of their lives were impoverished economically, educationally, and socially.

My assignment was to evaluate these men and to make recommendations as to their fitness for return to military service. Based on our evaluation procedures, we were required to make one of three recommendations: Restoration to military service after completion of the sentence, educational rehabilitation, or discharge. Among the evaluation procedures we used were personal interviews to get at the men's educational work and criminal history, as well as individual intelligence and literacy tests. I administered every one of these procedures and then had to integrate the diverse data in order to make a recommendation for future action. I was extremely lucky in that my immediate supervisor was the famous philosopher Nelson Goodman. He gave me invaluable on-the-job training by helping me relate the diverse materials we had gathered on the men in such a way that we were able to make educated recommendations for the disposal of their cases. I was also involved in the educational program teaching reading, writing, and arithmetic. Our goal was to bring the men to a fourth-grade literacy level, so that they could be returned to military duty. The program was a huge success, with almost every participant completing the program.

This Army experience had a profound impact on my subsequent views of intelligence and particularly of intelligence tests. I had come to realize that, at least in the case of these men, the results obtained from the Wechsler-Bellevue test seemed unrelated to their practical knowledge and competence. The test items and the tasks on that test just made no sense to them. They could not understand why they had to play with puzzles, or with blocks, or answer silly questions such as those on the similarities subtest. The most inappropriate were the tests of social comprehension, e.g., "What would you do if you found a stamped addressed envelope on the street?" This was totally meaningless for them because few of them ever received mail, bought stamps, or could read the address anyway. It was a type of knowledge they did not need or had any relevance for them. Their language was at times archaic and unclear, so that Wechsler's test items made no sense to them. They tested in the IQ range of seventy to eighty. These scores indicated mental retardation. Consequently, I asked myself and Nelson Goodman, "How could these men do all the things they claimed to be able to do and still be retarded?" I had discovered that many of them were subsistence farmers and could handle a lot of farm-related activities, such as assemble a rifle blindfolded, hunt with marksman skills, harness mules to a plow a straight furrow, harvest crops, raise animals, and even make moonshine. That was all the practical intelligence they needed to carry on their farm duties. I had trouble considering these prisoners as retarded. I thought they were culturally backward and needed to be educated.

Then I thought of Cattell's discussion of the dysgenic population trends. Were these men the instances of the dysgenic trend, or did they fail the definition of Aristotle's socio-political man á la Bühler, or did we need to approach them from a perspective that takes account of the context in which they have to live their daily lives? What did my college psychology teach me about these people? The psychology of these men provided narratives from a different world than that of academia; yet the two worlds were coexisting with each other.

After my discharge from the Army I was determined to go to graduate school where I could spend time studying the issues of intelligence and environment. I applied to many graduate schools and decided to go to the University of Chicago, which was known as an intellectually innovative and forward thinking institution (after all, they raided some of the best Clark faculty in the early days). I intended to work in the clinical program with the hope of getting some answers to my burning questions. Little did I realize then how naive I was to expect easy answers to these questions and how I would be pursuing them long after graduate school. When I arrived at the university to enroll, I discovered the existence of the Committee on Human Development. This was a real find and one I had not expected. It offered, according to the catalogue, an interdisciplinary program that emphasized the state of complexity of human behavior and the social context in which it developed. Since the policy at the university was very flexible about entering programs, I shifted my major from clinical psychology to the Committee on Human Development. Psychology, anthropology, sociology, genetics, physiology, and nutrition were areas the program covered. I believed that becoming acquainted with all of these disciplines would enable me to create a reconciliation between academic psychology and the practical experience gained during my service in the Army. I was convinced that I was on the way to get some insights on how to proceed. I soon discovered how difficult it was to think in intercultural and interdisciplinary terms and was reminded that Bühler had been explicit about the heuristics of adopting an eclectic approach to the study of psychology. One of my first attempts while at Chicago to do this was with my master's thesis in which I sought to find out what contributions cultural anthropology could make to our understanding of human reasoning. I did a very careful search of the literature and found that very few anthropologists had addressed the problem. However, I was able to find enough sources to document that culture and intellectual performance are intimately related.

This experience convinced me that an interdisciplinary approach was the only way to go, but the task would not be easy.

The second experience which set my thinking in the direction of an interdisciplinary approach to the study of intellectual performance has to be traced to my course work with Professor Helen Koch, a child psychologist. One of the requirements for her course was that we write a term paper on a topic of interest to us. As an undergraduate I had read the earlier work of Kurt Goldstein and from it I learned about his holistic approach. He had described his position in greater detail in his seminal volume, *The Organism* (Goldstein, 1939/1995). I decided to use this book as the basis of my term paper. Helen Koch supported my decision. Spending three months studying this book had a profound effect on my thinking. Goldstein documented, in some detail, the interdependence of the major scientific disciplines addressing development. The capstone that he proposed as the integrative construct was self-actualization. The study of Goldstein fortified my belief in the need for an interdisciplinary approach.

In fact, it was my study of Goldstein that gave me the idea for my dissertation. I became intrigued with his discussion of abstract and concrete thought and of the ways to differentiate them. I decided I wanted to study the development of abstract and concrete thought in young children. I also wanted to use his methodology because it seemed to me most appropriate for children. Goldstein had studied brain-injured soldiers in World War I and had identified the *sequelae* of brain damage on intellectual activities. These experiences led him and Martin Scheerer to develop the object sorting test as a diagnostic procedure for determining the degree of intellectual dysfunction suffered by the brain injured patients. This test was published in the monograph *Abstract-Concrete Behavior* (Goldstein and Sheerer, 1941). My intention was to adopt Goldstein's object sorting test and modify it for studying the development of abstract-concrete thinking among children. The reason this approach was very appealing to me is that the method of sorting familiar objects seemed like a more real life situation than the typical decontextualized method of question asking used for conventional assessment procedures. In addition, the opportunity to assess the language children would use in such tasks would provide some information on children's reasoning. I thought that this approach was a close analogy to real life. However, Goldstein and his coworkers did not grant me permission to modify the material or the procedure so I could use it with children. I then had to develop my own sorting tasks and select appropriate familiar objects. I also decided to expand the study to examine whether children would use different modes of organization when the symbolic modes of representation were in different modalities, e.g., three-dimensional miniatures (toys), words, or pictures. So with Helen Koch's encouragement, I proceeded to develop the dissertation.

It was during this period that I had occasion to discuss my project with Heinz Werner, whom I would visit whenever I came to Worcester. These visits proved to be important for me because Heinz Werner was very helpful. He discussed the crucial question of how to frame instructions for a sorting task in order to avoid biasing the types of groupings the child would make. His admonition resonated with me because in my pilot work I had observed that asking children to group items that "belong together" led to different types of responses than asking them to group things that "are alike." The choice of instructions is crucial since they create a set for the remaining responses. The findings from this pilot effort made me aware of the important role language communication plays in test situations and interviews. In such situations investigators have to be sure that: 1) the language used is clear and understood by the child; and, more important, 2) that the child and the interviewer attach the same meaning to the words used in the test situation. Shared meanings can never be taken for granted. The solution, which seems so obvious now, was to create an open-ended inquiry dialogue in order to maximize the opportunity for shared meanings to be assured.

My dissertation, *Developmental trends in the abstraction ability of children*, was completed in 1951 and published in 1953 (Sigel, 1953). A second article, "The dominance of meaning" (Sigel, 1954) followed, in which I argued that the child's attribution of meaning to an object can transcend the physicalistic properties of the object. For example, a child who sees a red plastic miniature toy horse still recognizes it as a horse without being disturbed by the incongruity of color and size. The meaning is dominant. Today I would cite such dominance of meaning as an example of representational competence.

I have no doubt that my study of Kurt Goldstein's organismic view played a crucial part in the development of my dissertation and, perhaps more importantly, it also contributed in major ways to the direction my subsequent research was to take. When in the interim I thought of other developmental psychologists who might have helped, however subtly, to shape and influence my thinking, I certainly would not have included Karl Bühler in such a list. I no longer had the notes I took during class or my visits at his hotel, and I had never read his works in the original. But when I was in preparation for this chapter, Jaan Valsiner introduced me to some of Bühler's writings which had recently been translated into English (Eschbach, 1989). I was struck by some similarities between his work and my research and began to wonder if his discussions had perhaps formed my interests in some uncanny way in which I had not been aware.

The Bühler-Sigel Compatibility

I will begin with a brief overview of my own work for the past few decades. I have studied the development of representational thinking in children and developed a model that I have labeled the *Distancing Model*. To my amazement, when I read some of the summaries and quotations from Bühler's work, especially his integrated theory of signs and representation of language and the place of language in the development of representational competence, I discovered a number of concepts and advocacy positions that overlap with mine.

The model describing the development of representational thinking evolved from observations of categorization behavior of preschool children from middle- and low-social class families. The tasks involving three-dimensional objects and life-sized pictures of these objects. Lower class children had no difficulty creating rational groupings with the three dimensional objects and labeling their groupings appropriately. However, they had considerable difficulty creating groupings with the pictures even though they could label them. Children from middle-income families had no such difficulty. They produced very similar groupings with the pictures. The problem for me was to explain the object-picture discrepancy among children from low-income families and why no such discrepancy was found among children from middle-class families. The reason this was such a perplexing problem was that all the children could label the objects and the pictures with the correct names. But why did knowing the names not help the poor children categorize the pictures and object items with similar categories? If having the name did not help the grouping of pictures, would words serve a representational function? Obviously they did not function similarly when working with types of materials. Why could the poor children not understand the class equivalence of the objects and their representation—the pictures? The labels they used were based on observable attributes of the objects. After all, they did understand the instructions of the task since they did organize the objects on some functional or perceived similarity. However, even when they used the correct names, they were rarely able to include all of the items available to them in the category. It was as though the items that could be grouped together were not. The children had only a limited understanding of the category, even though they knew the word. For example, the children would exclude two-legged animals when they used the animal label—limiting the members of the group to four-legged animals. I interpreted their performance as being an indicator of a perceptually dominant approach and the word was not understood as an abstraction.

I had no way to label this finding in the context of my research program. It was a serendipitous event that led me to create what I called a *Distancing Model*. I was on an airplane on my way to a meeting to report on my research on the categorization behaviors of preschoolers, which I described above. While I was thinking of the discrepancy problem, I was looking out of the window, watching the ground rapidly recede. In the process I realized that although the objects in view became smaller, I knew they did not shrink. My first inclination was to attribute this to the traditional object-constancy argument. The trouble with that concept was that it did not explain the fact that the objects really had not shrunk. They looked smaller because they were receding into the distance. Suddenly I could discount the perceptual discrepancy as related to the characteristics of the object. The paradox was that while the physical view was an external reality, viewed relative to the context, my internal reality was independent of the physical world. My internal knowledge of the constancy of object size enabled me to interpret the external reality as a here-and-now phenomenon. What instigated the shift in what I saw versus what I knew was the abrupt ascent. That upward movement of the plane was the instigator of the discrepancy. My ability to transcend that shift can be explained, not only by my awareness of my internal representation, but also by my confidence in my own internal knowledge of the conservation of the object in spite of a shift in retinal image. In other words, I knew that the objects did not become something different in spite of their change in retinal appearance or because of a shift in perspective. Suddenly, the term *distancing* popped into my head as a label for this phenomenon. The discrepancy between my internal and external image was not a conflict because of my awareness that this event was due to a change in the physical situation. So, internal reality did not change in spite of the external reality of what I saw.

This seminal event, and the subsequent labeling of it as distancing, brought together my previous work in classification, communication, and representation under one rubric. Distancing acts (the ascent in the airplane) were the instigator of a representation. I paired the constructs Distancing → Representational Competence, and offered the distancing hypothesis as a basic idea to set the direction for my research program on the development of representational competence. This realization brought me back to the fact that the development of representation might be related to the linguistic environment in which children were socialized. So, I reasoned that social class differences might be related to the way in which the parents interacted linguistically with their children. And it would not matter what social class I studied, the level of language interaction should have comparable effects. We discovered that middle-class parents were not a homogenous group in how they engaged with their children, so we had a range of distancing acts within a given social class. Consistent with my belief that socialization of cognition begins in the family, I decided to focus on the family linguistic environment as a primary source of influence. So, after much piloting and observing of preschool children in school and in the home, I concluded that parents use teaching and management strategies that seem to be analogous in their effect to what the airplane experience did for me, that is, they create mental distance by employing cognitive demands for the child to separate him- or herself from the ongoing here and now or place him- or herself in the future (anticipation), or reconstruct the past (hindsight), or transcend the immediate present. These cognitive demands function as distancing acts. Although these acts could be non-personal as in the airplane example, I was interested in studying them in a parent-child context, focusing on verbal interactions. Further, I argued that cognitive representational capabilities evolve within the socialization experiences in the family because of the dialogic practices in particular that create shared experiences within which a new representational systems develops. The quality of the child's representational competence depends on the quality and frequency of parental distancing utterances. The distancing acts used by the parent can either emphasize the ongoing here and now by an authoritative statement, or encourage the child to think for him- or herself through inquiry or Socratic-type dialogues. The more concrete and perceptually based the strategy, the more likely the child's representational competence will be limited. The more inferential and open-ended the inquiry in the dialogue, the more likely the child's representational competence will be enhanced. The results of our studies with parents teaching their children in our laboratory supported our hypotheses (Sigel, 1982).

I will not be able to offer an extensive and detailed comparison of Bühler's semiotic theory to show where all the comparable points of view are, but I will be able to show that the overlap is more than just superficial.

Let me begin with the following quotation by Eschbach (1989) which demonstrates the similarity with Bühler's interest in language:

> . . . he (Bühler) develops his concept of the three significatory functions in the language phenomena, the sign nature of language and the four part- model which unites . . . speech interaction with . . . language-product, and speech-act with . . . language-system (p.117).

My interpretation of this quotation is commensurate with my conceptualization of the distancing verbal acts. The act is a signal in a representational form that demands a mental transformation of a verbal message into some action or verbal response. Further, since distancing acts in verbal form are representations, if they are to be effective there must be an apprehension or an understanding of language.

Innis (1982), in reviewing Bühler's theory of integrated semiotics, presents a good summary statement:

> Apprehension of signs and the preconditions for the intersubjective use of signs . . . as bearers of content and sense. . . . language is an instrument used by a sender to communicate to an addressee about objects and states of affairs—involves intersubjective sharing, the ideal structures are social objects that have been produced by communicating subjects, though produced by a group and not by any one individual consciousness (p. 35).

In addition to these comments of Bühler regarding language resemblance, in his discussion of categorization he includes the principles of perception of similarity. Dissimilar objects or events are instances of relational cognition when organized into categories, which is "thinkable, however, when the percepts have already been interpreted as signs" (Eschbach, 1989 p. 128). I would interpret the responses of the children or the adults as not understanding or being aware that categories are constructions with a number of defining attributes. For instance, an animal is an abstraction which can have as its referent, for example, specific animals, or specific animal characteristics which can be shared by any of them, such as eyes, or brain, or bring capable of reproduction, etc. The items are grouped on the basis of perceived similarity, where the attribute selected for the classification depends on whether the individual uses a perceptually based character or one already abstracted and converted into some sign to refer to the object, such as a word, a picture, or some meaningfully shared notation. The knowledge of the sign is derived from the humans' social nature (inherently natural to the human socialization). Is this not reminiscent of Bühler's discussion of Aristotle in my seminar with him at Clark? In addition, another common interest is expressed in the following:

> The individuals of a social species exert behavioral control over one another. But, the mutual control of individuals' behavior can be affected only by the specific needs of individuals if these needs express themselves and are recognized by the others. This entails the specific means for communication. Communication assumes a new dimension when it allows for representation, it goes beyond what is perceptually give in the situation (Kurz, 1996, p. 181).

The characterization of language in representational terms is compatible. Even its subtext overlaps with the role representation plays in my distancing model.

Let me now elaborate some of the commonalities that add to the uncanny resemblance between Bühler's work and mine. We share the conception of language as signs, signaling some action, event, or object representation. Communication on any level requires shared meaning of these signs. We each ground the evolution of language and its development in the social nature of humans, an allusion to the cultural origins of language. Understanding the meaning of signs, and therefore of its representational nature, evolves through a series of transitions from infancy to adulthood as Kurz (1996) writes:

> Bühler's own research contribution to this late enterprise (child development) was focused on questions concerning representation. How can the transition between scribbling and drawing (i.e., the attempt to draw *something*) be described? What are the first indications of representational use of language in the child? Here as with the study of thinking, Bühler (1925) shifted his study of language for pragmatic reasons: "The first tool-related thinking . . . is unrelated and prior to thinking in terms of language. But soon language not only becomes the universal means for the expression of the higher mental processes but also the most useful tool of thinking: today it is still best if we proceed from thinking in terms of language" (p. 180).

So, Bühler holds that language is a universal tool for communication, for thinking, and for representing knowledge and experience. When I refer to the distancing model, I see it as basically dealing with the socialization of cognition. To fill out the details of the socialization model it would be necessary to describe the cast of characters involved, and show how they interact and mutually influence each other cognitively, emotionally, and socially. Then the detailing of psychological nature and *sequelae* of such actions will bring some order into the development of thought and language into this seemingly chaotic world.

Since I have yet to do a more detailed study of Bühler's work, I can only provide a relatively brief comparison of some other points of resemblance such as: the need for an interdisciplinary, or as he called it, an "eclectic approach," the binding quality of a thought to language, of the role of meaning in the communication process, and, particularly, intersubjectivity within social interaction That all of this occurs within a developmental framework is particularly compatible.

Of course this is a generally accepted perspective and not unique to Bühler. Rather, it is his conception of the development transitions with his eclectic approach to the study of human development (my interpretation), not just his advocacy of the eclectic approach to solve the problem of the bringing together the multiple voices of the schools of psychology. He wrote this in 1927 and it articulates with my paper on the need for conceptualization of developmental psychology with an active, integrative, interdisciplinary perspective (Sigel, 1956).

As I read his work now, I can only marvel at the many resemblances between Bühler and myself. Let me conclude with a brief summary of the distancing-representational model and the reader can judge whether the similarity is possibly somehow related to Bühler's early influence on me:

> Presumably, all knowledge is in the form of mental representations such as words, pictures, graphics, and notational systems. It follows that competence to understand the representational rule, to understand as well that signs and symbols are representations of experience (including specific knowledge systems), and to be able to work with symbols and their transformations are central to cognitive functioning. The competence to understand and to perform such cognitive acts is thought to be a product of the child's cultural-socialization experience, initially in the family, followed by experience with other individuals, groups, and institutions. In sum, the central argument is that distancing acts are critical and necessary, but not sufficient, for the development of representational competence. The model is one of reciprocal interaction and hence of mutual influence (Sigel, 1993, p. 143).

It may not really matter whether Bühler's influence has been dormant until aroused by this exercise in recollections of my early experiences with him. What has happened because of this effort at recollection is that my interest in Bühler has its own significance. This report should also highlight the fact that the return to some history of psychological ideas may offer us many valuable ideas. In my case, Jaan Valsiner's request has served as a distancing strategy instigating my reconstructive memory of my academic intellectual history with Bühler's work as the centerpiece. Finally, what is of particular interest is that Bühler's views are of more significance to me, as I know them, than those of any other theorist I have studied.

And so for now, I let matter rest.

Notes

1. Previously published in *From Past to Future, Vol. 1*(1), pp. 1–15. *Legacy of Karl Bühler.* © 1998 Frances L. Hiatt School of Psychology, Clark University. Author: late of Educational Testing Service, Princeton, NJ.
2. I describe this setting to highlight the distinction between Bühler's formality and the informal setting, but Bühler was consistently formal. He seemed oblivious to the setting as a place for informal intellectual discussions. I do not recall whether he ever talked about his own work. I do remember the development of the social and philosophical material he described.
3. Coser (1984) also reports that Karl Bühler's international reputation was such that during the 1920s he held visiting professorships in distinguished American universities such as Stanford, John Hopkins, the University of Chicago, and Harvard University. In 1930 Harvard offered him the MacDougall Professorship, but because he and Charlotte "were both deeply attached to Vienna he declined" (pp. 38-39). Coser reports that Bühler declined a similar offer of a professorship at Fordham University in 1938. That offer, however, was then withdrawn when University authorities discovered that although Karl was Catholic, his wife was Protestant and their children were being reared as Protestants.

References

Coser, L. A. (1984). *Refugees and scholars in America.* New Haven, CT: Yale University Press.

Eschbach, A. (1989). The characteristics of Karl Buhler's pragmatically integrated theory of signs. In G. Deledale (Ed.), *Semiotics and pragmatics: Proceedings of the Perpignan Symposium* (pp. 118-129). Philadelphia, PA: John Benjamin Publishing Company.

Goldstein, K. (1995). *The organism: A holistic approach to biology derived from pathological data in man.* New York, NY: Zone Books. (Original work published 1939)

Goldstein, K., and Scheerer, M. (1941). Abstract and concrete behaviors: An experimental study with special tests. *Psychological Monographs, 33* (Whole No. 239).

Innis, R. E. (1982). *Karl Bühler: Semiotic foundation of language theory.* New York, NY: Plenum.

Koelsch, W. A. (1987). *Clark University: A narrative history,* Worcester, MA: Clark University Press.

Kurz, E. M. (1996). Marginalizing discovery: Karl Popper's intellectual roots in psychology; or, how the study of discovery was banned from science studies. *Creativity Research Journal, 9,* 173-187.

Sigel, I. E. (1953). Developmental trends in the abstraction ability of children. *Child Development, 24*(2), 131-144.

Sigel, I. E. (1954). The dominance of meaning. *The Journal of Genetic Psychology, 85,* 201-207.

Sigel, I. E. (1956). The need for conceptualization in research on child development. *Child Development, 27*(2), 241-252, 1956.

Sigel, I. E. (1982). The relationship between parents' distancing strategies and the child's cognitive behavior. In L. M. Laosa and I. E. Sigel (Eds.), *Families as learning environments for children* (pp. 47-86). New York: Plenum.

Sigel, I. E. (1990). Journeys in serendipity: The development of the Distancing Model. In I. E. Sigel and G. H. Brody (Eds.), *Methods of family research: Biographies of research projects: Vol. 1. Normal families* (pp. 87-120). Hillsdale, NJ: Erlbaum.

Sigel, I. E. (1993). The Centrality of a distancing model for the development of representational competence. In R. R. Cocking and K. A. Renninger (Eds.), *The development and meaning of psychological distance* (pp. 141-158). Hillsdale, NJ: Erlbaum.

7

Bühler's Legacy: Full Circle and Ahead

Nancy Budwig[1]

In this paper I would like to play with the idea of how one might relate Karl Bühler's work to ongoing and future work in the area of psychology with a particular focus on issues of human development embedded within a sociocultural context. What is so fascinating to me about Bühler's work is that as a psychologist he gave serious consideration to language. While at first glance this may seem somewhat trivial given the current explosion of interest in what could be referred to as the discursive or narrative turn in the social sciences over the last two decades, I would claim that, nevertheless, most psychologists either ignore the issue of signs, and more particularly language, or treat it in a very superficial way. Thus, it is in this respect that Bühler's claims with regard to the centrality of language can be reconsidered in terms of recent changes in the landscape of the social sciences.

Nerlich and Clarke (1996) argue that Bühler can be viewed as "the most celebrated pragmatic thinker in Germany and an important link in a chain of thinkers that extents (*sic*) from Humboldt to Habermas" (p. 224). In turning attention to language functioning though it is important to keep in mind Bühler had very specific ideas about the nature of linguistic forms as well. Thus although he has primarily been discussed in terms of his contributions to issues of language functioning, Bühler also has made important points about the connections between linguistic forms and the semantic and pragmatic functions they serve. First, Bühler has contributed to the development of the notion of *fields* that we will see link forms with meanings in much the same way cognitive linguists currently are considering. In fact, cognitive linguists could benefit from a fuller understanding of Bühler's discussion of the notion of field. Second, Bühler's discussion of deixis and, in particular, the ways "*pointing words*" orient speaker and listener in terms of context could be viewed as having paved the way for much work going on currently in cultural and linguistic anthropology.

It is of interest to note that although Bühler, a psychologist, has been explicitly cited and praised by scholars in the neighboring disciplines of linguistics and anthropology, Bühler's work has received little attention from psychologists (see though Brock, 1994, for an exception). Jakobson (1973, p. 41) directly noted the significance of Bühler's work for linguists by claiming that Bühler's work was "for linguists probably the most inspiring among all contributions to the psychology of language." Most contemporary volumes on functional linguistics or linguistic anthropology at least briefly discuss Bühler's work. In the following, I will argue that the field would do well to return to some work of psychologists like Bühler who not only have something to offer, but also have played a central role in developing the very ideas we are "importing" from other fields today!

Bühler's Impact on Work in Related Disciplines

Bühler's work clearly has had an impact on subsequent work in the area referred to as pragmatics and subsequently functional linguistics. Similarly Bühler's work on deictics, followed by Jakobson's work on shifters, can be viewed as paving the way for the discussion of "transposition" in cultural anthropological work (see Gumperz and Levinson, 1996; Hanks, 1996b, Haviland, 1996). What I find intriguing, though, is the apparent but often uncited connection between Bühler's writings and current work in the area of cognitive linguistics.

Cognitive Linguistics

Cognitive linguists are concerned with the connection between language and the cognitive construal of the world. Langacker describes construal as "the relationship between a speaker (or hearer) and a situation he conceptualizes and portrays" (Langacker, 1987, p. 487-488). Focus is on the interface between particular linguistic items (either syntactic or lexical choices) and their relation to how events are conceived. Consider for instance the distinction in saying a person is *running* versus *jogging* or *sprinting*. Lakoff (1987) and Fillmore and his colleagues (see Goldberg, 1996; Palmer, 1996, for review) have discussed the construct of "ICMs"—"Idealized Cognitive Models." Here it is assumed that the use of particular lexical items such as "bachelor" convey more than a simple definition; rather they invoke a "theory" containing several components. Cognitive linguists have also focused on issues of viewpoint and perspective, claiming that language coding implies particular vantage points. Focus has been placed on figure/ground organization and the way in which certain items are foregrounded or backgrounded, based on systematic choices of linguistic items. For cognitive linguists the connection between language and cognition is one of examining how particular linguistic arrangements provide distinct slants on event construal.

Bühler's Legacy 117

Bühler's (1934/1990) discussion of the "field-theoretic approach" to language can be compared to current themes in cognitive linguistics. Bühler discusses the relationship between words or lexical items on the one hand, and "fields" on the other:

> But just as the painter's colors require a painting surface, so too do language symbols require a surrounding field in which they can be arranged. We call this the *symbolic field* of language (Bühler, 1990, p. 171).

> Aber ebenso wie die Farben des Malers einer Malflaeche, so beduerfen die sprachlichen Symbole eines Umfeldes, in dem sie angeordnet werden. Wir geben ihm den Namen *Symbolfeld* der Sprache (Bühler, 1934, p. 150-151).[2]

Bühler's discussion of the term "field" is compatible with Lakoff's (1987) use of the construct "Idealized Cognitive Models" and Langacker's (1987) "schema" to the extent that all are concerned with the ways of linking language with broader conceptually structured wholes or gestalts.

Bühler goes on in his discussion to outline the relationship between a number of linguistic elements, such as case systems, and how they play a significant role in construing particular vantage points. Bühler claims language cannot be viewed as representing a given reality, but rather linguistic forms in conjunction with symbolic fields help structure the nature of experience. Bühler's concerns with issues of linguistic universals and the stamp of individual languages is outlined in brief form in the following:

> The core of the inner form of language is in my opinion the fact that different language families *prefer* different intermediate and symbolic fields because they see what is to be represented, the world in which all speakers live, with different eyes ... In my opinion it is and remains nothing more than a preference. For it is by no means impossible for us as speakers of Indo-European languages to make sense of alien symbolic fields (Bühler, 1990, p. 172).

> Das ist nach meiner Meinung ... der Kern der inneren Sprachform, daß verschiedene Sprachfamilien verschiedene Mittler- und Symbolfelder *bevorzugen,* weil sie die Darzustellende, die Welt, in der alle Sprechenden leben, mit verschiedenen Augen sehen... Und es ist und bleibt nach meiner Meinung auch nicht mehr als eine Bevorzugung. Denn unmoeglich ist uns Indo-germanen das Nachdenken fremder Symbolfelder keineswegs (1934 p. 152).

For Bühler, as for cognitive linguists, language (viewed as a system consisting of lexical and syntactic units) plays a central role in constructing the world. In adopting a non-representational view of language, the idea is not that language can be viewed as a mapping of an "out there" experience, but rather it is claimed that through the complex linkage of sign and symbolic field, language plays a significant mediating role in the construction of reality. In sum, though the connection has not been typically made, Bühler can be viewed as a precursor to current work carried out in cognitive linguistics.

Pragmatics and Functional Linguistics

Bühler continually has been noted to have had tremendous impact on the field of pragmatics (see Nerlich and Clarke, 1996). As is discussed by Valsiner (this volume), Bühler outlined a pragmatic theory of language by suggesting three main functions of language: *expression (Ausdruck), appeal (Appell)* and *representation (Darstellung)* (see Bühler, 1934, pp. 28-29; 1990, p. 34). Bühler makes clear though, that he takes representation to be the dominant or most specifically human aspect of language. Nevertheless he took as a central goal to develop his "sematology" so that it linked with a theory of action.

It is this view of the various functions of language that is often absent in many psychological theories today. Many psychologists have worked with what Reddy (1979) has called the conduit metaphor of language—a metaphor that emphasizes the representational aspects of pragmatic functioning. At the same time, as many psychologists have continued to work with a representational view of language, others have struggled to understand the multifunctionality of language. More recently pragmatic theories have been developed to examine the performative quality of certain utterances in which saying something is simultaneously doing something, as for instance with certain speech acts like promising, baptizing, and the like (see Austin, 1962; Searle, 1969). In addition, many pragmatic theorists have given up on the strict division of language functioning as implied in Bühler's scheme and argued instead for the multifunctionality of language that was later discussed by Wittgenstein (1953) and his followers (see Duranti, 1997; Hanks, 1996a, for review).

Relating Bühler's work to more recent advances in the area of pragmatics and functional linguistics, one finds several points of further development. One major difference has been methodological. Clearly by the 1970s, functional linguists have become concerned with looking at language in natural contexts of use. Here the issue has become one of examining naturalistic data rather than the sort of constructed examples that Bühler made use of in his work—such as his famous *"Es regnet" (It is raining)* example. As researchers have begun examining language stemming from real-time interactions they have begun noticing the interface between particular grammatical devices and social interaction, as well as the interface between discourse and grammar (see Ochs, Schegloff, and Thompson, 1996, for review). This has led to discussion of the ways in which the selection of specific linguistic devices not only represents and achieves action but also contributes to the construal of context in particular ways.

What is particularly interesting is that Bühler made the linkage between the use of particular grammatical devices such as case markers and particular symbolic fields in terms of semantic considerations, although he did not draw the connection between form and function as most modern day functional linguists have in terms of more pragmatically charged uses of language. Nevertheless, his work on deixis can be seen as an important precursor to recent work doing exactly this.

Cultural and Linguistic Anthropology

Modern day cultural and linguistic anthropologists have been fascinated with the connection between meaning and context, with quite a lot of focus on the role of deixis in the contextualization process (see Duranti, 1997; Duranti and Goodwin, 1992; Gumperz and Levinson, 1996; Hanks, 1996a). Although such a link often is not made explicit, Bühler's discussion of deixis has played a central role in framing the range of questions currently being addressed. For Bühler (1990, p. 121) deictic words can be described as follows:

> To put it briefly: the formed deictic words, phonologically distinct from each other just as other words are, are expedient ways to guide the partners. The partner is called by them, and his gaze, and more generally, his searching perceptual activity, his readiness for sensory reception is referred by the deictic words to clues, gesture-like clues and their equivalents, which improve and supplement his orientation among the details of the situation. That is the function of the deictic words in verbal contact, if one insists upon reducing this function to a single general formula.

> Kurz gesagt: die geformten Zeigwoerter, phonologisch verschieden voneinander wie andere Woerter, steuernden Partner in zweckmaessiger Weise. Der Partner wird angerufen durch sie, und sein suchender Blick, allgemeiner seine suchende Wahrnehmungstaetigkeit, seine sinnliche Rezeptionsbereitschaft wird durch die Zeigwoerter auf Hilfen verwiesen, gestenartige Hilfen und deren Aequivalente, die seine Orientierung im Bereich der Situationsumstaende verbessern, ergaenzen. Das ist die Funktion der Zeigwoerter im Sprachverkehr, wenn man darauf besteht, diese Funktion auf eine einzige allgemeine Wortformel zu bringen (1934, pp. 105-106).

Since Bühler's discussion of deixis, several others have used a variety of terms to talk about related phenomena including Silverstein's discussion of "shifters" (1976), Goffman's discussion of "frames" (1974), Gumperz's use of "contextualization cues" (1982), and Hanks' (1996b) introduction of "deictic fields." What these authors share is a fascination with the ways in which language use itself creates context. Subtle variations in the use of deictic forms have been noted to index routine communicative practices themselves. Hanks (1996b), for instance, has illustrated this through his careful analysis of seemingly random use of deictic forms used by speakers in Yucatec Maya. The Maya deictic system is an extremely complex system involving the use of both terminal and initial deictic forms. Hanks suggests ways in which co-occurrence patterns in the use of these forms can best be explained as attempts on the part of conversational participants to index to one another how to identify discourse referents by focusing attention or drawing upon information based on perceptual or conversational knowledge. Ochs (1996) also provides illustration of a similar point, namely that indexical forms help assign situational meanings in complex ways that are intereactional achievements, through her detailed analyses of affective and epistemic stances. Ochs' research in a variety of communities leads her to the conclusion that linguistic resources for marking stance play an "especially privileged role in the constitution of social life" (p. 420). Such research marks a shift in thinking from Bühler's time of suggesting the need to examine the role of language as indexical, to the more radical claim that deictic forms themselves play a fundamental role in the co-construction of context dialogically by speakers and listeners.

This sort of perspective has been nicely laid out in Hanks' (1996a) discussion of language and communicative practices. He argues:

> Our starting point is the three-way division of language as a semiformal system, communicative activities as semistructured processes, and actors' evaluations of these two (see figure 7.1). These evaluations could be called *ideological* in the sense of embodying broader values, beliefs, and (sometimes) self-legitimating attitudes. They are metalinguistic, or metadiscursive, to the extent that they bear directly on language or discourse, serving to fix its meaning (p. 230).

Hanks goes on to suggest that the three elements are synthesized in the moment of "practice":

> We must remember as we enter into this synthesis that its three dimensions, though overlapping, are analytically distinct, and they require different modes of analysis. . . . The challenge of practice analysis is not reduction of this to a by-product of that but integration of distinct phenomena into a more holistic framework (pp. 230-231).

Figure 7.1
Three Dimensions of Communicative Practice. (Hanks, 1996a, p. 230)

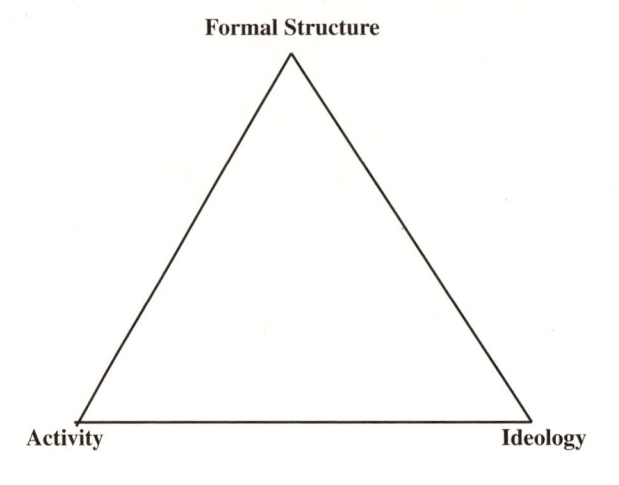

Formal Structure

Activity   **Ideology**

This sort of holistic view of human functioning is quite consistent with Bühler's view of the relationship between psychology and language. Similar too is the idea that in speaking, agents do more than represent—they also bring about changes, "connect" with others, and the like. Hanks' practice based view of communication pushes Bühler's plurifunctional view of language even further by adopting a more constructivist view that suggests talk plays a fundamental role in creating speaker-object relations. By using deictic forms (and other linguistic resources) speakers do not simply *point to* or draw attention to already existing or imagined objects as Bühler suggested. According to Hanks, the contrastive use of deictic forms simultaneously *produces* subjects, objects, and social relationships in the course of everyday communicative practices. Communicative practices are viewed as "invisible," and repeated or habitual use of everyday language can lead participants to think in particular ways. It is this sort of linkage that begins to make for intriguing discussion for the connection between language, thought, and practice based approaches to human development.

The Contributions of Bühler's Work to the Study of Human Development and Socialization

Although Bühler's work has received little discussion in psychological circles, it seems that over the last years the field has come to rely on ideas that in part can be traced to his ideas. There are at least three ways that Bühler can be viewed as having an impact on the study of human development. Only one of these ways is directly acknowledged. For the others, the road is less direct. Interestingly, these developments have existed side by side with little attempt to link them together—much as was the case with Bühler's own thinking on these issues.

The Study of Symbolic Development

One of the most explicit treatments in psychology of Bühler's work can be found in Werner and Kaplan's *Symbol Formation* (1963/1984). In their discussion of language development, Werner and Kaplan devote an entire chapter to a discussion of Bühler's treatment of the relationship between case marking systems and the introduction of his notion of symbolic fields (see above). When discussing the development of symbolic abilities, Werner and Kaplan, though drawing heavily on Bühler's discussion, are quick to note that Bühler's view of language is "agenetic" to the extent that he focuses on "ideal structure" (see Werner and Kaplan, 1963/1984, p. 52), while their own approach could be characterized as developmental. Bühler has noted, for instance, ways in which case markers are often used in languages to mark specific formula-like schemata. The use of transitive verbs for example "call for" the filling in of two slots in a syntactic model—first calling for "concrete" actions and later for more "abstract" ones. Werner and Kaplan prefer to view this development in terms of a *functional shift:*

> We maintain, as we have insisted throughout this work, that the latter view is more tenable. We believe that the shifts which take place from concrete action models to syntactic relations of a more abstract sort reflect the operation of the basic development principle pertaining to *form-function relationships*. As one will recall, according to this principle, wherever functional shifts occur during development, the novel function is first executed through old, available forms; sooner or later, of course, there is a pressure towards the development of new forms which are of a more function-specific character, that is, that will serve the new function better than the older forms (p. 60).

Werner and Kaplan go on to discuss their view that language development is just one example of a more general developmental process, namely children's desire to conceive of the world first in terms of "formula-like schemata" and only later in terms of more freedom from the concrete perceptual-motor contexts.

This perspective was developed and further refined years later by Dan Slobin in his crosslinguistic studies of children's language development (see Slobin, 1985). Interestingly, this work can primarily be traced in part to developments in cognitive and functional linguistics, where Bühler's work was more widely read, than to Werner and Kaplan's discussion within psychology. Slobin has argued that particular prototypical events provide a framework for children's early organization of linguistic forms. Based on a review of typologically distinct languages, Slobin provided intriguing evidence that children acquiring different languages begin to use case marking forms to mark a scene he referred to as the Manipulative Activity Scene. For instance, in a language that requires the use of a case marker on the objects of verbs, children were first noted to limit such usage to objects pertaining to scenes in which an agent willfully brought about a change of state. According to Slobin, children first give forms concrete meanings and only later use them in more abstract ways. In general this is not only consistent with Werner and Kaplan's discussion of the form-function relations, but also with Bühler's idea that language plays a major role in speakers adopting particular perspectives on events. While connecting with some of Bühler's work on the notion of *field* and syntactic models, this line of argumentation did not pick up on the plurifunctionality of language.

Sociocultural Practice and Human Development

Some recent discussions of human development have begun to emphasize the role of communication in development and socialization. Such views have emphasized that within ongoing interactions with significant others, children and other novices come to participate in new and more advanced forms of thinking, and engage in activities in a way more consistent with cultural ways of acting (see Valsiner, 1989; Wertsch, 1991, 1998). Influenced by Vygotsky's (1981) "general law of psychological development" in which development is viewed in terms of the transition from "intermental" to "intramental" functioning, this newer work has emphasized the role of practice in individuals' cognitive development in a way that has been largely absent in developmental discussions (see Duranti, 1997, for an interesting elaboration of the connection between Vygotsky, Bühler, and current work in linguistic anthropology).

More recently a variety of sociocultural researchers have stressed the role of communicative interchanges and semiotic means in developmental processes. Such a view depends on and elaborates Bühler's assumption that language is more than a representational system. While many developmental psychologists view language as something of a window onto underlying thought processes, sociocultural research has started from a more multifunctional view of language and its role in human development. Analyses of such communicative interchanges are not so much revealing of "underlying mental concepts," but rather, such analyses help us understand ways in which the *communicative interchanges themselves* play a pivotal role in the socialization process (see Rogoff, Mistry, Göncü, and Mosier, 1993, for an excellent illustration of this point).

Note that, as with Bühler's discussion of the plurifunctionality of language, there is no attempt within such sociocultural work to examine the relationship between particular linguistic devices and language functioning. We turn now to a group of researchers whose work supports the notion that such linkages play a fundamental role in human socialization.

Language Socialization

Language socialization research is guided by the belief that in learning to use language children are also simultaneously socialized into cultural ways of being (see Schieffelin and Ochs, 1986; and Miller and Hoogstra, 1992, for review). Similar to sociocultural approaches such as those reviewed above, language socialization work has emphasized the central role of practices in human development. In contrast, though, to most sociocultural research, language socialization approaches are more closely linked to the specific role of *language* practices.

The view of language within a language socialization perspective is quite broad. Language is more than the lexicon and syntax, and pragmatic functioning is central. Language socialization researchers are explicit in their focus on one or both of the following claims: 1) An examination of *language functioning* is central to an understanding of how language practices encode and socialize information about society and culture. 2) An examination of *language forms* can contribute to an understanding of the ways meaning is constructed in interactions. It is those approaches that focus on both claims that can be related to Bühler's writings in the most interesting ways, and it is these that I will focus on here.

The adherence to both assumptions outlined above draws upon Bühler's discussion of deixis and pointing much like other work stemming from cultural and linguistic anthropology. The assumption is that if deictic forms index culturally appropriate ways of acting, feeling, and knowing, then these indexicals simultaneously provide individuals with ways of co-constructing cultural meanings (see Budwig, in press; Goodwin, 1990; Ochs, 1996). Indexicals are said to play a central role in this process:

> A linguistic index is usually a structure (e.g., sentential voice, emphatic stress, diminutive affix) that is variably used from one situation to another and becomes conventionally associated with particular situational dimensions such that when that structure is used, the form invokes those situational dimensions (Ochs, 1996, p. 411).

To this extent, language is said to play a powerful not only role in researchers' processes of meaning construction, but also, because language is thought to play a dynamic role in the actual construction of the social order, for the participants as well. Ochs (1996) has demonstrated this in her discussion of the ways languages index social identity through pronominal systems and honorific morphology. Extending Bühler's (1990, p. 121) claims that deictic forms "are expedient ways to guide the partners," one can see that the sort of claim made by language socialization researchers is that experts, in their use of particular indexicals, give "clues" to novices about how to "orient" themselves in given situations. Although as Werner and Kaplan noted in their discussion of the links between early language meanings and cognition, Bühler was not concerned with the issue of development per se, language socialization researchers have been specifically focused on how experts and novices together work to construct cultural meaning systems. At the same time, although language socialization researchers have been interested in this process, their work has yet to be cast within a particular developmental framework. We will turn in the final section to consider how this might be an important direction for future research.

Circling Back Towards the Future: Bühler's Legacy

I have noted in the above that Bühler has received very little attention in psychology, although his work has had a significant impact on linguists and cultural anthropologists over the past decades. Why should it be the case that psychologists now attend to Bühler's ideas? Although there are many different answers that can be given, my focus will be on the significance of Bühler's work for rethinking the role of language in the study of human development.

There has begun to be a subtle shift in the way developmental psychologists view language and its role in human functioning over the last decade. Around the time Bühler was writing there was a sense that the study of language and its development intricately relates in important ways to other aspects of human functioning. Over the years however, language has been viewed more and more in terms of the conduit metaphor, and therefore as more peripheral to many aspects of human development. Several converging factors discussed above have led some developmental psychologists to reconsider a more dynamic view of language, one more consistent with the view Bühler was developing.

While the recent emphasis on the role of language cannot be directly traced to Bühler's work, what appears to be the case is that Bühler's work has had its impact via a slight detour. Recent studies in the areas of human development and socialization have drawn increasingly on the fields of linguists and cultural anthropology. Such work has clearly been influenced by Bühler's discussion of his notion of symbolic fields and indexicals. And it appears that via this indirect route, Bühler has found his way back into psychology. In some sense then Bühler's ideas, especially those concerning the indexicality of language, can be viewed as reentering psychology through the back door. With this in mind the time is ripe for psychologists to think freshly about them. In the remaining space I will discuss two ways such notions can be rethought.

Towards a Holistic Understanding of Language and Its Role in Human Development and Socialization

In returning to Bühler's ideas, what is striking is the breadth of his coverage as he discusses psychological aspects of language. The breadth of his work is significant when compared to some modern day monographs. One important aspect his work brings back into focus is the importance of considering language not only in terms of syntax, but also in terms of conceptual and pragmatic meanings. This serves as a reminder of the importance of adopting a more holistic view of human development and is quite consistent with some recent inter-disciplinary movements.

At the same time his work encourages a more holistic view of development, it is interesting to note that aspects of Bühler's *Sprachtheorie* (theory of language) were never linked together systematically in his own writings. This is to say, over the years he developed the Organon model, outlined the notions of symbolic field and deictic field, and emphasized the plurifunctionality of language. These aspects never were linked together as holistically as might be fruitful. This seems to have been accomplished more recently in practice-based models that link together forms, functions, and ideology as discussed by Hanks (1996) and others (see also Gumperz and Levinson, 1996).

As one begins to make such linkages in studying the synthesis of various aspects of communicative practices and the role of language in such accounts, it seems essential to also simultaneously consider the contributions of what have until now been relatively distinct traditions. For instance, currently there are few attempts to consider the overlaps between the aims of language development research, sociocultural theorizing, and recent trends in discursive and narrative psychology. Such consideration would aid in linking together what has been until now some separate areas of discussion. For instance, Cox and Lightfoot (1997) have taken an important first step in this direction by placing side by side in their discussion of sociogenetic approaches to internalization what has previously been kept distinct; these include consideration of approaches emphasizing social interaction stemming from sociocultural theorizing on the one hand, and approaches stemming from narrative and discursive psychology that have specifically focused on the role of symbolic action on the other. What all of these approaches have yet to integrate is the extent to which children's linkages of forms and functions are themselves undergoing important developmental shifts. In sum, to date, various aspects of Bühler's work have differently influenced cognitive, sociocultural, and discursive psychologists interested in human development and socialization. An attempt to link these separate attempts together to recognize their distinct and overlapping contributions will provide for a new round of intriguing debates on the role of language in human ontogenesis.

Viewing Language Socialization Developmentally

In the attempt to link Bühler's work to discussions of the development of symbolic functioning, I have noted the direct connection between Werner and Kaplan's (1963/1984) work and Bühler's discussion of symbolic fields. Werner and Kaplan were noted to have claimed that their work would extend Bühler's by adding a developmental component. The particular developmental framework they offered concerns the principle of form-function relationships, in which new forms first serve old functions and new functions are first served by old forms. It is exactly this sort of link that needs elaboration in current attempts within language socialization to understand the fundamental role of indexicals for human development. In other words, we have noted that Hanks' discussion of practice-based approaches to language integrates and draws upon several central aspects of Bühler's language theory. Yet what is still needed is a discussion of the sort of developmental principle discussed by Werner and Kaplan in their elaboration of symbolic fields. To know that forms, functions, and ideology come together "in practice" tells us little about developmental transformations. To this extent, a model such as Hanks' or Ochs' discussion of the principle of indexicality is an important *first step* towards understanding sociogenetic internalization. Nevertheless, a further account of the developmental process that would entail a careful examination of the co-constructive efforts of communicative partners of various levels of expertise is very much needed. It is here that future research needs to be directed.

My own research has pursued exactly this question: How is it that one might elaborate a practice-based account of language and link it with a view of development based on the construction of form-function relationships? Studying this issue involves crosslinguistic comparisons of children interacting with a range of communicative partners in ongoing and meaningful communicative interchanges over developmental time. My own work has been examining the changing nature of positioning of self and other in discourse of caregivers, their toddler children, and these children's peers over microgenetic and ontogenetic time. Looking at both typological (German, Hindi, English) and cultural differences in language patterning of forms and functions of talk about self and other, I have been highlighting the ways in which children and caregivers co-construct meaning over time. Such work allows for simultaneous attention to Bühler's discussion of symbolic fields and his discussion of deixis. By focusing on the use and development of case markers and other forms of self and other reference, such work has attempted to focus on caregivers' and children's active attempts at sense-making.

Let me illustrate this by considering some examples that summarize points I have made in more detail elsewhere (see Budwig, 1995, 1997, 2000). Looking at rather mundane play activities taking place between caregivers and their children, such as building with wooden blocks, I have noted the very different ways notions of personhood are marked through the use of grammatical devices by caregivers and their two-year-old children over longitudinal time in speech samples of English, German, and Hindi speakers. Three points are particularly noteworthy here. First, looking at the caregivers speech, pronouns and other linguistic devices were used by the caregivers of each speech community in systematically distinct ways. The American mothers frequently referred to the child in combination with action statements (*"Gee you are making a big tower"*), while references to themselves were linked with assertions about their own mental states (*"I think you could make it taller"*) and generic focus was found in attempts to directly change their children's behaviors (*"I don't think children are supposed to play with these like that"*).

Although consistent, it is important to note that these form-function patterns were not statically linked, but rather, were part of the caregivers' attempts to mark significant aspects of the communicative routines themselves and were significantly based on the very practices in which the caregiver and child were participating. This brings us to the second noteworthy point, namely that the use of deictic and other related forms were not tied in any one-to-one way to particular language functions but rather that meaning was emergent based on how such forms were used within the dynamic flow of ongoing interaction. The deictic forms I have examined were dynamically employed as ways to construct distinct ways of situating participants in the dialogue. For instance, I have noted ways in which the middle-class Anglo English-speaking caregivers downplayed their own agency and enhanced their children's by using joint forms of self and other reference (e.g., *We're making a big tower, aren't we*) or by limiting the use of first person reference to mental state verbs or, on occasion, action verbs in requests of permission (e.g., *I think you might want to build it this way, Can I put this here?*). In contrast, the German caregivers from ex-East Germany were more likely to ground the discourse about their own and their child's actions in terms of either joint or generic agency. For instance, these caregivers, when objectively carrying out similar actions (such as placing wooden blocks on towers they were building) frequently opted to employ the generic term *man* (one), such as in the example "*Jetzt kann man so was machen*" (*"Now one can make something like this"*), to highlight common ways agents could work toward agreed upon solutions, downplaying the child's specific agency in this process. In this sense, the caregivers drew upon typological options of their language to index routine aspects of the communicative routines thereby providing their children with important clues to cultural ways of being.

A third point that is particularly important to this work involves the attempt to link the practice based approach to indexicals with a developmental framework such as Werner and Kaplan's (1963/1984) discussion of the orthogenetic principle. What is central here are findings from my prior work suggesting that the children do not link forms and functions in the same way their caregivers do, nor in the same way over time. As would be predicted by Werner and Kaplan, early on the children used new forms to convey old functions, and new functions were first expressed by old forms. In general the children's development of indexical forms moved from a more concrete level to a more abstract level of symbolization. For instance, early on the use of *I* by the American children was primarily limited to the assertion of mental states. A separate form, *my*, was used in subject position in a way that deviated from adult input (e.g., *My build the tower*) to talk about self as agent. While the children's use was consistent with the aspects of communicative practice as marked by their caregivers, the specifics of the marking were not identical, and in fact showed systematic development over time moving from levels of rather global origins to more highly differentiated and then integrated systems of indexical usage (see Budwig, 1995, for further details). What this suggests is that the children are actively involved in the process of sense making and are not in any straightforward manner simply isolating meanings from caregiver speech and imitating such usage in their own speech.

It should go without saying that there are many details that need to be worked out in order to capture the related contributions of community, language typology, and level of development in this process. Research thus far has been restricted to small samples and many questions remain about the variation found not only within caregivers who speak the same language, but the impact such variation has on their children's usage of similar indexical expressions. Such work, even if quite preliminary, nevertheless shows that from their earliest forays into the use and understanding of deictic expressions, children are capable and likely to use them productively in their sense making activities.

Conclusions

In this article I have argued that Bühler has made a significant contribution to psychology in part because of his emphasis on the centrality of a theory of language to psychological work. Bühler's theory has yet to have had significant impact on the field of human development—in fact, his work is rarely cited in psychology texts. At the same time, Bühler's work has been recognized and made use of by cultural anthropologists and linguists. And ideas based on his work are slowly beginning to creep back into psychological discussions. My sense is that a solid reading of his work will provide our field with fresh approaches to old questions. As I have noted, important modifications will need to take place. For instance, Bühler, although emphasizing language, rarely studied it with the care that modern day researchers, do thanks to technological advances. So the work that lies ahead is one of reinterpreting his writings in light of modern day concerns. It is my hope that this volume, with its overview and suggested linkages to ongoing issues within psychology, will inspire a few to link past with future by reconsidering aspects of Karl Bühler's work. His work has offered linguists and cultural anthropologists a psychological theory of language. By coming full circle it is central to now take Bühler's ideas and move ahead.[3]

Notes

1. Previously published in *From Past to Future, Vol. 1*(1)*36-48. The Legacy of Karl Bühler*, pp. 36–48. © 1998. Frances L. Hiatt School of Psychology, Clark University. Author: Nancy Budwig, Department of Psychology, Clark University, 950 Main Street, Worcester, MA.
2. It is interesting to note that one of the few places that this aspect of Bühler's work is discussed is in a chapter by Werner and Kaplan's (1963/1984) book *Symbol Formation*—a point to which I will return below.
3. I am grateful to Michael Bamberg, Valerie Crawford, and Jaan Valsiner for comments on an earlier version of this paper.

References

Austin, J. (1962). *How to do things with words*. Oxford: Oxford University Press.
Brock, A. (1994). What ever happened to Karl Bühler? *Canadian Psychology/Psychologie Canadienne, 35*, 319-326.
Budwig, N. (1995). *A developmental-functionalist approach to child language*. Mahwah, NJ: Erlbaum.
Budwig, N. (1997, October). *Language, practices, and the construction of personhood*. Paper presented at Georgetown Symposium on "Psychological Development from Personalistic Perspective," Georgetown University, Washington, DC.
Budwig, N. (2000). Language and the construction of self: Linking forms and functions across development. In N. Budwig, I. Uzgiris, and J. Wertsch (Eds.), *Communication: An arena of development*. Stamford, CT: Ablex.
Bühler, K. (1934). *Sprachtheorie*. Jena-Stuttgart: Gustav Fischer.
Bühler, K. (1990). *Theory of language: The representational function of language*. [Translation of *Sprachtheorie*, by Donald Goodwin] Amsterdam: John Benjamins.

Cox, B., and Lightfoot, C. (Eds.) (1997). *Sociogenetic perspectives on internalization.* Mahwah, NJ: Erlbaum.
Duranti, A. (1997). *Linguistic anthropology.* Cambridge: Cambridge University Press.
Duranti, A., and Goodwin, C. (Eds.) (1992). *Rethinking context.* Cambridge: Cambridge University Press.
Goffman, E. (1974). *Frame analysis: An essay on the organization of experience.* New York: Harper & Row.
Goldberg, A. (1996). *Constructions: A construction grammar approach to argument structure.* Chicago, IL: University of Chicago Press.
Goodwin, M. H. (1990). *He-said-she-said: Talk as social organization among black children.* Bloomington, IN: Indiana University Press.
Gumperz, J. (1982). *Discourse strategies.* Cambridge: Cambridge University Press.
Gumperz, J., and Levinson, S. (Eds.). (1996). *Rethinking linguistic relativity.* Cambridge: Cambridge University Press.
Hanks, W. (1996a). *Language and communicative practices.* Boulder, CO: Westview Press.
Hanks, W. (1996b). Language form and communicative practices. In J. Gumperz and S. Levinson (Eds.), *Rethinking linguistic relativity* (pp. 232-270). Cambridge: Cambridge University Press.
Haviland, J. (1996). Projections, transpositions, and relativity. In J. Gumperz and S. Levinson (Eds.), *Rethinking linguistic relativity* (pp. 271-323). Cambridge: Cambridge University Press.
Jakobson, R. (1973). *Main trends in the science of language.* London: Allen and Unwin.
Lakoff, G. (1987). *Women, fire, and dangerous things: What categories reveal about the mind.* Chicago, IL: University of Chicago Press.
Langacker, R. (1987). *Foundations of cognitive grammar.* Volume 1. Stanford, CA: Stanford University Press.
Miller, P., and Hoogstra, L. (1992). Language as a tool in the socialization and apprehension of cultural meanings. In T. Schwarz, G. White, and C. Lutz (Eds.), *New directions in psychological anthropology* (pp. 83-101). Cambridge: Cambridge University Press.
Nerlich, B., and Clarke, D. (1996). *Language, action, and context: The early history of pragmatics in Europe and America, 1780-1930.* Amsterdam: John Benjamins.
Ochs, E. (1996). Linguistic resources for socializing humanity. In J. Gumperz and S. Levinson (Eds.), *Rethinking linguistic relativity* (pp. 407-437). Cambridge: Cambridge University Press.
Ochs, E., Schegloff, E., and Thompson, S. (Eds.). (1996). *Interaction and grammar.* Cambridge: Cambridge University Press.
Palmer, G. (1996). *Toward a theory of cultural linguistics.* Austin, TX: University of Texas Press.
Reddy, M. (1979). The conduit metaphor: A case of frame conflict in our language about language. In A. Ortony (Ed.), *Metaphor and thought* (pp. 284-324). Cambridge: Cambridge University Press.
Rogoff, B., Mistry, J. Goncü, A., and Mosier, C. (1993). Guided participation in cultural activity by toddlers and caregivers. *Monographs of the Society for Research in Child Development, 58,* 7, serial no. 236.
Schieffelin, B., and Ochs, E. (1986). Language socialization. *Annual Review of Anthropology, 15,* 163-246.
Searle, J. (1969). *Speech acts.* Cambridge: Cambridge University Press.

Silverstein, M. (1976). Shifters, linguistic categories, and cultural descriptions. In K. Basso and H. Selby (Eds.), *Meaning in anthropology* (pp. 11-56). Albuquerque, NM: New Mexico.

Slobin, D. (1985). Crosslinguistic evidence for the Language-Making Capacity. In D. Slobin (Ed.), *The crosslinguistic study of language acquisition* (Volume 2, pp. 1157-1256). Hillsdale, NJ: Erlbaum.

Valsiner, J. (1989). *Human development and culture: The social nature of personality and its study.* Lexington, MA: Lexington Books.

Vygotsky, L. (1981). The genesis of higher mental functions. In J. V. Wertsch (Ed.), *The concept of activity in Soviet psychology* (pp. 144-188). Armonk, NY: M.E. Sharpe.

Werner, H., and Kaplan, B. (1963/1984). *Symbol formation.* Hillsdale, NJ: Erlbaum.

Wertsch, J. V. (1991). *Voices of the mind: A sociocultural approach to mediated action.* Cambridge, MA: Harvard University Press.

Wertsch, J. V. (1998). *Mind as action.* New York: Oxford University Press.

Wittgenstein, L. (1953). *Philosophical investigations.* Oxford: Blackwell.

Part III

Thinking and Speaking: Development through Thinking, Acting, and Speaking

8

Arnold Gesell and the Maturation Controversy

Thomas C. Dalton[1]

Arnold Lucius Gesell was a pioneer in developmental psychology when the field was in its infancy. Gesell had a distinguished career that began after receiving a Ph.D. from Clark University, where he studied psychology under G. Stanley Hall. As a physician and experimentalist, Gesell blazed a trail of discoveries about early motor, cognitive and emotional development that is unrivaled. He provided a scientific foundation for the diagnosis and preventative clinical care of pre- and postnatal infants that has become the hallmark of modern pediatrics. His observational studies of how infants grow, attain motor coordination, and learn new skills furnished the first comprehensive theory of the interrelated sequences through which infants and children pass in their physical and mental development. Gesell worked tirelessly for the rights of physically and mentally challenged children to receive special education that would enable them to find gainful and meaningful employment. His books and writings in popular magazines increased public awareness of and support for preschool education and better foster care for orphans. Gesell's innovative use of photography and motion pictures to document the behavioral patterns of early development provided physicians and parents an important roadmap with which to understand the complex pathways involving the integration of physical and mental functions (Miles, 1964).

Despite these achievements, many of Gesell's successors have cast an unfavorable light on his views about infant development. Developmental psychologists have criticized Gesell for proposing a stage theory of infant growth that has fallen into disfavor among contemporary researchers (Clarke et al., 1993). His conception of development as a maturational process has been challenged for allegedly reducing complex behavioral, perceptual, and learning processes to genetic factors (Roberton, 1993; Thelen and Adolfs, 1994). But Cairns (1998, p. 71, has countered this overly simplistic interpretation by contending that Gesell believed that children's social interactions are more likely than motor or sensory systems to be influenced by early experiences.

To be certain, Gesell's attempt, as a physician, to provide an authoritative, even definitive account of development, led him to make pronouncements about heredity and environment that contributed to subsequent confusion and misinterpretation. Infant experimentalist Myrtle McGraw rectified some of these errors of emphasis. She showed that, if Gesell's theory takes into account the relationship between experience and the brain, growth and development can be shown to contribute fundamentally to learning and neurobehavioral integration.

Gesell's colleagues and collaborators, including Helen Thompson, Catherine Amatruda, Francis Ilg, and Louise Bates Ames, among many others, carried forward his work begun at Yale (see references for Gesell). McGraw inspired additional inquiries in America and abroad by Bert Touwen (1995; 1998), a neurologist, Ronald Oppenheim (1995), a neurobiologist and by Gilbert Gottlieb (1998) and Philip Zelazo (1998), who are psychologists. Moreover, the Gesell archive, which includes his correspondence with Myrtle McGraw and neuroanatomist George Coghill, who strongly influenced their research, reveals that Gesell adopted a more nuanced view of development involving the interaction of structure and function and genes and environment than is acknowledged by his detractors. My contentions in this essay are that Gesell not only paved the way for contemporary research in motor development, but he (and McGraw) anticipated the fundamental issues about growth that must be addressed theoretically and experimentally by psychologists and neuroscientists who are committed to the advancement of developmental science.

A Biographical Synopsis

It is worth reviewing the highlights of Gesell's diverse career, because the separate strands of his educational, scientific, and professional pursuits were intertwined. Gesell was born in Alma Wisconsin in June 1880. His father was a photographer and his mother was a teacher—two skills that would serve Gesell well later on. Gesell (1952, p. 124) noted in his autobiography that, as a child, he had a broad range of formative experiences that included "the dark as well as bright facets of our microcosm." According to Gesell (1952, p. 124), the traumatic incidents that he witnessed at "close range," included "funerals, devastating sickness, ominous quarantines, accidents, drownings, chronic alcoholism, and epileptic seizures." Gesell noted that "These strange and sobering" experiences possessed psychological significance, as they "cumulatively left a deposit of impressions, which sensitized a background for my clinical studies in later life" (p. 124).

After graduating from Stevens Point State Normal School in 1899, Gesell attended and graduated with a B. Ph. from the University of Wisconsin at

Madison in 1903. There he studied under Frederick Jackson Turner, intellectual leader of the history of the Western Movement in America. Turner inspired Gesell to conduct an archive study of the history of Mormonism, "which was carefully guarded," Gesell (1952, p. 126) recalled, "because of its apocryphal items." Gesell completed his senior thesis, which compared higher education in Ohio and Wisconsin, and gave a commencement oration on "Shaftsbury and Child Labor." Following graduation, he returned to Stevens Point to teach high school from 1898-1901 and then was appointed principle in Chippewa Falls from 1903-1904.

Edgar James Swift, Gesell's psychology instructor during his high school years, played an important role in Gesell's decision to enroll in the Ph.D. program in psychology at Clark University in 1904. Swift, a former student

Figure 8.1
G. Stanley Hall. Photo courtesy of Clark University Archives, Special Collections, Goddard Library, Worcester, Massachusetts.

of G. Stanley Hall at Clark University, extolled Hall's brilliance and urged Gesell to apply, furnishing him with an outstanding reference and letter of introduction. Gesell was not to be disappointed. He recalled that he greatly admired Hall's "empathic propensity" to get into the minds of other thinkers and to "penetrate into the mental life of children" (Gesell, 1952, p. 126). He commanded the undivided attention of students attending his graduate seminar with his exuberance and "Jovian countenance" (p. 126). Gesell excused Hall's literal construal of recapitulation because Hall was, nevertheless, a "naturalist Darwinian of the mind."

Swift seemed to have adopted a fatherly attitude toward Gesell by taking a strong personal interest in his progress during graduate school. He wrote frequently, offering insights about Hall's personality and expectations that would prove to be helpful in handling this exhilarating but intimidating intellectual environment. Swift (1905a, p. 1) advised Gesell to take Hall's seminars and to "select some subject with content enough to put two or three years of work on it." He reassured Gesell that Hall would offer his advice about methods when a topic was chosen. At one point, near the beginning of the second semester in 1905, Swift informed Gesell that he had heard from a mutual friend that he was considering dropping out for at least a year. Alarmed by Gesell's impending decision, Swift warned, "It will be the mistake of your life to do it. Now that you are in the swim keep going and finish next year" (Swift, 1905b, p. 1). Over the next year, Gesell struggled to propose a topic that would be personally rewarding and also receive Hall's support. He dropped one idea (a topic that remains undocumented) for fear that it would not get Hall's approval. Gesell eventually chose to study the evolutionary origins of jealousy from a comparative perspective—a topic well-suited to Hall's research interests (see Ross, 1978 for an excellent intellectual biography of Hall). Gesell (1952, p. 127) recalled that Hall suggested that he include in his study the observation of infants—a decision that he later regretted. Instead, he relied on questionnaire responses of young girls at two normal schools and drew on evidence from philosophical theories and novels.

A Dissertation on Jealousy

Gesell's dissertation "Jealousy" was published in the *American Journal of Psychology*, founded by Hall in 1887. Despite couching his analysis in the language of instincts favored in this era, Gesell displayed a surprisingly sophisticated understanding of the theoretical issues involved in tracing the evolution of this emotion in animals and man. While contending that jealousy arises from rivalry (not envy) involving a conflict of interests, and considering it to be one of the oldest emotions, Gesell (1906, p. 451) denied that jealousy can be reduced to fear or anger. Jealousy is "synonymous with the will to live," Gesell (p. 447) reasoned, but it can easily pass into anger, if an envied rival's success is perceived to have overshadowed unfairly one's own accomplishments or standing. Gesell speculated that jealousy may have been an emotional remnant of a behavioral reaction to an aggressive foe that involved a "slinking," "sulking," or grudging retreat whereby a temporary victory is defiantly acknowledged. But Gesell did not believe that jealousy was strongly associated with any one temperament or physical expression, as Darwin had contended. How jealously is expressed depends on contextual factors. Rivalry brings out boastful or even indignant attitudes, while feelings of injured pride contribute to sulking, mocking, and slandering. Significantly, Gesell argued that the human capacity to feel and express jealousy, unlike animals, presupposes the possibility of self-reflection and the knowledge of other minds that are acquired during early childhood. These are important capabilities that Gesell believed to make possible feelings of self-pity as well as sympathy. He reported that evidence of sympathy was observed in a sixteen-month-old Japanese infant, who apparently sought the concern and attention of the researcher while she was playing with a rattle. This same baby exhibited emotional distress and jealousy when she was left alone to play. These arguments are strikingly contemporary in their anticipation of research on how children acquire a theory of mind (see Wellman, 1990) and adopt prosocial behavior (see Eisenberg et al., 1999).

Professional psychologists were by no means guaranteed a teaching post in academia during its infancy as a field of study. Gesell taught two years at an elementary school (1907-1909) in New York City, before being enticed away by fellow Clark University graduate and expert in intelligence testing, Lewis Terman, for a professorship at Los Angeles State Normal School from 1909 to 1911. During this time Gesell met and married Beatrice Chandler, a University of Chicago graduate, and had two children. Gesell used his free time during the summer to collaborate with Henry Goddard, a pioneer in developmental disabilities. They co-directed a special training institute for teachers of mentally retarded children sponsored by New York University. This re-ignited Gesell's life-long interest in abnormal psychology, but according to Gesell (1952, p. 128), it also imparted "a vague sense of unpreparedness for a task which was taking shape in my mind," which was a study of the developmental stages of childhood. It was at this time that Gesell decided to attend medical school, first at the University of Wisconsin (1910-1911) and then transferring to Yale, where he obtained his M.D. in 1915. All the while he was teaching part-time in the Department of Education at Yale. This workload took its toll and Gesell was forced to take a two-year sabbatical (1916-1918) to recover from tuberculosis.

Gesell had the good fortune early in his career to have had supportive and prominent mentors like G. Stanley Hall, who attracted excellent students, including John Dewey at Johns Hopkins, and who promoted the professional careers of those he admired, such as Gesell. This gave Gesell the upper hand in negotiations regarding academic appointments. Not only did Hall give Gesell excellent references following graduate school, but he continually tried to recruit and attract Gesell away from Yale, even before he had completed his medical degree, to persuade Gesell to accept an academic appointment at Clark University. In 1912 Hall announced that he was looking for an "understudy," and promised to offer a full professorship and laboratory in applied psychology with special emphasis on the mentally retarded (Hall, 1912, p. 1). Hall (1914, p. 1) renewed his earlier offer in 1914 but hedged it by saying that he "could offer nothing that could for a moment compete with what you have in view in California." I think at this point that Gesell was more concerned about gaining his independence and creating his own identity as a research scientist and clinician.

Hall was alluding to Terman's vigorous attempts to lure him back to California and Stanford University. Although Terman did almost everything in his power to get Gesell to accept, Yale made a counteroffer that Gesell accepted as a professor of child hygiene. Terman (1918, p. 1) appealed to Gesell's commitment as an educational reformer to lure him away from Yale by saying that Yale "has done less for education than any other in the country." He added that "You would be in a state which is educationally progressive; your influence would be felt in every corner of it" (p. 1). Terman had promised earlier to arrange Gesell's appointment to a state commission for the mentally retarded that he found appealing. Although Gesell was clearly enthusiastic about the Stanford offer, he was divided about whether this commission would be sufficiently independent of the Board of Education to give him a free hand in undertaking state educational reforms. Gesell (1914, p. 2) asserted that his belief was that "the uniqueness and promise of the State position lay in the fact that the whole problem of recognition, [for the mentally retarded] special school care, after care, registration etc., would be worked out through the State public educational system, eventually perhaps through a state department. . . . Now it is easy to foresee what mischief as well as good an early law establishing a heralded public commission might do." Moreover, Stanford was not willing to match Yale's salary offer and rank of full professor.

Gesell gained notoriety at Yale for becoming the first school psychologist on the Connecticut Board of Education. This led to his appointment by the governor to the State Commission on Child Welfare in 1919 where he helped draft a two volume report dealing with the educational status and needs of handicapped children (see Fagan, 1987a; 1987b). During the next five years, Gesell and his colleagues conducted a series of comparative clinical investigations of the development of normal, deviant, and defective infants and young children. By assuming these leadership roles, Gesell was able to address the plight of children with special educational needs, which had been a personal passion. The results of these studies were published in 1925. The book, *The Mental Growth of the Pre-School Child: A Psychological Outline of Normal Development from Birth to the Sixth Year, Including a System of Developmental Diagnosis,* was illustrated with two hundred action photographs. This book generated significant popular interest and led to generous financial support for the establishment of a research institute at Yale. Benefactors included the Laura Spelman Rockefeller Memorial, The General Education Board, and the Carnegie Corporation. With this support, Gesell was able to hire a professional staff and conduct innovative longitudinal observational and experimental studies of infants for the next twenty-eight years. The nature, scope, and findings of this research and the controversies that it engendered are the subject of the remainder of this essay. It would be fair to say that Gesell's views about growth and development changed over time. His later theoretical formulations also exhibited an increasingly sophisticated appreciation for the dynamical and open-ended nature of developmental processes.

Pre-maturity, Precocity and Retardation

It is not surprising that Gesell adopted a clinical orientation toward development, as he was a trained physician. His collaboration with Goddard, who believed that intelligence was inborn, reinforced Gesell's proclivity to understand development and its disorders as originating in growth processes controlled by genetic endowment. Gesell spent a considerable amount of time between 1911 and 1925 examining babies and young children who had physical and mental defects. His intention was to develop a set of criteria that would furnish a diagnosis of an infant's level of maturation with respect to age-based norms of adequate neurological, behavioral, and emotional function. Gesell acknowledged that this approach made it much easier to detect gross defects in brain or behavioral function than to spot subtle variations due to differences in skill and attitude that may signal variations in neurobehavioral capacity. He posed the dilemma in the following terms:

> The application and interpretation of the examination situations may require adaptation to the child's disabilities. It is often difficult to distinguish between a performance, which fails for mechanical reasons and one, which fails from lack of insight and maturity (Gesell and Amatruda, 1947, p. 237).

In making this observation, Gesell was acknowledging that some children fail to perform a task because of physical or mental handicaps. However, other children may exhibit a delay in sensori-motor coordination that masks their true abilities. Indeed, Gesell noted that some children may refuse to attempt to do things that they believe are beyond their capabilities, even though they could succeed, if they were encouraged to make an extraordinary effort. Anticipating McGraw's frequent assertion, Gesell admitted that researchers often fail to discover "concealed abilities," because they are apt to excuse failure on the basis of motor incapacity (p. 237).

The strongest evidence supporting Gesell's argument that development obeyed invariable laws of growth is the fact that premature babies with no added complications continue the normal course of development and thrive, despite their early exposure to environmental influences. Gesell and Amatruda (1947, p. 292) asserted that "Prematurity, neither retards nor accelerates." Likewise, Gesell reasoned that infants born at post-term may be further developed, but this is not due to added growth or precocity, as the infant is simply performing normally for its true age. He acknowledged, of course, that there are examples of intellectual prodigies, such as Mozart, who showed exceptional growth potential, suggesting extraordinary adaptivity of the nervous system. Nevertheless, Gesell cautioned that the distinction must be preserved between "primary" acceleration that is due to natural or genetic causes and "environmental acceleration," due to parental solicitude, for example, that may result in an exaggerated emphasis on musical talent. In this instance, Gesell and Amatruda (1947, p. 308) contended, "such overstimulation can scarcely produce primary acceleration. It is more in the nature of excessive specification and over-organization." This was consistent with Gesell's tendency, as a physician, to view the environment as contributing to potentially adverse repercussions for early development, such as retardation, than to consider its positive and constructive effects on growth. Conversely, Gesell believed that enhancing environmental supports could mitigate the behavioral and emotional deficiencies resulting from poor nurturing. That is why Gesell and his associates believed that the developmental quotient was more sensitive to the "backstrokes of seriously inadequate environmental conditions" than other influences on growth processes (p. 319). Similarly, by conceiving growth as a physiological phenomenon, Gesell focused largely on endocrine disorders that impeded or distorted development, which are governed by metabolic processes.

In advancing these arguments, Gesell adopted an extremely narrow view of ontogenetic change that is no longer shared among contemporary developmental scientists. Gilbert Gottlieb (1997) argues decisively that heredity and environment reciprocally interact and that behavioral plasticity plays an important role in creating new organism-environmental relationships that subsequently alter the genome. Behavior that is considered normal or typical for a species can undergo extensive modifications or changes that do not result in consequences that are deleterious to survival.

Gesell believed that the "symptoms" of superior endowment, although subtle, could be detected and diagnosed in the form of developmental and dynamic signs. Unlike McGraw, he did not believe that advanced posture or early locomotion are reliable indicators of accelerated growth or development. Only in the second or third year does this become prominent, as suggested by speech, comprehension, and judgment. Significantly, the dynamic signs that Gesell considered indicative of superior endowment, such as emotional sensitivity, alertness, cooperativeness, rapport, and capacity to handle novel situations, are the very same attributes that McGraw claimed to have observed in the experimental twin Johnny, who was given special motor stimulation shortly after birth. I try to resolve this discrepancy later on in this essay, by closely examining the

**Figure 8.2
Arnold Gesell in the 1930s.**

Photo courtesy of Yale University, Harvey Cushing / John Hay Whitney Medical Library.

conceptual differences and empirical evidence that led them to adopt opposing positions on the role of experience in early development.

Growth, Development, and Maturation

Gesell (1945) traced the intellectual streams of influences to their sources in Darwin and Huxley, who led to his conceptualization of human growth and development as a morphogenetic, chemical, and physiological phenomena. Darwin made it possible to put development within an evolutionary and phylogenetic perspective. Huxley demonstrated that embryology is preeminently the science of morphology or form and that it must involve comparative (i.e., animal and human) methods of analysis. According to Gesell, Sir Kenelm Digby, a British physician, proposed the first modern, epigenetic conception of development in the 1600s by stressing the physiochemical nature of early growth. Joseph Needham (1942), a biochemist and embryologist, carried this line of inquiry forward in the twentieth century by investigating the biochemical and hereditary foundations of morphogenesis.

Several contemporary embryologists who studied the relationship between early growth and behavior strongly influenced Gesell's conception of development. German scientist Eugene Minkowski (1928) clinically interpreted the behavior of surgically removed fetuses. Davenport Hooker (1943), an American physician, was the first scientist to use motion pictures to document the effects of stimulation on briefly viable fetuses and premature babies. Gesell (1945; 1952) also acknowledged the influence of Z. Y. Kuo (1932), a Chinese expatriate, and Leonard Charmichael (1933), William Windle (1940), and George Coghill (1929), embryologists who also studied the effects of early stimulation. Kuo challenged Coghill's assertions about the integrated nature of early motor development and furnished important evidence that species specific behavior may be significantly altered before birth (see Gottlieb, 2000). Gesell acknowledged that Coghill's research and ideas were singularly important to his conceptualization of growth. For reasons that will become clear, Gesell gave greater emphasis to the maturational implications of Coghill's experimental findings than are warranted by Coghill's own theoretical perspective. Ironically, Coghill consistently interpreted Gesell's findings as evidence that they supported his view that learning occurs in the earliest stages of neural growth and behavioral development.

George Coghhill and Embryology

Coghill derived his theory involving the relationship among neural growth, behavioral development and experience from his studies of the lowly *Amblystoma*, a salamander whose larval stage lends it to an analysis of locomotion. He conducted detailed cellular studies of neural growth processes to determine the relation between sequence of growth and anatomical form. He also applied different modes of stimulation and restriction at different times to determine whether there is a common pattern of response. These studies led Coghill to propose a highly original theory about behavioral development that formed the centerpiece of Gesell's developmental analysis.

Coghill (1929) drew an important distinction between the *form* that neural structures and mechanisms assume, which enables activity to occur, and *function*, or the extent to which different behaviors may be performed. This distinction is easily glossed over by those who have claimed that Coghill was a nativist. Coghill contended that the form or characteristic patterns of flexion and extension of muscles that enable adoption of different postures and movements are governed by neural growth processes not directly influenced by experience. Form includes stereotyped motor actions, such as the contra-lateral motions of arms and legs involved in prone and erect locomotion. This is what Coghill (1929, p. 86) was referring to when he stated that, "The general pattern of the primary nervous mechanism of walking, is therefore, laid down before the animal can in the least respond to the environment." But how these postural mechanisms and neuromuscular capacities are used to perform different behaviors is directly influenced by experience.

Figure 8.3
George E. Coghill in the 1930s.

Photo courtesy of Dr. Robert Williamson.

Although Gesell acknowledged the difference that Coghill maintained between growth and learning, he tended to accord a much larger role to the form-shaping processes of neural growth than Coghill envisioned. This may have been because Gesell considered the growth of the brain to be a maturational process controlled by genetic factors. Coghill's claim that neural structures anticipate the acquisition of function no doubt strengthened Gesell's conviction that this was a correct interpretation of Coghill's theory. However, Coghill never used the terms 'maturation' or 'genes' to characterize neural growth processes, as he considered this to be an issue that could only be resolved by further research. Moreover, the crucial issue is not that the brain grows and matures but rather how it grows and the role of behavior and environmental contingencies in shaping its development.

This divergence of interpretation is clearly evident when their statements about the relation between growth and experience are compared. Gesell and Thompson's (1934) nativist interpretation of Coghill's ideas is evident in the following statement:

> Coghill found that the innate maturation of the nervous system determined its primary structure, and that function or exercise did not even hasten the various types of reaction. He infers that the specificity of nervous structures in terms of behavior

is "determined by the laws of growth in which the behavior values of the patterns of response have no part" (p. 360).

While acknowledging the interaction of heredity and environment, Gesell and Thompson (1934) clearly assigned more weight in development to genetic factors.

> There is a very reciprocal interrelationship between heredity and environment. The intimacy of this relationship may not, however, prevent us from ascribing a priority and possibly even some preponderance to hereditary factors in the patterning of human behavior. . . . Environmental factors support, inflect and modify, but do not generate the progressions of development. Growth is an impulsion" (pp. 294; 296).

Coghill (1929, p. 91) believed that neural growth processes performed two important functions that did not involve the predetermination of behavior. First, the capacity of neurons to grow in an embryonic fashion, Coghill stated, "gives to the organism as a whole its ability to subjugate new parts and thereby maintain its unity during the development of behavior." Hence "the primary function of the nervous system," according to Coghill, is "the maintenance of the integrity of the individual while the behavior pattern expands" (p. 91). This role is more properly characterized as regulatory than determinative. Second, the fact that the growth of neurons exceeds the capacity of the young organisms to channel this nervous energy effectively creates an enormous flexibility and potential for the development of alternative forms of behavior that can only be specified through experience. Coghill (1929, p. 109) was very clear that this apparent neural "overgrowth" constituted a "structural counterpart to future behavior forms." He contended that these "neural mechanisms of specific behavior. . . must be organized out of elements of experience" (p. 109). But Coghill then makes a perplexing and confounding statement that Gesell undoubtedly believed to have justified his genetic perspective. Coghill asserts that:

> They [neural mechanisms] represent such factors of behavior as attitudes which can come to an issue only in the more or less distant future, but which, at the appropriate time, issue in decisive, essentially predetermined action. This predetermination may be regarded, in mechanistic terms, as an act of will. . . . Growth, accordingly, may be conceived as the creative function of the nervous system, not only with regard to the form of the behavior pattern, but also with regard to its control. The creative component of thought, upon this hypothesis, is growth (p. 109).

This unusual statement, in my opinion, is indicative of Coghill's belief that the neural anticipation of function constitutes learning and signifies the essential freedom that organisms, which possess nervous systems and brains, have to attain their ends. James Mark Baldwin (1894) conceived development from a similar angle of vision. Each generation finds new value in recurring stimuli, according to Baldwin, through processes of habit, anticipation, and accommodation. He believed that neurobehavioral integration was a circular process whereby a stimulus and motor response tend to reproduce one another to form habits. But this circularity is not redundant, Baldwin argued, because some new feeling arises that introduces slight changes in behavior that benefits the whole organism. Infants learn how to reinstate, but attach new meaning to the recurring stimuli through *conscious imitation* to produce behavior that has adaptive value. Infants do so by channeling the excess energy of nervous discharge into new motor coordinations, expanding their skills beyond those of their predecessors. Baldwin was vague about how this reinstatement occurred neurophysiologically. Nevertheless, he was confident that he had solved the problem of how it is possible for ancient behaviors to persist that are based on pain and pleasure, thus upholding recaptulationism, and yet, to find new adaptive value in behaviors that express a more complex range of attitudes and emotions.

Ironically, Coghill (1933, p. 136) illustrated this point most forcefully by citing evidence from Gesell's infant studies of regarding and prehension—behaviors that first appear at six weeks. Coghill considered these behaviors to constitute the beginning of attention. He believed that they are made possible by a mechanism of total integration, which enables infants eventually to engage in synchronous action, involving the head, trunk, and arms. Significantly, in arguing that these emergent capacities constitute learning, Coghill (1933) approvingly cited Dewey's views about mind to support his assertions, when he said:

> This development of the process of optical fixation and prehension may be taken as a basic example of motor learning, and, in my judgment, the principle (i.e., partial patterns emerge from a prior integrated state) that is seen in operation here is involved in all motor learning. In non-motor learning, also, the principle becomes applicable if we bear in mind that knowing is a mode of doing—a thesis that is defended by Dewey and that permeates the psychology of Ogden. It is possible, therefore, that all learning consists of the expansion of a primarily integrated total pattern of action and of individuation of partial patterns within the total system" (p. 136).

To be certain, Gesell (1925) made numerous statements that his detractors have ignored, which clearly are in accord with Coghill's views of the importance of neural plasticity and experience in shaping behavior, as indicated in the following quotations.

> One of the prevalent quasi-primitive notions holds that growth is predetermined, that it is so natural that it takes care of itself.... Now the scientist would insist that growth is essentially lawful but also profoundly plastic ... it is marvelously adaptive, and likewise lawfully responsive to both internal and external conditions (p. 396).

> Not the least value of this conception of the growth of neurons in relation to behavior lies in the constructive effect, which it has on the nature versus nurture antithesis. Original growth potency is realized in no foreordained detail. Experience and milieu enter into the very process of growth (p. 365).

The two mechanisms (maturation and learning) are not discrete, nor does environment operate on one to the exclusion of the other. They function together as a single mechanism, which is constantly consolidated through the unifying process of growth (p. 300).

There is really no paradox or inconsistency in Gesell's foregoing statements that development is driven by maturational factors and that it is also shaped by experience. Gesell simply adopted an exceedingly narrow conception of learning and skill. This was at a time when American psychologists were adopting an increasingly wider notion of learning than that proposed by behaviorist theories of conditioning. Edward Tolman was leading the way towards a cognitive revolution that would undermine the reflex conception of learning. Gesell did not appear to be very well-informed about these advances in cognitive psychology.

Nevertheless, he believed that experience played a more prominent role in cognitive development than in motor development (as will be discussed below). For example, Gesell and Thompson (1934, p. 320) stated that, if the term "skill" is defined as "the refinement, facilitation, and specific improvement of a given behavior equipment or an existing set of capacities, then the term is highly relative, and in infancy skill is always highly transitory." He goes on to say that motor behaviors, such as plucking, are morphological phenomena in which learning plays little role:

"Training and experience will in a specific and always more or less transient sense perfect, modulate, and condition; but in its basic configuration the new pattern of plucking is not the architonic product of some mystical learning process; it is a morphological phenomenon, a topographical event in the mechanics of development" (Gesell, 1934, p. 320).

It is worth mentioning, at this point, that Gesell assumed that he and Coghill were in agreement that early stimulation does not accelerate the development of motor functions. Gesell and Thompson (1934, p. 309) observed somewhat tentatively that "Coghill doubts whether the appearance of a function like locomotion can be hastened in *Amblystoma* by exercise." Although this may have been true for technical or methodological reasons, Coghill did not rule out this possibility in other animals or humans. He cited evidence that nerve cells differed in the level of sensitivity to excitation and that dendrites grow in the direction of the sources of stimulation and continue to grow during adult life. He also stated that "the experience of the individual is a factor in determining the specificity of function of the constituent neurons" (Coghill, 1929, p. 98). But perhaps his most definitive statement about early experience was the following:

It would be difficult to prove that the extension and perfection of particular patterns of response are not facilitated by its performance—for the functioning of growing neurons may facilitate or excite their growth and thus the perfection of the pattern may be hastened through its exercise" (Coghill, 1926, p. 132).

In retrospect then, it is difficult to understand why psychologists continue to hold that Gesell and McGraw conducted essentially equivalent studies of development and learning processes, despite significant differences in methodology and findings. For example, Gesell and Thompson (1934a, p. 38) began their observational studies at four weeks rather than from birth. Gesell and Thompson (1934a, p. 315) did not introduce special training until the experimental twin was eleven and a half months (and after fourteen months for the control twin) compared to twenty days for Johnny and Jimmy (see McGraw 1935, p. 40). (Jimmy was not afforded special stimulation but he was tested in the same activities at the same interval as Johnny.) They also used repetitive training exercises, administered tests that heavily emphasized vision, perception, and memory, and conducted no follow-up studies (Gesell and Thompson 1934a, pp. 40-41). Their conclusions that training neither alters the sequence nor accelerates the processes of skill acquisition and that delayed practice results in greater gains should not be surprising given these differences in methodology (Gesell and Thompson 1934a, pp. 316-317). The twins in Gesell's studies had already attained some degree of sensori-motor development at the onset of their respective experimental training and testing programs. Nevertheless, many aspects of McGraw and Gesell's experimental investigations remain inconclusive regarding the effects of stimulation or restriction on learning.

Myrtle McGraw and the Maturation Controversy

To be certain, Gesell's attempt, as a physician, to provide an authoritative, even definitive account of development led him to make pronouncements about heredity and environment that contributed to subsequent confusion and misinterpretation. Infant experimentalist Myrtle McGraw rectified some of these errors of emphasis. She showed that, if Gesell's theory takes into account the relationship between experience and the brain, growth and development can be shown to contribute fundamentally to learning and neurobehavioral integration.

Coghill's Pivotal Role in the Nature Versus Nurture Debate

As noted before, Coghill played a decisive but widely misunderstood role in helping resolve the debate between Gesell and McGraw about the effects of early experience on the development and integration of brain and behavior (see Dalton, 1995). Coghill never took an explicit position on the maturation-learning debate during the 1930s, as Oppenheim points out, thus inviting different interpretations. Nevertheless, Coghill closely followed Gesell and McGraw's infant studies because of the ramifications for his work. Coghill (1933b) visited Gesell's laboratory at Yale on at least one occasion in 1933, combining it with his first visit with McGraw at Babies Hospital. Gesell's experimental studies were nearly finished by the time he met Coghill, unlike McGraw, who was just getting her studies underway and could incorporate Coghill's suggestions into the experimental design. It is evident that Coghill continued to be open-minded about the implications of his theory, even though Gesell urgently sought and received Coghill's approval. They exchanged several letters during the 1930s with evident personal admiration and esteem for one another. One of these exchanges was quite significant, as it appeared to furnish evidence of Coghill's unqualified endorsement of Gesell's maturationism. Gesell (1934) sent a reprint of his 1934 article on "Maturation and the Patterning of Behavior," that was published in *A Handbook of Child Psychology*. Coghill (1934, p.1) replied to Gesell by indicating that he took "pleasure in saying that the paper as a whole and in all its parts meets with my most favorable consideration. To cite special points would require me to refer to almost every page." Coghill (1934) had only one specific comment to make which was that:

> Your position on the relation of growth and environment is certainly sound, and you state it very clearly, when you say that environmental factors "inflect" but do not generate the progression of development, while growth is an impulsion. This seems to me to be a fundamental thesis for all studies of the development of behavior (p.1).

This statement was entirely consistent with Coghill's argument, discussed before, that environment does not directly influence the *form* of behavior. Not surprisingly, Gesell construed this more broadly as an endorsement of his maturationism, even though Coghill never used this term in his letter or in any publication. It is evident in his reply that Gesell (1934) was relieved and reassured (mistakenly so) that this was not a point of contention between them, when he wrote:

> The concept of maturation seems to be assuming some importance in the literature of behavior and I was very anxious for the benefit of your criticisms, if I had fallen into any errors of interpretation particularly of your own fundamental work. Needless to say I am pleased to have your approval (p. 1).

It is unlikely that Coghill would have gotten involved in McGraw's research, if he really was convinced that behavioral development was a maturational event, unless he believed that her research was capable of resolving the issue of whether it was possible to accelerate the acquisition of function. She was fortunate to be able to pursue this issue independently, because she tried desperately to work with Gesell. As a student, McGraw respected and admired Gesell's (1934) work. She came away from her first visit at Gesell's clinic in 1926 "with a renewed professional enthusiasm," reminding Gesell that, "It is after all this exchange of ideas that makes the wheels go round" (McGraw 1926, p. 1). McGraw (1927) followed up her visit the next year by unsuccessfully seeking employment on Gesell's staff. However, once McGraw assumed her position with the normal child development study, she found it increasingly difficult to maintain cordial relations with Gesell. He never cited any of McGraw's research. This professional disregard disappointed and annoyed McGraw and unfortunately contributed to the continuing confusion regarding the differences in their respective theories (McGraw 1980).

McGraw (1935, p. 10) readily adapted Coghill's methods in her infant studies, contending that "it is the experimental embryologists, not psychologists, who deserve credit for formulating the most adequate theory of behavior development." McGraw (1979) acknowledged Coghill's extensive influence by saying that: "Coghill visited my laboratory many, many, many times—sometimes with Tilney, [her supervisor and Director of the Neurological Institute of New York], sometimes not. We talked and exchanged ideas. It was he, John Dewey, and the babies that got me thinking of process, not end result, or achievement" (p. 1). Indeed, McGraw found evidence that infant behavior develops through the unraveling of general movements similar to those Coghill observed in the larval development of salamanders. McGraw (1979) stressed also that collaboration among them was essential to the success of the project by saying: "Had he [Tilney] lived longer, Tilney, Coghill and Dewey and I (let me say the babies) might have arrived at a synthesis of the meaning of structure and function" (p. 1).

The importance of Coghill's contribution to Gesell, and particularly to McGraw's studies, cannot be overstated. Coghill (1930a, p. 638) claimed to have discovered a fundamental law governing the growth and development of behavior. Briefly, Coghill (1930, p. 638) stated his principle in the following terms:

> This law or pattern of development consists in the expansion of a primarily integrated total pattern of action within which partial patterns arise by individuation through restriction of both the field of motor action and the field of adequate stimulation.

For example, a fetal salamander's earliest movements are instigated by endogenous feelings, producing a series of alternating contractions of the trunk that proceed tailward, eventuating in locomotion. When appendages first appear, sensory systems are relatively undeveloped. Consequently, the application of a local stimulus to the limb bud, for example, does not elicit a local response, but triggers a tight flexion or general inhibition of movement in the animal in its entirety. Only when sensori-motor functions and receptive fields become better differentiated does stimulation evoke a localized response. This enables the suspension or inhibition of general movement and the assumption of a fixed postural stance or orientation.

What is important to notice in the principle quoted above is that this process of individuation is brought about not only by changes in neuroanatomical structures that support movement associated with growth. The complete range of movements that the animal can deploy is also limited by virtue of this differentiation, as is its receptivity to stimuli that may support alternative behaviors. While this makes the animal much more susceptible to conditioning and amenable to learning, it also restricts the degree of freedom it possesses to acquire and extract relevant contextual information from its environment that would enable a more adequate or optimum response.

McGraw's Early Stimulation Experiments

Coghill furnished a crucial insight that McGraw exploited in her studies. She reasoned that the psychological foundations of learning processes could be better understood if infants were given the freedom to devise their own motor strategies to respond to unfamiliar situations. McGraw interpreted this experimentally to mean that, if infants are confronted with uncertain situations involving multiple sources of stimulation and alternative motor options, then they are likely to suppress or inhibit an immediate, reflexive response and to mount a coordinated response. Thus, when confronted with uncertainty, she thought that infants are likely to suppress an immediate response until they get a feeling for the situation as a whole. Consequently, McGraw challenged infants, through non-verbal gestures, to extend their proficiency beyond those conditions already under their control, by placing them in situations that required problem solving through inventive motor responses, such as that involved in climbing off a stool, roller skating, or riding a tricycle. These innovative techniques of suggestive stimulation revealed how infants learn by adopting different physical postures and attitudes, inhibiting impulsiveness, and by drawing out and elaborating the physical movements involved.

McGraw confronted her doubts about age-based norms by adopting methods that would more clearly identify how growth processes account for the transient forms that behavior assumes in the course of development. McGraw adopted different premises than did Gesell about growth and development, while retaining the holistic principles that led them to propose similar theories, which involved remarkably different conclusions about the effects of early experience. McGraw saw development as a continuous process of interaction between neuroanatomical structures and physiological functions, involving the construction, dissolution, and reintegration of the brain and behavior into more varied and complex patterns. Development involves functional differentiation and specialization. Growth determines the rate that energy is transformed to affect size and complexity (i.e., degree of functional specificity) from birth to old age. Differences in energy input and the rate or velocity of growth introduce elements of indeterminacy in development that, McGraw believed, made possible the modification of the sequence through which neuromuscular functions are combined to form a pattern of behavior (McGraw 1935, p. 16). She attempted to demonstrate that growth furnishes the energy and resources of intelligence that enable infants to deliberately control the pace and sequence of their development.

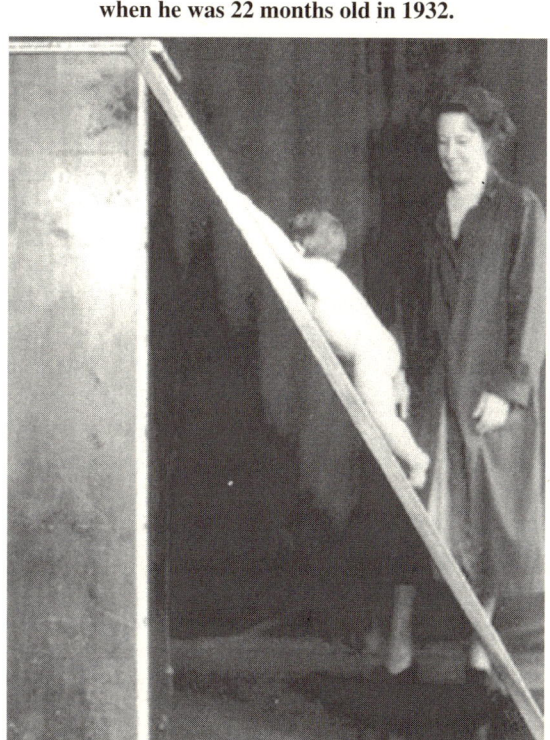

Figure 8.4
Myrtle McGraw assisting Johnny Woods on a step slide, when he was 22 months old in 1932.

Photo courtesy of Mitzi Wertheim.

This turned out to be a fruitful line of inquiry, which showed that sequential processes involved in early motor development are not preset and are subject to alteration through early experience. This finding does not in any way undermine the value of breaking development into stages, as Gesell advocated. This fact simply points out that the most significant phenomena in early development are the *interactions* that occur between factors in a series and not their *temporal* relationships. She discovered that phylogenetic traits previously considered useless, when taken in isolation from other behaviors, proved instrumental, when combined with other behaviors, to hasten the emergence and enhance the quality of its ontogenetic counterpart. For example, the seemingly disorganized swaying of the torso and alternating movements of legs and arms appearing in the early stages of prone locomotion enabled an infant to swim before being able to crawl. Johnny's (the twin receiving special exercise) ability to skate before he could walk smoothly, also demonstrated that the rhythmic stepping movements involved in skating could be stimulated to hasten the attainment of erect locomotion.

Through her innovative experiments, McGraw demonstrated that infants who are given adequate stimulation and freedom of movement do not strictly grow and behave according to the expected sequence in which they are predicted to do so. There is extensive variation among infants in how they attain motor achievements. Her discovery that babies could accomplish feats considered impossible at their age also challenged Gesell's contention that early stimulation is harmful or unnatural and that precocious performances or complex behaviors are controlled by genetic factors. Of course, numerous contemporary researchers have corroborated McGraw's theories. Gottlieb (1997) showed that prenatal ducklings use auditory stimulation to properly imitate and recognize their own species before birth. Greenough et al. (1993) have demonstrated that early, enriched experience induced synaptic change in the rat hippocampus, as compared to controls. Merzenich et al. (1988) discovered that experience can directly alter and reorganize somatosensory premotor cortical maps in humans, supporting McGraw's presumption that the brain retains its plasticity throughout development.

Gesell and McGraw's Theories of Development

Gesell and McGraw advanced extraordinarily powerful and elegant theories of the complex dynamics of neuromuscular development that, in many respects, complement one another. The metaphors that they employed to explain development are highly suggestive. Noteworthy is the fact that McGraw first employed a weaving metaphor in *Growth,* which was published four years *before* Gesell (1939a) advanced his own theory of the "spiral organization of reciprocal interweaving" to explain infant development. However, there are several crucial differences in their respective theories that explain why they adopted fundamentally different perspectives about the effects of early experience on development and learning and the importance of brain-behavior interaction for neuromuscular integration. There also is evidence in the Gesell archive that his views about the role of the brain and cortex were undergoing change, which narrowed the differences in their respective theories. This helps put Gesell's legacy in a more favorable historical and contemporary context.

Gesell employed the spiral metaphor to suggest how some traits are temporarily split off and diverge from one another as they come within the field of influence of other traits, before recombining to form a more complex pattern. Traits that become separated through divergence look like they are "retreating," according to Gesell (1939a, p. 179) but are actually "more mature" because they do not continue on the same trajectory but spiral upwards to a "higher level." For example, the pincer or plucking movement represents a higher form of prehension than indicated by the more oblique scissors closure (See Figure 8.1). Gesell believed that this process by which behavioral traits attain greater complexity occurs solely through mechanisms of reciprocal enervation and inhibition at the subcortical level. There is no cortical involvement and thus these attainments do not entail deliberate or purposeful control. At that time, Gesell saw only a limited role for environmental stimulation, individual experience, and learning in the attainment of developmental outcomes.

Unlike Gesell, McGraw (1935; 1943 and 1946) attempted to find out whether cortex is involved in early development. She found evidence that cortical inhibition is not only essential to voluntary action, but also indispensable to the formation of neuronal connections necessary for the coordination of feeling, movement, thought, and action. McGraw believed that cortical inhibition spreads selectively by alternating between upper and lower regions of the body, enabling infants and toddlers to gradually gain increased control over the amount, sequence and direction of their movement. She did not believe that this was a unilinear or structurally predetermined process. Instead she advanced a tentative *bidirectional* theory of structure and function that has been more fully elaborated by Gilbert Gottlieb (1997). She proposed that consciousness emerges through behaviorally mediated neurobiological and neuromuscular processes of reorganization that support the transition from uncontrolled movement and minimal consciousness to erect locomotion and self-consciousness (see figure 8.2). As cortical functions spread, new behaviors emerge, creating new centers of dominance and the exaggerated or excessive exercise associated with the acquisition of a new capability. The cross-pressures from these competitive processes frequently result in the regression toward more rudimentary and involuntary forms of behavior. Nevertheless, with each backward swing, older traits and emergent capabilities are actually recombined and reintegrated in slightly different ways, according to McGraw, to alter the form or configuration of a total pattern. These observations led McGraw to contend that infants and toddlers contribute to their own development by controlling how much conscious effort they put into combining alternative movements, and by obtaining novel experiences that contribute to increased awareness and motor and cognitive integration (see Dalton, 1998).

During the time when McGraw was conducting her studies, Le Roy Conel, a Harvard neuroanatomist, began his studies of the neural growth patterns of the cerebral cortex of newborns to six years. These were remarkably thorough studies, now corroborated by more powerful methods, (see Shankle et al., 1998) that McGraw specifically cited and used to establish that brain and behavior are integrated by the exercise of deliberate judgments initially involved in sitting up and the subsequent development of prone locomotion. Conel's (1939, p. 147) studies appeared to support McGraw's contentions about mind. His investigations indicated a correlative development in the brain, as the posterior central gyrus supporting a sitting posture was in the most advanced stage of development. However, by six months, areas of the premotor cortex that Conel examined, involving the regions of the lower trunk, hands and feet, assumed a dominant role, while movements in the upper body were inhibited. This was consistent with McGraw's (1941) findings that infants tend to push with their feet and pull with their hands at this stage of prone progression. Conel subsequently determined that by fifteen months these separate movements become well integrated in the hippocampus.

When Conel brought his studies to Gesell's attention in 1939, Gesell began to reexamine his assumptions about the timing of cortical involvement in early development. According to Gesell, he found "intriguing" the question that Conel had raised regarding "the functioning of the cerebral cortex of an infant at the end

Figure 8.5
Gossell's Spiral Organization of Reciprocally Interwoven Behavior: Prehension {adapted from Gesell 1945; 174}

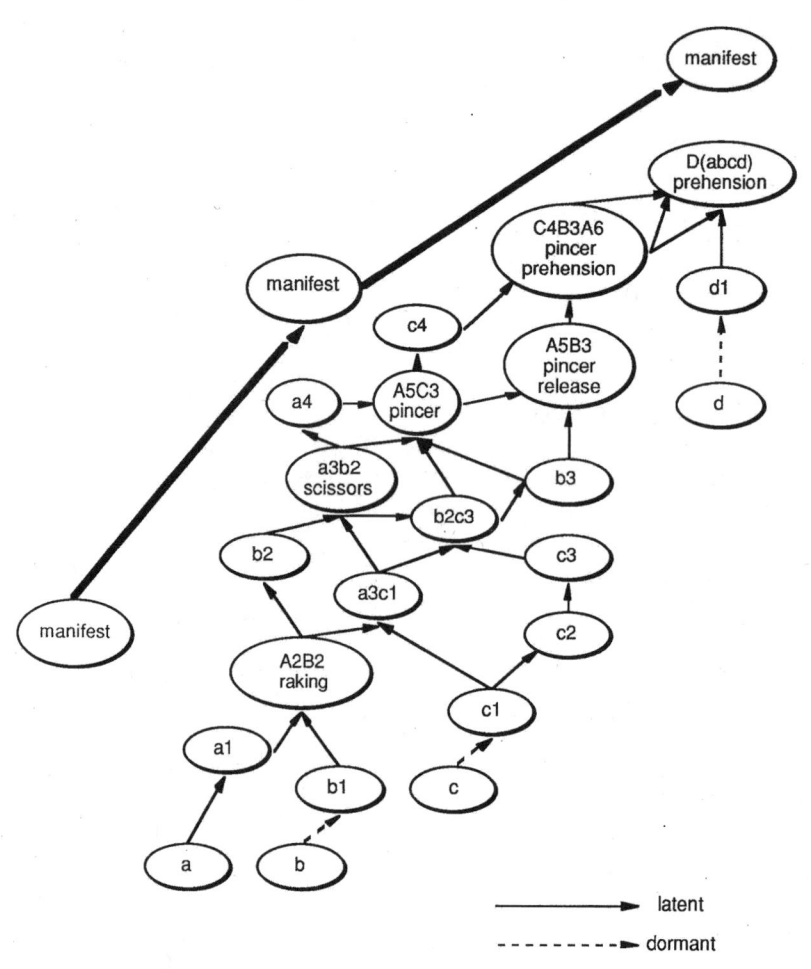

Arnold Gesell and the Maturation Controversy 157

of the first month of post-natal life." Gesell (1939b, p. 1) cautiously noted that an answer to the question about mind "takes us, inevitably, into philosophical neurology." He nevertheless agreed that he "would ascribe considerable function to the cortex of the month-old neonate," saying that "his behavior is too coherent, too integrated, and too personal in its individuality to be considered merely subcortical"(1939b, p. 2). Indeed, Gesell asserted that his own studies of premature babies led him to speculate that "the cortex may begin meagerly to function in the fetal period." Finally, in a concluding statement that is strikingly congruent with McGraw's assertions, Gesell indicated that:

> We think of the cortical cells as growing structures, which organize the behavior of the infant in both its more permanent and transient aspects. Indeed, the rate of

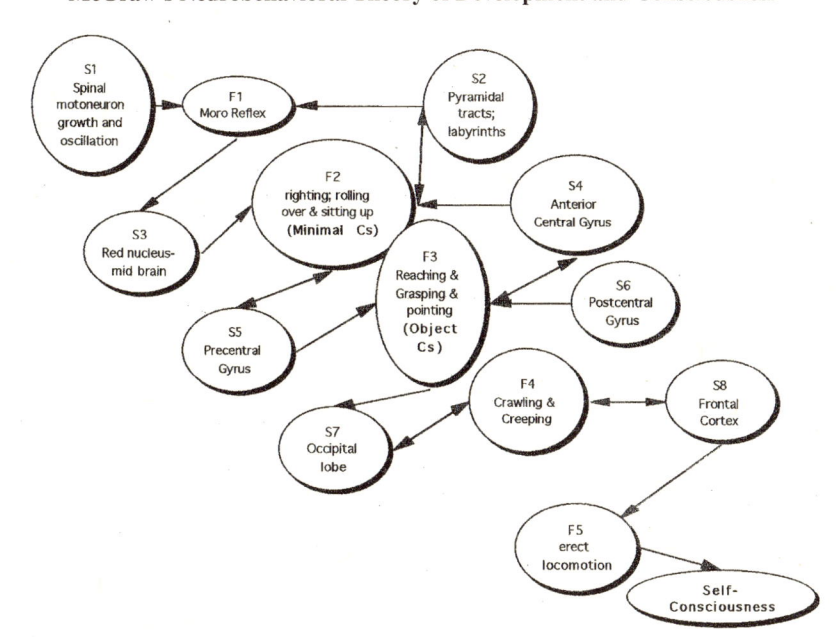

Figure 8.6
McGraw's Neurobehavioral Theory of Development and Consciousness

Motoneuron growth and oscillation along the spinal column commences a sequence of behaviorally mediated neuronanatomical and neuromuscular reorganizations that sustain successive forms of conscious activity, culminating in erect locomotion and selfconsciousness. Each functional pattern (F) constitutes the center of gravity of neural structures (5) undergoing differential growth (i.e., aXOns and dendritic connections), as illustrated by the neural complex 52-55 encircling F2. Reciprocal interactions occurring, for example, between F4 (crawling and creeping), and neuranatomic structures 54 and 57 enable antecedent structures to influence subsequent patterns. Consequently, erect locomotion at F5 entails re-solving the problem of balance by drawing on the energy of consciousness generated by antecedent stages of neuromuscular development occuring previously.

behavior growth is so swift that the distinction between maturation and learning cannot be arbitrarily drawn.

Assessing Gesell's Contribution to Developmental Science

It is hard to imagine how advancements in our scientific knowledge about neurobehavioral development could have been achieved without Gesell's pioneering studies. The theoretical perspectives of scientific pioneers are not always clearly understood by successors who sometimes express both awe and ingratitude. Esther Thelen, a prominent contemporary researcher in infant development, typifies this intellectual ambivalence by deriding Gesell's maturationism, while appropriating him as the unwitting and unsung father of dynamic systems theory. In her haste to dismiss and sometimes ridicule Gesell's ideas, however, she has failed to do justice to the complexity and sophistication of his ideas. In perhaps one of the more uncharitable appraisals of Gesell and McGraw's work yet to be advanced by a contemporary experimentalist, Thelen astonishingly asserts, "that the successes of the early pioneers also contributed to the decline of the field" (Thelen, 2000, p. 388). She reasoned that once major motor milestones were catalogued:

> There seemed to be little left to do. Moreover, both Gesell and McGraw's theoretical positions appeared to lead to dead-ends in terms of further empirical studies, but for different reasons. Once Gesell showed, through the descriptive topologies of behavior, that human development obeyed universal principles, the case was effectively closed (ibid).

Moreover, Thelen has changed her opinion several times about the relative merit of Gesell and McGraw's theories. At one time she considered McGraw to have adopted a "more prescriptive neural-maturationist model" than Gesell and that only "Gesell's ideas are worthy of serious consideration," because she contended that Gesell anticipated dynamic systems theory by emphasizing the self-generating patterning of behavior (Thelen, 1989, p. 10). More recently, Thelen (2000, P. 387) expressed agreement with this author (see Dalton, 1996) that "McGraw's legacy as a maturationist oversimplifies her more sophisticated view of development." But she still blames McGraw for having "put the role of maturation into the forefront." Thelen's inconsistency, and frankly erroneous, retrospective assessment of McGraw's work not only ignores McGraw's belated but well-deserved recognition as being Dewey's protégé and collaborator, (see Dalton and Bergenn, 1996; Dalton, 2000), but such misrepresentations impede rather than advance developmental science. Gesell's and McGraw's research can hardly be singled out as having brought about the death of motor studies, as their ideas never received a proper burial.

A fair assessment of Gesell's contribution to developmental science has been impeded by contemporary reconstructions that do not do justice to the comprehensive and integral nature of his work as a whole. Not since Freud has any American psychologist more boldly attempted to critically challenge and change popular beliefs and misconceptions about abnormal development, and to demonstrate that early learning is often constrained by motor limitations and emotional immaturity, than has Gesell. He did much to change how state institutions care for and educate children who suffer from mental retardation and to develop surer methods of diagnosis, which build on their strengths rather than dwell on their limitations. He was the first among other pioneering child psychologists, including Jean Piaget, to realize that little was known about the processes of normal development. His use of embryological evidence strengthened and deepened his knowledge of how early growth processes affect development. His attempt to construct a scale based on the sequence of observed relationship between motor and cognitive behaviors led researchers to become more knowledgeable and explicit about the underlying processes of growth. He also demonstrated that clinical and experimental perspectives could be combined to yield insights of much greater magnitude than when these approaches are employed independently. Gesell attempted to strike a balance between the excesses of behaviorism and Freudian psychoanalysis, even though he tended to give greater weight to maturational factors. And perhaps Gesell's greatest legacy then, is to have precipitated an intellectual rivalry about early development that put the nature versus nurture debate under intense scrutiny and scientific examination. The ensuing debate has now led many contemporary researchers to admit that this dichotomy has outlived its usefulness as a theoretical construct.

Notes

1. Previously published in *From Past to Future, Vol. 3*(2), *Beyond Observing Human Nature: Theoretical Contributions of Arnold Gesell to Developmental Science*, pp. 7-31. © 2001 Frances L. Hiatt School of Psychology, Clark University. Author: Thomas C. Dalton, Cal Poly State University, San Luis Obispo, CA.

References

Baldwin, J. M. (1894). *Mental development in the child and the race: Methods and processes.* New York and London: Macmillian.

Cairns, R. (1998). The making of developmental psychology. In R. M. Lerner, (Ed.), The handbook of child psychology. 5th ed. (pp. 25-106). New York: Wiley.

Carmichael, L. (1933). Origin and prenatal growth of behavior. In C. Murchison (Ed.), *A Handbook of Child Psychology*, 2nd ed. rev. (pp. 31-159). Worcester, MA: Clark University Press.

Clarke, J. E., Truly, T. L., and Phillips, S. J. (1993). On the development of walking as a limit-cycle system. In Thelen, E. and Smith L. B. (Eds.), *A dynamic systems approach to development: Applications.* (pp. 71-94). Cambridge, MA: MIT Press.

Coghill, G. E. (1926). The mechanism of integration in Amblystoma punctatum. *Journal of Comparative Neurology, 41*, 95-152.

Coghill, G. E. (1929). *Anatomy and the problem of behavior.* New York: Hafner.

Coghill, G. E. (1930). The structural basis of the integration of behavior. *Proceedings of the National Academy of Sciences, 16*, 637-643.
Coghill, G.E (1930a). The structural basis of the integration of behavior. *National Academy of Sciences Proceedings, 16*, 637-643.
Coghill, G. E. (1930b). Individuation versus integration in the development of behavior. *Journal of Genetic Psychology*, 3, 431-435.
Coghill, G. E. (1933a). The neuroembryonic study of behavior: principles, perspectives and aims. *Science*, 78, 131-138.
Coghill, G. E. (1933b, October 27). Letter to C. J. Herrick. Neurology Collection, C.Judson Herrick Papers, Spencer Research Library, University of Kansas, Lawrence, KN.
Coghill, G. E. (1934, April 23). Letter to A. Gesell, 1. General Correspondence, Arnold Gesell Papers, Manuscript Division, Library of Congress, Washington, DC.
Coghill, G. E. (1936). Integration and the motivation of behavior. *The Journal of Genetic Psychology, 48,* 3-19.
Coghill, G. E. (1938, May 25). Letter to A. Gesell. General Correspondence, Arnold Gesell Papers, Manuscript Division, Library of Congress Washington, DC.
Coghill, G. E. (1939, June 30). Letter to A. Gesell. General Correspondence, Arnold Gesell Papers, Manuscript Division, Library of Congress Washington, DC.
Conel, L. (1939). *The Post-Natal Development of the Human Cerebral Cortex. Vol. 1: Cortex of the Newborn.* Cambridge, MA: Harvard University Press.
Dalton, T. C. (1996). Was McGraw a maturationist? *American Psychologist, 51*, 551-552.
Dalton, T. C. (1998). Myrtle McGraw's neurobehavioral theory of development. *Developmental Review, 18*, 428-436
Dalton, T. C. (1999). The ontogeny of consciousness: John Dewey and Myrtle McGraw's contribution to a science of mind. *Journal of Consciousness Studies, 6,* 3-26.
Dalton, T. C. (1995). McGraw's alternative to Gesell's Maturationism. In T. C. Dalton and V. W. Bergenn, (Eds.), *Beyond heredity and environment: Myrtle Mcgraw and the maturation controversy.* Boulder, CO: Westview Press.
Dalton, T. C. and Bergenn, V. W. (1996). John Dewey, Myrtle McGraw and *Logic:* An unusual collaboration in the 1930s. *Studies in History and Philosophy of Science,* 27, 775-881.
Eisenberg, N., I. Guthrie, B. Murphy; S. Shepard, A. Cumberland and G. Carlo, (1999). Consistency and development of prosocial dispositions: A longitudinal study, *Child Development, 70,* 1360-1372.
Fagan, T.K. (1987a). Gesell: The first school psychologist. Part I. The road to Connecticut. *School Psychology Review, 16*, 103-107.
Fagan, T. K (1987). Gesell: The first school psychologist. Part II. Practice and significance. *School Psychology Review, 16,* 399-409.
Hall, G. S. (1912, September 7). Letter to Gesell, 1-2. Arnold Gesell Papers, Manuscript Division, Library of Congress, Washington, DC.
Hall, G. S. (1914, June 18). Letter to Gesell, 1. Arnold Gesell Papers, Manuscript Division, Library of Congress, Washington, DC.
Gesell, A. (1906). Jealousy. *Journal of Psychology*, 17, 337-496.
Gesell, A. (1914, June 14). Letter to Lewis Terman, 1-3. Arnold Gesell Papers, Manuscript Division, Library of Congress, Washington, DC.
Gesell, A. (1925). *The mental growth of the preschool child.* New York: Macmillan.
Gesell, A. (1933). Maturation and the patterning of behavior. In C. Murchison (Ed.), *A handbook of child psychology,* 2nd ed. rev. (pp. 209-235). Worcester, MA: Clark University Press.

Gesell, A. (1934, March 22). Letter to G. E.Coghill, 1. Arnold Gesell Papers, Manuscript Division, Library of Congress, Washington, DC.
Gesell, A. (1938, May 17). Letter to G.E. Coghill. Arnold Gesell Papers, Manuscript Division, Library of Congress, Washington, DC.
Gesell, A. (1939a). Reciprocal interweaving in neuromotor development. *The Journal of Comparative Neurology*, 10, 161-180.
Gesell, A. (1939b, October 28). Letter to J. LeRoy Conel, 1-3. Arnold Gesell Papers, Manuscript Division, Library of Congress, Washington, DC.
Gesell, A. (1945). *The Embryology of Behavior*. New York: Harper Brothers.
Gesell, A. and Thompson, H. (1934). *Infant Behavior: Its Genesis and Growth*. New York: McGraw-Hill.
Gesell, A. and Amatruda, C. (1947). *Developmental diagnosis: Normal and abnormal child development*. New York: Paul Hoeber.
Gesell, A. and Ilg, F. (1949). *Child development: An introduction to the study of human growth*. New York: Harper.
Gesell, A. (1952). Autobiography. In E. G. Boring, H. S. Langfield, H. Werner and R. M. Yerkes (Eds.), *A history of psychology in autobiography,* Vol. 4 (pp. 123-142). Worcester, MA: Clark University Press.
Gottlieb, G. (1997). *Synthesizing Nature/Nurture: Prenatal roots of instinctive behavior*. Mahwah, NJ; Erlbaum.
Gottlieb, G. (1998). Myrtle McGraw's unrecognized conceptual contribution to developmental psychology. *Developmental Review*, *18*, 337-448.
Gottlieb, G. (2000). Zing-Yang Kuo: Personal recollections and intimations of developmental science. *From Past to Future: Clark Papers on the History of Psychology*, 2, 1-12.
Greenough, W. T., Black, J. E. and Wallace, C. (1993). Experience and brain development. In M. H. Johnson (Ed.), *Brain development and cognition* (pp. 319-322). Cambridge, MA: Oxford.
Hall, G. S. (1912, September 7). Letter to Gesell. Arnold Gesell Papers, Manuscript Division, Library of Congress, Washington, DC.
Hall, G. S. (1914, June 18). Letter to Gesell. Arnold Gesell Papers, Manuscript Division, Library of Congress, Washington, DC.
Hooker, D. (1943). Reflex Activities in the human fetus. In R. Barker, J. S. Kounin and H. F. Wright, (Eds.), Child behavior and development (pp. 120-192). New York: McGraw-Hill.
Kuo, Z. Y. (1932). Ontogeny of embryonic behavior in Aves. The chronology and general nature of the behavior of the chick embryo. *Journal of Experimental Zoology*, 61, 395-430.
McGraw, M. B. (1926, March 19). Letter to Gesell, 1. Arnold Gesell Papers, Manuscript Division, Library of Congress, Washington, DC.
McGraw, M. B. (1927, March 2). Letter to Gesell. Arnold Gesell Papers, Manuscript Division, Library of Congress, Washington, DC.
McGraw, M. B. (1935/1975). Growth: A study of Johnny and Jimmy. New York: Appleton Century. Reprint, New York: Arno Press.
McGraw, M. B. (1939). Swimming behavior of the human infant. *Journal of Pediatrics,* 15, 485-490.
McGraw, M. B. (1941). Development of neuromuscular mechanisms as reflected in the crawling and creeping behavior of the human infant. *Journal of Genetic Psychology, 58*, 83-111.
McGraw, M. B. (1943). *The neuromuscular maturation of the human infant*. New York: Columbia University Press.

McGraw, M. B. (1946). Maturation of behavior. In L. Carmichael, (Ed.), *Manual of Child Development.* (pp. 332-369). New York: Wiley.

McGraw, M. B. (1979, December 31). Letter to R. Oppenheim,1-2. Myrtle B. McGraw Papers, Special Collections, Millbank Memorial Library, Teachers College, Columbia University, New York.

Merzenich, M., Recanzone, G., Jenkins, W., Allard, T. and Nudo, R. (1988). Cortical representational plasticity. In P. Rakic and W. Singer (Eds.), *Neurobiology of the neocortex* (pp. 41-67). New York: John Wiley and Sons.

Minkowski, M. Neurobiologische studien am menschlichen foetus. *Abderhaldens Handbuch d. biologischen Arbeitsmethoden, Lief,* 253 S. 511-563.

Miles, W. R. (1964). Arnold Lucius Gesell, 1880-1961: A biographical memior. *National Academy of Sciences, Biographical memiors,* Vo. 37 (pp. 55-96). New York: Columbia University Press.

Needham, J. (1942). *Biochemistry and morphogenesis.* Cambridge: Cambridge University Press.

Oppenheim, R. W. (1978). G. E. Coghill (1872-1941):Pioneer neuroembryologist and developmental psychobiologist. *Perspectives in Biology and Medicine,* 22, 45-64.

Oppenheim, R. W. (1995). Myrtle McGraw's nascent and pioneering use of embryology to understand human development. In T. C. Dalton and V. W. Bergenn, (Eds.), *Beyond Heredity and environment: Myrtle McGraw and the Maturation Controversy.* (pp. ix-xv). Boulder, CO: Westview Press.

Roberton, M. A. (1993). New ways to think about old questions. In Thelen, E. and Smith L. B. (Eds.), *A dynamic systems approach to development: Applications.* (pp. 95-118). Cambridge, MA: MIT Press.

Swift. E. J. (1905a, May 1). Letter to Gesell, 1-3. Arnold Gesell Papers. Manuscript Division, Library of Congress, Washington, DC.

Swift, E. J. (1905b, February 25). Letter to Gesell, 1. Arnold Gesell Papers. Manuscript Division, Library of Congress, Washington, DC.

Terman, L. (1918, March 22). Letter to Gesell, 1-3. Arnold Gesell Papers. Manuscript Division, Library of Congress, Washington, DC.

Thelen, E. (1987). The role of motor development in developmental psychology: A view of the past and an agenda for the future. In N. Eisenberg, (Ed.), *Contemporary topics in developmental psychology.* New York: Wiley.

Thelen, E. and Adolfs, K. (1994). Arnold L. Gesell: The paradox of nature and nurture. In R. D. Parke, P. A. Ornstein, J. J. Rieser and C. Zahn-Waxler, (Eds.), *A century of developmental psychology.* (pp. 357-388). Washington, DC: American Psychological Association.

Thelen, E. (2000). Motor development as foundation and future of developmental psychology. *International journal of behavioral development,* 24, 385-397.

Touwen, B. C. L. (1995). Epilogue: A Neurologist's "Homage." In T. C. Dalton and V. W. Bergenn, (Eds.), *Beyond Heredity and environment: Myrtle McGraw and the Maturation Controversy.* (pp. 271-283). Boulder, CO: Westview Press.

Touwen, B. C. L. (1998). The brain and the development of function. *Developmental Review,* 18, 504-526.

Wellman, H. M. (1990). The Child's Theory of Mind. Cambridge: MIT Press.

Windle, W. F. (1940). *Physiology of the fetus: Origin and extend of function in prenatal life.* Philadelphia, PA: W. B. Saunders.

Zelazo, P. R. (1998). McGraw and the development of unaided walking. *Developmental Review, 18,* 449-472.

9

Alexander F. Chamberlain: A Life's Work

Julia M. Berkman[1]

No one has written extensively about the life and work of Alexander Francis Chamberlain since the early 1900s, but the importance of this scholar should not be underestimated. The first person to receive a doctorate degree in anthropology in the United States, Alexander Chamberlain made considerable contributions to the body of knowledge in his field—a discipline that was then a combination of anthropological and psychological inquiry. His early work began with investigations into the cultures and languages of two Indian tribes indigenous to Canada and the northern United States and, within a few decades, positioned Chamberlain as the leading scholar in this domain.

Unlike many anthropologists in our time who focus their efforts on studying a single group, ethnicity, or region, Chamberlain followed the scientific tradition of his era, pursuing general inquiry in his field. He became well-versed in the practices, beliefs, and especially the folklore of peoples in all parts of the world. A devout believer in the existence of common human traits, he was especially capable of synthesizing what he knew of each group in a way that established a bridge between otherwise distinct regions of the globe.

Beyond his ethnographic insights, Chamberlain queried the development of the child and wrote on the subject of childhood in world folklore. He concerned himself with a scope of worthwhile subjects ranging from linguistics to women's suffrage. No topic was out of range as all forms of human study addressed the need for seeing each group as a contributing force to humanity at large. Chamberlain emphasized that no single racial, ethnic, or religious group should be singled out as inherently superior to another, a belief far ahead of his time. The following is an attempt at drawing a picture of a man whose scholarly achievements and strength of character are captured in the depth and breadth of his writing.

A Brief Biography

Alexander Francis Chamberlain was born in Norfolk, England on January 12, 1865. His parents, two siblings and Alexander immigrated to the United States while he was still a child, and within two years relocated on to Ontario where Alexander would eventually attend the Union School and the Collegiate Institute. When he received a prestigious scholarship to attend the University of Toronto, the Chamberlain family moved once more in order to facilitate their eldest son's studies. Alexander began his exemplary college career in the department of modern languages, his record marked by numerous academic honors. Finally earning a bachelor's degree in modern languages and ethnology in 1886, Alexander left the University proficient in German, French, and Italian. He held an appointment as fellow in modern languages in the University College, Toronto for the following three years, continuing his work towards a master's degree at the same time. In 1889, Alexander was awarded a master's degree by the University of Toronto after completing a thesis based upon his thorough studies of the Mississagas of Skugog, Ontario, a tribe of Canadian Indians. He held a position as fellow, doing tutorial and post-graduate work in modern languages, at University College, Toronto between the years of 1887 and 1890.

Chamberlain came to Clark University in 1890 to pursue his anthropological studies with Franz Boas. While Boas only remained at Clark long enough for Chamberlain to complete his doctorate, his research interests and ideologies would help shape the course of his student's career (see below for more on Boas). Chamberlain's dissertation, completed in 1892, was an in-depth analysis of the language of the Mississagas. While working on this project, Chamberlain began to investigate the Kootenay Indians, making his first field trip in the summer of 1891. He would continue to visit the Kootenay tribe throughout his lifetime, becoming the foremost authority on their language and culture at the time.

Chamberlain spent the rest of his life teaching and publishing at Clark University—contributing greatly to its fame as a place of serious scientific research. His status in the university quickly rose as he became lecturer in anthropology in 1892, acting assistant professor in 1900, assistant professor in 1904, and finally full professor in anthropology in 1911. Throughout these years, he also acted as editor of the *Journal of American Folklore* (1900-1908), co-editor of *the Journal of Religious Psychology* (1911-1914), and department editor for the *American Anthropologist* and the *American Journal of Archaeology* until the time of his death, to name just a few of his numerous contributions to scientific organizations. Chamberlain published prodigiously in American, as well as European, journals and encyclopedias, emphasizing the global significance of his cultural knowledge.

Chamberlain's dedication to his own work, and especially his desire to facilitate the work of others, guided his professional achievements. The *American*

Anthropologist, the *Journal of American Folklore*, and *Current Anthropological Literature* for years featured his annotated bibliographies of then-current anthropological periodical literature; a monumental effort which greatly served in the education of others. At the time of his death (caused by gangrenic diabetes) in 1914, Chamberlain "had practically completed his work of many years on a distribution-map of the South American aboriginal languages" and the first part of a Kootenay dictionary and grammar (Gilbertson, 1914, p. 339).[2]

The Role of Franz Boas in Anthropology at Clark

Franz Boas came to newly established Clark University in 1889. The circumstances around his appointment were quite befitting of G. Stanley Hall's notorious methods of actively recruiting the university's original faculty members:

> ... he [Boas] went to Cleveland, Ohio, to attend the meeting of the American Association [for the Advancement of Science], and, according to the story as he told it, chatted with a gentleman who shared his seat. As the train was coming into the station at Cleveland, his seat-mate introduced himself, and invited him to accept a teaching post in an institution of higher learning then being founded, which he headed. The seat-mate was G. Stanley Hall ... Boas accepted the offer ... (Herskovits, 1973, p. 13).

As no separate department of anthropology existed at the time, Boas taught his courses under Hall in the psychology department. From the late 1880s to early 1890s Boas published several papers on the topic of folklore and traditions (e.g., Boas, 1891; 1888), subjects with which Chamberlain was already becoming consistently more involved. In addition to work in the field (which was greatly limited due to the university's strict policy on professorial absence), Boas led a study of Worcester school children that later expanded to other parts of the United States and Canada. Through these anthropometric investigations, Boas hoped to study how the physical growth of children was influenced by various environmental conditions. The study was carried to completion with the help of Chamberlain, among others (Chamberlain, 1899).

Both Boas and Chamberlain led investigations into tribal cultures and wrote extensively on their findings,[3] but it was their philosophy on the causes of racial differences which linked them together intellectually. Although Boas did the majority of his theoretical writing after leaving Clark in 1892 (in fact, much of his published work in this domain appeared after Chamberlain's death), the foundations of his radical thinking can be glimpsed from statements made just before Chamberlain became his student. In 1889, Boas wrote "On Alternating Sounds," disputing the assumption that an inability to perceive culturally unfamiliar sounds was a sign of primitiveness. He maintained that previous experience and knowledge were critical influencing factors in human perception. Later in his career, Boas would repeatedly stress that racial differences were due to environmental effects rather than heredity (Boas, 1927). He would continue to: "search for similarities between various cultural groups, substantiating his belief in common human mental processes" (Herskovits, 1973).

As will be discussed later, Chamberlain thoroughly supported this view, expounding it within his own writing. In fact, many of Chamberlain's extensive arguments for historically-based (vs. biologically-based) racial differences predate those of Franz Boas. Nevertheless, it is clear that Chamberlain was influenced by his teacher in this respect, as he would later quote his mentor's writing to facilitate his own point (e.g., Chamberlain, 1900, p. 48).

Investigations into the Native Tribes of North America

Chamberlain began his studies of the Mississaga Indians as part of his Masters thesis work. The Mississaga were part of the Algonkian tribes of the northern shores of Lakes Huron and Superior. As early as 1648, they were "described as dwelling around the mouth of the river Mississaga" (Chamberlain, 1892, p. 7). Thus, as Chamberlain found, their name could be broken down into two parts: Missi, meaning great, and Saga, meaning mouth of the river.

The Mississagas had been converted to the Methodist faith in the early nineteenth century by European settlers, building their first church c.1824. By the time Chamberlain began his investigations into their native culture, many of the tribe's people spoke English, had taken on Christian names in addition to their Indian ones, and had begun to assimilate into the lifestyle of Western culture. In 1884, reports claimed that the tribe now consisted of only forty-three members.

In June, 1888, Chamberlain received communication from an Indian agent at the Mississaga settlement who wrote that the tribe had "no old songs, beliefs peculiar to them; some don't even speak the language" (Chamberlain, 1888a, p. 159). Rather than accepting this report, Chamberlain decided to visit the small tribe, now residing on the island of Skugog, and investigate for himself. Without delay, he made this trip the following August. He found that, although only the eldest members of the tribe could inform him about the traditional practices and beliefs of their ancestors, there still remained some (both young and old) who could not speak English. His main source of knowledge was Mrs. Bolin (Nawigishkoke in her native tongue), a sixty-five-year-old Mississaga woman who seemed most knowledgeable about the tribe's heritage. Along with her assistance, Chamberlain succeeded in translating some 700 Algonkian words and in recording numerous legends, including the following on the "Mississaga tradition of the origin of Indian corn":

> Our people used to make children fast for several days to see what god they would serve. Once, a long time ago, a man put his young son out to fast and dream. He built a little camp for him and left him there. He made him fast as long as he thought it safe. At first, when the father came to ask his son about his dream, the boy did not answer. Afterwards he said that he had seen a little old man coming towards him,

with only a little hair just over his forehead. He (the father) then lifted the corner of the blanket and pulled out an ear of corn. ... The corn was half worn off, no kernels at one part,—it was a time of drought, I suppose,—and the little silk grew right on top of the ear. It was the corn ... himself coming that the boy saw (Chamberlain, 1888b, p. 143).

Contrary to the letter he had received, Chamberlain was able to obtain enough information in that visit, and through subsequent inquiries, to publish a volume on the history, language, beliefs, and folklore of the Mississagas. In addition to tracing their etymology, this linguistic achievement involved classifying words and phrases into various domains, including both the tangible (e.g., food, animals, nature) and the abstract (e.g., words related to feelings, such as "glad"). A product of this examination was Chamberlain's dispute with those linguists who presumed that the rules of certain languages applied to all others:

... the rule assumed by some authorities that syllables should, as far as possible, close with a vowel sound does not hold in the Algonkian tongues, for in Mississaga the termination of a syllable in a consonant is very frequent ... (Chamberlain, 1892, p. 68).

Chamberlain was also concerned with onomatology, the study of the origin and history of proper names.[4] He stressed the importance of comparative onomatology "as evidence of the mental acquirements of the races of people compared" (Chamberlain, 1889, p. 351). As such, he paid careful attention to the Mississaga names of places, people, and mythological characters. This study, in all its facets, earned Chamberlain a doctorate in anthropology at Clark University.

For the remainder of his career, Chamberlain turned his attention to studies of the Kootenay Indians, inhabiting southeastern British Columbia, Canada and northern Idaho. He first visited the tribe in the summer and autumn of 1891. Much as he did with the Mississaga language, Chamberlain became proficient in the dialect of the Kootenay. In addition, he examined their cries and noises, plant names and uses, mythology, folklore, and drawings (Boas, 1918). He felt that this Indian tribe, unlike others, was better able to resist the "evil influences of white contact" (Chamberlain, 1901b, p. 248). Nevertheless, he did observe these influences in drawings of medicine men (who served as mediums, doctors, and prophets). Chamberlain (1901c) suggested that drawings of the shaman represented the result of contact between the Kootenay pagan religion and ideas introduced by the missionaries of Christianity. He recognized the need for a comparative study looking at the effects that the introduction of European faiths had upon the language, religious concepts, and artwork of American and Canadian Indians (see Valsiner, this issue).

Despite his efforts to capture the meaning of the Indian languages he studied, Chamberlain admitted to the limits of this search. In "Translation: A study in the transference of folk-thought," he conceded that one cannot truly understand a language, and what lies behind it, unless it is your own native tongue. For, "there are no two races upon the faces of the earth whose minds run in exactly the same channel, whose speech is cast in just the same mould" (Chamberlain, 1901a, p. 165).

Influence of the Conquered on the Conqueror

An important aspect of Chamberlain's professional and moral convictions was the attention he paid to the symbiotic relationship between contacting cultures. Rather than assuming that a colonized group solely benefited from the influences of a more advanced culture, as many others would have argued at the time, Chamberlain saw the oppressive qualities of the white man when in contact with native populations. In 1902, shortly after the United States' colonization of the Philippines, he penned a bold article that heavily criticized the historic practice of colonization, especially when falsely justified by economic gain. Chamberlain spoke of the transforming effect which a colonized society would have on the self-labeled victor:

> We know now how hard it is to exterminate a people; we are learning to what extent peoples supposed to be utterly extinct survive to influence in no insignificant way the physical, intellectual, and moral well-being of their conquerors and *soi-disant* exterminators (Chamberlain, 1902a, p. 511).

According to Chamberlain, the culture of a colonized civilization did not simply fade when its people were forced into the practices of a newly dominant society. The culture of the oppressor did not vanquish the other and thereby prevail. It was instead molded to include many of the beliefs and customs of the "conquered" group.

In several works, Chamberlain discussed the bidirectional transfer of symbols that occurred between once wholly distinct groups. In "Algonkian words in American English: A study in the contact of the White man and the Indian," Chamberlain (1902b) spoke of common words, used in everyday English speech, which were rarely acknowledged as coming from the Indian language (for example: caucus, hickory, moose, and pecan). Chamberlain intended this as "an effort to indicate how much we of the intrusive race really owe to the aborigines of the New World" (1902b, p. 267).

The Child Study Movement

Alexander Chamberlain began teaching at Clark University at the same time that the child study movement, propelled by G. Stanley Hall, began to form. In 1894, Hall initiated a study examining the development of children that would last for approximately a decade. Concerned with the inadequate state of education in the United States, Hall and colleagues endeavored to discover patterns in the nature of children which could be used as a guide for curriculum reform in the schools (for more on Hall's role, see Valsiner, this issue). This in-depth research was based upon the belief that all children possess a common set of instincts (White, 1990; 1992).

This movement did not bypass Chamberlain, who also delved into investigations of the child. His strong support for the "*genius* of the movement for 'Child-Study'" was voiced in the introduction to his 1895 book *The Child and Childhood in Folk-Thought*, which came out of a lecture series given at the summer school held at Clark University in 1894 (see below). Although they did not meet in all respects, several common elements can be seen between Hall and Chamberlain's work. For one, Chamberlain also relied upon observations of children and built his theories upon existing information (White, 1990). Rather than systematically investigating a hypothesis, Chamberlain presented a body of evidence and later applied a theory to the data. Another principle that Chamberlain seems to have taken from Hall is that children possess a unique and powerful imagination that guides their experience (Ross, 1972). As will be discussed later, this belief was echoed in Chamberlain's discussions of child play and in observations of his daughter's development.

The Role of the Child in Folk-Thought

Chamberlain's interest in the role of children and childhood as formative aspects of culture and myth first became apparent in *The Child and Childhood in Folk-Thought*. A dissection of myths from across the globe, this text drew out common themes in folk traditions. Chamberlain's aim was to show that human ideas and institutions had their origins in the consideration of childhood. Motherhood and fatherhood were necessitated by the needs of the child and, in turn, influenced the development of social structures and patterns. He believed this was true for all races and endeavored to prove so by including in his book a sampling of lore from around the world, all relating to the meanings which various cultures assigned to children, mothers and fathers. While he duly noted that not all cultures assign the same respect or traditions to these roles, Chamberlain did show that all cultures have some sort of hierarchical classification into which mothers, fathers, and children fall. Other common themes, such as the connection between motherhood and the earth, fatherhood and the sun, were pronounced as well.

This book is a prime exemplar of Chamberlain's immense fund of knowledge pertaining to the diverse cultures, languages, and beliefs of people from all over the earth. In discussing the child in folk-thought, he drew upon traditions of Asia, Africa, Western and Eastern Europe, South America, and the Mediterranean, finding shared motifs amongst different groups: "a familiar phrase in English is 'babes and sucklings,' the last term of which, cognate with German *Saugling*, meets with analogues far and wide among the peoples of the earth"

(Chamberlain, 1895, p. 78). Tracing the etymology of certain words, such as "child," Chamberlain was also able to illustrate a group's philosophy on the subject. For example, he noted that the Snanaimuq language, of Vancouver Island, used words for male and female infant whose literal meaning was "the weak one," implying that children in this culture were not viewed as contributing members until a certain age or physical ability was reached. The Modoc, of Oregon, referred to babies as "what is carried on one's self," connoting an inactive view of the child—quite different from the European understanding of the child as an active member of the family.

Chamberlain's opinion that women should be regarded with high esteem was also apparent in this volume. He doubtlessly had great respect for motherhood and held this as a venerable role in society:

> ... it is hoped, we shall ... wake up to the full consciousness that the great men of our land have had mothers, and proceed to re-write our biographical dictionaries and encyclopedias of life-history (Chamberlain, 1895, p. 17).

Chamberlain argued that mothers should have continuing input into the education of their children, that their influence on this matter should not halt when infancy ends and formal education outside of the home begins. Since mothers have guided the education of their children for centuries, they should be able to play a part in school-building as well (ibid, p. 236).

This liberal attitude towards the role of women in society was a recurring theme in Chamberlain's writing. Not only did he attribute evolutionary strides to women, but he also cited woman as being the first poet, the first priest, and the first painter (Chamberlain, 1897). He showed a deep appreciation for the role of women in history and for their contributions to society—beyond motherhood. Unlike G. Stanley Hall, who believed that innate differences between the sexes warranted "the separate education of women from puberty onward for their ultimate maternal role" (Ross, 1972, p. 302), Chamberlain championed equality in education and academic employment. He not only preached these beliefs, but also lived by them (see below, and Valsiner, Chapter 10).

Commendation and Criticism

It was usual for Chamberlain to insert small "position statements" all over his very voluminous, yet mostly descriptive, writings. He was clearly more of a collector of information rather than a scientist who would unite observed details with general theoretical explanations. Some of his contemporaries found his style quite favorable. The publication of *The Child and Childhood in Folk-Thought* led to a positive review by Donald Brinton, who captured Chamberlain's poetic touch:

> This work supplies a want in the literature of folklore, and supplies it well. ...It is astonishing to note what an important part he [the author] has played in the life and

opinions of his elders, and what diverse powers he has exhibited or been credited with ... [the author] ... is no gleaner of dry stubble, but delights in the literary and poetic sides of his inquiry, and brings under contribution the bards, the dramatists and the moralists of the world (Brinton, 1896, p. 484).

Yet Chamberlain's stance as a moralistic encyclopeadian drew criticism from his predecessor Franz Boas. In a direct rebuttal of Brinton's positive review, Boas emphasized in no uncertain terms that Chamberlain's tendency to collect together the massive knowledge about ideas of different societies was insufficient:

While this preparatory work is very meritorious, particularly in so far as it refers to uncommon books, the attempt at a scientific arrangement of the material thus obtained does not appear successful. If scientific description was the author's aim it was incumbent upon him to arrange his material from certain points of view in a systematic way. If he desired by inductive method to investigate certain phenomena it was his duty to array his facts for the purpose of finding the elements common to all of them. His book fills neither the one nor the other requirement (Boas, 1896, p. 741).

Boas pointed to the characteristic feature of Chamberlain's writing—the presentation of the richness of anthropological materials with a corresponding fear of bringing to it his own analytic interpretation. In reading the many small linguistic reports that Chamberlain published, one finds open-ended future-oriented statements, like the following:

The writer does not desire at present to discuss the remote origin and inter-relation of the "child words" brought together in this brief essay, but hopes that additions will be made to the data there given from other sources, and that on some future occasion the subject may be discussed in its wider aspect (Chamberlain, 1890, p. 241).

Studies of the Child

It was at the turn of the century that Alexander Chamberlain began to write on the subject of child development. In 1900, he published *The Child: A Study in the Evolution of Man*. As with the other subjects he studied, Chamberlain merged these insights with his knowledge of cultural development worldwide. Consistent with the times, his approach toward the subject of child study was a melding of both anthropology and psychology, two disciplines which, as Chamberlain successfully showed, share much in common. Although he did not believe in recapitulation theory (as advocated by Hall), which stated that "ontogeny repeats phylogeny, the individual the race" (Chamberlain, 1900, p. 51), he did draw a parallel between the process which a child goes through in maturation and the process which a culture goes through in the course of its development. Chamberlain viewed each stage of childhood as a metaphor for the evolution of mankind. As the child becomes an adult, so does primitive man become modern.

Chamberlain emphasized three explanations for the existence of a prolonged childhood in our species: 1) it provides the infant with enough time to shed his weaknesses and gain his strengths, becoming a contributing member of society, 2) it lengthens the time in which the child can play, and 3) it ensures the "sociability of the race" (Fiske, cf. Chamberlain, 1900, p. 441). The first of these is self-explanatory—the child must have enough time to develop the skills necessary for functioning in daily life, especially considering the complexities of human societies. The child must develop his own faculties as he matures to an adult. Infancy insured the adult human's great intellectuality "by making a considerable portion of his early life physically and even mentally helpless" (ibid., p. 442).

The Significance of Children's Play

The second argument concerns the role of play in the child's life. Play allows the child to experiment with roles that he or she will have to fill as an adult. This comes through imitation of elders and sex-appropriate role-play. Play is the child's labor—it educates him and initiates him into society. It is an efficient means for the child to explore his environment, making mistakes along the way, then finally deciding how he should act upon and within it. In the larger scheme, Chamberlain saw a correlation between childhood play and adult invention, both involving experimentation with existing knowledge in a search for the new:

> In a word, animals, and man more especially, possess youth because the creation of art and civilization was a necessity—and these had to be fashioned from instincts through the transforming power of play (ibid, p. 442).

Chamberlain contended that play was the root of all aspects of human life—language, art, science, poetry, and so on. This view may be compared with the notion that leisure among the upper classes gave way to invention that, in turn, furthered the development of modern society. Without this time for "play" the creative and functional industries of the world might not have progressed at the same rate. Chamberlain did point out that just as work exists in child play, so does play often exist in adult work; each is concerned with mastering some task or process.

Finally, Chamberlain asserted that "the helplessness of the child was necessary to bring about the helpfulness of mankind" (ibid, p. 441). Namely, in taking care of the infant, man was able to express and foster his compassion and benevolence, as Nature had intended for him. This morality separated the human race from other species whose young do not need the prolonged attention required by the human child.

As he did in the majority if his work, Chamberlain stressed the idea of basic human equality in *The Child*. He underscored that children, regardless of race, were born with the same intellectual capacity and that the environment determined their eventual ability. Circumstance, and not genetic predisposition, drives children apart developmentally and intellectually. In this respect, Chamberlain fully supported the teachings of Boas, whom he quoted as stating that "achievements of races do not warrant us to assume that the one race is more highly gifted than the other" (ibid, p. 48). Clearly, more weight is put upon certain types of achievements here than upon others (the more industrialized being better), but the aim of the statement lies more in affirming the basic sameness of both "primitive" and "evolved" peoples. Chamberlain certainly believed that both the physical and mental unity of mankind could be seen in the resemblance of children all over the world. In this respect, Chamberlain read Wordsworth's lines as: the child is not only the father of his own man, but also the father of mankind.

Studies of His Own Child

In 1904 and 1905, Alexander Chamberlain and his wife, Isabel Cushman Chamberlain, published a series of three articles detailing aspects of their only child's development during the first three years of life. While in the introduction to their first study they stated that "questions of psychological and pedagogical import ... are dealt with" (Chamberlain and Chamberlain, 1904a. p. 264), the study itself predominantly presented data collected by the Chamberlains concerning formation of the child's language ability, imagination, and emotional capacity. Unlike the later works of theorists such as Piaget, who used observations of their own children as building blocks for their developmental theories, the Chamberlain study did not strive to outline any model of development. There was no systematic attempt at explaining the process by which their daughter, Ruth, began to understand or interact with her world; nothing resembling a stage theory, only hints at certain types of learning relationships. For example, the Chamberlains noted when Ruth first spoke of fearing gnats. They credited this event to an occasion the previous week when she had played with a girl who feared these insects:

> About a week before a girl friend of hers who is afraid of spiders and mosquitoes was playing with her and this fear (?) of the gnat is to be attributed to that occasion (Chamberlain and Chamberlain, 1904a, p. 275).

In effect, they suggested that their daughter's newly found fear was modeled upon that of her friend. It was up to the reader, however, to extend this example into a model of learning for children, for no other mention of this particular phenomenon was made.

Much in line with Alexander's work on the Native Tribes of North America, the Chamberlains focused predominantly on Ruth's speech. The fact that their daughter often spoke in a language of her own creation (which her father termed "Chinese" for Ruth's ease of reference), greatly interested them. As Alexander Chamberlain had done numerous times before with tribal languages, the couple carefully recorded Ruth's "Chinese" words and sentences. For the first published study, they compiled an alphabetical list of 430 "Chinese" words that Ruth regularly spoke, attempting to break down her pretend language into syntactic patterns and rules. While her parents did speculate that some of these words were derived from Ruth's usual English speech patterns, they also drew parallels between Ruth's invented language and the 'primitive' languages of the American Indians.

After listing various English words that their daughter regularly used, and their implied meaning, the Chamberlains made the following statement concerning those words that did not seem to originate from the English language:

> In this category may be listed a number of words, which, standing by themselves, with no explanation of their history, might be taken for "original" inventions of the child, so primitive are they in appearance and so suggestive of the vocabularies of savage and barbarous peoples (Chamberlain and Chamberlain, 1904b, p. 481).

This comparison is reminiscent of Alexander's belief that the course of a child's development is analogous to the development of humankind. The growing child and the growing culture must both experiment with, and create, new forms and ideas before establishing a set pattern of activity. Once again, the introduction to the first study stated that Ruth's parents "avoided imposing things upon her by direct teaching" (Chamberlain and Chamberlain, 1904a, p. 264). As evidenced by their writing, the Chamberlains focused much more upon observation and inquiry of their daughter than upon a search for tasks which would shape her development. Rather than stifling her pretend language, they asked her questions about it, tried to understand it. In a similar vein, Alexander Chamberlain questioned Ruth's definitions of common objects and attempted to trace their roots, rather than simply teaching her the correct answers (for more detail on these studies, see Valsiner, this issue). This positive attitude toward free exploration in personal evolution coincided with Alexander Chamberlain's belief that development, whether an individual's or a culture's, should be allowed to progress at its own rate, without outside intrusion.

On Modesty

Alexander Chamberlain's writing is marked by modesty. Many of his journal articles are filled with extensive references to other researchers and theorists in his field whose work he considered preeminent. Disclaimers about his efforts only contributing one small part to a large body of thought are not uncommon in his publications. His humility can also be seen in his attitude toward other ethnicities and races of men and women. As Albert Gilbertson (1914) stated in a memoriam for his colleague, "beneath diversities of culture he recognized the generic, fundamental, universal human traits" (p. 340). In writing reviews of new books or articles, Chamberlain consistently praised those who, rather than simply describing something new about the culture they had been studying, addressed the contributions which that culture had made to the world. For example, in his review of Walter E. Roth's "The Structure of the Koko-Yimidir Language," Chamberlain wrote:

> Special studies like this must increase the interest of the comparative philologists in the Australian dialects, which afford so much valuable material for the investigation of primitive speech, and yet, by the striking analogues of thought they offer with languages so far advanced as the English of today, testify to the essential unity of the human mind, apart from century, clime, or race (Chamberlain, 1901d, p. 757).

It is necessary here to address Chamberlain's use of the word 'primitive' in his writings. Although today's standards deem this word derogatory in referring to those cultures unaffected by the modernity of Western civilization, one must remember that, for all of his progressive thinking, Chamberlain remained tied to the vocabulary of his era. While different terminology may be used by professionals in the field of anthropology today, the present author will assume that 'primitive' to Chamberlain connoted, "of or pertaining to a race, group, etc., having cultural or physical similarities with their early ancestors" (as defined in the Random House College Dictionary, 1980). Use of this word to convey a negative value judgment would have been inconsistent with Chamberlain's pronounced views.

Chamberlain did more than commend others for raising issues of race and gender equality. He himself wrote at length upon these topics. In protest to those men[5] who refused to believe that "the Negro has done anything decidedly and recognizably human during the long millenniums of his existence ... " (Chamberlain, 1911, p. 482), wrote a response entitled "The Contribution of the Negro to Human Civilization," (ibid) published in 1911. Chamberlain outlined achievement in areas such as political and social organization, commerce, and the arts, naming not only specific black individuals who played large roles in what had become world history, but also the contributions of black groups in certain parts of the world. While he may have believed that African development was delayed in comparison with European evolution, he did not attribute this to an inherent biological difference (as some do even today). Rather, Chamberlain believed that "differences between races ... depended upon historical opportunity" (Barnes, 1921, p. 215). Therefore, Africa's isolation was responsible for its decelerated development, while Europe's cultures were able to interact more readily. Although it is impossible to blindly accept this aspect of his reasoning, and thereby ignore the modern belief that industrialization does not define development, the following quote from the last paragraph of the same article should make Chamberlain's intentions clear:

> There shall, indeed, come a time when there will be no question of race, and when the loose threads of evolution will be gathered together in the skin of infinite beauty and loveliness. Such things must be. The ideal of the world's hopes is not the domination of so-called "lower" races by "higher," not the "new nationalism," or the "old imperialism," but the humanity that was intended in the beginning and shall be in the end (Chamberlain, 1911, p. 500-501).

Conclusion

The life's work of Alexander Chamberlain encompasses not only the goals of a great teacher, but also those of a great explorer and advocate of human equality. The linguistic, historical, and survey writing he did laid a critical framework for further investigations into numerous cultures across the globe. His ideas about child development served as a symbol for greater human evolution as he synthesized the ideas of many critical thinkers of the time, merging together both the anthropological and psychological research and theory of that era. Above all, Chamberlain was able to view the larger picture, the struggles which different groups (be they racially-, ethnically-, or gender-defined) faced in gaining their own ground, without the oppression of those individuals who, erroneously, thought themselves superior. Chamberlain considered himself to be an ordinary man, generic in the same way that all of humankind is, but he left a scholastic mark which doubtlessly sets him apart.[6]

Notes

1. Previously published in *From Past to Future, Vol. 3*(1), *Passionate Collector: Alexander F. Chamberlain and Child Study*, pp. 1-13. © 2000. Frances L. Hiatt School of Psychology, Clark University. Author: Julia M. Berkman, Department of Psychology, Clark University, 950 Main Street, Worcester, MA.
2. A memorial article written by Albert N. Gilbertson for the *American Anthropologist* shortly after Chamberlain's death serves as the primary source of biographic information on A.F.C.
3. Boas published *Kootenai Tales* in 1918, a book detailing the Kootenai Indian culture and language, which consisted in part upon investigations and writing completed by A.F.C. before his death.
4. As defined by the Random House College Dictionary (1980).
5. Chamberlain actually named some of these men in his article: Mr. Thomas Dixon, Mr. Thomas Watson, and Professor W. B. Smith.
6. Many thanks to Jaan Valsiner, whose guidance and comments on earlier versions of this paper were invaluable.

References

Barnes, H. E. (1921). Some contributions of American psychology to modern social and political theory. *Sociological Review, 13*, 204-227.

Boas, F. (1888). Chinook songs. *Journal of American Folklore, 1*, 220-226.
Boas, F. (1889). On alternating sounds. *The American Anthropologist, 2*, 47-53.
Boas, F. (1891). Dissemination of tales among the natives of North America. *Journal of American Folklore, 4*, 13-20.
Boas, F. (1896). [Review of the book *The child and childhood in folk-thought*.] *Science*, n.s., *6*, 741-742.
Boas, F. (1918). *Kutenai tales*. Smithsonian Institution, Bureau of American Ethnology, Bulletin 59.
Boas, F. (1927). *Primitive art*. (Instituttet for Sammenlignende Kulturforskning, Series B, Vol. 8). Cambridge, MA: H. Aschehoug and Co.
Brinton, D. (1896). [Review of the book *The child and childhood in folk-thought*.] *Science, n.s., 6*, 483-484.
Chamberlain, A. F. (1888a). Notes on the history, customs and beliefs of the Mississagua Indians, *Journal of American Folklore, 2*, 150-160.
Chamberlain, A. F. (1888b). Tales of the Mississagas. *Journal of American Folklore, 1*, 141-147.
Chamberlain, A. F. (1889). Algonkian onomatology, with some comparisons with Basque. *Proceedings of the American Association for the Advancement of Science, 38*, 351-353.
Chamberlain, A. F. (1890). Notes on Indian child language. *American Anthropologist, 3*, 237-241.
Chamberlain, A. F. (1892). *The Language of the Mississaga Indians of Skugog*. Philadelphia, PA: Press of MacCalla and Company.
Chamberlain, A. F. (1895). *The child and childhood in folk-thought*. New York, NY: MacMillan and Co.
Chamberlain, A. F. (1897). The mythology and folklore of invention. *Journal of American Folklore, 10*(37), 89-100.
Chamberlain, A. F. (1899). Anthropology. In *Clark University 1889-1899 Decennial Celebration* (pp. 148-160). Worcester, MA: Clark University.
Chamberlain, A. F. (1900). *The child: A study in the evolution of man*. New York, NY: Charles Scribner's Sons.
Chamberlain, A. F. (1901a). Translation: A study in the transference of folk-thought. *Journal of American Folklore, 14*, 165-171.
Chamberlain, A. F. (1901b). Kootenay group-drawings. *American Anthropologist, 3*, 248-256.
Chamberlain, A. F. (1901c). Kootenay "Medicine-Men." *Journal of American Folklore, 14*, 95-99.
Chamberlain, A. F. (1901d). [Review of the book *The structure of the Koko-Yimidir language*.] *American Anthropologist, 3*, 756-757.
Chamberlain, A. F. (1902a). The contact of "higher" and "lower" races. *Pedagogical Seminary, 9*, 507-520.
Chamberlain, A. F. (1902b). Algonkian words in American English: A study in the contact of the White man and the Indian. *Journal of American Folklore, 15*, 240-267.
Chamberlain, A. F. (1911). The contribution of the Negro to human civilization. *Journal of Race Development, 1*, 482-502.
Chamberlain, A. F. and Chamberlain, I. C. (1904a). Studies of a child - I. *The Pedagogical Seminary, 11*, 264-291.
Chamberlain, A. F. and Chamberlain, I. C. (1904b). Studies of a child - II. *The Pedagogical Seminary, 11*, 452-507.
Chamberlain, A. F. and Chamberlain, I. C. (1905). Studies of a child - III. *The Pedagogical Seminary, 12*, 427-453.

Gilbertson, A. N. (1914). In memoriam: Alexander Francis Chamberlain. *American Anthropologist, 16*, 336-348.

Herskovits, M. J. (1973). *Franz Boas: The science of man in the making.* Clifton, NJ: Augustus M. Kelly.

Hyatt, M. (1990). *Franz Boas, social activist: The dynamics of ethnicity.* New York, NY: Greenwood Press.

Ross, D. (1972). *G. Stanley Hall: The psychologist as prophet.* Chicago, IL: The University of Chicago Press.

White, S. (1990). Child Study at Clark University: 1894-1904. *Journal of the History of the Behavioral Sciences, 26*, 131-150.

White, S. (1992). G. Stanley Hall: From Philosophy to Developmental Psychology. *Developmental Psychology, 28*(1), 25-34.

10

The Fate of the Forgotten: Chamberlain's Work Reconsidered

Jaan Valsiner[1]

Both anthropology and cultural psychology keep up the idea that human beings are social. That notion of the social nature of the human psyche has been a general social representation that has at times organized psychologists' thinking, then disappeared, and later re-appeared as if it were a new idea (Valsiner and van der Veer, 2000). Thus, when the areas of socio-cultural studies (Wertsch, del Río and Alvarez, 1995) or cultural psychology (Cole, 1996; Shweder, 1990) were distinguished by their respective labels at the end of the twentieth century, they merely restored the focus of psychological research on topics that had already been present previously in the social sciences. It is true that our contemporary intellectual foci are phrased differently from their predecessors—versions of Völkerpsychologie of Wilhelm Wundt, Heyman Steinthal, Moritz Lazarus, or Hermann Paul, or "culture and personality" traditions in anthropology. Yet the object of investigation—person's psychological self-organization through culture—remains shared by past and present of traditions of thought. In that investigation, boundaries between disciplines become irrelevant, while the subject matter of the inquiry takes center stage.

It is the early psychological traditions developed at Clark under the guidance of G. Stanley Hall that constitute a brief episode of such unity of psychology and anthropology in the study of human language in its psychological functions. In that context, the diligent work of Alexander Chamberlain stands out as a major contribution (see Berkman, Chapter 9). His work—despite his recognized status as the first U.S. Ph.D. in anthropology—has been forgotten by both anthropologists and child psychologists. His work is at times mentioned in passing as a part of early "diary studies" of child language (e.g., Ingram, 1989), yet the empirical evidence that he had carefully accumulated has not put to productive use by later generations.

Aside from the usual tendency to forget one's predecessors in science—a kind of consensually approved historical myopia—there are various additional reasons why his work has been underestimated. Chamberlain—if viewed in the jargon of our contemporary social scientists—was deeply "interdisciplinary" in his work. Despite the positive halo of the term in our discussions about social sciences, the realities of social organization of any science entail separation rather than integration. An "interdisciplinary scholar" has the benefits of being *knowledgeable about* the different disciplines, yet need not be *known in* any of them. Chamberlain's work took place in parallel in anthropology and in developmental psychology under the interdisciplinary emphasis of "child study" as set up by G. Stanley Hall. Hall's efforts were given relatively superficial review later, while his complex character has been dissected in the writing of psychology's history (Ross, 1972). The remembering of Chamberlain seems to have vanished into oblivion together with that of the rest of Hall's army of co-workers in the "child study" area. Finally, some aspects of Chamberlain's own ways of thinking and presenting his work (as will be shown below) may have contributed to the collective forgetfulness.

Hall made child study the distinctive feature of the "Clark tradition" of psychology. Largely through that, Clark University in the beginning of the twentieth century became the leading U.S. center for psychology. Even if anthropology was at first an important component of psychology at Clark,[2] it slowly disappeared from the academic realm within the University. Chamberlain's work constituted both the beginning and the end of the (miniscule) "Clark tradition" in anthropology.

Beginnings of Cultural Anthropology

The general picture of the emerging anthropology of the 1890s is one that is similar to the natural sciences as known through the ways in which Charles Darwin moved towards his system of evolution. It entailed meticulous collection and preservation of specimens from different places in the World, and careful thinking about what theoretical constructs can be used to see the unity in this natural diversity. The beginnings of anthropology as a separate discipline in the United States were characterized by a number of features.

First, there was a very close connection between the studies of folklore and the new emerging anthropology. The first anthropologists were careful collectors of folklore texts. The work on folklore texts usually followed the standards of meticulous collectors of valuable treasures. Second, the focus on folklore and the general European-based cultural education allowed the early researchers to combine ideas from Shakespeare with those of any American Indian tribe. The study of cultures was not limited to the target society, but drawn freely from all historical and literary texts from all over the World. Third, the branches of physical and cultural anthropology were still united within the same whole—the same anthropologists would be active in both the cultural and physical realms of the discipline. This made it possible for the same researchers to address issues of anthropometry, folklore, religious beliefs, and activity practices of their target culture.

The emerging anthropology in the U.S. was a universalist science that was aimed at general knowledge about the cultural nature of humankind based on the empirical variability of specific collections. It even subsumed psychology within it. Daniel Brinton suggested the following general scheme of nomenclature of anthropology as a general science of human beings:

I. Somatology: Physical and experimental anthropology
    A. Internal somatology (study of body's internal organs)
    B. External somatology (anthropometry, color, hair, canons of proportions, etc.)
    C. Psychology—experimental and practical
    D. Developmental and comparative somatology (embryology, teratology, human biology, medical geography, vital statistics, etc.)
II. Ethnology: Historical and analytic anthropology
    A. Definitions and methods: stages of culture, ethnic psychology, etc.
    B. Sociology: governments, marriage relations, laws, institutions.
    C. Technology: utilitarian and the fine arts.
    D. Science of religion: primitive religions, mythology, symbolism, religious arts, etc.
    E. Linguistics: gestures and sign language, spoken and written language.
    F. Folklore
III. Ethnography: Geographic and descriptive anthropology
IV. Archaeology: Prehistoric and reconstructive anthropology
(Brinton, 1892, pp. 265-266)

As can be seen from this general nomenclature, the science of anthropology was meant to be an interdisciplinary synthesis. Now, a century later, the discussion about the need for "interdisciplinarity" is in the focus of attention again.

Such discussions at the end of the nineteenth century had an advantage over the ones in our time. Both anthropology and psychology were then in their stage of formation; their institutional power structures were not yet in place. For example, in an effort to define his discipline, Franz Boas claimed anthropology to be a part of a larger inter-disciplinary quest of knowledge about human beings. In his vision:

> ...a separation of anthropological methods from the methods of biology and psychology is impossible, and ... certain problems of anthropology can be approached only from the point of view of these sciences. ... If there are any laws determining the growth and development of the human mind, they can be only laws that act in the individual, and consequently they must be determined by the application of individual psychology (Boas, 1908, p. 6).

The research that Alexander Chamberlain established within the realm of G. Stanley Hall's empire of child study in the 1890s deserves a closer analysis as an example of just such a *de facto* attempt at integration. Notably, the relationship between psychology and anthropology at Clark was the reverse of that indicated in Brinton's nomenclature. Anthropology was part of psychology, and psychology in itself developed within the still wider context of *paedology*, or "child study."

The Goals of "Child Study": Morality Through Hygiene and Education

It is a curious question why children need to be singled out as objects of a special study and why a whole discipline was built around it in the 1880s and 1890s. An answer to this question necessarily needs to begin from the social demands for explicated—publicly disputable—knowledge during that historical period. The social context of late nineteenth century highlighted socio-moral issues of the new generation in an effort to maintain control over these issues through knowledge. Knowledge is a kind of social power—and when a new "social problem domain" becomes highlighted through social construction of it as "problematic," the quest for knowledge may get a boost.

The history of psychology, as well as that of "child study," is certainly intertwined with the texture of society. The social history of the child study movement in the United States has been well-documented (Siegel and White, 1982; White, 1990; Wiltse, 1894). The term ***paedology*** (or ***paidology***, as it was originally labeled) was established in the United States (in 1893—Chrisman, 1920, p. 7). In an early piece of writing on the history of the child study movement, Sara Wiltse commented:

> While the work of child study did not, perhaps, absolutely originate in this country, the foreign initiative was extremely slight. Darwin and Lazarus had indeed made their studies; Preyer had begun the publication of some of his observations before the years 1879 and 1880, when the work in this country began. In fact, child study is, in a peculiar sense, American. Not only has more been done in this country than in all of the world besides, but it seems the *instinct of our people is to take a fresh, independent look at primal facts of human nature and at growth itself* (Wiltse, 1894, p. 190, added emphasis).

That "peculiar sense" of the "instinct" for a "fresh look" stems from the specific cultural history of the United States, where religious and secular beliefs, group conformity and individualism (see Mead, 1930), moralism as well as free-thinking have established a complex set of social representations of the role of the child in a society.

The role of G. Stanley Hall in the organization of that movement in the 1890s and 1900s was formidable. Yet the movement itself emerged before he took over its control and directed it towards the educational philosophies of his preference (Ross, 1972, chapter 15). It was the context of the history of U.S. society in the latter decades of the nineteenth century—especially the tensions brought forth by urbanization and the move towards religious liberalization—that made the issue of the nature and education of children salient for societal discourse. That discourse had obvious overlay from the moralistic (religious) value system that surrounded it.

In the transitional culture in which Hall lived, the new standards of health and disease bore some of the same burden as the old standards of virtue and vice. The pervasive danger of disease and deviation which Hall and his colleagues pictured hanging over the younger generation had something to it of the old fear of sin (Ross, 1972, p. 295).

In the development of the child study movement as an ideology of practical suggestions for American education one can observe the intricate relationship between liberalizing religion and bureaucratizing education.

G. Stanley Hall's Quest

The questions of healthy ways of living—and bringing up children—became a moral imperative for the "child study" movement. The meaning of "healthy," beyond freedom from diseases, could be open to various interpretations. As such, it became an ideological football field for various value-based "teams" and their active crowds of spectators. Even in a closer literal sense, Hall turned the cultivation of the body into a socio-moral goal—reminiscent of the dieting and exercise calls of our time.

The human body and its powers has certainly been one of the main objects of the cultural organization of the human psyche. The movement of child study brought out into the realm of education simultaneously the focus on what children *are like* (i.e., the study focus), and the moralistic utopia of the end of the nineteenth century U.S. of what the children *should be like*, under the conditions of speedy social transformation of the U.S. society. Hall's liberalized theology, mixed with the general acceptance of the biogenetic law of Haeckel, and with his own personal embracing of the burgeoning sexualities of adolescents made the child study at Clark a unique venture.

Anthropology and Child Study

The anthropological direction that Franz Boas and Alexander Chamberlain brought to Clark in the early 1890s fitted very well into the bigger picture of Hall's child study initiative (Ross, 1972). Both anthropology and child study were to be synthetic, integrative sciences. For Hall's version of child study at Clark—which was the main center in North America for that study area—the anthropological knowledge about customs of child-care, education, and beliefs of parents in different societies provided a valuable background for the immediate concerns of educational kind.

The anthropological focus in Hall's child study movement was there from the very beginning, when Franz Boas and Alexander Chamberlain came to Clark (see Berkman, Chapter 9). It contained both the physical and cultural anthropology divisions. Within the first, it led to the first North American anthropometry project. At Boas' initiation, Chamberlain and a number of other fellows were involved in the locally notorious[3] measuring of the bodies of Worcester school children in 1890-1892 (see Tanner, 1959)[4]. That project also fitted the nature of study of large groups of persons within the population. The anthropometry project was from the beginning conceived as international; in the summer of 1891 researchers from Clark were measuring the bodies of North American Indians in Quebec, Ontario, British Columbia, Alaska, Labrador, Dakota, New Mexico, Yucatan, and other places (Chamberlain, 1899c, p. 149).

Being a scholar of folklore entailed collection of different anthropological materials: beliefs, artifacts, and stories from all over the world. This was the social sciences' equivalent of Darwinian natural science. The Boas/Chamberlain tradition fitted well into the inductive scheme of the natural science, where the variation in the specimens from different locations can be used to reconstruct the cultural history of humankind. Yet it was in conjunction with the failure of Hall—and of the University in general—to provide Boas with sufficient time for his fieldwork that the latter decided to leave his position at Clark. Chamberlain remained behind, and took over Boas' role as the anthropological pillar of the child study program. As such, he did not challenge Hall's leadership role in that movement, while providing the needed comparative-cultural breadth.

The Chamberlains and Child Study

In line with his claims for the equality of men and women (see below) and as a concrete example of the collective nature of research, the empirical study of a child that Alexander Chamberlain made constituted a joint project with his wife, Isabel Cushman Chamberlain (see Berkman, this book). Isabel Chamberlain was a folklorist of high quality like her husband (e.g., see I. Chamberlain, 1900). Their joint work exemplified Alexander Chamberlain's egalitarian life philosophy in practice.

In an explicit elaboration of the role ethnology plays in Hall's child study research project, Chamberlain likened it to the "natural laboratory" of human cultural history:

> Besides the anthropometric and psycho-physical investigations of the child carried on in the scientific laboratory with exact instruments and unexceptionable methods, there is another field of "Child-Study" well worthy our attention for the light it can shed upon some of the dark places in the wide expanse of pedagogical science and the art of education.
>
> Its laboratory of research has been the whole wide world, the experimenters and recorders the primitive peoples of all races and all centuries,—fathers and mothers

whom the wonderland of parenthood encompassed and entranced; the subjects, the children of all generations of mankind (Chamberlain, 1896a, p. 5).

The practice of folklore study within the child study movement took the form of careful collection and organization of ethnological materials from all available sources of the time—including the collections of North American Indians that Chamberlain himself, and Boas, had obtained.

As was the case with many child study enthusiasts, Chamberlain's own observations of children began with the parenting role of his own child. The reports—meticulous descriptions of a child's developing construction in speech (Chamberlain and Chamberlain, 1904a, 1904b), their understanding of meanings (Chamberlain and Chamberlain, 1909), and description of activities (Chamberlain and Chamberlain, 1905) as well as reports on dreams (Chamberlain and Chamberlain, 1906) were all extensions of the folklorist's collecting desire to the realm of child's life.

The informant (or—research participant) in their study was their daughter Ruth (born August, 3, 1901). It is noteworthy that the Chamberlains' accounts of their child's development concentrated on the issue of language use in everyday life contexts, around ages three and four years. The issue of child language interested Chamberlain already long before he had a chance to observe its development on his own child—in one of his first publications (Chamberlain, 1890a) he summarized different examples of American Indian languages focusing on the expressions used by children in different settings.

In their clear researcher stance as naturalists (in the field of developing child), the Chamberlains introduced their series of child observations, by claiming:

> The data here presented have been obtained and recorded with due care and precision, and *in no case has theory been allowed to twist facts*. The sections on spontaneous word-forming and spontaneous language are believed to contain some new and interesting data, *which may contribute somewhat* to the solution of the problems of "invention" in child's speech (Chamberlain and Chamberlain, 1904a, p. 264, added italics).

In a characteristic Chamberlainian twist, the declarative overstatement (about theories) and understatement (about the relevance of their data) go hand in hand here. It reflects the author's modesty (see Berkman, this book), yet in our retrospect it becomes clear that a collector need not trust others to do the hard work of integrating the knowledge made possible by the careful collection effort. All forward-oriented statements in a discipline are predictions with no guarantees, and the "default value" of the reliance upon other scholars of the future is to be forgotten. It is only in the circumscribed knowledge domain of the "history of psychology" that one may rediscover long-lost data. Yet the historian has one's own focus, and aside from highlighting some work from the past for the present readers, might not change the historical myopia of the research enterprise of the given science.

There can be explicit benefits for contemporary science to consider earlier collections of materials. A careful reading of Chamberlains' observations reveals that the description of Ruth's language use was documented in meticulous detail even in areas that our contemporary child language researchers might give up. This documentation entailed both naturalistic observations of Ruth's language use in everyday contexts and specific sessions of questioning about meanings. The latter were accomplished by recording her answers to questions of the form "What is [word depicting something] for?" when she was two years ten months (Chamberlain and Chamberlain, 1904a, p. 271) and again at three years three weeks (Chamberlain and Chamberlain, 1904b). When she was almost four years—and while she was "innocent as yet of day and of Sunday school," the interview question was changed to "What does ____ mean?" (Chamberlain and Chamberlain, 1909, p. 64). The latter testing was extensive (including 1,185 words, tested over twenty-four days in July 1905). The Chamberlains were really after charting out the full dictionary of Ruth's meanings. In contrast, the earlier testing included only 100 (Chamberlain and Chamberlain, 1904a) and 106 words (Chamberlain and Chamberlain, 1904b, pp. 458-460).

Inventiveness in Speech

The construction of novel speech forms occurred largely in the context of the situated activities that Ruth experienced in her daily life. Those included participation in many verbal interactions: being read to by parents, pretending to read a book by herself, singing and being sung to. Like most other observers of child language development, the Chamberlains noted the constructive creativity of the child's word invention and extensions in meanings. Yet the crucial domain of development that was described entailed the move to story creation.

The parents-researchers made use of the spontaneously occurring contexts, turning a child-initiated event spontaneously into a probe of the child's construction of language use. Thus, on March 4, 1904, Ruth spontaneously began telling a story to her mother, who recorded it, and asked her to tell another one. As a result, seven stories were produced (No. 1 spontaneously, the others prompted by the mother):

1. Once upon a time there wuz a efful (elephant). A great big efful and a little efful. The little efful was climbing on the big efful's tummy (stomach). And they began to ting, Dooley-ooley. And they began to drow (grow) a *long-long* trunk out in tront (front).
2. Once upon a time there wuz a titty out in ze back zhard. There wuz two titties, a big titty an a little titty. And the little titty wuz climbing on the ozzer one's head. And they bedan to sing, Doy-oy-oy.
3. Once upon a time there was a black tat (cat) from Bayville. He jumped around all the trees. Dess (guess) he broken a tree.

4. Once upon a time there wuz anuzzer black tat. He lived down to Bayville. I dess he didn't broken a tree.
5. Once upon a time there wuz a black tiger. And he bedan to try (cry). And he climbed up in a tree and taid, wasn't that a dood tiger? And then he ran home to tind (find) his mama and his tater (father), and Helen. And he tat in a chair, and Helen taid, Who is zat?
6. Once upon a time there was a *leopard*! And a piger. [Here her mother asked, What is a piger?] A piger is a dog. And he bedan to tind their mother in their own home and their tather.
7. Once upon a time there wuz tcheep (sheep), wight (right) in the middle. And anuzzer tcheep. And they bedan to tick (kick) up their teet an tay tiddlee-dee. There wuz anuzzer black tcheep tat up in a tree an tay tiddle-dee-dee. (Chamberlain and Chamberlain, 1904b, pp. 281-282)

This description of consecutive reconstruction of a story antedates the classic work of Frederick Bartlett by two decades (Bartlett, 1920). The development of a holistic constructed matrix of the story—filled in by changing characters (elephant—kitty—cat—cat—tiger—leopard—sheep), and activities becomes evident in this sequence.

Knowledge of Things and Meanings

It is trivial to state that our (adult researchers') knowledge about children's minds is limited to interpreting their communication efforts; as well as their actions. Access to children's spontaneous display of knowledge is certainly the highest for those adults who share the children's life environments. Thus, parents as researchers—or "baby biographers"—have advantage over those researchers who pay cursory visits to children's environments and are assigned the social role of guests.

> *Skeleton.* On April 7, 1904, she picked up an archaeological pamphlet, opening it at a page containing a picture of a skeleton lying in a grave. She exclaimed at once: "Like zose at nuwersity!" About a month before, she had been taken by her father to his room in the University, where were several mounted skeletons of infants (Chamberlain and Chamberlain, 1904a, p. 268).

Obviously it takes the "insider's knowledge" that parents as child observers can provide to be able to interpret the child's linkages of the here-and-now experiences with those of the past.

Language Used as a Tool in Activity Contexts

The Chamberlains documented Ruth's narrations of stories that substantiated ongoing actions. For example:

While at the dinner table on March 28, 1904, Ruth said "I want to eat this, so a leopard won't det it." Her father asked her if she was afraid of a leopard, to which she replied no. He then asked her if she had seen a leopard, whereupon she said "no," but continued "I did see a tiger this months." In answer to the question, where? She replied, "In a tore" (store). When asked what the tiger was doing, she said,

"Buying tometin to' his mother." On the evening of the same day at the tea-table the tiger came up again. Her father asked her if she was afraid of a tiger. She answered "no," whereupon her father said, "take father's hand, and let's go find the tiger." She acceded readily enough, and although the sitting-room was not at all well-lighted, crawled up to the sofa and stuck her head under to see if the tiger was there. Then she said she had the tiger in her hand and brought it into the kitchen. Finally she found her mother's bag and put the tiger into that, bringing him again into the kitchen and dining-room (Chamberlain and Chamberlain, 1904a, pp. 274-275).

This episode was preceded some five months before by an episode of scared of the dark—substantiated by the idea that "there is a tiger" in the back yard. The episode itself can be considered an example of "genetic dramatism" (Cirillo and Kaplan, 1983). The confabulation of a new story is what substantiates ongoing action ("finding' the 'tiger'"). The child's construction—obviously with the support of the parents—was shown also to include the creation of new holistic speech flows, or "new languages."

The Child as Language Inventor: From "Chinese" to "Skov'n"

The question of children's inventiveness in creating whole new communicative systems interested Chamberlain already from the very beginning of his anthropological investigations.[5] Thus the emergence of such "new languages" right at home was a rewarding birth of the phenomenon. Ruth's invention of her own language is described (and transcribed) in detail resembling anthropologists' presentation of aboriginal languages at the time.

Ruth moved from a phase of inventing names for her scribbles and toys (at two years eight months/ two years nine months of age) to creating a "language of her own" (which her father labeled "Chinese"—a name that the daughter accepted). She would use meta-language markers in switching between English and "Chinese" (e.g., by declaring to her father "Tather, I want to talk Chinese"—Chamberlain and Chamberlain, 1904a, p. 284). As an example:

On May 25, 1904, she said to her father "I want to talk Chinese." And, pretending to "read" from Fiske's "History of the United States" for schools, delivered herself a long talk of which he was able to record the following:

Romlin maswa wasma mamin pamblin doosin preerlam rosin hasin tooli. O madrin noofri tomatlin tindlins. O bafres omlin toofres disin dalrin dalrin toosin. Memli cawsun tosin. Babri batlin toosin toosin pelbrin tamidawsin. Bambin toosin hemblin toosin toonding goosin. Amlantin tatrin balintoodrin goodrin avan jaisli. Pamlin deedee tree peerin deezin chai whosin jeesin bopres in tees. Pwasrain cawsin mbrasin wosin. Tambli shamplus. Desden doling dadza dadza. Bafron hamlin toosin hoosin dawsin. Dewsin bamin primlin toos. Waslin toomin pemlin tomlin tusin (Chamberlain and Chamberlain, 1904a, p. 285).

This (and similar) excerpts from Ruth's language invention led the Chamberlains to view language construction as a kind of "intermediate gestalt" (in terms of Friedrich Sander's notion of microgenesis—see Valsiner and Van der Veer, 2000, chapter 7). Thus, they viewed Ruth's "Chinese" as:

... a sort of matrix from which an inflected language could, perhaps, with no great difficulty be shaped. Its exact relation to her own English speech cannot be absolutely determined, but it is safe to say that few of the characteristic "words" of her "Chinese" seem to be derived from or connected with her usual speech-forms (Chamberlain and Chamberlain, 1904a, p. 288).

The child's language invention went even further. On September 9, 1904, the parents noticed a change in Ruth's use of "Chinese":

Shov an ov gov an ov. Jov an nov kow ka. Skov an jov an nov. Skov an ov an jov'nov'n. Skov'n nov an jov'n joltin an bov a log. Kov an jov an nov. Jov en nov an nik an jons. Skun nov an gog an gains. Kog an gog an kosh an dawlin. Skov an jov an nov an jov. Gov an yov an nokut bov an jawbun. Gov an nol an chaufun nawl an bob an nog. Gok an gok an gok an gatin. O kus gov'n nov. Skov'n nov an jon. Skov'n nov an non. Skov'n vu an nov'n jods (Chamberlain and Chamberlain, 1904b, pp. 477-478).

When asked whether she was speaking "Chinese," Ruth replied, "No! it's skov'n." This "new language" was built around the "o" (in contrast with the "Chinese" which had no univocalism in it). Furthermore, as the parents observed Ruth was "almost singing" the "skov'n."

The fact that children produce long strings of vocal production from their babbling period (second half of the first life-year) onwards is no news for child researchers. However, few of them (e.g., Weir, 1962) have attempted to transcribe and analyze the phonemic content of these long vocalization strings. Chamberlain's work on different American Indian language transcription surely made him a fitting observer of such strings. A further interesting moment in these observations is the child's meta-knowledge—the new invented language is explicitly re-named (no more "Chinese" but "skov'n").

The conscious move from one language (English) to the first invented one, and further to a third one, provides evidence for the child's construction of ***generative platforms*** for alternative sign systems. Once a previous platform becomes shifted into anew form (such as the "o-language" of the "skov'n"), generativity of the actual vocal production can explode instantly. Surely which new generative platforms can emerge depends upon the previously established ones, and on language teaching. In that respect, Chamberlain adamantly supported the natural sequence of development of generative platforms. In his devastating criticism of the ways English was taught, at his time, in schools (Chamberlain, 1902c) he pointed to the futility of connecting it with Latin and Greek, and called for the "full use" being used of the "evolutionary aspect of English" (p. 165). That evolutionary aspect can be viewed as a language-historical emergence of new generative platforms—surely a result of new challenges to the language users.

Role of Culture Contact

Challenges for emergence of new generative language platforms are most likely wrought thanks to needs to communicate differently from the usual, established patterns. Communication between people of different language backgrounds—or what is often labeled "culture contact"—would create such necessity. In the history of the North American aboriginal languages it was their mutual encounters – warfare and trade—that facilitated the transfer of knowledge through the repeated themes of myths as well as the development of new generative language platforms. The enforced culture contact by the acts of colonization added further necessities for development of communicative systems. When the European traders and other functionaries reached the territories of (our present-day) Oregon and Washington State, they were confronted with a myriad of aboriginal languages. As a solution to the task of communication, a *lingua franca*—a new version of the Chinook language—developed (see Boas, 1888). It was a jargon consisting of English, French, Chinook (in its aboriginal version), Nutka and Sahapatin words. A similar history can be charted for the *pidgin English* in the Pacific.

The primacy of the "situated activity contexts"—the jargon widespread in the socio-cultural studies of our present time—for language uses was obvious for the pioneers of the "culture contact" with the American aboriginal people. Of course these pioneers enforced *their* form of such contact by the power of might and persuasion. Drawing or forcing the aborigines into "situated activity contexts," such as Christian religious services, led to introduction of new words into the Amerindian languages. Chamberlain's interest in the construction of meanings in different languages led him to analyze Bible translation nuances into these languages. Largely based on the work of others (e.g., Baraga's *A Grammar and Dictionary of the Ojibwa language*, 1878) Chamberlain paid attention to the differences in the agent/recipient relationship in the translation context of "salute to Holy Mary." Translation of Bible stories encountered language complications. For the Ojibwa, two versions of salute were differentiated:

Anamikãgewin = salute as **given by**
[somebody, e.g. Holy Mary]
Anamikãgowin = salute as **received by**
[somebody e.g. Holy Mary]

Aside from forcing any Bible translator to ponder upon the vagueness of the English language, such semantic differentiations in Amerindian languages indicate the necessity of being clear about who acts upon whom, and with what results. As Chamberlain (1901b, p. 168) indicated, the taken-for-granted Christian concept of the *amor Dei* in Latin forces the translator into Nahuatl (Aztec) to specify whether "somebody's love towards God" or "God's love towards somebody" is being meant. Simpler distinctions are possible on the basis of verification based on observable behavior—the Ojibwa notion of "Christian"—*enamiad*—means "one who prays" (versus pagan—*enamiassig*—"one who does not pray," ibid., p. 169).

The "Primitives"

In line with respecting the mutual historical enrichment between languages, Chamberlain was ethically opposed to the efforts to eradicate the cultural traditions of different aboriginal societies for the general goal of "melting" them down into the dominant Anglo-Saxon societies (see Berkman, Chapter 9). His rhetorical equivalence:

"educating primitives" = "killing children"

would obviously insult many a dedicated educationalist of that time (as well as our own), who was dedicated to the goal of "bringing" the American Indian children "up to the standards" of the "civilized" society. Yet the warlike orientation can be traced in the rhetoric of some of such fighters for cultural assimilation. For example, a statement describing the missionary fervent of a school district administrator in the U.S. from the end of nineteenth century Oklahoma illustrates the ideology of warlike intervention. Talking of educating American Indian children, a local school administrator suggested:

> If we propose [sic] to educate Indian children, let us educate them all. If we look to the schools as one of the chief factors of the great transformation, why not establish at once to embrace the entire body of available Indian youth? ... If there could be gathered by the end of 1893 ... nearly all of the Indian children and they be kept there for ten years, the work would be substantially accomplished; for ... there would grow up a generation of English speaking Indians, accustomed to the ways of civilized life. ... Forever after this [they will be] the ... dominant force among them (Ellis, 1996, p. 15).

This kind of attitude towards the native inhabitants of North America was precisely the target for Chamberlain's anti-war campaign. He understood the basic nature of education: its **violence through opportunities**. Introduction of any new form of education is necessarily an act of violence in relation to the previous state of affairs, while undoubtedly it opens up a set of new opportunities for the newly educated persons.

Chamberlain's comparison of education of the aborigines with war against children had another extension. He disliked war as much as he reproached alcohol:

> War is like alcohol. Its glow is followed by a dangerous refrigeration of the social organism. Like alcohol, war stimulates for the moment, giving a false sense of exhilaration, but, as is the case with alcohol in the system of the individual, this brief and temporary exaltation is followed by a much longer period of depression which is often of the greatest possible danger. The medicine, indeed, is worse than the disease. The after-effects of the war more than cancel its immediate seeming benefits (Chamberlain, 1902a, p. 510).

Of course nice metaphors do not change social realities. Introduction of formal education is the best equivalent of gaining control over the minds of the conquered people—yet it need not remain permanent. In any new generation, based on the transposition of the unofficial history of the ethnic group (Wertsch, 1998), revitalization of the seemingly eradicated aspects of ethnic identity can be re-born. Meanings once lost can be reconstructed, and the preservation of oral literary traditions in that process is substantial in creating that basis for renewed meaning construction.

Construction of Cultural Tools

Chamberlain's collector's habits led him to the discovery of very early descriptions of the invention of semiotic devices by American Indians, as he referenced a French missionary describing the process in 1655:

> ... Our Lord inspired me with that method the second year of my mission, when, being greatly embarrassed as to the mode in which I should teach the Indians to pray, I noticed some children making marks on birch-bark with coal, and they pointed to them with their fingers at every word of the prayer which they pronounced. This made me think that, by giving them some form which would aid their memory by fixed characters, I should advance much more rapidly than by teaching on the plan of making them repeat over what I said (quoted in Chamberlain, 1906, pp. 69-70).

This may be one of the early elaborate descriptions of both of the "stimulus-means" role of written signs (in the sense of Lev Vygotsky—see Van der Veer and Valsiner, 1991). Chamberlain brought to his readership the summary of the efforts of providing different American Indian groups with written versions of their languages. Literacy was surely the beneficial effect of the White-Indian culture contact. Furthermore, encounters with new objects—brought in through such culture contacts—lead the development of the languages since these objects become named. Chamberlain traced the different ways in which American Indians named the elephant—an animal foreign to North America, who was made available through traveling circuses, pictures in books, etc. The

Cherokee called the elephant "great butterfly" (because of the ears resembling the wings), the Micmac term translated as "a sea cow," and the Ojibwa—"great pig" (Chamberlain, 1907, p. 443). In contrast to an elephant, objects linked with the activities of Catholic missionaries were more difficult to render. For example, the clear notion of the Pope in the Ojibwa language has been rendered as "first-chief-great-black-robed"—in contrast to a regular priest, "the black-robed" (Chamberlain, 1901b, p. 171). The use of analogical reasoning allows different language users to create names for the same object in different contexts of known objects. In the mode of reverse innovations, Chamberlain (1902b) showed how American English has benefited from loans from various American Indian languages.

The Solemn Nature of Language

Behind the collector's mind was that of a poet. It is not coincidental that Chamberlain selected an epigraph from Oliver Wendell Holmes for the front page of his doctoral dissertation:

> Language is a solemn thing; it grows out of life—out of its agonies and ecstasies, its wants and its weariness. Every language is a temple, in which the soul of those who speak it is enshrined (Chamberlain, 1892b, p. 0).

Chamberlain was himself a poet of distinction,[6] and in his presentation of ethnographic evidence the theme of poetry was considered the highest level of human psychological functioning. He demonstrated that that highest level was present among American aborigines (Native Indians—see Chamberlain, 1896b) and women (Chamberlain, 1903a). The role of language for him was basic for human psychological life:

> There are two aspects of the poetry of speech, poetry of thought and poetry of sound—the word that *epitomizes an epic*, and the word that *embryonizes a symphony*. (Chamberlain, 1896b, p. 43, added emphases)

One can see parallels here with an effort, decades later, to capture the language-based complexity through the notion of "genetic dramatism" (see above, and also in Kaplan, 1983). Kaplan's focus on the latter as the "*idealization of the actual*" could encompass both the epitomizing and embryonizing sides of the word in Chamberlain's thinking.

History of Language

Chamberlain supported the idea of the emergence of human language in history as a result of singing that accompanied rhythmic action—Chamberlain relied upon Bücher's (1899) ***Work and rhythm*** (Chamberlain, 1903a, p. 219). The gender division of different activities—among which child-caring and food preparations historically belonged to women's social roles—led to gender differences in the orientation to singing, and poetry. As Chamberlain, in his characteristic brief inserts of basic ideas into elaborate presentations of ethnographic evidence, remarked:

> To the mother beside the cradle, where lies her tender offspring, song comes as natural as speech itself to man (Chamberlain, 1903a, p. 205).

Earlier in his course of studies, Chamberlain had claimed, following Raoul de la Grasserie, that an evolutionary process was involved in the making of the grammatical gender in human languages. That early hypothesis was basically a differentiation idea encoded into the assumed history of everyday life practices of men and women:

> Man first distinguished the *ego* and the *non-ego*, and along with this the *like-me* and *unlike-me*. Then he separated the animate and the inanimate into two great groups, himself included in the first. The next step was to discover the rationalistic distinction between himself and other and the other animals; this led to his esteeming himself higher in dignity and intelligence to woman, and again to a distinction based upon the degree of intensity and vitality which finally led up to the differentiation of masculine and feminine (Chamberlain, 1890b, p. 5).

Phylogenetic speculation as it was, it must have fitted well with G. Stanley Hall's evolutionary discourse at the beginning of Chamberlain's move to Clark. At the same time, behind the question of grammatical gender is of course the question of social gender.

Inventions and Language

The relevance of words in the making of new experiences (in his terms—**embryonizing of the symphony**) found its way into a number of research *foci* of Chamberlain's. As was shown above, child's inventiveness in the process of speaking fascinated Chamberlain in his day-to-day encounters with his daughter. A similar issue is of crucial value for human cultural history.

Given the history of inventions in the practical lives of people in "primitive societies" how could these technical inventions emerge if the psyche of the "primitive man" was supposed to be closed to novelty? Chamberlain undertook an excursion into the question of how invention occurs in the folk texts of the "primitive people," indicating that the notion of open-ended imitation (á la Gabriel Tarde) is evident in the folktales (Chamberlain, 1897). He analyzed the notions of knowledge (and knowing) in different languages of the "primitive societies" (Chamberlain, 1903b), and provided empirical accounts into new proverbs that were evident in the changing of his contemporary society (Chamberlain, 1904a, 1904b). Chamberlain also took an interest in the ways in which basic emotions—anger (Chamberlain, 1894b) and fear (Chamberlain,

1899b)—are encoded in different languages of the world. That effort antedates the concerns about cultural construction of emotions a hundred years later (Wierzbicka, 1999).

Men and Women

In his treatment of gender differentiation, Chamberlain was adamantly opposed to discrimination (see Berkman, this issue). He found a very innovative solution to the usual question of male/female dominance/sub-dominance. Following the lead of another folklorist of his time, Daniel Brinton,[7] Chamberlain created an intransitive "power cycle" between men and women—utilizing the notion of child (see Valsiner, 1997b on intransitive hierarchies).

In its generic form, that cycle was of the following form:

MEN ARE DIFFERENT FROM WOMEN
WOMEN ARE LIKE CHILDREN
(=men > women and children)
and CHILDREN ARE GOD-LIKE

⇓

GOD-LIKE CREATURES DOMINATE OVER MEN
HENCE:
WOMEN (like children) ARE HIGHER BEINGS THAN MEN

Chamberlain's disdain for dominance of the powerful over the powerless (whites > Indians, adults > children, university president > faculty, etc) was a basic moral stance. At the same time, it was a standpoint informed by the variety of nuances in gender relations that can be observed worldwide.

The Color of the Devil

A crucial object whose characteristics of color could be illuminated by analysis was the Devil:

> ... in the old days the preachers devoted a good deal of their time to the giving of detailed descriptions of the Devil, and the approximation of his form to that of man, and the folklore connected with the various divergences comes quite within our field. With the white races, the Devil is painted black, but we are assured by more than one authority that he is "not so black as he is painted;" indeed, when we reach the Hottentots, we find that their Devil is quite white (Chamberlain, 1893, p. 17).

Folklore gives much evidence for the making of distinctions between the in-group and out-group in terms of projecting some characteristics of "monstrosity" upon the out-group members (Jahoda, 1999). The connections made, that way, between the supernatural malevolent agents and the members of the out-group serve as powerful social-psychological mechanisms of stigmatization (see Thomsen, 1987). The non-self "foreignness" of "the other" have both horrifying and appealing valences to them.

Drawings

Chamberlain collected drawings from the Kootenay during his fieldwork in British Columbia in 1891. Among those were a few which Chamberlain found relevant for a general point. First, were the drawings of Kootenay "medicine men" (see figures 10.1 and 10.2) by an old Upper Kootenay man who, "formerly as a great warrior ... reputed as having been more skillful with the bow and arrow ... than with the pencil to-day" (Chamberlain, 1901d, p. 97). Figure 10.1 represents a "medicine-man" of the Kootenay wearing a special shirt of the shaman, and "horns" that characterize his role. The drawing was completed by the old man in twenty minutes, in Chamberlain's presence, and without any interference or suggestion.

**Figure 10.1
Drawing of a Kootenay "medicine man" (pure case)
(from Chamberlain, 1901d, p. 97).**

Figure 10.2
Drawing of a Kootenay "medicine man" (interference from Christian traditions) (from Chamberlain, 1901d, p. 97).

In contrast, figure 10.2 (drawn by the same informant, in seventeen minutes, under similar conditions) indicated to Chamberlain interference between Kootenay and Christian traditions:

> The artist who drew it said it was another "medicine-man" picture, and did not differentiate it particularly from the other drawing of a shaman. In the left hand is a small cup or basket (?)— ... —containing "medicine" (*awumo*). In the right hand is some other article. The expression of the face, the beard, the outstretched arms, etc., suggest that the Indian has here given us a copy of the figure on the cross or crucifix ... (Chamberlain, 1901d, p. 98).

The mutual interference of traditional and appropriated religious practices can certainly be traced through drawings. At the time of Chamberlain's fieldwork in 1891, it was precisely the Upper Kootenay tribe that was undergoing change due to Catholic missionary efforts.

Drawings also serve as mediating devices between the present and the past. The same old Kootenay warrior drew a picture of the war dance (figure 10.3), being actively involved in memory-work:

While executing this drawing the old Indian's countenance evinced time and again the pleasurability of the recollections it called up. After he had completed his work, Bläswã ... was so affected by the old associations recalled by it that, starting up with the paper in his hand, he danced and yelled for a few minutes to his heart's delight (Chamberlain, 1901c, p. 253).

The fashionable talk in contemporary cultural psychology—in reincarnation of the ideas of Lev Vygotsky—about semiotic mediation of activity could use this drawing event described by Chamberlain as a good example of the power of signs in uniting the past and the present (e.g., see Cole, 1995, figure 3 on p. 38). The uniqueness of this event is exemplified by the general absence of drawings as part of the Kootenay cultural tool-box—thus, the researcher introduced a new medium that was used by the person as a sign-construction device, resulting in the sign as controlling conduct.

The drawing itself, as Chamberlain pointed out, entailed the living Kootenay (line A) and the dead Blackfoot Indians (line B). The second and fourth of the Kootenay dancers wear ceremonial "horns" of weasel-fur. The dead Blackfoot Indians are drawn mostly without eyebrows. The two rows of figures face away from each other (whereas in another drawing—Kootenay dance—two lines of dancers are depicted facing each other—Chamberlain, 1901c, p. 254).

Figure 10.3
Kootenay picture of a war dance (from Chamberlain, 1901c, p. 253)

Chamberlain also made the point about the psychological sophistication of the Indian's "drawing from memory" and that it included multiple objects in the composition.

Tobacco in Context

It may well be that social fashions for different health campaigns have a tendency to recur. In the end of the twentieth century, those faced with the witch hunt on the people who elect to smoke—and the regulations that smokers can only smoke outside, in the harsh Worcester winter—would have found a sympathetic supporter in Chamberlain. In 1905, he described the situation in U.S. in terms similar to our times:

> Today efforts are being strenuously made throughout the country to prevent the use of tobacco in any form by pupils in the public schools, and innumerable restrictive regulations have been passed by municipal and legislative authorities with this end in view. ... This is because certain noxious effects of the weed upon children and youth have been generally recognized, and public opinion *is ready to add penal enactment to scientific evidence* (Chamberlain, 1905b, p. 184, italics added).

Yet tobacco has been considered to belong to the class of food in many societies—and as food it has had its own ambiguities. The grand "health fights" of our contemporary societies are largely indicators of totem-based social regulation efforts of human conduct, rather than actual issues of tobacco per se. In the histories of human societies, the role of tobacco has fluctuated between being considered FOOD at times, and POISON at others (Lévi-Strauss, 1983, p. 68). Chamberlain reiterates a story from a school context from England (Gloucester) soon after tobacco had been introduced in Europe.

> After tobacco came into use, the children carried pipes in the satchels with their books, which the mothers took care to fill, that might serve instead of breakfast. At the accustomed hour every one laid aside his book and took his pipe, the master smoking with them, and teaching them how to hold their pipes and draw in the tobacco.

> This spectacle of a schoolmaster suspending the intellectual activities of his house of learning in order to teach his pupils how to smoke properly is something hardly conceivable nowadays, yet many of our good old English forefathers seem to have regarded such a proceeding as a necessary and useful part of the curriculum (Chamberlain, 1905b, p. 185).

Obviously this description of an educational context is a far cry from our contemporary fights for the pure souls and good health of our children in schools. Yet the message from the human cultural history remains clear: tobacco as any other useful plant has played both positively (food, medicine) and negatively (poison, cause of illnesses) valenced roles. The specific organization of these valences is a socio-political and historical particular. Smokers for Chamberlain were similar to the "primitives," women, and children—mistreated by the powerful "social others" for some socially highlighted features.

Yet in other matters Chamberlain did not pass by an opportunity to embed his feelings against some personal practices. While siding with smokers, he seemed by far less positive of the people who pierced their earlobes. Summarizing some ideas of Italian educators, he suddenly launched into a crusade against ear-piercing:

> A polemic against ear-rings is more necessary in Italy than it is in America. In southern Europe ear-piercing survives for all kinds of reasons, some of them connected with folk-superstitions, and the barbaric custom of wearing ear-rings is still much in vogue (Chamberlain, 1901a, p. 416).

Surely Chamberlain would have been disappointed seeing the wealth of body-piercing techniques coming into vogue a hundred years later. The strength of psychological construction of meaningfulness on one's own body makes use of any invasive or masking technique that is made available. The difference of aboriginal body painting and contemporary cosmetics is not so great as our usual rendering of such techniques might lead us to believe.

Chamberlain at Home

Chamberlain was certainly one of the encyclopedic minds who left behind a wealth of knowledge he had carefully collected and integrated, but very few—if any—followers. His knowledge was appreciated by the graduate students of the time—in the very free context of learning and teaching at Clark. Yet his wide knowledge, and collectionist's attitude, seemed not to have been a great asset in his teaching of seminars. Some of the students mention him in their retrospects upon their education:

> Chamberlain, in anthropology, was notable for his warm and catholic protagonisms (Gesell, 1952, p. 126).

> Nearly all the courses [at Clark at in early 1900s] started out with an attendance of twenty or thirty, which in some cases was reduced to ten or less before the middle of the semester. A course by Chamberlain in anthropology dwindled to four, and finally to two. It might have been one instead of two, only I had stayed too long to drop out without embarrassment. ... Chamberlain gave only two lectures a week... [which were] unorganized and sometimes rambling (Terman, 1930, pp. 313-314).

> From the somewhat erratic but erudite Chamberlain I got little directly, though partly as a result of my contacts with him, I browsed rather extensively in anthropological literature (Terman, 1930, p. 320).

Not surprisingly, Chamberlain supervised only two Ph.D. theses during his quarter of a century at Clark. One of them—Miriam Van Waters (who later became a recognized voice in the U.S. juvenile justice and parenting discourse—see Van Waters, 1925, 1927) combined Hall's interest in adolescence with Chamberlain's worldwide focus. Van Waters has been described as having Chamberlain as a main doctoral advisor because of G. Stanley Hall's disapproval of case studies (Ross, 1972, p. 354). Yet that claim need not be accurate; Van Waters' doctoral dissertation was not devoted to case studies. In it, she explicitly disproved Hall's claims about adolescent sexuality, while providing support to Hall's explanations of adolescents' religious sentiments (Van Waters, 1913). In ways reminiscent of Chamberlain's own doctoral dissertation, Van Waters provided a thorough worldwide overview of adolescent initiation ceremonies.

The other doctoral advisee, Albert N. Gilbertson, worked largely on the cultural patterns of ethics among the Eskimo (Gilbertson, 1914a), as well as took interest in themes of folklore (e.g., Gilbertson, 1913). He was supposed to become the successor to Chamberlain in the area of anthropology at Clark, yet this succession failed because—as usual—of financial constraints (Koelsch, 1987, p. 57). Part of these constraints were due to the economic effects of World War I, so the extinction of anthropology as an institutionally distinct area of studies at Clark University could be considered a casualty of the war.

Gilbertson is one of the few sources illuminating Chamberlain's relations with Hall in the later part of his scientific life:

> Their mutual helpfulness and cooperation did not preclude marked differences of opinion, as for example on the recapitulation theory, which Dr. Chamberlain regarded as essentially unsound as a pedagogic doctrine, no matter what might be its biological utility (Gilbertson, 1914b, p. 341).

This is a more benevolent depiction of Chamberlain's relations with Hall than has been encoded into the institutional history of Clark University.[8] While it was indeed the case that the "Hall times" at Clark were filled with frictions between Hall and Jonas Clark, and between Hall and the faculty (e.g., Ross, 1972), it still remains notable that in spite of such frictions the intellectual climate was intellectually vigorous, with strong yet varied opinions expressed and tolerated (see Averill, 1990). In fact, Hall mastered the freedom of access to higher education in ways that fitted his own complex character (Sokal, 1990)—bringing to Clark in general (and to the Psychology Department in particular) faculty members who would be the very best in their areas of expertise, agreed to come (and stay) for relatively low salary because of their personal loyalty to Hall. They were parts of a vigorous—which included acceptance of many conflicting viewpoints—intellectual atmosphere that was certainly dominated by Hall, but not to the detriment of the longer-term intellectual contributions of the students who finished their Ph.D. at Clark at that time (see Terman, 1930, p. 317 for an outcome summary of "the Clarkies" of the Hall time).

Chamberlain seemed to fit into the social context of the University very well. He complemented Hall's activities throughout his career at Clark—despite his criticisms of the "great black-robed chief" of his Department and of the University as a whole. It is not to be forgotten that in his 1896 book he praised the "distinguished president" of Clark University (and the "genius of the movement of child study"—Chamberlain, 1896a, p. vii) with no British understatement. Their shared religiosity of the free minds may have united the differences of opinion into a communal community identification. The latter seems to come out into the public domain in Chamberlain's vicious critique of the ways in which American universities dealt with salary and pension issues of their faculties (Chamberlain, 1909). Although these comments were general and representing the U.S. universities as a whole, it need not be forgotten that Chamberlain worked basically all his life in one university—Clark. His dramatic description of the life of academics—in their "servitude ... to the whims of governing bodies, the gross and petty tyrannies of presidents, and the time-destroying and soul-sickening vanities of faculties" (Chamberlain, 1909, p. 754) may bear some resemblance to the context of Clark in the first decade of the twentieth century.[9]

General Conclusions: Collectors, Collections, and Development of Science

It might be an exaggeration to claim that Alexander Chamberlain, in his role as the first Ph.D. in Anthropology in the United States, moved the disciplines he was involved in—anthropology and paedology—forward during his lifetime. The forgetting of his work in the later renderings of the histories of psychology and anthropology has effectively created an oversight of the potential value of his work. Yet the value remained unexplored also by Chamberlain himself. He may himself have contributed to the forgetting of his work by his reluctance to provide interpretations for his carefully collected empirical evidence. Often bald hypotheses—many of which are proven inadequate—are needed for science. Through the active disputes of any hypotheses sciences move closer to adequate knowledge. Sometimes most of the intellectual work of scientists is devoted to the adequacy of the connection between hypotheses and empirical evidence (e.g., in high-energy physics, Knorr-Cetina, 1999). Thus, mere amassing of collections of data solves no problems.

Yet such collections are useful for re-interpretations by new generations of scientists who—differently from Chamberlain—may test their hypotheses on the carefully established collections. Chamberlain's sensitivity to issues of cultural modification through culture contacts—documented in the historical changes in American Indian languages, and in the American Anglo-borrowings from the Indian languages—chart out a basis for an open-ended, developmental direction that is currently slowly emerging in the soul-searching in contemporary cultural anthropology.

Chamberlain's involvement in Hall's "child study" research program was substantial in providing a wider context for the phenomena studied on the basis of local New England children. The observations of the Chamberlains on the development of their own child were at the forefront of the empirical traditions of "child biographies" of the time—and in some respects may have surpassed later similar efforts. When comparing the "child biography" created by the Chamberlains with the ways in which child language is studied in our time, we may note the thoroughness of observations then—but not always now.

Chamberlain's refusal to make general sense of his rich collections was a target of criticism of his work already at the time the work appeared (see Berkman, Chapter 9). Franz Boas was the most vocal critic of the preponderance of collectionism. Boas' critique of Chamberlain was linked with the important issue of convergence in human cultural development that was an object of discussions around the time (Boas, 1896b; Goldenweiser, 1913).

The issue—difference between immediately observable features of an object (or—phenotype), its underlying generating mechanisms (or—genotype), and the process of the emergence of the former on the basis of the latter (or—development) are as burning (and unsolved) in anthropology and psychology at the end of the twentieth century as those were a 100 years before. The problem is unsolved because the *being* and *becoming* sides of the objects of investigation are not united into one scheme of thought. Two developmental processes—psychological or cultural—can lead to a similar-looking outcome (and hence can be classified into the same class if only the *being* side of the observations is considered). If the *becoming* side becomes emphasized, similar starting states may lead by the same process to vastly different outcomes.

The issue of convergence occupied the minds of psychologists at around the same time as well. In his definitive statement about differential psychology, William Stern (1911) used the principle of convergence as the theoretical bridge between the foci on universal psychological laws and their individual-specific manifestations. In this context emerges the formula—variability entails universality. Later in the twentieth century, the developmental orientation in psychology largely disappeared from the minds of psychologists (Valsiner, 1997a), and thus the issue of convergence has become one of the key problems for contemporary thought—and (again) one with promises for the future.

The principle of convergence becomes theoretically highlighted when the developmental and ontological perspectives in a given area—be it anthropology or psychology—become integrated. Convergence represents a direction of (at least two) developmental trajectories in relation to an ontological state (of similarity). Anthropological collections of the kind Chamberlain liked to produce revealed the ontological *status quo* of the outcomes of otherwise hidden underlying processes.

Similar tension between explanatory universal theory building and documentation of empirical differences and similarities between societies can be found in our contemporary chasm between cultural and cross-cultural directions in psychology. The latter—as primarily an empirical enterprise—produces data similar to those of collections of folklore. Only here it is no longer the original phenomena that are described, collected, and compared with one another. Instead, the collections are those of *aggregated data* from different societies-averaged scores on some psychological indicator, compared for their difference (by statistical criteria). As a result of such comparisons of the aggregates, statements about the ontological manifestations of abstracted images of societies (labeled "cultures") become tautologically causal. For example, statements about "the American culture" in contrast with "the Japanese culture" as found (empirically) to be different lead to causal implication of some posited general causal-cultural property—"the *Americanness*" of the "American culture" and "the *Japaneseness*" of the "Japanese culture."

In contrast, different versions of cultural psychology take a developmental-systemic view on the cultural nature of psychological functions. Here universal processes of personal self-construction through cultural means (signs and tools) are embedded in the inter-individually variable developmental trajectories. Persons construct cultural meanings (and social rules), which—in their outcomes—may indeed look similar across large geographical distances, yet their origins need not be the same. Neither are differences between persons living next door to one another proof of different origins—but may constitute a case of divergent manifestations of the same underlying functions.

The social practice of data accumulation across different studies has found its habitual role in contemporary social sciences. This is evident in the efforts of developing techniques of meta-analysis of data that are accumulated across different studies (see Lytton, 1994). The goal of these tactics of meta-aggregation (aggregation of already aggregated data) is to arrive at essentialistic large-N based generalizations that fit the assumed underlying populations by the standards of statistical inference. The Boasian/Sternian strategy of viewing unity in diversity would find little use from such Aristotelian aggregation efforts. The notion of theory-based look for the crucial case—critical for the hypothesis—(or setting up an experiment to test the hypothesis) is foreign to the collectionist and meta-analytic tactics in the social sciences.

Chamberlain's moralistic orientation was certainly in line with the efforts of his contemporaries to change the U.S. society in a direction of greater freedoms for the underprivileged, and under-considered—women, children, and aboriginal tribes. His rhetoric acquired poetic boldness when it came to the social fight—no trace was left from the hesitancy about "going beyond the data given" as was the case in the empirical collections. Chamberlain can be considered to fit well into our contemporary movements of feminism and multi-culturalism—for better or worse (for him, as well as for these movements).

In sum, Chamberlain was dedicated to the wisdom of the folk, and its lore—

> ... the "folk" have been pursuing this proper course of study for not a few thousand years, and some of them may continue to do so for as many millennia in the future. If

we are to take in the accounts of man and his faculties that the wise men of the "folk" have prepared for us, we should be fain to assent to the declaration of Solomon, the folklorist of old Israel,—*I am fearfully and wonderfully made* (Chamberlain,1893, p. 13).

The same can be said about the theoretically fearful and wonderfully folkloric collections of materials that Alexander Francis Chamberlain left as his contribution to the sciences of anthropology and developmental psychology.[10]

Notes

1. Previously published in *From Past to Future, Vol. 3* (1), pp. 15-39. *Passionate Collector: Alexander F. Chamberlain and Child Study.* © 2000 Frances L. Hiatt School of Psychology, Clark University. Author: Jaan Valsiner, Department of Psychology, Clark University.
2. From the beginning—through the subject "The Psychology of Language; Myth, custom, and belief anthropologically considered" (Chamberlain, 1899c, p. 148).
3. The local Worcester community was presented with a message by the *Worcester Telegram*, the local newspaper, about the dubious intentions of the "foreign" professor who would force Worcester children to undress in order to measure their bodies (Ross, 1972, p. 210).
4. Chamberlain also took anthropometric measurements from the Kootenay Indians during the expedition to British Columbia in the summer of 1891 (see Chamberlain, 1905b, p. 179).
5. He quoted Farrar (from 1873), who had claimed "It is well known that the neglected children in some Canadian and Indian villages, who are often left alone for days, can and do invent for themselves a lingua franca, partially or wholly unintelligible to all except themselves" (Chamberlain, 1890a, p. 237).
6. In 1904 he published a book of poems Gilbertson, 1914, p. 341).
7. Brinton (1894, p. 533), reviewing Havelock Ellis' *Man and woman* (Ellis, 1894), points to the "infantile diathesis" of women—and points out Ellis' solution—that women, due to their child-likeness, alone possess "the chief distinctive characters of humanity." Chamberlain was also thinking about the psychology of women issue as he reviewed Giuseppe Sergi's pamphlet *Per l'Educazione e la cultura della Donna* (Rome, 1892—see Chamberlain, 1892a).
8. Chamberlain, "in spite of his cranky temperament" was involved in the Worcester city politics, where "his ability to speak to audiences in English, French, German and Italian in the same evening made his services as a political speaker valuable in a city with an ethnically fragmented electorate." At Clark, it was a different story—as it is described: "In his twice-weekly lectures he spent much of his time criticizing Hall's ideas, and also worked individually with psychology and education students, especially in bibliography and guided readings" (Koelsch, 1987, p. 57).
9. It also indicates that the academics like Chamberlain were confronted with the same issue of how their creativity is hindered by fragmenting their time by different institutional activities—meetings, committees, and so on. This issue as a basic social control mechanism was analyzed only eighty years later (see Bourdieu, 1988).
10. I am grateful to Nancy Budwig and Julia Berkman for their suggestions upon the earlier version of this paper.

References

Averill, L. A. (1990). Recollections of Clark's G. Stanley Hall. *Journal of the History of the Behavioral Sciences, 26*, 125-130.
Bartlett, F. C. (1920). Some experiments on the reproduction of folk-stories. *Folklore, 31*, 30-47.
Boas, F. (1888). Chinook songs. *Journal of American Folklore, 1*, 220-226.
Boas, F. (1896). The limitations of the comparative method of anthropology. *Science, 4*, 901-908.
Boas, F. (1908). *Anthropology*. New York: Columbia University Press.
Bourdieu, P. (1988). *Homo academicus*. Stanford, CA: Stanford University Press.
Brinton, D. (1894). [Review of the book *Man and woman*.] *Psychological Review, 1*, 532-534.
Brinton, D. (1896). [Review of the book *The child and childhood in folk-thought*.] *Science*, n.s., *6*, 483-484.
Chamberlain, A. F. (1890a). Notes on Indian child-language. *American Anthropologist, 3*, 237-241.
Chamberlain, A. F. (1890b). The origin and development of grammatical gender. *Proceedings of the Canadian Institute*, pp. 4-5.
Chamberlain, A. F. (1892a). Summary of *Per l'educazione e la cultura della Donna* by G. Sergi. *Pedagogical Seminary, 2*, 477-479.
Chamberlain, A. F. (1892b). *The language of the Missisaga Indians of Skugog*. Philadelphia, PA: Press of McCalla and Co.
Chamberlain, A. F. (1893). Human physiognomy and physical characteristics in folklore and folk-speech. *Journal of American Folklore, 6*, 13-24. [Presented at the Third Annual Meeting of the American Folklore Society on December, 29, 1891]
Chamberlain, A. F. (1894a). Anthropology in universities and colleges. *Pedagogical Seminary, 3*, 48-60.
Chamberlain, A. F. (1894b). On the words for "anger" in certain languages: A study in linguistic psychology. *American Journal of Psychology, 6*, 585-592.
Chamberlain, A. F. (1896a). *The child and childhood in folk-thought* (The child in primitive culture). New York: MacMillan.
Chamberlain, A. F. (1896b). The poetry of American aboriginal speech. *Journal of American Folklore, 9*, 43-47
Chamberlain, A. F. (1897). The mythology and folklore of invention. *Journal of American Folklore, 10*, 88-100.
Chamberlain, A. F. (1899a). American Indian names of white men and women. *Journal of American Folklore, 12*, 24-31.
Chamberlain, A. F. (1899b). On the words for "fear" in certain languages. A study of linguistic psychology. *American Journal of Psychology, 10*, 302-305.
Chamberlain, A. F. (1899c). Anthropology. In *Clark University 1889-1899 Decennial Celebration* (pp. 148-160). Worcester, MA: Clark University
Chamberlain, A. F. (1900). *The child: A study in the evolution of man*. London, UK: Walter Scott.
Chamberlain, A. F. (1901a). Notes on Italian educational literature. *Pedagogical Seminary, 8*, 412-423.
Chamberlain, A. F. (1901b). Translation: a study in the transference of folk-thought. *Journal of American Folklore, 14*, 165-171.
Chamberlain, A. F. (1901c). Kootenay group-drawings. *American Anthropologist*, n.s., *3*, 248-256.
Chamberlain, A. F. (1901d). Kootenay "medicine-men." *Journal of American Folklore, 14*, 95-99.

Chamberlain, A. F. (1902a). The contact between "higher" and "lower" races. *Pedagogical Seminary, 9*, 507-520.
Chamberlain, A. F. (1902b). Algonkian words in American English: A study in the contact of the white man and the Indian. *Journal of American Folklore, 15*, 240-267.
Chamberlain, A. F. (1902c). The teaching of English. *Pedagogical Seminary, 9*, 161-168.
Chamberlain, A. F. (1903a). Primitive woman as poet. *Journal of American Folklore, 16*, 205-221.
Chamberlain, A. F. (1903b). Primitive theories of knowledge: a study in linguistic psychology. *The Monist, 13*, 295-302.
Chamberlain, A. F. (1904a). Race-character and local color in proverbs. *Journal of American Folklore, 17*, 28-31.
Chamberlain, A. F. (1904b). Proverbs in the making: Some scientific commonplaces, I and II. *Journal of American Folklore, 17*, 161-170 and 268-278.
Chamberlain, A. F. (1905a). The Kootenay Indians. In *Ethnology of Canada and Newfoundland* (pp. 178-187). Toronto: Ontario Archaeological Report.
Chamberlain, A. F. (1905b). Variation in early human culture. *Journal of American Folklore, 19*, 177-190.
Chamberlain, A. F. (1906). Acquisition of written language by primitive peoples. *American Journal of Psychology, 17*, 69-80.
Chamberlain, A. F. (1907). Analogy in the languages of primitive peoples. *American Journal of Psychology, 18*, 442-446.
Chamberlain, A. F. (1909). The endowment of men and women, a check to the institutional "exploitation" of genius. *Science*, n.s., *30*, 754-759.
Chamberlain, A. F. (1913). "New religions" among the North American Indians, etc. *Journal of Religious Psychology, 6*(1), 1-49.
Chamberlain, A. F., and Chamberlain, I. C. (1904a). Studies of a child I. *Pedagogical Seminary, 11*, 264-291.
Chamberlain, A. F., and Chamberlain, I. C. (1904b). Studies of a child II. *Pedagogical Seminary, 11*, 452-483.
Chamberlain, A. F., and Chamberlain, I. C. (1905). Studies of a child III. *Pedagogical Seminary, 12*, 427-453.
Chamberlain, A. F., and Chamberlain, I. C. (1906). Hypnagogic images and bi-vision in early childhood. *American Journal of Psychology, 17*, 272-273.
Chamberlain, A. F., and Chamberlain, I. C. (1909). Studies of a child IV. *Pedagogical Seminary, 16*, 65-103.
Chamberlain, I. C. (1900). The devil's grandmother. *Journal of American Folklore, 13*, 278-280.
Chrisman, O. (1920). *The historical child*. Boston, MA: Richard G. Badger.
Cirillo, L., and Kaplan, B. (1983). Figurative action from the perspective of genetic-dramatism. In S. Wapner and B. Kaplan (Eds.), *Toward a holistic developmental psychology* (pp. 235-252). Hillsdale, NJ: Erlbaum.
Cole, M. (1995). Culture and cognitive development: From cross-cultural research to creating systems of cultural mediation. *Culture and Psychology, 1*(1), 25-54.
Cole, M. (1996). *Cultural psychology*. Cambridge, MA: Harvard University Press.
Ellis, H. (1894). *Man and woman*. New York: Charles Scribner's Sons.
Ellis, C. (1996). *To change them forever: Indian education in the Rainy Mountain Boarding School, 1893-1920*. Norman, OK: University of Oklahoma Press.
Gesell, A. (1952). Arnold Gesell. In E. G. Boring, H. Werner, H. S. Langfeld and R. M. Yerkes (Eds.), *A history of psychology in autobiography* (pp. 123-142). Worcester, MA: Clark University Press

Gilbertson, A. N. (1913). The pitfall: An Old World folklore cycle. *Journal of Religious Psychology, 6*, 3, 273-278.
Gilbertson, A. N. (1914a). Some ethical phases of Eskimo culture. A PhD Dissertation in Anthropology, Clark University. [Published in *Journal of Religious Psychology, 6*, 4, 321-374 and *7*, 1, 45-74.]
Gilbertson, A. N. (1914b). In memoriam: Alexander Francis Chamberlain. *American Anthropologist*, n.s., *16*, 337-348.
Goldenweiser, A. A. (1913). The principle of limited possibilities in the development. *Journal of American Folklore, 26*, 259-290.
Ingram, D. (1989). *First language acquisition: method, description, and explanation.* Cambridge, MA: Cambridge University Press.
Jahoda, G. (1999). *Images of savages: Ancient roots of modern prejudice in Western culture.* London: Routledge.
Kaplan, B. (1983). Genetic-dramatism: Old wine in new bottles. In S. Wapner and B. Kaplan (Eds.), *Toward a holistic developmental psychology* (pp. 53-74). Hilldale, NJ: Erlbaum.
Knorr-Cetina, K. (1999). *Epistemic cultures: How the sciences make knowledge.* Cambridge, MA: Harvard University Press.
Koelsch, W. A. (1987). *Clark University, 1887-1987.* Worcester, MA: Clark University Press.
Lévi-Strauss, C. (1983). *From honey to ashes.* Chicago, IL: University of Chicago Press.
Lytton, H. (1994). Replication and meta-analysis: The story of a meta-analysis of parents' socialization practices. In R. van der Veer, M. H. van Ijzendoorn, and J. Valsiner (Eds.), *Reconstructing the mind: Replicability in research on human development* (pp. 117-149). Norwood, N.J.: Ablex.
Mead, G. H. (1930). The philosophies of Royce, James, and Dewey in their American setting. *International Journal of Ethics, 40*, 211-231.
Ross, D. (1972). *G. Stanley Hall: The psychologist as prophet.* Chicago, IL: University of Chicago Press.
Shweder, R. A. (1990). Cultural psychology-- what is it? In J. W. Stigler, R. A. Shweder, and G. Herdt (Eds.), *Cultural psychology* (pp. 1-43). Cambridge, MA: Cambridge University Press.
Siegel, A. W., and White, S. H. (1982). The child study movement: early growth and development of the symbolized child. In H. Reese and L. Lipsitt (Eds.), *Advances in child behavior and development.* Vol. 17 (pp. 233-285). New York: Academic Press.
Sokal, M. M. (1990). G. Stanley Hall and the Institutional Character of Psychology at Clark 1889-1920. *Journal of the History of the Behavioral Sciences, 26*(2), 114-124.
Stern, W. (1911). *Differentielle Psychologie.* Leipzig: J. A. Barth
Tanner, J. M. (1959). Boas' contribution to knowledge of human growth and form. In W. Goldschmidt (Ed.), *The anthropology of Franz Boas* (pp. 76-111). San Francisco, CA: Howard Chandler.
Terman, L. M. (1930). Trails to psychology. In C. Murchison (Ed.), *A history of psychology in autobiography.* Vol. 2. (pp. 297-331). Worcester, MA: Clark University Press.
Thomsen, C. W. (1987). "Man-eating" and the myths of the "New World"-- anthropological, pictorial, and literary variants. In C. F. Graumann and S. Moscovici (Eds.), *Changing conceptions of conspiracy* (pp. 39-69). New York: Springer.
Valsiner, J. (1997a, August). Well-kept hostages: developmental ideas in the twentieth century. In W. F. Overton (Chair) *Developmental Psychology: History as context for*

the 21st century. Symposium conducted at the Golden Anniversary of meeting of the American Psychological Association, Chicago, IL.

Valsiner, J. (1997b). The development of the concept of development: Historical and epistemological perspectives. In W. Damon and R. Lerner (Eds.*), Handbook of child psychology: Vol. 1. Theoretical models of human development* (5th ed., pp. 189-232). New York: Wiley.

Valsiner, J., and Van der Veer, R. (2000). *The social mind.* New York: Cambridge University Press.

Van der Veer, R., and Valsiner, J. (1991*). Understanding Vygotsky: A quest for synthesis.* Oxford, UK: Blackwell.

Van Waters, M. (1913). The adolescent girl among primitive peoples. *Journal of Religious Psychology, 6*(4), 375-418.

Van Waters, M. (1925). *Youth in conflict.* New York, NY: Republic Publishing Company.

Van Waters, M. (1927). *Parents on probation.* New York, NY: Republic Publishing Company.

Weir, R. H. (1962). *Language in the crib.* The Hague: Mouton.

Wertsch, J. V., del Río, P., and Alvarez, A. (1995). Sociocultural studies: History, action, and mediation. In J. V. Wertsch, P. del Río, and A. Alvarez (Eds.), *Sociocultural studies of mind* (pp.1-34). Cambridge, MA: Cambridge University Press.

White, S. H. (1990). Child study at Clark University: 1894-1904. *Journal of the History of the Behavioral Sciences, 26*, 131-150.

Wierzbicka, A. (1999). *Emotions across languages and cultures: Diversity and universals.* Cambridge, MA: Cambridge University Press.

Wiltse, S. E. (1894). A preliminary sketch of the history of child study in America. *Pedagogical Seminary, 3*, 189-212.

Part IV

The Dynamic Whole: Gestalt Ideas and Social Practices

11

Tamara Dembo's European Years

René Van der Veer[1]

When Tamara Dembo arrived in Berlin in 1921, she was about nineteen years old. She had spent her childhood and youth in Baku, where she was born on May 28, 1902, as the daughter of the Jewish merchant Wulf Dembo and his wife Sophie, née Woltschkina. In Baku she received private tuition—as a young girl she was diagnosed as having a heart condition and she was not allowed to go to school (Wertsch, 1993)—and passed the finals at the second boys' gymnasium in 1920. Having arrived in Berlin, she went to study at the University of Berlin, first mathematics and natural sciences, then psychology, philosophy, national economy, and the history of art (Dembo, 1931b). She was at first drawn to industrial psychology, specifically the field that we would now call ergonomics, but after hearing of Lewin's work from Ovsiankina and Zeigarnik (see below) she began attending Lewin's classes. Although Tamara Dembo apparently had no political reasons to leave the Soviet Union for Berlin (Marrow, 1969, pp. 20–21)—to study at a German university was rather common for Russians at the beginning of this century (cf. Valsiner, 1988)—it is nevertheless instructive to consider her decision to emigrate against the background of the political and socioeconomic developments of that time.[2]

It must be remembered that Russia went through a period of turmoil in the late 1910s and early 1920s. As a result of the October Revolution and the subsequent civil war, about 2 million Russians fled their native country. Others were expelled in subsequent years. Large numbers of Russians ended up in Manchurian Kharbin, Prague (via Istanbul and Belgrade), the Baltic countries, and Poland. But from about 1918 to 1925 it was Berlin that became what may be called the capital of émigré Russia. Many of the approximately 250,000 Russians who had moved to Germany settled in Berlin (where they tended to cluster together in certain quarters much like present-day refugees and foreign workers) and tried to resume their previous life, thus creating a rich Russian subculture in the German society. In Berlin, younger Russian children could visit Russian or bilingual Russian-German primary schools, older children might go to one of the available Russian *gimnazia*, and students could take courses at either the Russian Institute (which was allied with the University of Berlin and the Technische Hochschule) or the Free Spiritual and Philosophical Academy founded by the émigré philosopher Berdiaev. These institutes also served as institutional umbrellas for lecture tours of Soviet citizens and published their own proceedings (Raeff, 1990, p. 60).

Outside the educational system, Russian culture flourished as well. There were several Russian daily newspapers (one of them with Vladimir Nabokov's father as the editor), Russian literary journals, various Russian publishing houses, Russian theaters, and exhibitions of Russian modern art. From 1921 to 1926, during the period of the New Economic Policy (when Lenin for economic reasons temporarily allowed some forms of private enterprise and a more 'liberal' social climate), Soviet citizens who obtained permission to travel were likely to visit Berlin. Businessmen, academic scholars, artists, musicians, chess players, and writers all paid their visit to the German capital and often lived there for longer periods. Of the writers, the novelists and poets Belyj, Berberova, Bunin, Ehrenburg, Esenin, Gershenzon, Gorky, Khodasevich, Mayakovsky, Nabokov, Pasternak, Remizov, Shklovsky, Tsvetaeva, and A. Tolstoy deserve mentioning (Field, 1977; Raeff, 1990). Among the scholars we might mention Semyon Frank, Roman Jakobson, Aleksandr Luria, Lev Vygotsky, and Dmitri Uznadze (cf. Aşh, 1997; Van der Veer and Valsiner, 1991).

Thus, during that brief period in the early 1920s, a period that coincided with Tamara Dembo's student days, Berlin was a center of Russian culture where those who had left were in an excellent position to follow the recent cultural and political developments in their native country and where Soviet visitors could still feel more or less free to intermingle with émigrés (who still were their "natural" audience in a way, at least in the case of visiting novelists and poets). All this, however, gradually changed for economic and political reasons. First, the growing prices in Berlin forced the generally poor Russian emigrants to leave the German capital for cheaper places, mainly Paris and Prague. Second, for ordinary Soviet citizens it became increasingly difficult and eventually virtually impossible to travel outside the Soviet Union. The departure of the bulk of the Russian refugees and the strongly diminished number of visits from Soviet citizens naturally brought many Russian cultural activities to a stop and by the time Tamara Dembo had finished her studies Russian cultural life in Berlin was already losing much of its impetus (for detailed descriptions of Russian culture abroad, see Field, 1977; Raeff, 1990).

The Berlin Period: Working with Kurt Lewin

Having finished her studies, Tamara Dembo began doing research at the University of Berlin under the supervision of Kurt Lewin. From 1925 to 1928 she carried out a number of experiments that eventually formed the empirical basis for her dissertation (Dembo, 1931b). She was not the only Russian working with Lewin: Gita Birenbaum, Maria Ovsiankina, and Bluma Zeigarnik were there as well. Birenbaum and Zeigarnik would later return to the Soviet Union to become close collaborators of Lev Vygotsky. Elsewhere (Van der Veer and Valsiner, 1991) we have pointed out that Lewin and Vygotsky knew each other personally and corresponded about scientific matters. Just like Tamara Dembo (1931a), Birenbaum (1930), Ovsiankina (1928), and Zeigarnik (1927) published their research findings in *Psychologische Forschung*, the major new journal edited by Goldstein, Gruhle, Köhler, Koffka, and Wertheimer. Their papers were published as part of a longer series of publications in that journal, called "Investigations into the psychology of action and affect" (*Untersuchungen zur Handlungs- und Affektpsychologie*), and under the editorship of Lewin.

The journal *Psychologische Forschung* deserves a few more words, as it was the first truly internationally oriented German journal and, in a way, reflected the cosmopolitan character of Berlin as sketched above. Thus, the editors of *Psychologische Forschung* published not only the papers by Lewin's Russian co-workers mentioned above, but also papers by Soviet researchers such as Kravkov (1928; 1932; Kravkov et al., 1929), Luria (1929), Samojlov (1923), and Uznadze (1924; 1930), and by Russian émigrés such as Grünbaum (1927). For about a decade, then,—until further political developments in both the Soviet Union and Germany would make it impossible—the journal served as a publication outlet for Russians of different denominations. More generally, it can be said that the editorial policy of *Psychologische Forschung* reflected the international orientation of the Berlin Gestalt school and Kurt Lewin. As is known, the Berlin Institute of Psychology, more than other German research institutes, served as a meeting place for international psychologists (Ash, 1997, pp. 210-211).

Thus, we may say that Tamara Dembo's psychological training and research took place in the cosmopolitan atmosphere of Berlin and the Berlin school of Gestalt psychology (Sprung and Sprung, 1997). In her dissertation (Dembo, 1931b), she mentions Köhler, Lewin, Rupp, and Wertheimer as her most important teachers of psychology.[3] However, as we shall see below, in her actual research efforts she closely followed the principles of Kurt Lewin's topological or field psychology (cf. Boring, 1950, pp. 723-728; Lewin, 1933). The setup of her investigations, the way she analyzed the findings, and her entire theoretical approach reflected Lewin's dynamic approach of the time. The readers (*Referenten*) of Tamara Dembo's dissertation were Lewin and Köhler, while the American psychologist J.F. Brown (a Yale Ph.D. who later worked at Kansas; see Boring, 1950, p. 600) assisted her in carrying out several of the experiments (Dembo, 1931, p. 10).

The Development of Anger

Tamara Dembo began her dissertation by outlining her theoretical outlook in a brief introductory chapter. She explained that she wished to study the origin and genesis of anger (*Ärgerniss*; literally vexation, irritation, or annoyance). She claimed that the psychology of feelings and emotions was underdeveloped and that mere classifications dominated the scene. This she explained on the basis of the prevailing Aristotelian approach in psychology. Characteristic of that approach is that the universal (*das Allgemeine*) is seen as the opposite of the individual and that one seeks for some abstract average. The dynamics of a phenomenon are not investigated, possibly because of the Aristotelian emphasis on frequency as the basis for lawfulness and the linked thesis of replicability as requirement for any experiment. With Lewin (1927/1981; 1931/1981; 1931), Tamara Dembo emphasized another scientific approach (the Galileian approach) in which one follows concrete singular cases and their individual course or genesis. Establishing the "abstract average of as many historically given cases as possible" is not necessary. Instead, researchers should try to reproduce the pure concrete phenomenon under experimental, artificial conditions. Such reproductions would form the basis for deriving formal descriptions of their dynamics (Ash, 1995; Lewin, 1927/1981). Lewin, following Cassirer (1910/1953) and Mach, believed that Galileo was the originator of such an approach,[4] hence his opposition of the Aristotelian and Galileian approach.

In accordance with the Galileian approach, Dembo decided to provoke anger in the laboratory. This was done by confronting subjects with problems that were either impossible or very difficult to solve and at times by actively hampering their efforts at solution. During the problem solving process the subjects were being watched by the experimenter and her assistant. The assistant made shorthand reports of everything that was said and the experimenter made note of the global events that took place. This resulted in protocols of about fifteen pages per session. Afterwards the subjects were questioned about their feelings during the experiment. Dembo explained that it would have been ideal to film the experiments but that trials showed that this method was technically still too difficult and too expensive. All in all, twenty-seven subjects were subjected to sixty-four experiments (each experiment lasting about one or two hours) over a period of four years (1925-1928).[5] The subjects did not know that the development of anger was the topic of the investigation.

Dembo used two tasks, "ring throwing" and "flower grasping." In the ring throwing experiment the subject's task was to throw ten rings in a row onto a bottle from a distance of 3.5 m. This proved impossible for most subjects. Moreover, the experimenter would sometimes actively hamper the task solution by catching rings thrown by the subject, etc. In the flower grasping experiment the task was to grasp a flowerpot with the hand without the feet leaving a prescribed area. Here there were two allowed solutions (sitting on the knees outside the area and reaching for the pot or using a chair standing outside the area as support and then reaching for the pot) but the experimenter insisted on finding a third solution. This solution did not exist, however, and all the subject's further proposals were dismissed as violating the rules. Both tasks thus ensured that subjects would be busy for one or more hours trying to solve the task. It was further hypothesized that the subjects' repeated failure and the at times teasing behavior of the experimenter (e.g., laughing after subjects' failure) would lead to anger and irritation in the subjects.

Before Dembo decided to use these two tasks to provoke anger she had experimented with another, third task, the "waiting experiment." In this task the subjects were invited to come to the experimental room and then given no instruction at all. They were free to do what they wanted and the experimenter did no more than making meticulous notes of their behavior. Subjects reported that they felt they were being watched and had difficulty concentrating on the activities they set out to do. One subject, for example, began solving a crossword puzzle from the newspaper he had brought with him but felt unable to think clearly in the presence of the writing experimenter. When she left the room for a few minutes he immediately found two words. Others tried to read books and felt equally hindered. Still other subjects made no attempt to do something meaningful and simply watched out of the window for one and a half hours or tried to begin a conversation with the experimenter.

According to Dembo (1925), the experimental setting did not, however, provoke strong emotions. Unlike in the ring or flower experiments, the subjects did not become angry at the experimenter. The sole effect she noted was that subjects—there were twenty-five of them, about half of them members of the staff of the Berlin Institute—tended to become somewhat depressed and began ruminating about what they believed were their personal shortcomings. In a meeting at the Institute, on December 7, 1925 (Dembo, 1925), she presented her preliminary findings for the three experiments and asked her colleagues what they felt were the crucial differences between the ring throwing and flower grasping experiments, on the one side, and the waiting experiment, on the other side. The minutes of this meeting—led by Wertheimer—are interesting, because they reveal to what extent the experiments elicited a psychological struggle between subject and experimenter. The subjects—at least those who were members of the Institute as well—entered the experimental situations with explicit hypotheses about their goal (e.g., "she wants to make me angry," "she wants to see how long she can keep me here," or "it is an intelligence test") and at times engaged in what they saw as subversive activities. One subject in the waiting experiment, for example, began telling Dembo jokes and triumphed when she finally laughed. The minutes are also interesting as they show to what extent at that stage—by the end of 1925—the findings were still open to theoretical speculation. There was not yet a trace of the vector psychology that Dembo would eventually use to analyze her findings. Nor was there an exclusive focus on anger: Wertheimer, Gottschaldt, Lewin, Dembo, and the other members of the Institute who were present at the meeting tried to think of experimental settings that might elicit *pleasant* feelings in the subject. As to the difference between the first two experiments and the waiting experiments, it was decided that the waiting experiment lacked a strong goal whose frustration can provoke anger. For the same reason, that is, the lack of a clear goal, the mildly frustrated and utterly bored subjects can drift away in depressive thoughts. For these reasons, Dembo apparently decided to skip the third task.

In analyzing the experimental situations, one would be tempted to believe, Dembo said, that the behavior of subjects is regular in the sense that *b* always follows *a*. But such regularities we do not find, as development is *cumulative*; e.g., the same environmental event may lead to vastly different reactions depending on the tension that has accumulated in the subject. We do better to look at the topology of the *Umfeld*, that is, we must investigate the forces that are operative in the experimental situation and that influence the mental state (*innere Zustand*) of the subject. What are these forces? How can we analyze the experimental situation? (see figure 11.1).

First, there is the goal A. For subjects who have accepted the conditions of the experiment A acquires a strongly positive valence (*Aufforderungscharakter*), that is, subjects strongly wish to reach the goal. They are hindered in their attempts by the internal barrier B, which may acquire negative valence. Finally, if the negative valence of the internal barrier B surpasses the positive valence of the goal A, subjects may want to leave the whole experimental situation. They almost never do, however. The experimenter insists that they continue, the subjects may feel obliged to continue as they have agreed to participate, to leave would mean to admit total failure, and so on. The fact that subjects virtually never discontinue the experiment (i.e., leave the room) suggests that there is another, external barrier present in the situation, barrier C. Thus the subject is caught between various forces and barriers: forces (vectors) that draw him toward and away from the goal, and barriers that prevent him from reaching the goal or leaving. The result is increasing tension. The subject may begin to "pendulate," that is, he may alternatively feel drawn toward the goal and drawn toward leaving.

The strength of the various tendencies (vectors) will vary—e.g., the subject will feel more strongly drawn toward the goal if he feels that his chances of

Figure 11.1
The Topology of the Experimental Situation (after Dembo, 1931b).

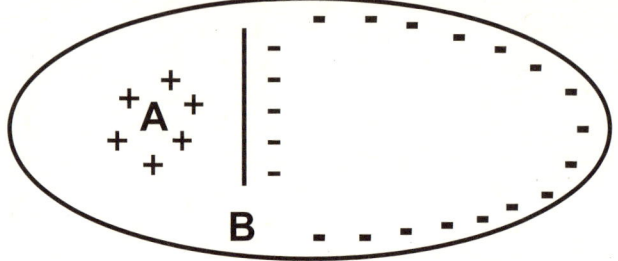

reaching it have become somehow better—and the behavior of the subject will depend on the momentary constellation of forces. A large part of Dembo's dissertation consisted of giving a detailed description of what subjects do when the psychological tension is mounting in terms of the existing forces and barriers. For example, after repeated failure to reach the goal subjects will come up with unrealistic or *Ersatz* solutions. An unrealistic solution would be to hypnotize the flowers to leave the pot. Subjects who are obsessed by the goal come up with such suggestions. An *Ersatz* solution would be to throw a ring around an irrelevant object. Subjects often feel drawn to irrelevant objects (which then serve as an inferior substitute for the goal) but are at the same time irritated by them as they distract them from reaching the real goal.

Dembo also described how subjects may "leave" the experimental situation without actually leaving the room. Unable to solve the task and feeling incapable of leaving the room, some subjects, for example, will begin reading the newspaper, or begin daydreaming. Others try to escape the situation physically by suddenly recalling urgent phone calls they have to make. The inflexible attitude of the experimenter (e.g., "we must continue the experiment," "there is another solution") eventually makes virtually all subjects resume their efforts.[6] However, subjects become increasingly aware of the experimenter's role in restricting their freedom of action and now little more is required to elicit outbursts of anger and annoyance.

Tamara Dembo describes how subjects display occasional expressions of annoyance (e.g., cursing, throwing a ring against the experimenter), but how they still try to control themselves. It is vital for the subject's self-esteem to hide his feelings, to pretend that he is not really involved in the problem solving process. In Dembo's terms, the subjects encapsulate their mind, create a barrier between the inner psychic system and the *Umwelt*. The growing tension causes pressure on this and the other barriers and now it needs only little additional pressure (*Zusatzdruck*) by the experimenter (e.g., laughing mockingly when yet another of the subject's attempts to solve the task fails) to make the subject break down. The barrier between the inner system and the outer world dissolves, subjects may become highly emotional and rude, begin talking about their private affairs, act childishly, and so on. Dembo dryly remarked that such emotional outbursts undoubtedly involve a strong release of energy but that she was not sure that Freud was right in claiming that such discharges always bring relaxation.

In sum, what Dembo offered was an analysis of the subjects' behavior in terms of a complex dynamic system of field forces and barriers. The strength of these forces and barriers varies over time, which makes claims of the type "environmental stimulus a will always be followed by response b" utterly useless. By creating the adequate conditions and manipulating and needling the subjects Tamara Dembo was able to lay bare the genesis of anger. It was her claim that the insights she gained in her experimental setup would hold in real-life situations as well.

It is clear that Dembo's analysis of the experimental situation and the behavior of subjects was fully in the tradition of Lewin's vector psychology. When she began her pilot experiments in the summer of 1925 this conceptual apparatus did not yet exist but in her analysis of the results five years later she was able to make use of it. This is not to say, however, that she necessarily contributed little to the conceptual apparatus or the analysis of the findings. From accounts of contemporaries and from minutes of meetings that have been preserved it is well known that the concepts of vector psychology and the plans for investigations often came about in lively and informal discussions between Lewin, his colleagues, and his students, and that afterwards it was often difficult to say who advanced which idea (Ash, 1995; Dembo, 1925; Marrow, 1969). But it does mean that Dembo was initially trained in a certain mode of thinking that seemed very promising at the time. And it is very understandable that she attempted to use the same conceptual apparatus in subsequent investigations that dealt with at first sight totally different situations. This brings us to a thus far little known episode in Dembo's European years as a researcher.

The Groningen Period: Working with F.J.J. Buytendijk

Tamara Dembo defended her dissertation, "*Der Ärger als dynamisches Problem*" (Dembo, 1931b), on July 25, 1930. We know, however, that she finished the empirical part of her investigation in 1928. To take two years to write down and interpret the results of her research (which in itself was conducted over a—to modern standards—quite protracted period) seems excessively long. The fact is, however, that Tamara Dembo did not devote these two years exclusively to the completion of her dissertation. In that same period she moved to Groningen in the Netherlands to work as an assistant at the Physiological Institute of the University of Groningen. Judging by her notebooks and letters she worked there from at least early February to August 1929.

The head of that institute there was no other than F.J.J. Buytendijk (1887-1974), the famous Dutch zoopsychologist and later founder of the Utrecht phenomenological school in psychology (Dehue, 1995). Buytendijk had become professor of physiology at the University of Groningen in 1925 and by the time that Tamara Dembo arrived there had already published widely on strictly physiological topics and on topics that would now be viewed as belonging to animal psychology or ethology (e.g., on habit formation in birds and fish; on form perception in dogs).

From Tamara Dembo's letters to Buytendijk and from other sources we can infer that Buytendijk had quite intensive contacts with prominent members of the Gestalt movement (and with a host of other international psychologists).[7] He personally knew Koffka, Lewin, and Goldstein and corresponded with them. Buytendijk's interest in the Gestalt approach was somewhat critical (Dekkers, 1985), but he was clearly inspired by it and for some time used Gestalt concepts to describe and analyze his own experimental findings in animal psychology (e.g., Buytendijk and Fischel, 1931a; 1931b; 1931c; 1931d; 1932a; 1932b). Eventually, he felt most drawn to the work of Kurt Goldstein (1878-1965), who by that time was slowly developing his own conception. Both Buytendijk and Goldstein were critical of the traditional stimulus and reflex concepts and defended a more holistic approach of the organism (claiming, for example, that the meaning of a stimulus is dependent on its significance for the whole organism in a specific situation; see Ash, 1995). Buytendijk corresponded with Goldstein and was instrumental in getting Goldstein to the Netherlands in 1934 when his further stay in Germany became too dangerous (Dekkers, 1985).

We do not know how Tamara Dembo ended up at the Groningen Physiological Institute but given the intensive contacts between Gestalt figures and Buytendijk sketched above, it would not come as a surprise if one of the Gestalt psychologists had recommended her to Buytendijk. Goldstein, for example,—who knew of Dembo's work and also would work with her compatriots Ovsiankina and Hanfmann (cf. Hanfmann, Rickers-Ovsiankina, and Goldstein, 1944)—may have played a role.[8] However that may be, the fact is that she befriended Buytendijk and his family[9] and spent her time doing research into animal intelligence at Buytendijk's physiological institute.

Rats in a Spacious Maze

The only publication that resulted from the stay at Groningen (Dembo, 1930), shows clear traces of the work of both the first and the second of Tamara Dembo's supervisors. From Buytendijk (1918), she borrowed a device (box) that he had used to investigate the behavior of toads and his general anti-associationist stance. From Lewin, she borrowed the analysis in terms of field forces. The topic of her research was the "goal-directed behavior of rats in a free situation." Tamara Dembo remarked that in the traditional learning experiments with rats in T-mazes the freedom of movement of the rats is very limited (one of Buytendijk's themes; see below). As a consequence, the difference between purposeful behavior and non-purposeful behavior is not as clear as would be possible in situations where the rats have more freedom. In order to be able to study the development of purposeful behavior over time in a less restricted environment, Dembo decided to use Buytendijk's box (see figure 11.2).

The glass plates 1 and 2 served as a barrier for the rat, but enabled it to see the goal (i.e. food) at q. The box was sufficiently large (120 x 70 cm.) to allow the rat plenty of freedom to move around. It always entered the box through door p and was removed from the box one minute after it had reached the goal, that is, it was allowed to eat for a minute. Tamara Dembo worked with three rats—according to her notebooks they went by the names Ada, Biba, and Boba—who each visited the box for five to eight trials a day over a period of twenty days. The bulk of her paper consists of a discussion of the trajectories that the rats followed while walking from p to q.

222   Thinking in Psychological Science

Figure 11.2
Spacious Maze Allowing for Free Behavior (after Dembo, 1930).

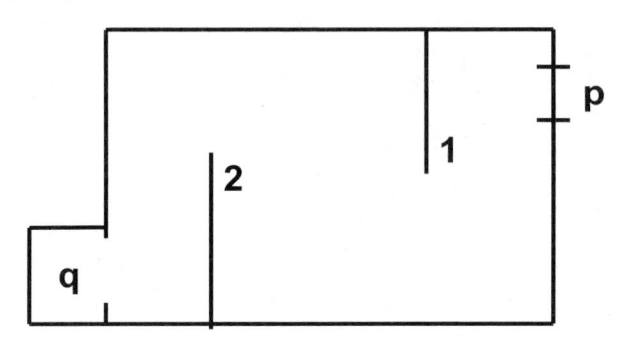

Not surprisingly, a rat that was placed in the box for the first time would move around in a seemingly erratic manner, that is, it did not run directly to the goal but walked to and fro sniffing the walls, glass plates, etc. In sum, in the first trial the novice takes a genuine interest in the environment itself and explores it. The goal is reached only accidentally. In Dembo's terms, there is not yet a single vector that determines the whole of the rat's behavior but many small vectors that "distract" it. Up from the second trial, however, the rats' behavior changed dramatically: they would now follow a more or less direct route to the goal zigzagging around the glass plates. This goal-directed behavior lasted until the animals were satiated (say, four or five trials). After that, the animals again showed great interest in their environment, and re-began exploring the box, following unpredictable routes.

To Tamara Dembo, this simple finding showed that an explanation in terms of the formation of chains of associations or reflexes was mistaken: According to the associationist explanation the repetition of the direct trajectory and its reinforcement by the food would only strengthen this trajectory. It is incapable of explaining why the animal resumes the original "erratic" route after a number of trials. In her terms, the rat has not forgotten the direct trajectory but just does not display it: the rat will only follow the direct route when the vector (or field force) towards the goal happens to be the strongest in the constellation of field forces. In a way, then, she made the distinction between manifest and latent learning that Tolman (Tolman and Honzik, 1930) would make that same year, although without using these terms.

There is another way to demonstrate that the rats' behavior is determined by the momentary constellation of field forces operative in the environment and not by simple habit formation. Linking up to Maier (1929), Dembo wanted to investigate whether the rat's behavior is still determined by the goal vector even when it is already following an older, habitual trajectory. To this end, she removed one of the glass plates after the rats had learned to follow the direct, zigzag route to the goal. The results showed that two of the rats followed the original trajectory during the first one or two trials after the plate had been removed, thus making an unnecessary detour. In the subsequent trial they investigated the place where the plate had been and then proceeded following the shortest possible trajectory towards the goal. The remaining third rat immediately paused in the first trial after the plate had been removed, sniffed around, and then followed a direct route to the goal. This result again showed to Dembo that the rats' behavior is not determined by in learned chains of associations but by the dynamic interplay of forces in a specific situation. As long as the animal is not satiated, it is the vector towards the goal that will determine the global behavior of the animal.

Thus, in this tiny simple experiment Tamara Dembo showed that a reflexological or associationist account is unable to explain the behavior of rats in a maze—a theme that much appealed to her Dutch mentor Buytendijk, who pursued this theme in several of his own publications (Buytendijk, 1931b; Buytendijk and Plessner, 1935). She argued that Lewin's notion of dynamic field forces is able to shed more light on the rats' behavior than the associationist approach can do. It was Lewin himself who had suggested such an interpretation of the results. From Tamara Dembo's correspondence with Buytendijk, we know that she discussed the draft version of her paper with Lewin and that he suggested numerous changes. This resulted in the final, fully rewritten version (Dembo, 1930b; 1930c; 1930d; 1930e).

Rats in an Amusement Park

Above we mentioned that Tamara Dembo's stay in Groningen resulted in one publication. This is not strictly true, however. During her stay at the Physiological Institute, Tamara Dembo carried out numerous other rat experiments the results of some of which she planned to publish. Thus, we see her investigating whether rats can learn to pull a string to obtain some biscuit attached to the string, whether they jump a glass barrier to obtain some food; whether they can make detours; whether they can discriminate between two objects, etc. The experiments were clearly inspired by the work of Köhler and the rats displayed a variety of skills that cannot be observed in a T-maze.

One particular set of observations took place in a large box that contained very many, diverse, and for rats presumably attractive objects (see below). For this reason, Dembo and Buytendijk referred to the box and to the whole investigation as to the "amusement park" (Dembo, 1930d; 1930e; 1931c; 1932). While in Groningen, Dembo apparently did not find the time to finish a paper about this series of observations and when back in Berlin she was too much occupied by the preparation for her dissertation defense and (eventually) her departure for the United States to work on it any further. In letters to Buytendijk (Dembo, 1930b; 1930d; 1930e) she apologizes for the delay, claims that she discussed the content of the paper with Lewin, and promises to finish it[10] as soon as possible. When Buytendijk finally writes to her about his intention to publish the draft version of the paper under her name if he does not receive a revision on short notice (he could do so as he was co-editor of the journal in question), Tamara Dembo (1931c) replies that in her opinion it would be better if another person would do some additional experiments and publish the whole investigation under his own name ("there is no need at all to publish the work under my name—it is the right of the person who will continue the work and write the article"). And this, in fact, is how it happened. Buytendijk (1931a) published the paper under his own name (but without doing additional experiments), mentioning in the subheading that the paper was written "on the basis of experiments by Tamara Dembo." In view of these circumstances, we will briefly review Buytendijk's paper.

Buytendijk began by criticizing the experiments by American behaviorists and Pavlov for their exclusive emphasis on simple and measurable behavior. Dogs can salivate or not, rats can turn left or right in a T-maze, but otherwise the animals are left very little choice. They cannot display the complete range of their natural behavior. Such an approach, Buytendijk argued, is bound to underestimate the lower animals' intelligence and does harm to a genuine comparative psychology. Rather than experiment with large amounts of rats in exceedingly restricted situations we should observe individual rats in situations that leave them many more degrees of freedom (and that can still be manipulated by the experimenter).

To this end Tamara Dembo and Buytendijk devised a large box of 2 X 2 m (and 1 m high), which was filled with objects and devices that might interest a rat. These included various sorts of food, a piece of wood, a glass of water, little bags filled with sand, objects to climb on, pieces of metal, etc. Sometimes an animal of another species (a frog or a rabbit) would be placed in the box as well. Rats were placed in the box either alone or together with one or five other rats.

The whole investigation consisted in observing what rats would do under various circumstances, e.g., when placed in the box for the first time or when confronted with a frog. Buytendijk claimed that under such circumstances rats show much more varied and also more intelligent behavior than under the usual contrived circumstances. He described, for example, how a rat explores its new environment (i.e., first a nervous rapid inspection of the whole box, then a somewhat less superficial and more relaxed next round of inspection, and finally a detailed investigation of several of its principal objects), how rats may "hesitate" between various options (e.g., between dragging A or B to their nest), how they can be utterly amazed, how they show "insight," and how they jump up and down in nervous anxiety when confronted with a live frog.

Buytendijk concluded that we should not confine ourselves to the study of situations that leave the animals few degrees of freedom. The observation of behavior in "rich" situations that leave them more choice can yield new insights.

Rats may show "emotional" behavior similar to that observed in other animals and humans, they may be capable of more intelligent behavior than commonly observed, and we may observe their social behavior. He warned against the tendency to study the average animal in trivial situations just because the results of such experiments are easier to describe statistically.

Birdwatching in the Lab

Even more surprising than Tamara Dembo's rat studies—about whose existence few people seem to have known until now—are her bird observations. To our knowledge these observations have not been published and the following account is based on a typed manuscript found in her archives. The manuscript is written in German and follows the format that was used by the *Archives Néerlandaises de Physiologie de l'Homme et des Animaux*, the journal co-edited by Buytendijk that also published Dembo's rat article (e.g., the final paragraph consisted of a list of numbered conclusions). On the first page of the typed manuscript Dembo has added in handwriting that its author was "Tamara Dembo (from the Physiological Institute of the University of Groningen)," but in the text we find several indications that it was intended as a joint product by Buytendijk and Dembo. Thus, in her introduction she writes that "one of us" found that fish can discriminate between various movements of objects and she refers to "our" previous studies of dogs. Buytendijk was the one, of course, who had published widely on fish and dogs (and, inspired by R.M. Yerkes comparative approach, on many other species, such as ants, birds, octopuses, and women).

The object of the article was to describe whether a bird (a siskin) can find food that is hidden by the experimenter but, like in the rat studies, Dembo supplied detailed descriptions of behavior that was not directly related to that goal. The emphasis was on lengthy unobtrusive observation and in discussing the bird's behavior Dembo (and Buytendijk) took great pains not to make the mistake of anthropomorphism. This approach, although it lacked the naturalistic field observations, had much in common with that of the then emerging ethology of Tinbergen and Lorenz.[11]

Dembo studied the siskin in a cage of 50 X 50 X 35 cm. Attached to the cage were 4 boxes A, B, C, and D, that could contain food behind little doors (see Figure 11.3).

The bird was first taught that the food was behind the door of box B. No changes were subsequently made during four months. After that, the whole cage (which was located on a table) was turned 180 degrees. Food was still placed in box B, which now, however, occupied the spot previously occupied by box D. The question was what the bird would do. Dembo explained that merely listing the various actions that the bird displays does not provide genuine insight in its behavior. For this reason she chose to discuss sequences of

Figure 11.3
Bird Cage for the Study of Food Searching (after Dembo, 1929).

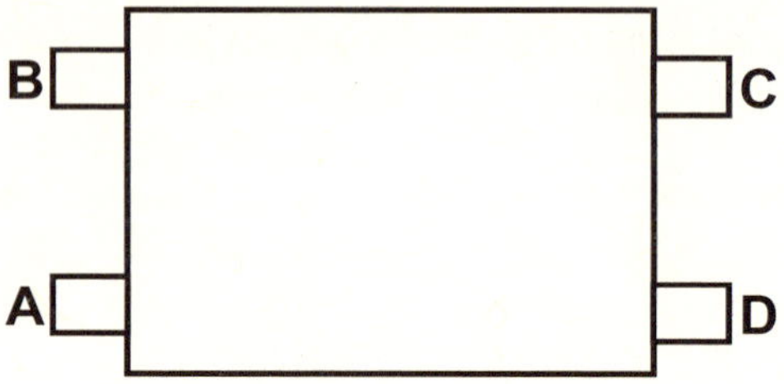

behavior (*Geschehensschnitten*) and the transitions from one type of behavior to another. In themselves these descriptions of sequences of bird behavior are perhaps as interesting as the answer to the question whether the bird can find the food in its new location (it can).

Being in an impoverished environment, the number of activities the bird could display was, of course, rather limited: it could fly around, sit still and look around, sharpen its beak against the bars, drink, eat, take a bath and little more. Dembo nevertheless provided us with several interesting observations. To illustrate her elaborate descriptions and interpretations of bird behavior we give an excerpt of one observation (which started at 3.00 hours):

> The bird flies to the middle perch. *As said before, this is equivalent to occupying a secure, comfortable location.* The bird *preens itself and looks around. Sharpens its beak against the bars.* Continues preening, looks around. *The bird can behave uniformly quietly.* Sharpen its beak for a long time and look around.
>
> 3.05. During the further sharpening the bird looks around once and then continues preening. Jumps on the right perch, then on the left, looks around, jumps back on the middle en continues sharpening its beak. After some time it briefly extends its neck and continues sharpening its beak. Then it [missing word] its wings, folds them together and sits quietly, looking around, but otherwise motionless. Later it looks down for a moment and opens and closes its beak, then continues sharpening its beak or preening. Once it jumps up and down in a way that it now sits with its back to the observer, then it turns back and continues sharpening its beak.
>
> A certain behavior of the bird, e.g., sharpening of the beak or quiet behavior (sitting), can be *showered with* very brief (spark-like) actions. The grounds for these spark actions cannot be inferred. Characteristically, they often occur, and also in this case, during a phase of transition from one lengthy *action* (sharpening) to another (approaching of food).
>
> 3.15. The bird jumps on the right, then on the left perch, again on the right one and back on the middle one. The bird has become more lively. The sharpening is meanwhile continued, but also more energetically.

In this case the transition to a new action is not just characterized by the fact that the total behavior of the bird becomes more lively and by 'doing something else for brief moments," but by a phase of *"hidden interweaving"* of the beginning of the new action with the old one. Thus, as if by accident the bird jumps on the perch in the vicinity of the food tray, seemingly not paying notice to the food. And only because the bird immediately afterwards occupies itself with the food, one sees that the jumping on the perch was no "accident." *The gradual transition form one action to another* can in general be described as follows: First, there is a stage of being exclusively occupied with the first action, then (2) begins a phase when the first action (in our case, the sharpening) is being interrupted by brief spark-like actions. Then (3) the bird generally becomes more lively and as if by accident draws essential "preliminary stages" of the second action into the range of the first action (the bird leaves the spot of the first action and literally approaches the second action. But the "approaching" of the second action does not always have to be spatial). Then (4) the beginning of the second action is no longer carried out as if by accident, but it gets the emphasis in the action complex and it alone remains (Dembo, 1929, pp. 4-6).

Dembo described various other behaviors that are equally interesting and that demonstrate her abilities as a bird watcher. We will mention a few of them. She discussed how the siskin regularly pecked the bottom of the cage after a failure to find food behind one of the doors and coined it "Ersatzpecking." She mentioned how the bird "pendulated" between the goal and other activities, i.e., how goal-directed activity is interspersed with bouts of other activity. She observed that the bird frenetically pecked the bottom after yet another failure to find the food and suggested that the bird was frustrated and in anger. Finally, she argued that one psychic process can be temporarily suppressed (she used the term "Verdrängung" or displacement) by another one and subsequently become re-activated again. Thus, on the basis of her careful and lengthy observations she postulated that needs or drives may be operative at time it even when this cannot be inferred from the actual behavior at time t. The reason is that various behaviors can suppress or inhibit each other.

Very similar observations and explanations are, of course, quite common in modern ethology. Analyses in terms of competition between and inhibition of activities abound in ethology and the term "displacement activity" has been advanced to describe the seemingly irrelevant behavior that often occurs when ongoing behavior is temporarily inhibited (Hinde, 1982). This once again demonstrates the remark made above, that is, that many psychologists and biologists in the late 1920s and early 1930s advanced ideas that came quite close to or were identical with the concepts that would be propagated by Tinbergen and Lorenz somewhat later and that would be used to declare the need for the new science of ethology. As is often the case, the birth of this new science was as much due to clever propagandizing by its originators as to genuine novel insights (Röell, 1996).

The bird manuscript was never finished. The typewritten version found in Dembo's archives is full of handwritten corrections, remarks in the margin etc., and it is followed by two pages in handwriting in that she tries to reformulate her introduction to the paper. We have no idea why the paper was not completed and published nor why no mention is made of it in the Dembo-Buytendijk correspondence at our disposal.[12] The reason may have simply been that Tamara Dembo was generally slow in writing. But it does seem a pity that it was not published at the time, if only because it clearly demonstrates that the animal psychologists of that period were able to do interesting observational studies in the laboratory that ethologists would later claim were only possible in field studies.

Leaving for the United States

> Sehr geehrter Herr Professor, you were not quite mistaken when you suspected that I was ill. In fact, I have a fever and this fever will last for another 7 weeks ... until the examination (Dembo, 1930e).

With these words written on May 31, 1930, in a letter to Buytendijk, Tamara Dembo jokingly referred to her dissertation defense which would take place on July 25 of that same year. As we know, Tamara Dembo defended her dissertation successfully, and two days after the event she was happy to mention this fact to Buytendijk:

> A few days ago I successfully defended my dissertation and I feel that a big weight has been taken off my shoulders. I cannot stand examinations and hope never in my life to have to do another one. But all is well that ends well. The nice thing is that I am immediately very busy after the examination. In six weeks I will go to Professor Koffka in Northampton and before that I must prepare my paper for printing, I must "restore" my English, see some things in Berlin, and prepare everything for the trip. I travel via Hoek van Holland, London, Liverpool ... and hope to be in New York on September 22, from there it is only four hours to Smith College (Dembo, 1930f).

Thus ended the European period of Tamara Dembo. She would be back occasionally (cf. Dembo, 1931c; Rosa and Wertsch, 1993), but continued her scientific career in the United States, first at Smith College with Koffka, then at the Worcester State Hospital (1932-1934), Cornell University (1934-1943), the University of Iowa (1934-1943), Mount Holyoke College (1943-1945), Stanford University (1945-1948), the New School for Social Research (1948-1951), Harvard University (1951-1953), and finally at Clark University (1953-1980).

She had felt drawn to Clark University much earlier. In a letter to Buytendijk (Dembo, 1932), she explained that Worcester was just sixty miles from Northampton and that she wanted to learn more about American animal psychology via Hunter's experiments at Clark (cf. Hunter, 1920, 1928, 1929). Perhaps, she wrote, I will ask him whether I can attend his colloquia. Whether she carried out this intention we do not know but it seems to show that her interest in animal psychology was not a fleeting affair. Her publications, however, would henceforward make no mention of this field. Via the research of perception (Dembo and Hanfmann, 1933), she went to the problems of newly admitted patients (Dembo and Hanfmann, 1936; Hanfmann and Dembo, 1934), to end up in the field for which she would become known in the United States, that is, the field of rehabilitation psychology.

In the introduction to this paper we sketched how hundreds of thousands of Russians left their native country at the beginning of this century. Many of them were forced to leave, others left voluntarily, and in still others the complex of reasons and causes that played a role in what turned out to be their emigration cannot be described in these simple terms. But all of them faced the hardships of adjusting to one or even several new countries and their cultures, of finding a job, of struggling to learn a new language, and so forth, in a historical period when the world economy was heading for a crisis. And many of them must have been lonely and longing to return at times,[13] perhaps to relatives and friends that meanwhile had perished in Soviet concentration camps or in the atrocities of World War II. The situation must have been even more difficult for young single women such as Tamara Dembo (Wertsch, 1993). In dedicating this issue to Tamara Dembo we pay tribute to the adventurous and not so adventurous young women such as Gita Birenbaum, Tamara Dembo, Eugenia Hanfmann, Maria Ovsiankina, Gertruda Vakar (cf. Friedrich, 1984), and Blyuma Zeigarnik, who struggled hard to adjust to entirely new and often difficult circumstances and nevertheless left their trace in the history of psychology.[14]

Notes

1. Previously published in *From Past to Future, 2(1),1-17. Tension in the Field: The Dynamic World of Tamara Dembo.* © 1999 Frances L. Hiatt School of Psychology, Clark University. Author: Rene Van der Veer Faculty of Social Sciences (FSW) Rijksuniversiteit Leiden, Postbus 9555, 2300 RB Leiden, The Netherlands.
2. According to other accounts (Anonymous, 1993; Kennedy, 1993; Rosa and Wertsch, 1993), she spent part of her youth in St. Petersburg. I am here following her own very brief autobiographical account in Dembo (1931b), which makes no mention of St. Petersburg.
3. Hans Rupp (1880-1954) was a student of G.E. Müller and the head of the laboratory of applied psychology in Stumpf's institute in Berlin (Behrens, 1997; Sprung, 1997).
4. Subsequent historians of science have advanced quite different views of Galileo's approach and some have even seen him as continuing Aristotle's mode of thinking (Cohen, 1994).
5. That subjects participated in two or more experiments can be explained by the fact that they sometimes came back to continue the task. We have no idea why it took Tamara Dembo four years to carry out sixty-four experiments of one or two hours duration.
6. Reading Dembo's (1931b) meticulous accounts of individual subjects who despair of finding the solution and obviously want to stop the experiment as soon as possible (imagine having to think of ways to grasp a flowerpot for approximately two hours), one realizes that her experiments were, apart from showing the genesis of anger, at the same time demonstrating obedience to authority.

7. In Tamara Dembo's letters to Buytendijk, Lewin and Koffka repeatedly send their greetings, promise to send films (in the case of Lewin), papers, etc. Tamara Dembo herself kept Buytendijk informed about her colleagues' activities. She mentioned, for example, that in May 1932 Koffka had left for Moscow to take part in a psychological expedition in "Turkestan" (Dembo, 1932). This was no other than the expedition to Uzbekistan, iniated and organized by Vygotsky and Luria to investigate the mental processes of so-called primitive people (see Van der Veer and Valsiner, 1991, for a detailed description).
8. But there are plenty of other possibilities. There was, for example, the figure of A. A. Grünbaum. Grünbaum (1885-1932), a Russian Jewish psychologist from Odessa, who worked with Külpe in Würzburg, emigrated to the Netherlands in 1914. He became a prominent member of Dutch academia and brought Buytendijk into contact with the German philosopher Max Scheler (Dekkers, 1985). Grünbaum, with his excellent contacts in both Germany and Holland, may have been instrumental in getting Tamara Dembo her position in Groningen.
9. The eldest son of Buytendijk, Frits Buytendijk, now eighty-five years old, still remembers her as a pleasant, modest, and intelligent young woman who visited their home. He was sixteen at the time.
10. In Dembo's archives a typewritten draft version of the paper published under Buytendijk's name was found. Its author is not given. The published version is clearly a polished and trimmed (e.g., names of rats and excessive empirical detail have been deleted) version of this draft version to which a one-page conclusion paragraph has been added. Onto this manuscript numerous corrections and changes have been written by Dembo (judging by the handwriting). She also makes suggestions in the margin, like "Do we really need this example?" and so on. None of these changes has been carried through in the published version, however, which consequently still contains several (grammatical) errors. What may have happened, then, is that Dembo was working on a revision of a joint version of the paper or on a version already produced by Buytendijk, but in the end failed to send her comments to Buytendijk in time.
11. In their efforts to establish a new discipline, Tinbergen and Lorenz tended to exaggerate the differences between animal psychology and ethology, an attitude which did not improve the emotional atmosphere in Dutch academia (Röell, 1996).
12. We have just one indirect reference to the bird studies. In her letter to Buytendijk of July 27, 1930, almost a year after she had left Groningen, Dembo (1930f) inquired "How the little bird is doing?" (Und was macht das Vögelein?).
13. In a letter dated 9 April 1932, Luria (1932) wrote to Dembo "I heard that you plan to come to us. If this is *serious* and *for a long time*, then we must discuss all possibilities of your move."
14. I would like to thank the following persons for their help in locating and gathering archival materials: Willem J.M. Dings of the Katholiek Documentatie Centrum in Nijmegen (where the letters of Tamara Dembo to Buytendijk can be found), Jacques Dane of the Archief en Documentatiecentrum Nederlandse Psychologie in Groningen, and Simone de Lima and Jaan Valsiner of Clark University (who supplied me with Dembo's notebooks about the experiments conducted in Berlin and Groningen and with part of her correspondence).
15. All of Dembo's letters to Buytendijk are written in German.

References

Anonymous (1993). Tamara Dembo, ninety-one, leading figure of Gestalt therapy in this century. *The Boston Globe*, Monday, October 18.

Ash, M.G. (1995). Gestalt psychology in German culture 1890-1967: *Holism and the quest for objectivity.* Cambridge: Cambridge University Press.

Behrings, P.J. (1997). G.E. Müller: The third pillar of experimental psychology. In W.G. Bringmann, H.E. Lück, R. Miller, and Ch.E. Early (Eds.), A pictorial history of psychology (pp. 171-176). Chicago, IL: Quintessence Publishing Co.

Birenbaum, G. (1930). Das Vergessen einer Vornahme. *Psychologische Forschung, 13,* 218-284.

Boring, E.G. (1950). A history of experimental psychology. New York: Appleton-Century-Crofts. (second edition)

Buytendijk, F.J.J. (1918). Instinct de la recherche du nid et expérience chez les crapauds. *Archives Néerlandaises de Physiologie de l'Homme et des Animaux, 2,* 521-529.

Buytendijk, F.J.J. (1931a). Eine Methode zur Beobachtung von Ratten in aufgabefreien Situationen (Nach Versuchen von Tamara Dembo). *Archives Néerlandaises de Physiologie de l'Homme et des Animaux, 16,* 574-596.

Buytendijk, F.J.J. (1931b). Kritik der Reflextheorie auf Grund der Erforschung der Verhaltungsweisen beim Tiere. In: *Verhandlungen der Deutschen Gesellschaft für innere Medizin.* XLIII. Kongress, Wiesbaden 1931 (pp. 24-33). München: Bergmann.

Buytendijk, F.J.J., and Fischel, W. (1931a). Strukturgemässes Verhalten von Ratten. *Archives Néerlandaises de Physiologie de l'Homme et des Animaux, 16,* 55-83.

Buytendijk, F.J.J., and Fischel, W. (1931b). Teil und Ganzes bei der Orientierung von Ratten. *Archives Néerlandaises de Physiologie de l'Homme et des Animaux, 16,* 214-233.

Buytendijk, F.J.J., and Fischel, W. (1931c). Versuch einer neuen Analyse der tierischen Einsicht. *Archives Néerlandaises de Physiologie de l'Homme et des Animaux, 16,* 449-476.

Buytendijk, F.J.J., and Fischel, W. (1931d). Die optische Ferneinstellung der Ratte. *Archives Néerlandaises de Physiologie de l'Homme et des Animaux, 16,* 510-527.

Buytendijk, F.J.J., and Fischel, W. (1932a). Versuche über die Steuerung der Bewegungen. Archives *Néerlandaises de Physiologie de l'Homme et des Animaux, 17,* 63-96.

Buytendijk, F.J.J., and Fischel, W. (1932b). Die Bedeutung der Feldkräfte und der Intentionalität für das Verhalten des Hundes. *Archives Néerlandaises de Physiologie de l'Homme et des Animaux, 17,* 459-494.

Buytendijk, F.J.J., and Plessner, H. (1935). Die physiologische Erklärung des Verhalten. Eine Kritik an der Theorie Pawlows. *Acta Biotheoretica, 1,* 151-172.

Cassirer, E. (1910/1953). Substance and function. In E. Cassirer, Substance and Function and Einstein's theory of relativity (pp. 3-346). New York: Dover Publications.

Cohen, H.F. (1994). *The scientific revolution: A historiographical inquiry.* Chicago, IL: University of Chicago Press.

Dehue, T. (1995). *Changing the rules: Psychology in the Netherlands, 1900-1985.* Cambridge: Cambridge University Press.

Dekkers, W.J.M. (1985). Het bezielde lichaam: Het ontwerp van een antropologische fysiologie en geneeskunde volgens F.J.J. Buytendijk. Zeist: Kerckebosch.

Dembo, T. (1925). Vortrag von Fräulein Dembo, über ihre Versuche, mit anschliessenden Fragen. Im Psychologischen Institut der Universität, Montag d. 7. Dez. 25. Minutes of a meeting on 7 December 1925.

Dembo, T. (1929). Futtersuche nach indirekte Merkmalen beim Vogel. Unpublished manuscript.

Dembo, T. (1930a). Zielgerichtetes Verhalten der Ratten in einer freien Situation. *Archives Néerlandaises de Physiologie de l'Homme et des Animaux, 15,* 402-412.

Dembo, T. (1930b). Letter to F.J.J. Buytendijk, dated 24 January 1930[15].

Dembo, T. (1930c). Letter to F.J.J. Buytendijk, dated 12 March 1930.

Dembo, T. (1930d). Letter to F.J.J. Buytendijk, dated 8 April 1930.
Dembo, T. (1930e). Letter to F.J.J. Buytendijk, dated 31 May 1930.
Dembo, T. (1930f). Letter to F.J.J. Buytendijk, dated 27 July 1930.
Dembo, T. (1931a). Der Ärger als dynamisches Problem. *Psychologische Forschung, 15*, 1-144.
Dembo, T. (1931b). Der Ärger als dynamisches Problem. Berlin: Julius Springer.
Dembo, T. (1931c). Letter to F.J.J. Buytendijk, dated 20 September 1931.
Dembo, T. (1932). Letter to F.J.J. Buytendijk, dated 3 June 1932.
Dembo, T., and Hanfmann, E. (1933). Intuitive halving and doubling of figures. *Psychologische Forschung, 17*, 306-318.
Dembo, T., and Hanfmann, E. (1936). The patient's psychological situation upon admission to a mental hospital. *American Journal of Psychology, 47*, 381-408.
De Rivera, J. (1995). Tamara Dembo (1902-1993). *American Psychologist, 50*, 386.
Field, A. (1977). Nabokov: His life in part. Harmondsworth: Penguin Books.
Friedrich, P. (1984). Biograficheskyj ocherk. In G. Vakar, Stikhotvoreniia. East Lansing, MI: Russian Language Journal.
Grünbaum, A.A. (1927). Über das Verhalten der Spinne (Epeira diademata) besonders gegenüber vibratorischen Reizen. *Psychologische Forschung, 9*, 275-299.
Hanfmann, E., and Dembo, T. (1934). The value of an orientational letter for newly admitted patients. *Psychiatrical Quarterly, 8,* 703-721.
Hanfmann, E., Rickers-Ovsiankina, M, and Goldstein, K. (1944). Case Lanuti: Extreme concretization of behavior due to damage of the brain cortex. *Psychological Monographs, 57*, 1-72.
Hinde, R.A. (1982). *Ethology*. Oxford: Oxford University Press.
Hoppe, F. (1930). Erfolg und Misserfolg. *Psychologische Forschung, 14,* 1-62.
Hunter, W.S. (1920). The temporal maze and kinaesthetic sensory processes in the white rat. *Psychobiology, 2*, 1-17.
Hunter, W.S. (1928). The behavior of raccoons in a double alternation temporal maze. *Journal of Genetic Psychology, 35*, 374-388.
Hunter, W.S. (1929). The sensory control of the maze habit in the white rat. *Journal of Genetic Psychology, 36*, 505-537.
Kennedy, R. (1993). Tamara Dembo, 91, Gestalt psychologist who studied anger. *New York Times*, Tuesday, October 19.
Kravkov, S.V. (1928). Über die Richtung der Farbentransformation. *Psychologische Forschung, 10*, 20-31.
Kravkov, S.V. (1932). Über ein Grundgesetz der Farbentransformation. *Psychologische Forschung, 16*, 160-165.
Kravkov, S.V., and Paulsen-Bashmakova, V.A. (1929). Über die kontrasterregende Wirkung der transformierten Farben. *Psychologische Forschung, 12*, 88-93.
Lewin, K. (1927/1981). Gesetz und Experiment in der Psychologie. In C.F. Graumann and A. Métraux (Eds.), *Kurt Lewin Werkausgabe. Bd. 1. Wissenschafstheorie 1* (pp. 279-321). Bern: Hans Huber.
Lewin, K. (1931). The conflict between Aristotelian and Galileian modes of thought in contemporary psychology. *Journal of Genetic Psychology, 5*, 141-177.
Lewin, K. (1931/1981). Der Übergang von der aristotelischen zur galileischen Denkweise in Biologie und Psychologie. In C.F. Graumann and A. Métraux (Eds.), *Kurt Lewin Werkausgabe. Bd. 1. Wissenschafstheorie 1* (pp. 233-278). Bern: Hans Huber.
Lewin, K. (1933). Environmental forces. In C. Murchison (Ed.), *A handbook of child psychology* (pp. 590-625). Worcester, MA: Clark University Press. (second revised edition)

Luria, A.R. (1929). Die Methode der abbildenden Motorik bei Kommunikation der Systeme und ihre Anwendung auf die Affektpsychologie. *Psychologische Forschung, 12*, 127-179.
Luria, A.R. (1932). Letter to T.V. Dembo, dated 9 April 1932.
Luria, A.R. (1958). Letter to T.V. Dembo, dated 29 June 1958.
Maier, N.R.F. (1929). Reasoning in white rats. *Comparative Psychology Monographs, 6*, 1-93.
Marrow, A.J. (1969). *The practical theorist: The life and work of Kurt Lewin.* New York-London: Basic Books.
Ovsiankina, M. (1928). Die Wiederaufnahme unterbrochener Handlungen. *Psychologische Forschung, 11*, 302-379.
Raeff, M. (1990). *Russia abroad: A cultural history of the Russian emigration, 1919-1939.* New York-Oxford: Oxford University Press.
Röell, D.R. (1996). *De wereld van instinct: Niko Tinbergen en het ontstaan van de ethologie in Nederland* (1920-1950). Rotterdam: Erasmus Publishing.
Rosa, A., and Wertsch, J.V. (1993). Tamara Dembo and her work. *Journal of Russian and East European Psychology, 31*, 5-13.
Samojlov, A. (1923). Die Anordnung der musikalischen Intervalle im Raume. *Psychologische Forschung, 3*, 231-240.
Sprung, H. (1997). Carl Stumpf. In W.G. Bringmann, H.E. Lück, R. Miller, and Ch.E. Early (Eds.), *A pictorial history of psychology* (pp. 247-250). Chicago, IL: Quintessence Publishing Co.
Sprung, L., and Sprung, H. (1997). The Berlin school of Gestalt psychology. In W.G. Bringmann, H.E. Lück, R. Miller, and Ch.E. Early (Eds.), *A pictorial history of psychology* (pp. 268-272). Chicago, IL: Quintessence Publishing Co.
Tolman, E.C., and Honzik, C.H. (1930). Introduction and removal of reward, and maze performance in rats. University of California *Publications in Psychology, 4*, 257-275.
Uznadze, D. (1924). Ein experimenteller Beitrag zum Problem der psychologischen Grundlagen der Namengebung. *Psychologische Forschung, 5*, 24-43.
Uznadze, D. (1930). Über die Gewichtstäuschung und ihre Analogen. *Psychologische Forschung, 14*, 366-379.
Valsiner, J. (1988). *Developmental psychology in the Soviet Union.* Brighton, England: The Harvester Press.
Van der Veer, R., and Valsiner, J. (1991). *Understanding Vygotsky. A quest for synthesis.* Oxford: Blackwell.
Wertsch. J.V. (1993). Tamara Dembo: In memoriam. *Journal of Russian and East European Psychology, 31*, 3-4.
Zeigarnik, B. (1927). Das Behalten erledigter und unerledigter Handlungen. *Psychologische Forschung, 9*, 1-85.
Zeigarnik, B. (1931). Letter to T.V. Dembo, dated 9 January 1931.

12

Between Scylla and Charybdis: Tamara Dembo and Rehabilitation Psychology

Simone de Lima[1]

According to the Greek myth, Scylla and Charybdis were monsters lurking at the opposite margins of a strait through which only the boldest adventurers tried to navigate—often unsuccessfully. This image was used to characterize the task of the researcher at a conference held at Clark University on the relationship between rehabilitation and psychology. There, Alfred Baldwin discussed with Tamara Dembo, Kurt Goldstein, Heinz Werner, and others the dangers lurking in the strait. On the one side, by pursuing applications of knowledge atheoretically, one loses the basic mechanisms underlying the process of change; on the other, being dragged into the "coldly detached atmosphere" of basic research, one may become split from—and uninspired by—any connections to real human problems (Levinton, 1959).

This careful, dangerous steering is what seems to have challenged, troubled, and advanced Tamara Dembo in her several decades of work on the interface of applied and theoretical psychology, most outstandingly in the area of rehabilitation. In her early years of scientific education with Lewin, Koffka, Köhler, Wertheimer, and others of the Berlin Gestalt School (see van der Veer, Chapter 11), she developed the concern for careful theoretical analysis that she maintained throughout her work. Her subsequent years in the U.S. led her to encounter challenges such as the reintegration into social life of those disabled by accidents in World War II, which fundamentally influenced her position on the role of psychology.

Psychology, Dembo often and vehemently argued, should use its existing theoretical and methodological instruments to analyze and help solve genuine problems encountered by real persons. In a spiraling fashion, dealing with such problems would foster the re-elaboration of theoretical frameworks and require methodological adjustment—and advancement.

Rather than seeing applications as an "escape" from sound theory construction, her approach amalgamates theory and application in a line compatible with that posed by her advisor, Kurt Lewin:

> The greatest handicap of applied psychology has been the fact that, without theoretical help, it had to follow the costly, inefficient, and limited method of trial and error. Many psychologists working today in an applied field are keenly aware of the need for close cooperation between theoretical and applied psychology. This can be accomplished in psychology, as it has been accomplished in physics, if the theorist does not look toward applied problems with highbrow aversion or with a fear of social problems, and if the applied psychologist realizes that there is nothing so practical as a good theory (Lewin, 1951/1943, p. 169).

Dembo's classic volume on the psychology of anger (Dembo, 1931) was developed under the advice of Kurt Lewin and the influence and teachings of Koffka, Köhler, and Wertheimer at the Berlin Institute of Psychology. This period (see Van der Veer, this issue) set the guidelines for much of her later work on rehabilitation, the focus of this paper, and it is therefore useful to outline some of the central tenets of Dembo's take on field theoretical psychology.

In this approach, all behavior (encompassing actions, thoughts, intentions, etc.) is viewed from a structural-dynamic perspective; that is, the emergence, development, and resolution of a psychological phenomenon, such as anger, are analyzed through the examination of the changing configurations in the *person-in-environment field*. In other words, behavior is a function of change of the state of the *field* in time, the field of the person being constituted by his life space—not merely the environment "around" the person, but the environment as it exists *for the person*. Theory-derived methodological construction is a major concern, as the task becomes to describe the structure of the field with its interrelated elements, boundaries and zones of free movement and the dynamics (forces, directed by valences, and tensions, in the encounter of opposing forces) leading to change in the field and consequently in the person (Lewin 1936, 1938, 1939, 1951/1946).

Dembo's work in rehabilitation would also continue to show its Lewinian roots in that focus on the reconceptualization of real life, concrete phenomena was the goal. This reconceptualization was seen as entailing the building of constructs that would integrate different phenotypic manifestations of the interrelated elements, rather than focusing on description and listing of similarities. Finally, the Lewinian legacy is present in Dembo's concern with the relevance of *experience* as psychological phenomena, and the mediating role of *meaning* in field structural change.

From Perception to Schizophrenia: The Early Years in the U.S.

After completing her Ph.D., Dembo moved from Germany to the U.S. in 1930, to work as a research associate under Koffka at Smith College, in

Northampton, Massachusetts. Eugenia Hanfmann, also from Berlin, worked with her on issues of perception and emotion. Together they published *Intuitive Halving and Doubling of Figures* (Dembo and Hanfmann, 1933), a study in which the factors leading to the errors in the estimation of sizes of different geometric figures is investigated in children and adults.

Besides the traditional quantitative report, a good part of the paper is devoted to a qualitative description of the different strategies employed by children of different ages to solve the tasks, the richness of which can be seen exactly in the valuation of a discussion of processes over the classification of the children as achievers or non-achievers. The same attention to a rich description of behavior preceding analysis can be seen in her unpublished work from this period on values and authority in preschool. Dembo was to take up her interest in child development again in two different periods, first with Lewin in Cornell and Iowa, with her work on frustration and regression, and later, at Clark University, working on the issue of the psychological development of cerebral palsied children.

In 1932 Dembo and Hanfmann both obtained positions as research associates at Worcester State Hospital, also in Massachusetts, then a bustling research institution for the study of schizophrenia, under David Shakow. Shakow was to become a central figure in the establishment of clinical psychology in the U.S. after World War II, presiding over the Committee on Training in Clinical Psychology of the American Psychological Association that led to the Boulder Report (Raimy, 1950). They were assigned to the admissions sector of the psychiatric ward, and struggled for the director's acceptance of a project that would go beyond "immediate results"—the directors' main concern. In a memorandum to Hanfmann and Dembo, R.G. Hoskins, Director of Research, wrote:

> ... may I state that my primary desire is to initiate the use of your technics in a psychiatric setting with the introduction of a drug variable of proved potency—to test the potentiality of the technic. At this stage, however, it is desirable to restrict the problem to something that can be accomplished without undue indirection and that promises to yield fairly early tangible results" (Hoskins, 1933, p.1).

Exactly how the pragmatic culture of this new setting was negotiated with Dembo and Hanfmann's ideas about science is not known; the public results are that in studying the role of the orientation letter for new patients and the their psychological situation upon admission, Dembo and Hanfmann co-authored two papers (Dembo and Hanfmann, 1934; Dembo and Hanfmann, 1936).

In "The value of an orientation letter" Dembo and Hanfmann (1934) surpass what could have been a bureaucratic paper by rejecting dichotomous classifications of the reactions of incoming patients to the informational text (letter useful/not useful; understood/not understood) and exploring the establishment of different meanings by each patient upon the reading of the letter, thereby highlighting the heterogeneity of functions the same text may serve for different persons—or even the same person. The broader study, published in the *American Journal of Psychology* (Dembo and Hanfmann, 1936), is classically field-theoretical: the attempt is to unravel how the mental hospital constitutes a psychological field for each patient. Using observations of 100 incoming patients in several routines including the reading of the orientational letters, the authors propose a characterization of different psychological groups in regard to their structuring of the field constituting their experience of being hospitalized.

The fields that characterize each group are represented hodollogicaly, that is, through a topological representation that goes beyond the structure of the field to include dynamic concepts such as direction, distance, and force.[2] The situation upon admission is theorized to be a frustration situation constituted by the interplay of objective physical and social facts and the subjective state of the individual. The distinct hodological representations of the fields contrast the groups that vary in degree of analysis of the situation, concreteness versus abstraction of the representation (e.g. is the barrier perceived as the hospital door, hospital rules, or broader, societal rules?), time perspective, orientational relations with other patients and hospital workers, establishing differences in the forces present in each group and in the and valences acting for each group (for example, where efforts at "escape" are directed to, and if they exist at all depends on this structuration of the field). For each group, the hodological representations characterize the situation of the field upon admission, synthesizing the general character of the hospital situation and outstanding objects in the field; the enclosed field; the surrounding barrier and the outside field. Although the movement resultant from vectors is not characterized—it is not the agenda of the work—the analysis pinpoints the locus of possible origins of movement that may lead to field change.

Studies in Frustration and Regression: The Cornell/Iowa Years

Meanwhile, Dembo and Hanfmann had kept in close contact with their mentor, Kurt Lewin, and others such as Fritz and Grace Heider, in the American version of Lewin's "Quaselstrippe." These weekly meeting with former graduate students and colleagues were described as "a continuous scientific festival" (Dembo, 1982, p.132). When Lewin moved to Cornell, in Ithaca, New York, Tamara Dembo was able to obtain a fellowship to work as his research assistant there, pursuing the topic of the adjustment of the nursery school child to the social-institutional relations and rules, focusing especially on the eating situation. This unpublished work (Dembo, Frank, Lewin, and Waring, n.d.) is discussed by Lewin (1936, p. 96-97) and was a site for the development of ideas related to the child's resistance or acceptance of social pressure or suggestions related to her movement across different psychological regions, which Lewin later expanded in his writings on social and political tensions. In 1934, the same fellowship was renewed and allowed Dembo to follow Lewin to the Iowa Child Study Research Station, at the University of Iowa.

At Iowa, the study that had begun at Cornell of young children's actions and movements in fields fundamentally shaped by barriers—social and/or physical—developed into an extensive project, with Roger Barker, on the emergence of frustration due to modifications of the child-world field at a given moment (Barker, Dembo, and Lewin, 1941; Barker, Dembo, and Lewin, 1943). This paper fundamentally brings together Dembo's early work on anger as a dynamic phenomenon and Lewin's exploration into the constructs of development, regression, and retrogression founded on a hierarchical whole-part analysis derived from the Gestalt School, especially Koffka's idea of the "executive" and Goldstein's organismic approach.

The work, first published in 1941, is an experimental manipulation of the feeling of frustration in children with the intent of exploring the hypothesis that frustration leads to a temporary primitivization—or inversion of development. Development is posited as a process of differentiation, hierarchization, lengthening of life perspective, and differentiation of reality and fantasy catalyzed by changes in the person-environment field. The implicit assumption, then, is that this catalysis is reversible, and that experimental manipulation of this field in the direction of regression can lead to insights into the dynamics of development. With procedures that manipulate access of the children to luring toys, the authors analyze the activities of free play and emotional expression topologically, in terms of goals, barriers, valences, and movement as function of the person-goal relation.

In this analysis, Barker, Dembo, and Lewin are able to analyze the decreased degree of differentiation and stasis in parts of the whole resultant from the increased tension of frustration, pointing out (and this is not an unimportant problem) that there are considerable personal differences in what is experienced by each individual as frustrating.

In her later work on rehabilitation, Dembo found it useful to continue to analyze the issue of recovery and adjustment to injury as one fundamentally shaped by the person's relations to barriers, which (as already pointed out by the article) may be not only physical, but also social. Another important aspect is that this relationship to barriers is described dynamically, that is, subject to change in the person-environment field.

This is especially important to note today, when frustration has become seen as a *variables to be manipulated* with the intent of *classifying* children into static and dichotic groups (emotionally mature or immature), which are then used as predictors for success in schooling or in life (e.g. the delay of gratification studies by Shoda, Mischel, and Peake, 1990). Alternatively, Dembo's work, both in this paper and later, with injured adults, raises the important points that: 1) control over the emotional expression of frustration *develops* and is not an ability statically present or absent in people; 2) this development is fundamentally influenced by real occurrences in a person's life, in which he or she has to deal with situations of frustration, so *interpersonal variation* in emotional expression and control is a necessary aspect of the phenomenon, rather than a problem to be "averaged out" by dichotic groups; and 3) this development is not a linear path, always progressing to an ideal state phenomenon, but is marked by temporary regressions. In other words, there is marked *intrapersonal* variation in such expressions.

Dembo continued to work at the University of Iowa with Lewin and then independently until the year of 1943. In this period she also participated, with Lewin, Leon Festinger, and Sears in the writing of *Level of Aspiration* (Lewin, Dembo, Festinger, and Sears, 1944), a paper that would also have repercussions upon her work on adjustment to loss in rehabilitation. In this work, which builds on earlier efforts in the German context to analyze the phenomenon, the intriguing issue of aspiration as a driving force for change—with its possible positive and negative aspects—is discussed. Aspiration is characterized when the result of an action is seen as an achievement reflecting one's own ability. As there are different levels of difficulty and of aspiration, frustration is characterized as a mismatch between the level of aspiration and the possibility. Level of aspiration is thus a personally constituted frame of reference for "gauging" success or failure.

Studies in Adjustment to Loss: The Stanford Period

Paradoxically, it was the dynamics of World War II, which had caused and would cause Dembo so much concern and anguish[3], that was to open for her a job position and later the research area for which she became most well-known. In 1943 Dembo was invited to Mount Holyoke College, in Massachusetts, to fill a position had been left open first by a professor then by his substitute, both of whom had joined the military forces. Mt. Holyoke was her first exclusively teaching job, and as much as Dembo seems to have enjoyed the experience, she was soon writing to several agencies requesting funding for a project in which she would investigate the problems of physically handicapped discharged soldiers upon their return to the community.

The objective of the project as she presented it (Dembo, 1944) was twofold: to generate knowledge to be applied in rehabilitation and to guide the development of a theory of social adjustment. It was finally approved by the Committee on Medical Research of the Office of Scientific Research and Development and funded by a long-term grant from the Army, the Office of the Surgeon General, and Stanford University, to be executed by a team to be put together by Dembo at Stanford, where she had previously taught a summer session.

It was from this period on that Dembo dedicated herself to issues of rehabilitation, the theme for which she would be best known. Loss was all around her in these post war years; several later occasions she refers to the war as the event that sensitized her to direct her theoretical and methodological skills to the solution of human problems.[4]

The research team, established in 1945, was composed of Dan Adler, Gloria Leviton, Beatrice Wright, Ralph White, Gloria Ladieu, and Eugenia Hanfmann (then at Harvard). Their task was to understand, with the objective of promoting, the social-psychological rehabilitation of the physically handicapped. Besides the volume *Adjustment to Misfortune: A Problem of Social Psychological Rehabilitation* (Dembo, Leviton, and Wright, 1956), the group produced several papers based on this and related research designs (Adler, Ladieu and Dembo, 1948; Dembo, Ladieu, and Wright, 1951; Ladieu, Hanfmann, and Dembo, 1947; White, Wright and Dembo 1948). The publications *Adjustment to Misfortune*, the *Studies in Adjustment* "triad" and *Acceptance of Loss* were all outcomes of the major project, which situated the problems of the injured not as existing *in* the injury or the injured but constituted within the relationship between the injured and the non-injured.

The task was thus re-defined as an investigation into the meaning of the social-emotional relationship between the injured and non-injured, to be carried out through interviews and other qualitative procedures (group discussions, psychodrama) with handicapped and non-injured people, aligned with quasi-experimental probes in which the subjects situate themselves on a scale of fortune/misfortune.

Conceptual analyses led the group to identify the central problem of "misfortune" as entailing a relationship between one who regards the other as unfortunate and the self as fortunate. This includes a dimension of value loss, that is, the loss of something that is not considered, in a determined society, merely a neutral variation but as something that holds a positive valence and is perhaps even necessary: a *comparative value*. Those who the group finds to have become adjusted to the injury are exactly those who have gone through a process that entails value change—the scope of values are enlarged, and/or the *values lost* are reconceptualized as *asset*[5] *values*—holding a positive valence but relatively *inessential*.

The *Studies in Acceptance* series (Adler, Ladieu, and Dembo, 1948; Ladieu, Hanfmann, and Dembo, 1947; White, Wright, and Dembo, 1948) are a set of three articles that investigate more closely the evaluation of curiosity and help by the injured and the impact of this on their social acceptance. Here the group dives into the world of the injured, especially attempting to understand how they conceptualize others' (the non-injureds') misconceptions and biases regarding their injuries as the major barriers to their adjustment. Starting from very practical questions (When is it right to help the injured? When is it acceptable to ask questions?), the group refuses to provide neat rules and recipes. Rather, they defend the need to understand the phenomena of help and demonstration of curiosity more fully, as social relationships that are embedded in a field of meaning for both the donor and the recipient. It is basically the degree of congruity of these fields that will allow, for example, for productive help, and this congruity can only be established by the encounter of these fields and the possible re-structuration of both.

Back to the Northeast: Meanings and Values

Funding was suspended for the Stanford project in 1947, and in 1948 Dembo was invited for a position at the Political and Social Science Department at the New School of Social Research in New York. The department had a long-standing connection with the European theoretical tradition, especially as it had been established by Wertheimer, and had received Asch and Köhler as visitors. Very little is documented of the two-year period in which Dembo was at the New School, except for her work on the *Noticeability of the Cosmetic Glove* (Dembo and Tane-Baskin, 1955). In this paper, the usefulness of a prosthesis is discussed not in its technical aspects (as is and was usually the case) but in terms of its social-psychological usefulness.

This is established through the investigation of the personal meaning of the glove for the amputee, which is constructed, among other things, in relation to the reaction of observers. Via extremely naturalistic experiments in which the amputees are seen in public places and even drawn by art students, the research establishes that the noticeability of these prostheses is low enough for them to serve a social function, although they admit that there are other aspects to its function that are not covered by the study.

In 1950 Dembo left the New School to spend a period (1950-1952) as a Research Fellow at the Department of Social Relations, Harvard University, where she interacted with Henry Murray, Gordon Allport, and Talcott Parsons. Her work there, which was to be published later in a collection of works in homage to H. Werner (Dembo, 1960), revisits the concept of value, which had been central in *Adjustment to Loss*. Here, a theoretical and experimental attempt is carried out to conceptualize values as complex qualities with sub-components and inserted in value systems.

A series of eight experiments were conducted to investigate wished-for ideals—equated with values—their components, systems, and relations to *disvalues*. While maintaining the part-whole gestalt analysis (and here lies its strength) this is probably Dembo's least Lewinian paper, in that a dynamic/field analysis is virtually absent; on the contrary, the paper strives to identify those "pure" values, with an existence that is quasi-independent of the subject. This precludes any discussion of change or constitution of values, even though it is, interestingly, clear in the experimental set-up that the active reflection upon values may indeed transform them.

It is in fact ironic that in regarding values not as processes but as reified things, they become practically equated with traits possessed or not ("beauty"—which is not constituted but inherited)—in fact, the definition of a value is never made explicit. However, the paper has merits, especially in its attitude to experimentation as an endeavor that yields rich material through the emotional involvement of the subject. Considering how often in the paper issues such as "outside influence"; "origin" "change" of values are brought up and then suppressed, this seems to be an example of work that is "straitjacketed" into a theoretical framework that does not accommodate the richness of the phenomenon.

The Clark Years

In 1952, Dembo joined the Department of Psychology at Clark University, at the time directed by Heinz Werner, the prominent developmental psychologist who had worked with William Stern in Hamburg. With Werner, the Psychology Department was being revitalized in exciting, interdisciplinary ways, with research encompassing, to mention just a few areas, aesthetics, family relations, comparative psychology, psychopathology, and perceptual and symbolic development, all with strong theoretical and developmental nuances (Kaplan and Wapner, 1960).

At Clark, Dembo worked for four decades, for, although she officially retired in 1972, she continued to contribute to the field as Emerita Professor until her death in 1993. In this context, the decades at Clark were marked by her activity within the Psychological Aspects of Disability Section (22) of the APA, in which she played a leading role in defining the scope and problems of rehabilitation psychology (Dembo, 1968a, 1968b, 1969b; Dembo, Diller, Gordon, Leviton, and Sherr, 1973; Executive Committee of Div. 22, 1975); the direction of the Rehabilitation Psychology Training Program (cf. Dembo, 1980 for the program project; cf. Follini, Bergstein, Epstein, and Dembo, n.d, for one of its most outstanding productions), writings and coordination of symposia on the relation between applied and theoretical psychology (Dembo, 1970, 1974, 1993, 1982; Leviton, 1959) and, last but definitely not least, studies of the role of mother–child interaction on the development of intentionality and knowledge through action in children with cerebral palsy, which she developed with Heinz Werner and John Bell (Bell, Dembo, and Werner, 1955; Dembo, 1962); which also yielded reflections on professional-client relations (Dembo, 1964a, 1964b/1984).

As will be seen, if her previous work in the area of rehabilitation had mostly concentrated on laying down the theoretical and methodological foundations for unraveling the experience of being handicapped, her work at Clark definitely constituted a passage into intervention, while at the same time maintaining the concern with careful theoretical structuration of the problem being studied.

The Training Program in Rehabilitation Psychology

In 1962, recognizing the need to carve out a field of professional training that was not focused—as she saw clinical psychology to be—on the individual or personality, and that was aimed at intervention firmly subsidized by conceptualization, Dembo established a graduate and undergraduate training program in rehabilitation. The program's tenets were very much guided by Dembo's take on topological psychology (Dembo, 1980) and focused on the understanding and promotion of change of social-emotional relationships between the disabled and the non-disabled. Besides the seminars, the internships (characterized as research-internships) had the objective of advancing theorization while at the same time training students to perceive their own and others' feelings—while promoting Dembo's faith in the meeting of different viewpoints which we shall discuss later.

A notable representative of this period is the work in a mental institution by students in the program under Dembo (Follini, Bergstein, Epstein, and Dembo, n.d.). Starting from the assertion that psychology rarely goes beyond paying lip service to interactionist accounts of behavior, the authors criticized the regular attribution of deviations from the norm to problems *in* people, not — as they would defend—constituted in the interactions in the person-and-environment field, and go on to discuss the asymmetry of power between the mental patients and the administrators of the institutions.

They identify two views of custodial care of the mental patient: one that devaluates the patient to the extent that he/she is deemed unworthy of anything but subsistence, and another that retains the value of the person in misfortune, and therefore subscribes to the affirmation of basic human rights (not mere subsistence) for even the most severely disturbed patients.

Holding the second, person-centered perspective, the authors start research in one of the units of an institution of mental patients, which was organized under the tenets of the first, restrictive-custodial view. The unit was occupied by the most severe cases of "mental retardation" and the author's description of the situation they meet is both vivid and horrifying: "it resembled a nineteenth century poorhouse that reformers such as Charles Dickens had helped to eliminate" (p. 8), while the section for the gravest patients among the gravest resembled "the eighteenth century Salpetriere, the insane asylum in Paris before Dr. Pinel removed the chains" (p. 9).

In filthy installations, infested with vermin and feces, the women who were considered not able to profit from any training were crammed together, in a situation that, in the group's view, curtailed basic psychological functions. The team identified that the women lacked freedom of movement, power of choice/decision-making, privacy, possession, opportunities, self-care, comfort, and social communication, and their behavior, oscillating between apathy and aggression, was seen by the team as an attempt to escape the field in which conditions built up frustration and tension, as Dembo had elaborated earlier on in her work with anger and in *Frustration and Regression*. In fact, we can view the situation in itself as a tragic, a "natural" experiment in the development of anger and frustration.

The "operational" research involved establishing a demonstration program, in which activities and opportunities were offered to a sub-group of the women, at the same time conducting careful work with the administration, aiming at a change that would not disappear after the intervention, but that would be taken up by the staff. The demonstration program allowed the women to engage in activities that involved, required, and/or developed self-initiation, sustainment, structuring, sequencing, social, and especially verbal interaction, and emotional involvement. Several principles are outlined for work aiming change in institutional environment, including, as would be expected in Dembo's work, the respect and understanding of the life-space of the staff (as opposed to accusations and blaming processes); at the end of the project, although the building was still in dire need of reform, the staff had taken over the demonstrational program and was working—independently—to expand it to include other women.

It would be absolutely fascinating to have seen Dembo combine this research with her early work in the schizophrenic admissions ward. There, the rich topological characterization of the hospital situation as experienced by the different types of patients were a "snapshot" of the situation upon admittance; here, the bird's eye view of the impressive and inspiring change would gain from a microgenetic consideration of the dynamics of the wholes and their component units being restructured in the change.

Investigations in Cerebral Palsy

A year after Dembo's arrival at Clark, the project "The emotional and value aspects of interpersonal relationships between the cerebral palsied child and his parents" was initiated, under the direction of Werner, Dembo, and John Elderkin Bell, the psychologist distinguished for his theory and clinical practice in the area of family relations (Bell, Dembo, and Werner, 1955). The project involved interviews and home observations of families with young children diagnosed with cerebral palsy, and continued through 1955 when the coordinators issued a final report.

John Bell (Bell, 1955) contributed with a study of the cerebral palsied child situated in the family, focusing especially on the impact of societal depreciation of the child on the parents and the parents' forms of handling their diseases, identifying a pattern of *judgment* and *defense against judgment* that he modeled theoretically.

Dembo brought her theory of value loss and value change to the analysis of the parents' suffering concerning the child and forms of alleviating it (Dembo, 1955). The parents' suffering is situated as a problem of loss and this suffering is analyzed into several component elements—holding a value as a wished for and necessary versus coming to terms with its temporary and possibly permanent unattainability. Change in suffering can occur in the complex interplay between attainment of the value (i.e. the child's development) and change in values held by the parents, drawing special attention to the complex role played complex dynamics played by hope—with a fine line between unrealistic and realistic expectations for the future.

Concerning the relation (sometimes better stated as clash) between the parents' values and those of the professionals dealing with them, Dembo was drawn to the importance of recognizing the fundamental differences in the standpoint of the two sides of this interaction (the sufferer versus the observer; the professional versus the "client"; the insider versus the outsider) and recommended a fundamental shift in understanding the insider's standpoint in any fruitful intervention. She elaborates on this theme repeatedly, and—as we shall discuss—extends this into epistemological and methodological claims about the nature of the researcher's and the subject's knowledge (Dembo 1964a, 1964b/1984, 1969b, 1970, 1974).[6]

The other source of alleviation of parents' suffering, change in the development of children, constitutes the core of the research project that is outlined at the closure of the report by Dembo and Heinz Werner (Dembo and Werner, 1955). It is important to mention that at the time, severely cerebral-palsied children were usually considered "hopeless" cases of mental deficiency, and institutionalization was the routine recommendation. Working within a framework that used the Piagetian proposal of the origins of cognition in sensory-motor schemata formed in interaction with objects and the Wernerian notion of the early "world-of-action" as fundamental to later development, the study centers on the role of spontaneous, self-initiated actions of the child, which, in cerebral palsy, are hindered not only because of the child's physical limitations, but also possibly because of the mother's lack of promoting and fostering such activities. The project (Dembo and Werner, 1955) therefore aimed at studying the effects of a guidance program for mothers aimed at the cognitive and emotional change in their beliefs about their child's development and the role of intentional action therein on the development of intentional action in children and the relations between intentional action and cognition.

The project was carried out through 1962. In the final, extensive report (Dembo, 1962), unfortunately never "translated" into a publication. Dembo recognized that there is far more to the project that was executed, but gives priority to what she considers to be the main theoretical outcome of the project: an articulation of an extensive qualitative, structural and hierarchical analysis of the very basic intentional activities performed by (or in the case of CP, often lacking in) very young children.

Dembo (1962) posits that intentional activities—for which she attempts to elaborate criteria—play a fundamental and dual role in human development in that they that they are: 1) forms-in-process of knowledge[7] about the world, and 2) forms of development of knowledge about the world. The activity-knowledge relation is built from an interactionist and constructivist position in which activity is constrained by the physical properties of objects and by the person's physical body, and holds that cognition is in interaction with these properties—constrained but also reorganized by them. Cognition is therefore a process of permanent tension with such constraints—its reason for being is the transcendence of physical limitations; nevertheless, in order to do this, the properties of objects and of the body impose limits and boundaries on such "transcendence."

In positing such an interaction, Dembo strongly criticized learning theories which focus on ideas of reward and success of repetitive outcomes—rather, it is in the moments of emergence of the unexpected that the researcher should look for signs of reorganization of knowledge, a formulation close to Baldwin's (1894) focus on *persistent imitation*. Another important aspect of her discussion of the criteria of intentional behavior is her interest in those "borderline' activities that are neither clearly intentional nor non-intentional—and for which "inter-observer agreement" cannot be established. Dembo argued that these very outliers may be the most important indications of intentionality-in-the-making, a claim with important repercussions not only for general psychology but notably in cerebral palsy, where the overlooking of attempts at intentionality by caretakers may have devastating effects on this development.

An important consequence of this theorizing is the breakdown of the dualistic conceptualization of a " physical" versus a "mental" handicap in development—if cognition develops in action, many of the problems categorized as "physical" or "cognitive" may have to be further analyzed into components that include physical and cognitive elements and the interactions of both.

Dembo expressed her concern with the area having long been obliterated by ideas of development in which unspecified complexity or sequence in time are treated as a criterion for development: "Arriving at a criteria of development is not an empirical but a conceptual matter. Whether or not developmental changes in everyday life follow the sequence in time is an empirical question, but temporal sequence as such is an *arbitrary* and not intrinsic criterion of development" (Dembo 1962, p. 181, emphasis in the original). The conceptual task, in this case, is thus outlined in terms of defining, in a series of "basic" activities, what understanding on the part of the child is required for its execution, and establishing a hierarchical scheme of relations between activities so that it is possible to identify what elements of the old activity are reorganized in the production of the new one.

This analysis led to the establishment of the *families* of activities: *touch, grasp,* and *hold*, organized in increasing levels of *connection* with object, *control* of object and *inclusion* (the last family includes, and is derived from, the previous, and so on). For each member of the families, an analysis is made of the *intent of the action* and the *executive plan*. The intent of the activity delimits the *what* of the change, and the executive, the *how*. For example, her simplest activity, *touch*, has as its intent contacting object and as its executive plan transversing region between person and object. The analysis of the components of intent—*environmental components*—lists the knowledge that is necessary and materially defined by the physical nature of the objects and the person for the action to be developed. Thus, to contact an object, the world must be differentiated between entities; the person must be differentiated as agent; the object must be differentiated as goal; additionally, the region to be transversed between the object and the child must be known; the person must be differentiated into different bodily parts, for example, arm-body differentiation (note that this is one form of distinguishing intentional touching from bumping into); and the selection of *an* arm for the execution of the activity. In terms of the executive components, they are basically characterized as forces that have a point of application, a direction, a magnitude and duration.

This analysis is carried out for each and every one of the sixty-six basic activities selected, and although—as Dembo recognizes—it is in some cases tentative and cumbersome, it does have important theoretical and practical implications. Theoretically, it foregrounds the need for a more thorough specification of what is meant by development—a concept that involves not only the domains of qualitative change in the direction of progression or increase, but is also fundamentally delineated by value systems. In other words, development in children's actions is not only conceptualized as an increase in *number, structural complexity and hierarchical structure of the activities*, but also as a result of personal and societal values that judge each activity in terms of their positive and negative valences.

This complex analysis also brings to the foreground differences at different levels of accomplishment of the "same" action that may be overlooked if analyzed superficially. For example, contrast a baby banging onto a piano keyboard with an adult playing the piano. Consideration the hierarchical structure of the submission to the differentiated movements of the fingers to a plan, in the adult, is necessary to distinguish this from the child's banging even if eventually the outcome may be coincidentally the same; the amount of knowledge to be implied is different.

The "practical" importance of the study goes beyond cases of cerebral palsy and is extended to cases of breakdown, or delay of behavioral development in the sense that it stresses the importance of not only identifying vaguely a motor problem, but pinpointing the component(s) of the activity that are hampered, in a systemic view that allows for hypothesis about other related activities which will also be expected to be hindered—and, most importantly, guiding the forms of intervention that can be fostered in its development, substituted or circumvented. It also places a heavy emphasis on the need to explicit the values by which "development" is judged. Her perspective was clearly compatible and might be profitably articulated with Vygotsky's seminal ideas on the creation of roundabout routes of development (1929/1993), serving as a model for the provision of greater detail to what needs to change and how (see, for example, Kaplan, 1988 and Holmes-Bernstein, 1990, for different albeit related efforts in constructing systemic perspectives in neuropsychology).

In a half a century of work on rehabilitation, Tamara Dembo transited among many ideas, some in more elaborated and publicized form, some more tentative and less known. In the next part of this paper, I will attempt to situate her main theoretical contributions.

The Social Constitution of the Handicap

"Within laws and buildings there is room for people to further hinder the handicapped or provide them with opportunities" (Dembo, 1969b, p. 27).

One of the most important aspects of Dembo's stance on handicaps and rehabilitation is one that stems from her attributing central importance to a person-in-environment field. Therefore, despite the "trendiness" to do so at the time when she entered the field of rehabilitation, she decried a "pragmatic" view of rehabilitation, which would place the problem in the person and hurry to find "quick" methods of social reintegration. Such "reintegration" was usually restricted to "vocational" testing and placement —not actually finding "vocations" but surveying the scope of necessary jobs and "fitting" disabled people into them, by methods—so prevalent at the time—of behavioral modification, under the ethos of control and prediction.[8] This ethos is described by Myers (1968) and Lowenfeld (Leviton, 1959) as having its roots the notions of utility and economic feasibility, and its consequence is the creation of, in Dembo's terms (1968b), a *handicapped elite*—those who are handicapped but considered *worthwhile investing* in, with the consequent exclusion of those who are not.

Dembo set forth an alternative view (Dembo, 1968b; Dembo, 1982; Dembo, Leviton, and Wright, 1956/1975; Ladieu, Adler, and Dembo, 1948; Ladieu, Hanfmann, and Dembo, 1947; White, Wright, and Dembo, 1948), stating that the handicap is structurally located in the person-and environment life space, especially between person and others (Dembo, 1982). Disability is primarily a problem of locomotion and accessibility, not as located in the body but as a disability of social others to make the world more accessible to a diversity of people. People in this sense are less disabled than marginalized, in consonance with the Lewinian analysis of the marginalized man (Lewin, 1939). Lewin defined the marginal man as someone who lives on the boundary of two defined life-spaces, neither belonging nor being completely separate from each. He furthered this view into the analysis of adolescents, their instability and crises derived from the movement through the boundary of the different life-spaces of adulthood and childhood, with their different boundaries and zones of free movement.

For Dembo, in considering that Life Space is quasi-social, quasi-physical, quasi-conceptual in nature, it follows that the boundaries that delimit the movement of the handicapped are not only stairs, but values, laws, beliefs, and acts such as staring, ridiculing, offering help in a devaluative way, etc. This radical view is consonant with a social constructionist critiques of the concept of normality (Foulcault, 1976; Hacking, 1996; McDermott and Varenee, 1996; Pessotti, 1981), that is, views that situate the societal and historical construction of concepts such a mental deficiency, madness, normalcy, etc. They also reverberate with psychological and neuropsychological propositions that situate the problems of mental or physical disability in a mismatch between environmental, social, historical demands and the abilities of the person (Holmes-Bernstein and Wader, 1990; Sacks, 1996; Vygotsky, 1929/1933).

With such a conceptualization, Dembo understood that the task of psychology in the area of rehabilitation became one of deciphering and acting upon the relations that give rise to, hinder, and/or enable the adjustment to loss by the injured. Here, she moved from considering intervention at the *dyadic* level, where what should be changed were basically the relations between the injured and their non-injured relatives, friends, co-workers (Dembo, Leviton, and Wright, 1956/1975) to the level of *local* (Follini et al., n.d.) and *societal institutions* (Dembo, Diller, Gordon, Leviton, and Sherr, 1973; Dembo, 1968b). Over the years she presented growing concern about issues of power differences between those who are handicapped and those who establish the barriers for the handicapped (Dembo, 1982). The climate of overriding belief in social reform that was around at the establishment of Section 22 of APA (Dembo, 1968b; Usdane, 1968)—with the naïve idea of "rehabilitation" of the handicapped, the poor, the minority groups, etc.—substituted, at least in Dembo, for a growing awareness of the specificities of these different groups of people discriminated (Wertsch and Tulviste, 1991) and outright impatience for broader changes (Dembo, 1993) by the end of her life.

The Subject as a Positioned Knower

Dembo's understanding of the subject as an active, experiential, positioned *knower* capable of fruitful introspection has repercussions on her views of theory construction, methodology, and intervention. The subject, as conceptualized by Dembo, is a full *participant* in the study of human processes, a claim that has its roots not in empty "political correctness" but in an epistemological view rooted in the culture of German psychologists in the days of Wilhelm Wundt. Danziger (1985, 1987), contrasting the different courses of historical development of research practices in the U.S. and Germany, narrates how, in the Wundtian paradigm, knowledge about the processes of interest was to be obtained with the subjects, who were considered to detain the volitional, or agentic qualities fundamental to the causalities investigated. Therefore, it was common for the subject and the researcher to reverse roles, the subjects occupied a high status position (for example, in Luria and other professors acting as research subjects for Dembo in her early work) and were each viewed as a "personally identified individual" (p. 17).[9]

Wertsch and Rosa (1993) discuss how Dembo, in her many years of work in the U.S., continued to value the subject as occupying such a volitional, agentive and unique position, criticizing the paradox of modernity, in which the discourse of individuality coexists with statistical norms, and ideals of control and prediction. But, wary of the reactions against such an alien view, *Adjustment to Misfortune* dedicates several chapters to the explication of this view on the subject, as can be seen in the following quotation:

> There is nothing unscientific about being a subject and an investigator at the same time. In perception psychology, for example, the investigator frequently takes this double role. He can perceive and then cognize what he perceives (Dembo, Leviton, and Wright, 1956/1975, p. 18).

Dembo's Lewinian heritage adds that, since each individual can only be understood when one includes the person's life space in the analysis, the researcher/researched injured/non-injured, professional/client are dyads whose individuals occupy different positions, with consequently different conceptualizations, experiences, and relations to the "same phenomenon." Dembo characterizes this as the difference between the donor and the recipient, in the context of social-emotional relationships, and as an extension, in the difference between the insider/outsider, in the context of patient/professional relations.

The value attributed to experience is central to this point, both theoretically and methodologically; Dembo and colleagues particularly countered the prevalent norm for studying only overt behavior (interaction data), as opposed to including reflection unit data. This exclusion is not possible, in their view, because the establishment of goals, the planning, the struggling with one's moods, evaluations and expectations are as real psychological phenomena as the actual physical, external carrying out of those. Their importance as psychological phenomena are that they have effects—be these effects the doing of an action, or the blocking of an action. Effects are thus defined not as overt outcomes, but as the constant modification of the future by the psychological phenomena in the present.

Therefore much of her work revolved around the need to understand processes of adjustment to loss and difficulties as it constitutes an experience for the person who has suffered the loss, and to the persons around his or her, for example:

> Loss is usually seen as an end-point of unsuccessful, goal-directed behavior (failure) or else it is investigated in terms of the effect of failure on further goal-directed behavior. ... But it is important to know what loss means to the person himself, how it affects the opinions and behavior of others toward him, and what acceptance of loss implies (Dembo, Leviton and Wright, 1975, p. 2).

But the centrality of experience is not exclusively linked to the experience of the researched. The researcher also is an experiential being. The idea of research as a human and therefore, value-laden and positioned enterprise, is currently a central topic of theorization, in diverse approaches to the social sciences. In this line, a recent debate (Günther, 1998; Hong, 1998; Kojima, 1998) unveils the "untold" and often convoluted story of contacting and obtaining "informed consent" from subjects. Günther (1998) narrates the distinctly different dynamics involved in the phase of contacting subjects of different ethnicities in a cross-cultural study. Her narrative situates the contacting process as one which is worthy of analysis in and of itself, but that gets expelled from the reports of most research, substituted by a formulaic phrase in the procedures section. Hong (1998) criticizes what has become the dogma of informed consent, imagined as a universal ethical device, but in many cases, conflicting with the socially approved norms of different cultures. In the issue of informed consent as in the previously discussed anonymity of subjects, the central problem is the reification of some research procedures guided at standardization of results and the promotion of ethics, which however may become detached or even antithetical to these concerns if applied in a cookbook manner.

Stemming from another tradition, Dembo was a precursor of such concerns, and elaborated on the implications in the areas of research and intervention. First, the "modern" conceptualization of the neutral, disengaged researcher is questioned:

> Traditional psychology is the one-sided psychology of a particular kind of observer, namely an aloof, objective observer. The traditional psychologist, strictly behavioristically and observationally inclined, considers no other psychology but his to be scientifically legitimate. The scientific psychologist is ready to accuse his experimental subject of having a biased view, and he tends to reject the subjects' statements as egocentric and emotional. Further, he believes that he himself is not emotional and evaluative in his choice of problems, selection of data, and method of dealing with problems. ... In actuality, he sees things from a given angle, that of an objective observer whose observations are stripped of everyday connotations by his aloofness (Dembo 1970, p. 3).

and:

> The "ought" of traditional research—choice of the problem because of its theoretical importance, demand for objectivity in the performance of the research, the emphasis on dealing with reliable and most probable occurrences, and the like, all accepted as "ought" by the scientific psychologist—are values guiding psychologists in what they do (Dembo, 1970, p. 4).

Recognizing that the positions of the researcher and of the subject entail different views of the world and of the problem being investigated does not entail, for Dembo, a leap into nihilistic negation of encounter, as would a postmodern "multiplicity" view led to its extreme. She admits that one of the great hurdles in psychological research, especially that which investigates emotional relations, is the possibility of emotional engagement in the analysis:

> The whole flavor of the emotional meanings which one was at such pains to obtain can be lost if the approach to the data is unwisely rigid. The investigator is forced to perceive and to feel emotional relationships from the point of view of the donor and the recipient before he can understand the meanings and evaluations ascribed to them. ... In investigating emotional relationships, to feel is at least as essential as to think (Dembo, Leviton, and Wright, 1956/1975, p. 17-18).

However, for such an encounter of views, experiences and feelings—which she admits will always be partial—she proposes (Dembo, 1970) the need for a conceptual analysis, by the investigator, of these qualitative differences between the views.

First, the very meaning of problem is different for the researcher and for the researched—one is intrigued by a problem, the other may suffer from it; second, the subject thinks about the problem in "differently inclusive units," in the populational, temporal, and conceptual domains; for example, the researcher is concerned about handicapped people in general, in a relatively long time span, and in a more abstract way; the subject is concerned with a specific handicapped he himself may be experiencing, and involved with immediate, daily problems, as well as long-term ones. They are also positioned in different contiguities (temporal, physical) to the problem: for one, it is a constantly present and tangible problem; for the other, perhaps one-of-a-many interests in a research program.

The researcher, and especially the professional in intervention, may operate under the dictum of probability (expecting the most probable to happen, based on cumulative experiences with other cases); the subject, or patient, may organize his hopes in the direction of operating under the dictum of the possible as expecting the exceptional outcome may be the person's only hope.[10]

Dembo expects that with this process, which values the role of experience in the constitution of each person's life space, and the valuation of such different (and sometimes divergent) experiences, there is the possibility of encounter between the two views, (Dembo, 1955, 1964b/1984, 1964a, 1970, 1974; Dembo et al., 1956/1975) with the enrichment of the research and intervention enterprises. The realization that there are limits to the possibility of interpenetration of views, moreover, leads to the call for more involvement of and negotiation with the research subjects in many stages of research and intervention from the definition of the problem, to the forms of analysis, to the evaluation of usefulness and precision of results.

Such a negotiation also entails the necessary recognition, by researchers and professionals, that there are limits to their knowledge, and that they must be aware, in occupying a position of authority, and communicating with subjects and patients, to seriously scrutinize these limits. This is a process in which both parties are engaged in a restructuration of the phenomena, contrasting currently held values and beliefs with the consideration of values of the other, which may, optimally, lead to what Wertheimer called the aha-experience (Dembo 1969b) or Lewin (1946) terms change in cognitive structure.

The Relations Between Theory, Methodology, and Application

One of the central themes of the conference "The Relationship between Rehabilitation and Psychology," held at Clark University in 1959 and chaired by Dembo, was, as the name implies, the cross-fertilization between basic and applied concerns in psychology. The mix of speakers testifies that the time was propitious for such cross-fertilization: from the rehabilitation arena, Beatrice Wright, Lee Meyerson, and Berthold Lowenfeld joined researchers of high caliber better known for their theoretical contributions such as Heinz Werner, Alfred Baldwin, Lawrence Frank, and Kurt Goldstein. (Leviton, 1959).

In the debate, Goldstein, the eminent organismic neuropsychologist, situates the war as a fundamental turning point in psychology because of the ethical demands it brought to bear on psychology (when studying but not helping was not enough) and highlighted that pathology had motivated research which had resulted in advanced understanding not only of the pathological, but also, of "normal" processes (Leviton, 1959). To Dembo, amalgamating theoretical development and application of psychological ideas involved an ethical re-evaluation of the purposes of research; she urged scientists to scrutinize the purposes and values involved in the enterprise (Dembo 1969, 1970).

In fact, the mismatch that exists between a "problem" for research and a "real-life" problem is one of the starting points of her criticism to the problems of rehabilitation psychology. The difficulty of applying research to practice, Dembo claimed, did not lie, as was the usual interpretation, in "translation" of abstract knowledge into concrete one. A deeper analysis (Dembo, 1969, 1974) reveals that application involves: 1) possession of knowledge, 2) knowledge of the particular life situation in which knowledge should be applied, and 3) the relations between the two.

The real problem, to Dembo, lay in the lack of useful knowledge both about real-life phenomena and the context of application of such knowledge, since research developed with different constraints and presuppositions from those that operate in real-life problems are limited in their possibility of shedding light on the latter. This does not entail the demise of basic research but research in which there is "a permanent liaison between the scientific endeavor and life, an interrelating of the two throughout investigation" (Dembo, 1970, p. 1), with theoreticians that are willing to be constrained and challenged by problems that effectively affect people's daily lives.

In Dembo's scheme, applied research, however, is highly theoretical in that problems are not changed if not through a careful identification of the system that needs to change, its constitutive units and elements encompassed, and the vectors acting on the system and lending it dynamicity. All this, while keeping in mind that for each step of abstraction and detachment from the problem, necessary for theory, there must be the construction of steps back into the "real" phenomena (Dembo, 1982).

What Constitutes a Problem

There are tremendously intriguing problems in this field. But there is lacking, in most of the work, not only the relationship between theory and empirical endeavors; there is also lacking a serious conceptualization of the basic problems in education. Most of the education research is done in this way: You think of a certain educational method and then ask the question: "how efficient will this method be?" and study its efficiency statistically. Now this is not, what we could call in the academic field, research at all. This is just something we would call human engineering. (Werner, in Leviton, 1959, p. 103.)

Dembo does not propose the straightforward "adoption" of problems as viewed by those who suffer from them, but proposes that from these, scientific problems may be constructed. This redefinition of the problem is itself a fundamental methodological task, as it entails the positing of a question that will lead not to the "orderly catalog "of answers, but a system of interrelated concepts referring to dynamic processes. She uses one of her favorite issues: that of integrating theory and method in solid and fruitful ways, and criticizes harshly the practical but illusionary premature and primitive quantifications—those that are done on data "before the necessary qualitative description of problems and concepts" and those done on "systematically unimportant questions" (Dembo et al. 1956/1975, p.11).

On the development of a research problem, Dembo et al.. (1956/1975) note:

> The candidate problems are thoughts of the investigator, fed by qualitative observations and checked by them. For this type of work, an armchair and pencil are more appropriate than a straight chair and a calculating machine. It might require self control on the part of the investigator to go on with conceptualization and qualitative analysis of data when he is constantly lured by more easily quantify able, non-systematic, isolated problems (Dembo et al., 1956/1975, p. 9).

The criteria for the "fruitfulness" of a problem, therefore, is its ability to engender an interrelated set of concepts, in the Lewinian sense—Lewin proposed that rather than classify " data" or "facts" by similarity, one must posit an underlying mechanism which will be able to relate the different, sometimes even apparently opposing, coexisting "facts" in the phenomena being studied. This is what he attempts to do when connecting such things as physical growth, adventurousness, insecurity and cognitive development in adolescence through the construct of the changing life space of the subject (Lewin, 1939).

Such a systemic linkage of "facts" precedes, both in Lewin's and in Dembo's views, mathematical processing of the data; besides, careful analysis of the kind of mathematical representation adequate for each kind of data is to be carried out. A field theoretical stance will usually better benefit from a topological or hodological manipulations, rather than metrification – the " size" of many of the constructs are just not meaningful although psychology may benefit from formalization of geometry, (the space of a field) forces and vectors (the valences). Measurement, Dembo argued, was not to be confused with attribution of numerical values (Dembo, 1993); there are qualitative dimensions of change that can be measured (for example, depth and breadth of a conceptualization) where numerical values would add very little.

With methodology subserving a theoretical system rather than the other way around, it is of no surprise throughout her research, Dembo utilized a variety of methods of accessing the phenomena she was interested in, from experiments in the lab and in the field, interviews, group discussions, psychodrama, and observation. The main unifying point in all of these procedures was the importance attributed to the emotional involvement of both the researcher and the subject in the phenomena being studied, lest it be "stripped" of its real content, (i.e., the closeness allowed by being an "insider" or by sympathizing with an "insider"), and the ability of the method to provide insight into the qualitative nature of the phenomenon being focused.

Structure in Process

Emerging in varied forms throughout her work, the construct of development and related constructs played different roles in Dembo's writings. At times the structural analyses overshadowed a dynamic perspective; at others, they served to ground dynamicity.

Early on, in *Frustration and Regression*, Barker, Dembo, and Lewin (1943) focus explicitly on processes of development using the principles of differentiation, hierarchization, increase in scope and differentiation of fantasy and reality and the opposite processes arising from certain manipulations to the field, including those that are the result of past manipulations acting on the expectations and goal-orientedness in the light of which the present field is viewed and the future field imagined. In this theoretical treatment, they bring together the embriologically inspired ideas of part-whole differentiation of the Berlin Gestalt school with issues of fantasy and desire rooted in psychoanalysis. The focus on differentiation/integration mechanisms submerges, to reappear only in much later works.

In her dealings with rehabilitation, the central pragmatic and theoretical concern becomes that of change. Dembo, Leviton, and Wright (1956/1975) recognize that they have been more successful in characterizing the beginning and end states (of maladjustment and adjustment) than in analyzing the process of transformation from one state to another, a task for further research. It does not follow, however, that there are no lessons to be gained from this careful characterization, especially as its dynamic elements—the valences and vectorial forces—can potentially orient research and intervention.

Change is therefore conceptualized as a restructuration of the person-environment field that occurs as a function of the vectorial forces of valences. The emphasis given to valences, unique, experiential (but socially constituted) relations to objects in the world, is of topical importance. Rather than viewing the environment as a homogeneous, intra-individual "stimulus," generally subsumed under the label of motivation, the subjective nature of goals and attributions of value to regions in the field are brought into the investigators' agenda. In the process of restructuration, Dembo focuses on the importance of the encounter, clash, and renegotiations of the values, meanings and goal orientations of at least two interacting persons. It is only in the (emotionally tinted) negotiation of such differing meanings and goals in the dyad that adjustment can germinate. In fact, in her later years, she claimed (Wertsch and Tulviste, 1991) to have moved from the Gestalt idea of person-in-environment field to the idea of duality as the unit of analysis of psychology.

Finally, Dembo revisits the principles of development through differentiation and hierarchical integration, now clearly under the influence of Werner, in her work in the development of intentional action in cerebral palsy. In this work, Dembo's persistence in attempting to capture the complexity of the phenomena she was studying through a careful and painstaking description of structures is highlighted. This was more than a scientific "technique" and seems to have been extended into her very personal take on thinking about the scientific process. She refers to her own thought processes as including minute steps that can be integrated into insights or lead her astray. In an interview with Wertsch and Tulviste and (1991), and, below:

> Although the process of analysis is very tedious and difficult one achieves great deal of pleasure from it when components are found. One arrives at enjoyment similar to that in finding a mathematical proof, namely, that it is as it is and cannot be thought of differently (Dembo, 1962 p. 8).

The importance of such careful analytical descriptions of the complex structures involved even in simple acts such as touching, grasping, and holding cannot be sufficiently underscored in times as ours when much of developmental psychology is equated with tugs-of-war over the age-of-onset of the "possession" of this or that behavior without due consideration of the underlying, perhaps markedly distinct structural and functional organizations of apparently similar "external" behaviors. Furthermore, in her final writings, Dembo (1962) underscores the importance of scrutinizing the value-laden character of what are "elected" to be the hallmarks of development or complexification. Situating the lenses through which behavior is analyzed as socially constituted, Dembo heeds researchers against sweeping generalizations about what constitute the criterion for development.

Half a Century of Psychology

Although she officially retired in 1972, Tamara Dembo continued to work until her death in 1993 at the age of ninety-two. In half a century of psychology, Dembo's legacy is a set of ideas—in different degrees of elaboration—that still pose a stimulating challenge to our research and intervention practices. By socially situating disabilities, Dembo draws our attention to ways of resisting dichotomous accounts in which the site of intervention is either in the person or in the environment. In this perspective, her theoretical perspective led her to amplify her intervention strategies, in order to include partners, institutions, and the legal aspects of the disabilities. Yet, this amplification did not suggest a de-personalization of the intervention, and this is a good reminder in times when contemporary rehabilitation psychology faces the danger of being overridden by a legalistic approach where the intricacies of the person-and-environment relation are lost in favor of general, pre-established categories and modes of knowledge "molded" by the requirements of the legal system.

In situating personal meanings within the central agenda of psychology, research and intervention become referenced towards finding mechanisms at different levels that will provide unique, personal solutions for the restructuring of a field involving personal relations. Homogenizing, normative recommendations that say much about the average and little about each individual are substituted for the serious investigation of the single case and the ambiguous. The ambiguous, the hard to classify, the borderline, rather than being viewed as the researcher's nightmares, are viewed as indexing change-in-process, and requiring the theoretical restructuration of conceptual schemes that will integrate the newly observed, ill-defined phenomena. With the field-theoretical understanding of the individual, Dembo navigated successfully between the search for general mechanisms and the encounter with unpredictable outcomes.

A related set of ideas that Dembo leaves for further development in the area of communication are the implications of the structure of the field of personal meanings—the life space—which constitutes the person's viewpoint towards a problem and toward others' (different) understanding of the (same) problem. The mental restructurations that she posits necessary for communication are not disjunct from the mental restructuration involved in creative research. On this line we may conclude by remembering that Dembo's mentor and colleague, Lewin (1951), had defined the task of the psychologist as that of being a novelist with scientific means, and accordingly Dembo's work can be seen as a systematic, detective–like investigation into the details and complexities of the constitution of the real feelings of real people. The main tool for this, as she noted in her late interviews, was constituted by the researcher basically exploring the possibilities of generation of novel meanings for old problems. She exemplifies by discussing an instance in which the word for a problem she had been "battling" with suddenly became associated to a second, seemingly unrelated meaning, and from this second meaning the clue for the solution of the problem stemmed. Hopefully, in our contemporary dialogue with Dembo's ideas, new syntheses on the old but persistent problems of psychology may arise.[11]

Notes

1. Previously published in *From Past to Future, Vol. 2*(1), pp. 19-41. *Tension in the Field: The Dynamic World of Tamara Dembo*. © 1999 Frances L. Hiatt School of

Psychology, Clark University. Author: Simone de Lima, Instituto de Psicologia-PED, Universidade de Brasilia, Brasilia.
2. Lewin (1938) proposed the term "hodological space" for an expansion of the non-quantitative but mathematical representation of structure and position in psychology to allow for the inclusion of dynamic, and more specifically, vectorial aspects of the field.
3. It is noteworthy though not the topic of this paper the role played by Tamara Dembo in articulating the emigration of some of her ex-colleagues form Germany, especially Dr Susanne Libmann, who had been Wertheimer's student. The plight to bring Dr. Libmann took two years, between 1938 and 1940 and involved Tamara's efforts to raise support, an affidavit, money and a job amongst various figures in America, including Lewin, Wertheimer, Stuart Stoke, Ernst Simmel, Gregory Bateson, and Margaret Mead.
4. She cites this as her *conscious* motivation at the time of the Stanford studies. However, in her later years, she comes to realize that she herself had for many years been considered an invalid due to her poor health in childhood and reflects that probably influenced her sensitivity to the field (Dembo, 1991; Rosa and Wertsch, 1993).
5. More "transparent" terms for comparative versus asset values are, perhaps, essential and inessential values.
6. See also the articles in the 1975 issue of *Rehabilitation Psychology* (Diller, 1975), *a Festschrift* in honor of Tamara Dembo, in which other authors elaborate on the insider-outsider relations.
7. Although she does not mention the nature of such knowledge explicitly, one assumes, from her previous project, that she is describing knowledge that is primarily sensory motor, i.e. composed of sensory- motor, non-verbal, schemata.
8. Note that the end of WWII marked a problem for the placement of the disabled in the work space not only because there was an increase in the number of disabled people due to war casualties, but also because of the "return" of the "able" from the war, taking back the slots in the workplace that might have "tolerated" the presence of the disabled. (See Linton, 1998, for a historical discussion of the modes of participation of the disabled in society.)
9. Another important aspect discussed by Danziger (1985) is the genesis of the anonymous subject, "washed out" of the study by statistical distributions, in the context of American psychology. Dembo's work is an example of a clash of cultures in this sense both in her discussion of individual, outlying cases (*Frustration and Regression*) and in one of her early studies, when the subject is identified by name and picture, a reflection of the high prestige position occupied by the subject. (Dembo and Tane-Baskin, 1955).
10. The importance of the complex process of gaining hope after value loss (e.g. after an amputation) is central in Dembo's account of rehabilitation. She describes this experience as "doing away with the weight of the high frequency of the most probable occurrence and the acceptance of the dictum of possibility as a guide in thinking and planning" (Dembo, 1964/1984) and is instrumental as a coping strategy in the long and short term.
11. I wish to thank Pat Pulda, Mott Linn, and an anonymous librarian at the Goddard Library at Clark University who helped me obtain access to Dembo's archival materials. I am grateful also to Professor Roger Bibace, Professor Jaan Valsiner, and the *kitchen meeting* members, all of who contributed their extremely useful comments and suggestions on earlier versions of this paper.

I gratefully acknowledge funding from the CAPES Foundation, Brasilia, DF, Brazil.

References

Adler, D.L., Ladieu, G. and Dembo, T. (1948). Studies in adjustment to visible injuries: Social acceptance of the injured. *Journal of Social Issues, 4,* 55-61.

Baldwin (1894). Imitation: A chapter in the natural history of consciousness. *Mind,* n.s., *3,* 26-55.

Barker, R., Dembo, T., and Lewin, K. (1941). Frustration and regression: An experiment with young children. *University of Iowa Studies: Studies in Child Welfare, XVIII* (1).

Barker, R. G., Dembo, T., and Lewin, K. (1943). Frustration and regression. In R. G. Barker and J. S. Kounin (Eds.), *Child behavior and development A Course of representative studies* (pp. 441–458). New York: McGraw-Hill Book Company.

Bell, J.E. (1955). The nature of social depreciation and of defenses in being adjudged: A study of the cerebral palsied child in his family. In J.E. Bell, T. Dembo and H. Werner, *The emotional and value aspects of interpersonal relationships between cerebral palsied child and his parents: Final report on exploratory studies (1953-1955).* Unpublished manuscript.

Bell, J. E., Dembo, T., and Werner, H. (1955). *The emotional and value aspects of interpersonal relationships between cerebral palsied child and his parents: Final report on exploratory studies (1953-1955).* Unpublished manuscript.

Danziger, K. (1985). The origins of the psychological experiment as a social institution. *American Psychologist, 40,* 2, 133-140.

Danziger, K. (1987). Social context and investigative practice in early twentieth-century psychology. In M.G. Ash and W.R. Woodward (Eds.), *Psychology in twentieth-century thought and society.* Cambridge University Press.

De Rivera, J. (1995). Tamara Dembo (1902-1993). *American psychologist, 50,* 386.

Dembo, T. (1931). Der Aerger als Dynamisches Problem. *Psych. Forsch. 15,*(Whole No. pp. 1-114).(English version: T. Dembo, The dynamics of anger. In J. de Rivera (Ed.), *Field Theory as Human Science: Contributions by Lewin's Berlin Group.* New York, Gardner Press.

Dembo, T. (1944). *Letter to Dr. A. Gregg of the Rockefeller Foundation dated March 31, 1944.*

Dembo, T. (1955). Suffering and its alleviation. In J. E. Bell, T. Dembo, and H. Werner (Eds.), *The emotional and value aspects of interpersonal relationships between the cerebral palsied child and his parents. Final report on exploratory studies (1953-1955).* Unpublished manuscript.

Dembo, T. (1960). A theoretical and experimental inquiry into concrete values and value systems. In B. Kaplan and S. Wapner (Eds.), *Perspectives in psychological theory. Essays in honor of Heinz Werner* (pp. 78–114). New York, NY: International Universities Press.

Dembo, T. (1962). *Psychological development in cerebral palsy: Touch, grasp and hold (The role of intentional activities in the psychological development of small severely handicapped children.).* Unpublished Final Report to the INH, U.S.PHS, Grant M1149.

Dembo, T. (1964a). On studying professional-client relationships. *Bulletin, Division 22, APA, 11,* 19–24.

Dembo, T. (1964b/1984). Sensitivity of one person to another. *Rehabilitation Literature, 25,* 231–235.

Dembo, T. (1968a). The prophetic mission of rehabilitation - curse or blessing? First reply. *Journal of Rehabilitation, 34(1),* 34–35.

Dembo, T. (1968b). *Rehabilitation in 3 minutes 20 seconds and a spilled bottle of wine.* Talk delivered on March 1.

Dembo, T. (1969a). Psychological aspects of disability. *Bulletin, Division 22, APA, 16,* 39–43.
Dembo, T. (1969b). *Rehabilitation psychology and its immediate future.* Presidential Address, APA Division 22, delivered September 1.
Dembo, T. (1970). The utilization of psychological knowledge in rehabilitation. *Welfare in Review, 8 (4),* 1–7.
Dembo, T. (1974). The paths to useful knowledge. *Rehabilitation psychology, 21,* 4, 124–128.
Dembo, T. (1980). *Statement of need and approach—Rehabilitation psychology training program.* Unpublished report.
Dembo, T. (1982). Some problems in rehabilitation as seen by a Lewinian. *Journal of Social Issues, 38 (1),* 131–139.
Dembo, T. (1993). Thoughts on qualitative determinants in psychology: A methodological study. *Journal of Russian and east European psychology, 31,* 6, 15–70.
Dembo, T., Frank, J.D., Lewin, K. and Waring, E.B. Studies in social pressure. *Unpublished work,* referenced in Lewin, K. (1936). Principles of Topological Psychology. New York.McGraw Hill Book Co Inc.(p.96)
Dembo, T., and Hanfmann, E. (1933). Intuitive Halving and Doubling of Figures. *Psych. forsch., 17,* 306–318.
Dembo, T., and Hanfmann, E. (1934). The Value of an Orientational Letter for Newly Admitted Patients. *Psychiat. quarterly, 8,* 703–721.
Dembo, T., and Hanfmann, E. (1936). The Patient's Psychological Situation upon Admission to Hospital. *American Journal of Psychology, 47,* 381–408.
Dembo, T., and Tane-Baskin, E. (1955). Social usefulness of the cosmetic glove. *Artificial Limbs, 2,* 47–56.
Dembo, T. and Werner, H. (1955). Research plan on promotion of psychological development in children with cerebral palsy. Evolved on the basis of observations made during the exploratory studies. In J.E. Bell, T. Dembo and H. Werner, *The emotional and value aspects of interpersonal relationships between cerebral palsied child and his parents: Final report on exploratory studies (1953-1955).* Unpublished manuscript.
Dembo, T., Diller, L., Gordon, W. A., Levinton, G. and Sherr, R. (1973). A view of rehabilitation psychology. *American Psychologist, 28,* 8, 719–722.
Dembo, T., Ladieu-Levinton, G., and Wright, B. (1951). Acceptance of loss: Amputations. In J. F. Garret (Ed.), *Psychological aspects of physical disability* (pp. 80–96). Washington, DC: Federal Security Agency, Office of Vocational Rehabilitation.
Dembo, T., Levinton, G. L., and Wright, B. A. (1975). Adjustment to misfortune: A problem of social-psychological rehabilitation. *Rehabilitation Psychologist, 22, 1,* 1–101. (Original text published 1956).
Diller, L. (Ed.). (1975). Festschrift for Dr Tamara Dembo. *Rehabilitation Psychology, 22,* 2.
Executive Committee of Division 22. (1975). Psychology in action: Statement of beliefs and objectives of APA Division 22. *American Psychologist,* 1020–1021.
Follini, M., Bergstein, M., Epstein, H., and Dembo, T. (n.d.). *Operational studies in institutions for the disabled and the deprived: The effect of enriched environment upon custodial cases: A study in an institution for the mentally retarded.* Unpublished research report: Rehabilitation psychology training program. Department of psychology, Clark University.
Foucault, M. (1976). *Mental illness and Psychology.* New York: Harper and Row.
Gunther, I. A. (1998) Contacting subjects: the untold story. *Culture and Psychology, Vol. 4, 1.*65-74.
Hacking, I. (1996). Normal people. In D.R. Olson and N. Torrance (Eds.), *Modes of thought: Explorations in culture and cognition.* Cambridge University Press.

Holmes-Bernstein, J. and Waber, D.P. (1990). Developmental neuropsychological assessment: The systemic approach. In A.A. Boulton, G.B. Baker and M. Hiscock (Eds.),

Hong, G.Y. (1998). Logisitcs and researchers as legitimate tools for doing intercultural research: a rejoinder to Gunther. *Culture and Psychology, Vol. 4, 1., 81-90.*

Hoskins, R.G. (1933). *Memorandum to Drs. Hanfmann and Denbo.* August, 31, 1933.

Kaplan, B. and Wapner, S. (1960). *Perspectives in psychological theory: Essays in honor of Heinz Werner.* New York. International Universities Press.

Kaplan, E. (1988). A process approach to neuropsychological assessment. In T. Boll and B. Bryant (Eds.), *Clinical neuropsychology and brain function: Research, measurement, and practice.* Washington, DC: American Psychological Association.

Kojima, H. (1998). Researcher's story told and participants' story still untold: commentary on Gunther. *Culture and Psychology, Vol. 4(1),* 75-80.

Ladieu, G., Adler, D. L., and Dembo, T. (1948). Studies in adjustment to visible injuries: Social acceptance of the injured. *Journal of Social Issues, 4,* 55–61.

Ladieu, G., Hanfmann, E., and Dembo, T. (1947). Studies in adjustment to visible injuries: evaluation of help by the injured. *Journal of Abnormal and Social Psychology, 42,* 169–191.

Leviton, L.(1959). Conference: *The Relationship between Rehabilitation and Psychology* (155 p). Worcester, MA: Edited Conference proceedings, Clark University.

Lewin, K. (1936). Principles of Topological Psychology. New York: Mc Graw-Hill.

Lewin K. (1938) The conceptual representation and measurement of psychological forces. *Contributions to Psychological Theory,* Vol. I, No 4, Durham, NC, Duke University Press.

Lewin, K. (1939). Field theory and experiment in social psychology: Concepts and methods. *American Journal of Sociology, 44,* 868–896.

Lewin, K. (1951). Problems of research in social psychology. In D. Cartwright (Ed.) *Field theory in social science: Selected theoretical papers by Kurt Lewin.* New York: Harper and Row. (Original text published in 1944)

Lewin, K. (1951). Behavior and development as a function of the total situation. In D. Cartwright (Ed.), *Field theory in social sciences.* New York: Harper and Bro.(Original text published 1946).

Lewin, K., Dembo, T., Festinger, L., and Sears, P. (1944). Level of aspiration. J. McV. Hunt (Vol. Ed.), *Personality and Behavior Disorders: Vol. 1.* New York: Ronald Press.

Linton, S. (1998). *Claiming disability: Knowledge and identity.* New York University Press.

McDermott, R. and Varenne, H. (1996). Culture, development, disability. In R. Jessor, A. Colby and R. Shweder (Eds.), *Ethnography and human development: Context and meaning in social inquiry.* University of Chicago Press.

Myers, J.K. (1968). Statement. *Journal of rehabilitation, 34,* 1, 34.

Obituary: Tamara Dembo, ninety-one, Clark University Psychologist. (1993, October 18). *Telegram and Gazette,*

Obituary: Tamara Dembo, ninety-one, Gestalt psychologist who studied anger. (1993, October 19). *New York Times*

Obituary: Tamara Dembo, ninety-one, leading figure of gestalt therapy in this century. (1993, October 18). *Boston Globe.*

Pessoti, I. (1981). Sobre a genese e evolucao historica do conceito de deficiencia mental. [On the genesis and historical evolution of the concept of mental deficiency]. *Revista Brasiliera de Deficiencia Mental, 16,* 1, 54-69.

Raimy, V.C. (Ed.) *Training in Clinical Psychology: Report to the Conference on graduate Education in Clinical Psychology held at Boulder Colorado, August 1949.* New York: Prentice-Hall.

Rosa, A., and Wertsch, J. V. (1993, November-December). Tamara Dembo and her Work. *Journal of Russian and East European Psychology, 31, No. 6,* 5-14.

Sacks, O. (1996). *The island of the colorblind.* New York: Alfred A. Knopf.

Shoda, Y., Mischel, W. and P.K. Peake. (1990). Predicting adolescent cognitive and self-regulatory competencies from preschool delay of gratification. *Developmental Psychology,* 26, 6 pp 978-986.

Usdane, W.S. (1968). Second reply. *Journal of Rehabilitation, 34,* 1, 35.

Van der Veer, R. (1999) Tamara Dembo's European Years. *From Past to Future: Clark Papers on the History of Psychology 2,* 1–17.

Vygotsky, L.S. (1993). The fundamental problems of defectology. In R.W. Rieber and A.S. Carton (Eds.), *The collected works of L.S. Vygotsky, vol.2: The fundamentals of defectology (Abnormal psychology and learning disabilities).* New York: Plenum Press. (Original text published in 1929).

Wertsch, J.V and Tulviste, P. (1991). Interview with Tamara Dembo. February 18, 1991.

White, R. K., Wright, B. A., and Dembo, T. (1948). Studies in adjustment to visible injuries: Evaluation of curiosity by the injured. *The Journal of Abnormal and Social Psychology, 43,* 13–28.

13

Tamara Dembo's Socio-Emotional Relationships

Joseph de Rivera[1]

After Tamara Dembo arrived at Clark she secured a grant to train students in rehabilitation psychology. Many graduate students participated in this training and were teaching assistants in her undergraduate seminar and laboratory in rehabilitation psychology and interpersonal relations. She repeatedly attempted to write a book on her approach to rehabilitation and there are many tables of contents, half-written chapters, unfinished papers, and class notes in boxes in the Clark archives. This article is about one of the most pervasive themes in these papers and class notes, the concept of socio-emotional relations.

Dembo often wrote about the relationship between the person and the environment and is known for emphasizing that handicaps may be seen as existing in the environmental rather than personal part of the life space. She argued that a "handicapped person" should really be seen as a person handicapped by an environment. She pointed out that a person without legs was not handicapped in reaching a goal if the environment provided access by means of a wheelchair and ramps. However, Dembo knew that handicaps are not only in the physical environment. She wrote, "The suffering of deprived and handicapped people (or in other words, the handicap itself) entails particular social-emotional relationships such as being devalued, being dependent, being a burden, needing help, respect and acceptance" (Dembo, 1971, p.1). She began to focus on these relationships and they preoccupied her for the rest of her life. In her will she left money for the publication of one of her unfinished papers on how to investigate the quality of such relationships (Dembo, 1993) and it seems clear that she saw the concept as an important part of her legacy. To accept this gift we must ask about socio-emotional relations. What exactly are they?

Conceptualizing Socio-Emotional Relationships

Dembo points out that a person is in relationships with strangers, acquaintances, co-workers, professionals, friends, and family members, and that these others may be disinterested, mildly interested in one, or personally concerned and involved. She distinguishes between these role relationships (teacher-student, professional-client, etc.) and incidental relations such as one person accepting, devaluing or helping another person. Role relations, with their obligations, responsibilities, privileges, and social distance, are more inclusive and enduring than incidental relations.[2] She also distinguishes between instrumental or factual relations (e.g., asking directions, buying a ticket) and emotional relations (respecting a person, being repulsed by a facial scar). By socio-emotional relations she means incidental, emotional relations. Having distinguished them as one type of relationship, she is interested in the various kinds there are and the specific qualitative characteristics, properties, ingredients, that constitute kinds of relations such as trust, admiration, and helping, and give these the specificity that enables us to distinguish them from each other (class notes 10/19/1984).

Socio-emotional relations can be complementary; cooperation is an example. However, Dembo focuses on what she terms asymmetrical relations, where one person initiates the relation the "donor" and the other receives the relationship, the "recipient." Thus, the person who helps, accepts, devalues, is the donor while the one who is helped, accepted, devalued, is the recipient. While the donor carries a kind of responsibility for initiating the relationship, and may be blamed or praised, it should be noted that asymmetry does not refer to a difference in power or status the way it would if we were discussing role relations. Thus, a person with a handicap and low status, may be the donor, accepting or rejecting a professional who is trying to be of help.

As conceived by Dembo, socio-emotional relationships have objective properties. She is concerned with incidents where one person actually accepts, rejects, trusts, another person.

Any concrete incident of such a relation occurs in a particular setting, in privacy or public, during a time of stress or calmness, within a particular role relationship, with another who has similar or different ideological relations. However, she emphasizes that acceptance and other socio-emotional relations are experienced differently by those involved in the relationship. The donor of help may feel good about helping while the recipient is feeling badly because he or she dislikes an implied dependence.

If Dembo had simply been interested in helping persons she might have been content with coining a useful term, but she was committed to developing a science of experience that would be useful to persons who want to help others. The idea of socio-emotional relations seems important and straightforward. However, it is much more challenging to theoretical psychology than one might expect. Donor-recipient relations, such as to accept—to be accepted, or to devalue—to be devalued, are as empirically evident as friendship or anger. However, friendship may be regarded as an objective fact that, like power or status, may be measured by a social psychologist. And we are prone to refer feelings of anger or other emotions to the subjective experience of individuals. By contrast, socio-emotional relations are meant as relational units that are both interpersonally objective and experiential. To accept-to be accepted is at one and the same time both objectively interpersonal and experiential. Thus, it cannot be conceptualized simply as a unit to be observed by a social psychologist or as subjective feeling.

Of course, Dembo was mindful that Kurt Lewin had created a unit that combined the objective and subjective. His "life-space," or person-in-environment, allowed psychologists to understand behavior as dependent on subjective experience, and Dembo's seminal thesis on anger showed how emotion could be understood as an outburst of tension that broke through normal boundaries and unified the life-space (Dembo, 1976). But socio-emotional relations involve two persons in a situation, two subjectivities, and this is impossible to represent with one life-space. I believe it was this fact, as much as any other, that prevented Dembo from really developing the concept and publishing her ideas.

It might be objected that phenomenological psychologists often deal with persons who experience the same thing in different ways. Thus, Keen (1977) insightfully describes the same event as seen through different eyes. However, in a socio-emotional relation the persons are experiencing each other, experiencing an other's subjectivity, rather than a common event. For example, one person is experiencing being helped by another who is simultaneously experiencing being helpful. Could one represent this by placing two persons in the same life space? No, because the environmental part of the life space is the environment as perceived by, or as affecting, the person part, so each person necessarily has a different environment, perceives the situation somewhat differently.

Further, while the boundaries, barriers, and forces of the life-space are just as pertinent to an analysis of socio-emotional relations, one also needs a way to represent concepts such as dependency, trust, and devaluation. It is interesting to note how Dembo represents interpersonal forces in her dissertation on anger. In order to represent how the experimenter's field of power influences the life space of the experimental subject, she draws a series of concentric circles emanating from the experimenter, outside the life space but profoundly influencing that space by establishing valences and barriers. She points out that as subjects becomes aware of how this power is trapping them in a frustrating situation, they begin to enter into a struggle with the experimenter, attempting to break the latter's power over the situation. Dembo presents a fascinating diagram of this field of struggle. The diagram successfully captures the situation for the subject and objectively, between subject and experimenter, but lacks a portrayal of the experimenter's life space. I believe it is the best attempt to portray a dyadic interaction by Lewinian type diagrams (see de Rivera, 1976, p. 384).

Dembo was, of course, well aware of the representational problem. Reflecting on the problems that injured persons have with others, Dembo writes, "This I saw, not as a problem of a person and his environment, not as a problem of one's life space, but as the problem of matching the life space of two persons who were meeting and interacting with each other" (class notes, 7/18/1974, p.11). She asks how things appear to persons on both sides of a relation, to the donor and the recipient, the injured and the non-injured, as well as to an observer who is free to abstractly reflect about the relation. At one point she reflects on our tendency to use the self as the unit of psychology, as reflected in terms like "self-fulfillment." She contrasts this with the fact that we are always in relationships. She writes, "Two-ness-the original and perhaps natural unit of our own existence" (class notes, 7/18/1924, p. 42).

Of course, in everyday life this "twoness" goes on all the time. However, Dembo observes that one must slow the pace of everyday living in order to see the rich psychological material that is involved. And it is not the subject matter of much psychology. Krause (1970) has noted that most psychology is either the "first person" psychology of experience, as reflected by the psychologies of Freud or Lewin, or the "third person" psychology of behaviorists such as Skinner. Nevertheless, there is some "second person" psychology, as represented in the writings of Carl Rogers and Martin Buber, and it seems a shame that Dembo did not recognize these natural allies. Rogers, like Dembo, deals with acceptance, understanding, and the importance of the relationship between professional and client. Further, he suggests important dynamics, as when he postulates that change only occurs when the other is accepted.

Dembo was interested in what she called the "ingredients" of socio-emotional relationships and she saw these as interrelated. Thus, she points out (class notes, Spring 1983, p. 37) that a person (p) helping another (o) may involve p feeling closer to o. Each relation is subject to evaluations (helping is good, envy is bad). They entail both feelings that characterize the relationship (helping necessarily involves dependence) and feelings about what is going on (such dependence may be avoided or sought.) They also involve beliefs and expectancies. Dembo is quite clear that she has two different purposes: To gain knowledge about the characteristics and constitution of these real-life relations in their own right, and to gain knowledge in the hope of being able to improve relations. In order to slow down enough to grasp the qualitative properties of socio-emotional relations she uses interviews with persons whom she or her students enlisted as co-investigators.

The Relation of Acceptance

Unfortunately, Dembo never spelled out the ingredients of most of the dozens of key relations she and her students investigated. The closest she comes to doing this is in a section on acceptance in an unpublished 1971 paper (with an unknown co-author). In this paper she notes, " ... difficulty in acceptance pervades all relationships between the disabled and non-disabled" (Dembo, 1971, p. 4). She clearly distinguishes between acceptance on a merely intellectual level and on an emotional level, observing, "It is therefore quite possible for someone to be totally unaware of the negative feelings or aversions they have masked with a tolerant attitude until spontaneously confronted by a person with a disability in a life situation" (Dembo, 1971, p. 2). She notes that feelings of aversion, resentment, or that the other is inferior, are often masked and get in the way of emotional acceptance, and that in the early stages of acceptance there is some insecurity which is gradually replaced by people feeling more comfortable and free to act naturally.

Dembo's students were required to visit persons with disabilities (they were given the task of comparing the environment in a college dorm with, for example, a home for the elderly) and to conduct both self-interviews and interviews with others on incidents of acceptance, being accepted, and other socio-emotional relations. Dembo summarizes the results of numerous interviews on acceptance by making the following observations:

- Acceptance entails an openness for more inclusive communication.
- It involves an overlooking, a tolerating, or being patient with, what is perceived as negative or different.
- Acceptance leads to a more positive perception of the other.
- There are levels to this acceptance.
- The acceptor may feel insecure in opening his or her self to an other who may be "unworthy."
- In order for a person to be accepted they cannot be playing a role. That is, genuineness is a precondition for acceptance to occur.
- The person who is being accepted feels insecure until his or her acceptance has been confirmed.
- The security that is gained by being accepted spreads so that the accepted person can explore new situations.
- The accepted's self esteem is elevated by acceptance from a highly valued other.
- Being accepted leads the accepted to perceive the other as admirable, respected, warm, personal, attractive.
- However, if the accepted lacks self-esteem, the acceptance can be devalued and perceived as weird.
- One negative feature of being accepted is that it may induce a need for more acceptance.

Acceptance only occurs under certain conditions (such as self-acceptance). It has neighboring relations that are congruent (such as trust) and it cannot occur when there are incongruent relations (such as devaluation). Further, it is more likely to occur in certain favorable circumstances (such as liking the other), although these facilitative relations are not essential.

Dembo specifies the preconditions for acceptance as follows:
The donor must have:

- Self-acceptance and security
- Perceived status/role equality
- Minimal perceived "obligation"
- The recipient must have:
- The moral right to be accepted

The following factors are not essential but facilitate acceptance:
For the donor:

- Appreciation of
- Liking and respect
- Mutuality and sharing
- Openness and self disclosure
- Tolerance, ability to overlook
- Trust in other
- Curiosity, wish to understand

For the recipient:

- Mutuality and sharing
- Openness and self disclosure
- Sincerity
- Situational need (e.g., loneliness)
- Membership in family, group
- Undergoing rites of passage

Dembo also specifies the processes that the donor undergoes in the process of acceptance. If the reader imagines meeting with a person who has a severe handicap, such as the absence of both arms or severe facial scarring, s/he may be better able to follow Dembo's description of the process. Her list indicates the process as involving the following:

The donor begins to overlook negative aspects, to become more intimate, and eliminate judgments. Gradually s/he gains understanding, becoming closer yet keeping some distance. If the other is considered as acting appropriately, and the person does not impose his/her own standards, empathizing will occur. Dembo notes that this process is incongruent with rejecting, prejudging, perceiving narrowly, and being demanding. She raises the question of what might happen if a person experiences a discrepancy in his/her favorable view of the other. What if, perhaps, the other has committed a crime? In such a case the person will devalue and reject the other unless the person can see the discrepancy as out of character or change the meaning of the act in a way that will allow it to be integrated in with a favorable impression.

As the process proceeds there are specific results that Dembo lists as: The development of "twoness," new perceptions of the recipient, an increase in valuing the recipient, feeling closer, feelings of warmth, caring for, supporting, being needed, trust and confidence, and being attracted to the recipient.

Dembo does not indicate whether these processes and results follow particular patterns, and it would be interesting to see if some sequences were more likely and if the same processes are involved in less stressful incidents of acceptance such as the acceptance of a new member into a group.

The list of processes and results for the recipient of acceptance are somewhat different. As processes, Dembo only lists becoming more intimate, and getting closer but keeping some distance. However, she lists as incongruent: being rejected, prejudged and pitied, and also feeling subordinate, helpless, and devalued. That is, while the recipient experiences these relations, the socio-emotional relationship of acceptance cannot occur. As acceptance does occur it results in the recipient experiencing: "twoness," being valued, validation/confirmation of value, greater freedom to act naturally, the experience of being listened to, feelings of warmth and being cared for, support, security, feelings of comfort and relaxation, an increase in self-esteem, respect admiration, and gratitude for the donor, and depending on the donor. Dembo notes these results are incongruent with feeling vulnerable.

It seems unfortunate that Dembo confines herself to listing the properties of acceptance rather than exploring some of the relationships that are hinted at by her analysis. For example, the idea that the donor of acceptance may be insecure in opening the self to what is "unworthy," and the difficulty in dealing with discrepancies such as criminal acts, suggests that there may be a fear of contamination from the other. This implies that acceptance involves an opening of the boundaries surrounding self-identity, that one is accepting something into the self and that this may be why acceptance may be quite difficult. Such dynamics might then be related to the analysis of acceptance as an emotion. For example, the emotional act of acceptance may be understood as conferring being on another by granting the existence of something whose essence seems undesirable (see de Rivera, 1997). The other may appear so flawed that we hesitate to grant the existence of the flawed aspect of his or her behavior or physiognomy. Our refusal to admit protects our ideals, but at the expense of the other, who in a vital sense does not exist for us. The emotion of acceptance involves stopping our insistence that the other meet our ideal. We allow the other to be the way s/he is and stop insisting how they ought to be. It is fascinating to note how prior to acceptance persons believe that they will lose something of value, yet after the act of acceptance there does not seem to be any such loss of what is ideal. Rather persons report a greater sense of freedom.

While it seems useful to analyze the emotional act of acceptance and its implications for the self, viewing acceptance as a socio-emotional relationship, and not simply as an emotional act, emphasizes how acceptance changes the relationship between self and other, and hence may alter the other. Thus, as Rogers (1961) emphasizes, acceptance creates conditions that often lead the other to behave in more ideal ways. In this regard, it should be noted that Rogers does not mean overlooking destructive behavior (such as abusive behavior or a drug habit). Such overlooking actually implies a denial that the behavior exists and has impact. Acceptance means realizing the behavior (and taking whatever steps may be appropriate) without rejecting the personhood of the other. For Dembo, acceptance of persons who were disadvantaged often played a crucial role in restoring a damaged sense of self-worth.

Interrelations Between Socio-Emotional Relations

Dembo notes that tolerance, appreciation, and respect are "neighboring" relations to acceptance. She wondered how many socio-emotional relations there are. She observes that hundreds are named, and that others do not have names but are clearly implied, such as the relationship implied by one person being "restrained" in the presence of an other. While she was concerned about discovering the properties of each, she also wondered about the interrelations among them and hoped to describe this network or field. She believed that if we knew the structural and dynamic properties of individual relations we could see how they were related, if they composed a system of relations. If we understood such a system we might be able to change one relation by changing how it was "rooted" in the system (class notes, 10/19/1984). The class notes for the spring of 1983 indicate that she presented her class with some eighty-five socio-emotional relations that had been chosen by previous students. These are listed in table 13.1.

In the fall of 1984, she attempted to categorize these as abstract relations. She found that she sometimes focused on the intent of the donor (e.g., to advise, to take care of), sometimes on the emotional state of the donor (to distrust, to envy), and sometimes on the relation itself (to abandon, to confide). She found herself making fourteen categories and attempted to place the eighty-five relations in these categories, " ... in an attempt to arrive at a tentative example of a system of interrelations of interpersonal relations" (class notes, 10/11/84, p. 2). Searching for how the relations may be interrelated she decided to choose a category she terms "stabilization" as a building stone on which to build a system of interrelationships. The relation of trust is in this category and Dembo states, "I was surprised at how frequently the students in the class chose for analysis the interpersonal relation of trust, and only slowly did I realize what importance it can have." "Trust means feeling, thinking, and expecting that one can count on, rely on ... that one is secure ... will not be surprised. Trust shows the first building stone is intended to promote positive change ... has an effect beyond itself ... beyond an incident of trust as a more inclusive relation...effecting many other relations." She observes, "I was not aware that many of the interpersonal relations deal with stabilization and also destabilization of relations, that stability

Table 13.1
Socio-Emotional Relations Chosen by Students

abandon	deceive	fear	pity
abuse	defeat	flatter	praise
accept	defend	forgive	pressure
accuse	degrade	frustrate	pretend
admire	demand	give false	reassure
advise	depend on	impression	reject
aggress	disappoint	hate	respect
anger	disapprove	help	ridicule
annoy	disgust	humiliate	supervise
apologize	dislike	hurt	sympathize
assure	distrust	ignore	take advantage of
attack	disvalue	insult	take care of
betray	dominate	intimidate	teach
blame	doubt	(be) jealous	tease
comfort	educate	judge	tell someone what
compliment	embarrass	lead	to do
confide	empathize	lie	tolerate
confront	encourage	like	trust
console	entertain	manipulate	understand
counsel	envy	neglect	use
		oversee	

of a relation is at least of (as much) concern to people as, for instance, control or power relations" (class notes, 10/11/84 p. 3).

After such a promising beginning, the reader expects that Dembo will organize the categories about stabilization. However, she does not! She does not develop any system of interrelationships and we are left with only the list of fourteen categories and the relations that she placed in each. This list is presented in table 13.2. It may be noted that a few terms are placed in more than one category.

I have been unwilling to let these categories rest and have attempted to develop the system as best I can. I assume that categories such as change (when it gives benefit), assigning characteristics, feelings (when positive) and support, may be placed under stabilization, while change (when it threatens or destroys), devaluation, feelings (when negative), hindering, intrusion, trying-to-get-something, and compete in the sense of "defeat" are aspects of destabilization.[3] Further, while distance can be related to stabilization it seems to me that it can be organized in its own right and may include the category called give a false impression. This gives the system of interrelations shown in table 13.3.

Table 13.2
Dembo's Categorization of Socio-Emotional Relations

Category	Socio-emotional Relations
1. Change	
Give benefit	To advise, counsel, comfort, educate, take care of, teach.
Negative	To abuse, accuse, aggress, attack, confront, hurt, intimidate.(threaten, destroy)
2. Distance	
Closeness	To abandon, accept, confide, reject, understand
Inequality	To envy
3. Stabilization	To admire, apologize, assure, comfort, complement, console, defend, forgive, reassure, trust
A. Destabilize	To annoy, confront, disgust, distrust, doubt, embarrass, humiliate, ignore, ridicule, tease.
4. Assign characteristics	
Negative	To blame
5. Control	To dominate, lead, oversee, supervise, tell someone what to do.
6. Give a false impression	To deceive, flatter, lie, play a role, pretend.
7. Compete	To defeat.
8. Evaluate	To judge, praise
A. Devaluate	To degrade, disvalue, insult, neglect, pity
9. Try and get something from someone	To demand, manipulate, pressure, take advantage of, use
10. Give something to someone (positive, negative)	To disgust, entertain, help, teach
11. To support	To empathize, encourage, respect, sympathize
12. Feeling states	To dislike, fear, hate, be jealous, like, tolerate, feel uncomfortable with
13. To hinder	To frustrate.
14. To intrude into someone's privacy	
Unclassified	To anger, betray, depend on, disappoint

The Dyad as a Unit of Analysis

Dembo's emphasis on "twoness" suggests that her work can be related to that of Macmurray (1957), who argued that the dyad was the basic unit of the personal and made dyadic relations the basis of his philosophy. For Macmurray, a person qua person does not exist as either an individual nor as a member of a group, but only in relation to other persons. He asserted that these dyadic

Table 13.3
Interrelations of Socio-Emotional Relationships

Stabilization	Destabilization
To trust, apologize, assure, forgive, reassure	To distrust, doubt, confront
Positive Feeling states	Negative Feeling states
To like, tolerate	To dislike, envy, fear, feel uncomfortable with, hate, be jealous of
Be vulnerable	Try and Get Something
To depend on, (ask advise of), (request)	To demand, manipulate, pressure, take advantage of, use [Note how these imply a lack of trust that one is cared for]
Assign Positive Characteristics	Threaten
To admire, compliment, praise	To abuse, blame, accuse, aggress, attack, disapprove of, humiliate, intimidate, judge, ridicule, tease
Support	Injure
To comfort, console, defend, empathize, encourage, respect, sympathize	To betray, defeat, disappoint, hurt
Benefit	Molest
To advise, counsel, educate, entertain, help, take care of, teach	To frustrate, anger, annoy, intrude, disgust, embarrass
Closeness	Distance
I. To (attend to), confide in	To ignore
II. To understand	To give a false impression
	Deceive, flatter, lie, play a role, pretend
III. To accept	To reject, abandon
Equality	Inequality
(To consider an equal)	To Devaluate
	Degrade, disvalue, insult, neglect, pity

relations had a common structure that always involved two motivational strands, a caring for the other (love) and a concern for the self (fear). At any moment in time in any given relationship, one of these strands was dominant with the other subordinated to it. Normally, a child begins with love dominate and an assumption of the other's love, but when he or she is hurt by either an actual or apparent abandonment of the other's caring, the fear for the self becomes dominant. This fear can be manifested in two quite different ways. The person can either decide that one should avoid depending on the other and, instead, look out for one's self, or that one should be "good," and conform to what the other wants, in order to restore the other's love. Whole societies are oriented to these options, and develop congruent systems of morality and politics. Individualistic societies, such as our own, emphasize the moral duty of Kant and the politics of Hobbes, while a collectivistic society, such as Japan, emphasizes a morality of manners and a politics of conformity (see de Rivera, 1989). In either case, the fact that the underlying motivation is the dominance of fear is evidenced by splits that develop within the person and society. For example, Western civilization suffers from splits between mind and body, emotion and reason, liberals and conservatives, etc. These splits are only overcome, and unity achieved, to the extent that one is able to restore the dominance of love for the other. Then mutuality and true cooperation are possible. This restoration is the function of religion, which ideally operates to provide the faith and encourage the forbearance and forgiveness necessary for caring for other to recover a position of dominance.

The possible connection between Macmurray and Dembo is reinforced by a side point. Dembo observes that wishing to help may stem from three different motives: from duty, from a need to be needed, and from two-ness (class notes, 7/18/1974). It is interesting to note that, for Macmurray, duty is an aspect of the sort of morality generated by individualistic societies, while the need to be needed reflects conformity, and "twoness" appears to be referring to the sort of mutuality that Macmurray sees as occurring when caring for the other dominates our self-concern.

When Dembo organizes socio-emotional relations about the idea of stabilization she is emphasizing what Macmurray might term the maintenance of mutual relationships by relations that encourage the dominance of love. From this perspective, it may be observed that the socio-emotional relations that destabilize a relationship all reflect a fear for the self or will lead the other to fear for his or her self. They will lead a person to either withdraw from the relationship or submit out of conformity. Conversely, the socio-emotional relations that stabilize a relationship, do so by placing caring for the other over fear for the self.

Relations that involve distance are obviously related to stabilization. Those that involve closeness ordinarily stabilize while those involving distance ordinarily destabilize. Some exceptions will be discussed below. I have treated these relations separately because distance is a clear category that lends itself to separate analysis. Dembo distinguishes between two types of distance, one that is created by abandonment and rejection, and an other which has to do with inequality. However, Kreilkamp (1981, 1984) has distinguished three different dimensions for the first type of distance. He distinguishes:

The closeness involved in one person directing behavior toward a particular other (as when attention is given to specific needs) versus the distance involved in not attending to or being emotionally involved with, or attached to, the other as a particular human being.

The closeness of persons who communicate and understand one another versus the distance involved when barriers to this communication prevent a person from taking the other's point of view.

The closeness of persons being together in the same unit versus the distance involved when persons are not in the same unit. In this regard, it may be noted that a person must accept the other into the unit and this implies a certain equality of worthiness, some commitment to the maintenance of the unit, and an assumption that one can depend on the other. Distance prevents the attendant obligations.

It may be noted that distance is sometimes used to stabilize a relationship. For example, persons may avoid the discussion of subjects, on which they adamantly disagree, thus maintaining the distance involved in a lack of understanding, in order to maintain cordiality and prevent the divisiveness that might fracture a unit. And some societies, such as the Japanese, maintain harmony by utilizing status inequalities.

Why do not all socio-emotional relations involve aspects of distance? It may be argued that all do involve the dimensions of distance, but that only some involve changes in distance and, hence, lead a person to experience closeness or distance. Sympathy implies understanding, and hence a closeness on the second distance dimension, but it does not necessarily increase that closeness. Anger may or may not involve the distance of misunderstanding, but always implies a closeness on Kreilkamp's first dimension, because the anger is directed at a particular person with whom the person is emotionally involved. Further, de Rivera (1981, 1984) has argued that anger maintains the third type of closeness because it implies the two persons are in a unit with shared values. The angry person is asserting that the other ought to be responsible that there are shared values. Rather than becoming angry she/he may increase distance by no longer caring about how the other behaves, by no longer perceiving them as intelligible, by no longer seeing them as a responsible member of the unit, or by devaluing them. Often, important distinctions are involved. To "blame," implies a certain lack of trust or forgiveness, and hence a distance, that is not implied by "to hold responsible."

Socio-Emotional Relations, Emotions, and Relationships

While some socio-emotional relations stress action (to blame, comfort, demand, help), there are always implied emotions, such as anger or jealousy, sympathy, or liking. While for others such as anger, envy, or fear, these emotions are always directed in some specific way. Thus, anger may be directed as a blaming, a demanding, an insult, etc. Still other relations clearly imply both action and emotion, such as to admire, reject, sympathize. Whatever relation we name simply leads us to focus on a particular aspect of what is happening. In any case, Dembo wants to emphasize that a dyadic unit is involved. She is not interested in blaming or comforting as actions, or in anger, envy, or sympathy as subjective feelings. She is interested in one person directing anger, blame, admiration, envy, or sympathy toward a receptive other.

There is an interesting problem inherent in Dembo's analysis. In her analysis there is always a donor and a recipient who experience the same relation. Her description of acceptance involves what is necessary for one person to accept an other who feels accepted. But this way of framing relations avoids important problems in the description of inter-personal relations. What if p accepts o, but o takes advantage of p? What if o does not realize that they are the target of p's envy or rejection? Or what if p rejects o, and o realizes this rejection but does not feel rejected but anger, loneliness, or sadness? Or if o feels rejected when p feels uncomfortable? From an objective standpoint, socio-emotional relationships are more complex than Dembo's socio-emotional relations. They involve two separate individuals. Each has personal emotions and engages in actions which may or may not address what the other person is doing. Each affects the degree of closeness as exhibited on Kreilkamp's dimensions of distance. If socio-emotional relations, really refers to a dyad with objective status, than must not these relations always be described as occurring within a dyadic relationship where there is a certain objective degree of closeness and distance?

In fact, some of Dembo's writings illustrate this necessity because, paradoxically, the closeness of understanding often involves a realization of the distance implicit in persons being in quite different positions. One of Dembo's most important points is that there are times when one person is within a situation and experiencing feelings that are quite different from one who is outside the situation. The person within a situation of loss can only be helped if those outside that situation are aware of these differences. The sympathetic offering of a cup of tea at the right time may be of far more support than the assumption that one knows how the other is feeling, and professionals need to be aware that these positional differences affect how their advice is perceived. Dembo discusses the situation of a mother who is wondering how to deal with a baby with severe cerebral palsy. The professional, standing outside the situation, may know that there is no chance that the child will ever be able to talk. Fearing that wishful thinking may influence the mother's decision about whether to keep or institutionalize the child, the professional may emphasize that there is no real chance of the child ever communicating. However, for the mother, inside the situation, the thought that the child may someday be able to relate to her, even if it is only to reach out to touch her, provides the hope that buoys her spirit and allows her to continue providing care.[4]

From the standpoint of a third-person observer we might note that if a professional is sensitive to the distance involved in being outside the situation, then he or she may be engaged in the socio-emotional relation of to-understand rather than to-advise. However, it would be a mistake to end this article with such a third-person observation. Rather, following Dembo's emphasis, we may note that the professional is in a dyadic relationship with the client. Whatever socio-emotional relation he or she initiates will be embedded in the sort of personal relationship described by Macmurray. He or she, like you and I, will have to wrestle with the emotional forces inherent in these relationships, will have to pray for compassion to be stronger than the temptation to distance and advice.

Notes

1. Previously published in *From Past to Future, 1999, Vol. 2*(1), pp. 43-54. *Tension in the Field: The Dynamic World of Tamara Dembo*. © 1999 Frances L. Hiatt School of Psychology, Clark University. Author: Joseph de Rivera, Department of Psychology, Clark University, 950 Main St. Worcester, MA.
2. Both may also be distinguished from what Dembo (class notes, Spring 1983, p.30) terms, "ideological" relations, such as espousing equality or elitism, independence or dependence, etc., inclusive relations that determine preferences and evaluations that are imposed on incidental relations.
3. Parenthetically, it may be noted that Dembo distinguishes three kinds of help persons can provide those with handicaps: Help in performing an activity, help in improving the environment, and listening.
4. Parenthetically, it should be noted that this is why Tamara undertook her studies on the development of intentionality. Is the uncommunicative child just a "vegetable?" If a person with severe cerebral palsy flails about in a way that suggests he or she is trying to touch something, what is implied about personhood?

References

de Rivera, J. (1976). *Field theory as human-science*. New York: Gardner Press, Inc.

de Rivera, J. (1977). *A structural theory of the emotions*. New York: International Universities Press.

de Rivera, J. (1981). The structure of anger. In J. de Rivera (Ed.), *Conceptual encounter: A method for the exploration of human experience* (pp. 35-82). Washington, DC: University Press of America.

de Rivera, J. (1989). Love, fear, and justice: Transforming selves for the new world. *Social Justice Research, 3*(4), 387-426.

Dembo, T. 1971, Social-emotional relationships analysis. Unpublished manuscript, Clark University Archives, Worcester, MA.

Dembo, T. (1976). The dynamics of anger In J. de Rivera (Ed.), *Field theory as human-science: Contributions of Lewin's Berlin group* (pp. 324-422).

Dembo, T. (1993). Thoughts on qualitative determinants in psychology: A methodological study. *Journal of Russian and East European Psychology, 31*(6), 15-70.

Keen, E. (1977). Studying unique events. *Journal of Phenomenological Psychology, 8*, 27-43.

Krause, M. S. (1970). The three psychologies. Philosophical Psychologist, 4(1), 21-24.

Kreilkamp, T. (1981). Psychological distance. In J. de Rivera (Ed.), *Conceptual encounter: A method for the exploration of human experience* (pp. 273-342). Washington, DC: University Press of America.

Kreilkamp, T. (1984). Psychological closeness. *American Behavioral Scientist, 27*(6), 771-784.

Macmurray, J. (1979). *Persons in relation*. Atlantic Highlands, NJ: Humanities Press.

Rogers, C. R. (1961). *On becoming a person*. Boston, MA: Houghton Mifflin.

Part V

Dissecting Methodology and Thinking of Development

14

The Legacy of Adolf Meyer's Comparative Approach: Worcester Rats and the Strange Birth of the Animal Model

Cheryl A. Logan[1,2]

In 1892, a group of prominent Clark University faculty wore a now famous path between Worcester and Chicago. A break with Clark president G. Stanley Hall had led to a mass resignation of Clark science faculty, and half of the disgruntled men moved immediately to the newly-founded University of Chicago (Maienschein, 1988; Ross, 1972, chapter 12). They were an impressive group that included biologist C. O. Whitman, neurologist Henry Donaldson, anthropologist Franz Boaz, and anatomist Franklin Mall. But the life sciences were to be transformed as much by the animals as by the men who traveled this path. For it was at these institutions and at the Worcester Hospital for the Insane that albino rats were selected as the 'best' choice for a 'standard animal' for laboratory research in neurology, psychology and physiology.

The breeding of albino rats had an enormous impact on experimental psychology in the twentieth century. Rats were, and for many questions still remain, the modern animal model through which animal research provides an experimental foundation for human psychology. But the animal model tradition has recently been seriously questioned by new advances in the biological sciences (e.g., Bolker and Raff, 1997; Burian, 1993; Gottlieb, 2003, Chapter 15; Preuss, 1995, 2000). And the current debate is also the legacy of the Clark and Chicago scientists who pioneered research on albino rats in the mid-1890s. The two most important among those individuals were Henry Donaldson and Adolf Meyer. Together they promoted albino rats as an excellent test animal through which life science might extend experimental analysis to the solution of important human problems. Donaldson's impact is well-known. Between 1895 and 1910, he developed albino rats as one of the first test animals bred for science in psychology, neurology and physiology. In 1906, he left Chicago for Philadelphia to become the scientific director of the Wistar Institute of Anatomy. There he supervised the breeding of the first commercially-bred laboratory rat, the Wistar rat (Clause, 1993; Lindsey, 1979; Logan, 2001). By 1920, the Wistar Institute had sold thousands of albino rats to laboratories across North America. But it was Meyer who, after using rats in Worcester in the 1890s, first convinced Donaldson that rats would be an ideal test animal for scientific analyses of human brain and mind.

Adolf Meyer was not among the group that moved to Chicago in 1892. In fact, in 1892, he was newly arrived in America, a young Swiss immigrant who sought an academic position at the University of Chicago. Neurologist Henry Donaldson helped him secure a part time teaching post at Chicago. But in 1895 he left Illinois, going in the other direction, from Chicago to Worcester, to take a position as Director of Pathology at the Worcester State Hospital (then called the Worcester Lunatic Hospital). Meyer's career was spent primarily in clinics, but he always sought close contacts with universities. Worcester was no exception. Even before obtaining an appointment at the hospital, Meyer negotiated an appointment as an adjunct professor at Clark. In this position he taught clinical pathology and neurology and supervised Clark graduate students from 1895 until he left Worcester for New York in 1902.

Despite the pioneering impact of albino rats, Meyer's rat research has received no attention, and little is known about the way in which the animal served his more well-known psychiatric program. In what follows I discuss the role that albino rats played in Meyer's animal research. I then turn to the contrast between the way in which Meyer viewed the animal's role in research and the way rats were later used as a laboratory 'standard' to assure scientific generality. This comparison highlights the changes that occurred in comparative psychology in the twentieth century, and it further clarifies some of the concerns associated with the use of animal models today.

Meyer's Tools: The Worcester Rats

Meyer first used albino rats in Donaldson's Chicago laboratory in 1893. But in Chicago, rats were not central to his systematic research program.[3] Rather, it was in Worcester that the animals became a part of Meyer's vision for the fusion of psychiatry, neurology and psychology. Clark physiologist C. F. Hodge had already begun research on activity and fatigue in rats at Clark around 1894. Hodge became Meyer's close friend. They co-supervised Clark graduate students and exchanged research materials. During Meyer's first few years in Worcester, Hodge's student, Colin Stewart, continued Hodge's rat work. Their research was begun on wild-caught gray rats, but Stewart switched to albinos in 1896-1897. At just about the same time (October 1896), Meyer's diary first mentions research on a wild caught rat. And from August of 1897 through 1898, his research notes contain dated accounts of neurological manipulations on newborn and fetal albino rats. This indicates that he was breeding rats at the Worcester Hospital by August 1897, and Stewart may have obtained some of his albinos from Meyer's colony.[4] So, though others had already used the animals at Clark and his Clark colleagues no doubt piqued Meyer's interest in rats, it was Meyer who established what probably was the first breeding colony of albino rats in the United States at the Worcester State Hospital in 1897.

In the same year, 1897, Meyer convinced Donaldson that albino rats would be an excellent test animal for research in developmental neurology (Logan, 1999). Twice, once in 1897 and once in 1900, Meyer sent shipments of as many as fifty to 100 rats to Donaldson's Chicago lab. The first group was ill-fated; most of the animals died in transit. But the second arrived successfully. With them, Donaldson began a series of projects on rat brain development that defined the rest of his career. These animals also decisively shaped American psychology; they or their descendants were almost surely the rats used in John B. Watson's doctoral dissertation, completed in Donaldson's Chicago laboratory under the joint direction of Donaldson and James R. Angell (Boakes, 1984; Cohen, 1979). From these beginnings, the animal quickly became a foundational tool for research in neurology, physiology, and psychology. Through his rats, therefore, Meyer indirectly shaped the discipline of psychology. But that shape sometimes took a form that he never imagined and of which he might greatly disapprove.

Meyer's Pragmatic Functionalism

Adolf Meyer founded the integrative psychobiological school of American psychiatry, which dominated the field for the first half of the twentieth century. He is regarded by many as the central figure in American Psychiatry in the first half of the twentieth century (Grob, 1966; Klerman, 1979; Lidz, 1966; Shorter, 1997). When he entered psychiatry, therapeutic nihilism and restraints dominated an American asylum bureaucracy that was almost completely divorced from the advances then occurring in the rest of medicine. Meyer turned that around, beginning at Worcester, where he reformed hospital procedures for the care of the mentally ill (Grob, 1963, 1966; Shorter, 1997).

It is for psychiatry, and not his animal research, that we know Adolf Meyer today (Lidz, 1966; Lief, 1948). But he began his career as a comparative neurologist who was deeply committed to integrating basic brain research into psychiatric practice. His commitment to research was central both to his conceptual grounding and to the institutional reforms for the treatment of the mentally ill that he pioneered. But Meyer's approach to research differed greatly from the hereditarian custodialism anchored in autopsies and the assessment of blood and urine that dominated much of psychiatry at the time. Instead, under the influence of American functionalism and pragmatism, he argued that progress in treatment was possible only if the whole patient were considered (Leys, 1990; Lidz, 1966; Meyer, 1948). Without a problem, no complex of methods could succeed, and patients—their entire life course, medical, evolutionary, developmental, psychological, and cultural—defined the problem. Patients were the critical 'experiments of nature'; and without living persons providing a problem structure to center the inquiry, any method risked aimless wandering. He therefore advocated for consideration of developmental history, psychological function, nutrition, general health, and even culture, alongside the post mortem autopsy, which at the time dominated psychiatric research.

Meyer's holistic and functionalist emphasis on the patient entailed a methodological pluralism that was increasingly out of step with the growing tide of positivism. In physiology and in psychology, American positivism emphasized analysis, control, experimentation, and an engineering approach that rendered laboratories more important than explanation in science (e.g., Leys, 1990; Pauly, 1987). But his emphasis on the patient made Meyer critical of methodological dogmatism in any form, including that promoting only laboratories and control. He was, for example, critical of defining psychology solely in terms of experiments. In correspondence with Hall, in which Meyer established his Clark teaching responsibilities, Meyer stressed to Hall that the patients' problems "must be clearly before [the students] to avoid the idea that 'experiments' make a psychologist."[5] Too much else, culture, developmental history, habit, was involved that could not be accessed solely with experiments. Similarly, despite his emphasis on the brain, he was also critical of reductionism. In lecture notes from 1897, he criticized an overly mechanistic approach to psychopathology that was anchored entirely in physics and chemistry. He told students: "Even if we drop the old 'Lebenskraft,' we cannot help recognizing that the chemical and physical energies are so combined in it as to constitute an essentially new quality: we have a new 'Lebenskraft.' The only difference is that we have it understood that quantitatively it can be represented by chemical and physical terms."[6] Indeed, for him the fundamental problem of biology was whether in physiology and psychology "plasticity and activity and will . . . have any ultramechanical character" or whether they must be addressed with an inherently vitalistic principle manifest in "the self direction of organization."[7]

Meyer regarded simplification and dogmatism as the enemies of truth in understanding complexity, and his sensitivity to dogmatism led him to reject some of the major distinctions of the day that had been used by others to differentiate psychology from neurology and physiology (Meyer, 1926). In the classification of mental disorders, for example, he mistrusted both the distinction between the 'functional' and the 'organic' and that between symptoms that are subjective and those that are objective. Such dichotomies implied to him a hidden dualism that was inconsistent with his view that mental life is an aspect of biological unity.[8] Instead, he accepted a monism in which all mental processes were associated with corresponding physiological ones. On this view, any "purely psychical disorder . . . was just as well a disorder of the brain as any organic lesion" (Meyer, 1896-97, p. 275). Unity required that "the development of the mind goes hand in hand with the anatomical and physiological development, not merely as a parallelism, but as a oneness . . . " (Meyer, 1896-97, p. 273).

Meyer's pragmatic synthesis is reflected in a three-pronged research program that included longitudinal evidence on the diseased person, for which Meyer is known, but much else as well. To understand the living person he also needed parallel evidence on normal human brain and normal psychological processes, as well as converging animal research. The latter required experimental animals, and this was where the rats came in. The animal work would provide him with comparative evidence on the evolution of brain and with experimental evidence on basic processes in developmental neurology, which ethically could not be obtained with humans. His multifaceted approach is illustrated in an early sketch of his research plan for the Worcester Hospital laboratories. In it, he listed "macroscopic series" of anatomical sections of both normal human brain and brains with various lesions, plus "animal brains-mainly rat, rabbit, cat, dog, horse, monkey," microscopic sections from human children and fetuses, and those from adults with lesions. Finally, he listed microscopic stains of animal brains and autopsies from deceased patients.[9] All of these would be integrated with comprehensive 'field' data on the medical and psychological histories of individual patients.

Meyer's Clark connection was critical to this approach, because through Clark he would be able to add research on normal psychological processes. Extreme psycho-pathological phenomena, such as delusions and hallucinations, were certainly very clinically important. But Meyer did not consider them a good starting point for basic research: "[They are] not open to accurate methods, while the elementary psychical reactions, as voluntary movements, perception, choice of movements, and . . . the associations, are accessible" (Meyer, 1896-97, p. 276). And, under the directorship of E.C. Sanford, Clark provided working psychological laboratories that were among the first institutional foundations of experimental psychology in America. Habit was a central concept of early American experimental psychology, and Meyer noted that Hall and Hodge were beginning a scientific analysis of habit. Meyer viewed the laws governing the development of habits to be one of the most fundamental psychological questions. He asked his Clark students: "How—according to what laws—do habits grow? How can they be implanted and guided? On what difficulties are habits of life apt to become wrecked? Such are the questions raised in a discussion of the mental aspect of our constitution."[10]

Others began using rats to study habits at Clark in the late 1890s, but Meyer's own animal research was exclusively neurological. How, in 1897, did rats fit into his research program? Understanding their role requires appreciating two aspects of Meyer's early career: the central role he gave development and the specific research question he asked. I discuss each in turn.

Meyer's Epigenetic Perspective

Meyer was deeply committed to the importance of developmental analysis. He shared this commitment with the other early rat researchers (Logan, 2001), and the emphasis on development is clearly evident in his writings (Lidz, 1966; Meyer, 1926). His teaching notes from the Clark courses caution against a purely hereditarian view of mental illness. In assessing hereditary influences on mental disease, he stated:

> ... we are throwing hereditary and educational factors together. I am quite satisfied that many of the so-called hereditary features are acquired through the association of the children with their parents.[11]

Stressing the importance of etiology, in 1902, he wrote:

> ... when we know better what to look out for we may undertake studies of *developing* abnormalities which are not insanity yet and follow them out so as to accumulate materials of *actual observation* on which to build a solid theory of constitution (Lief, 1948, p. 108, italics in original).

Meyer stressed that human development begins with the fertilization of the ovum. Among the factors influencing development are "the development of the individual Anlage. . . . the creation of the surroundings, and more especially in mental life, the creation of an appropriate mental atmosphere."[12] He illustrated the power of that atmosphere in a thought experiment in which he described a "second Adam." The second Adam is a human being that Meyer imagined developing without the human atmosphere of "culture, literature, language, technology"; that is, a person developing without other people, but nonetheless surviving. He asserted that his second Adam would have an inconceivable intellectual life because it would not have been influenced by culture—a culture that instills "an individual mental atmosphere" and that shapes us developmentally: "Our words and methods of thought are chosen and trained from the psychical atmosphere existing independent from us."[13]

In an 1897 lecture on the pathology of nervous and mental phenomena, he distinguished between "a negative assumption" based in circumstantial evidence, which presumes causation in the absence of something, from the more positive approach of looking at contributions to "defective formation" [abnormal development]. As examples of the former he listed "defective *Anlage* [blueprint]," "degeneracy" and "heredity." Such negative assumptions are "block[s] in the way of much-needed knowledge (Lief, 1948, p. 109)." Development, on the other hand, offered the positive approach (Lief, 1948). In stressing this, Meyer often cited Wilhelm Roux's developmental mechanics:

> A recent science, the mechanics of development, and the studies of growth furnish the positive elements for us, as far as fetal life is concerned, and the study of the growth and development of man in the later periods.[14]

Even in pathology, Meyer believed, one must look at an influence that has been added to produce the negative outcome, not just speculate on something that is missing. He asserted that "defective formation" could coexist with normal *Anlage* when positive influences trigger defective development that interferes with the integration of the whole.

> This interference . . . may be due to mechanical or thermic influences and traumatism, to defective nutrition generally, to toxic influences, . . . to overfunction with insufficient repair, to faulty imitation in activity, to exercise in abnormal directions and proportions.[15]

His approach avoided a presumed blueprint (*Anlage*) representing explanation in terms of an all-powerful missing force. Instead of inferring a negative, he examined the relations among a number of positive developmental influences at many levels, some of which might act to send the developing system in an abnormal direction:

> Roux's mechanics of development stood out as a call for an experimental formulation of the interrelation and balance of the components of a living being, and also of maladaptations (Meyer, 1926, p. 64-65).

Rats, Development, and Evolution

Meyer became convinced of the rats' value in 1897, the same year in which he started his colony and the year in which he convinced Donaldson that rats would serve his neurological research well. But why rats? What did rats have to do with development? In 1900, the application of the experimental method to the phenomena of development was very controversial. Several camps debated the value of experiments on development. Detractors believed that intervening in the already dynamic and orderly sequences of development would produce abnormal monstrosities. Intervention was needed to perturb a static system; but, the thinking went, development was never static, and intervening might do serious damage when change was already so prominent (Querner, 1974). To illustrate that experiments could shed light on the causes of development, the proponents of experimentation needed an altricial mammal, one, like rats, that developed very slowly and in which many outcomes remained underdeveloped at birth. An emphasis on development typified all of the early rat researchers. All chose rats because rats develop so slowly and so late, and slow development would make experiments feasible (Logan, 2001).

Meyer was no exception. Because much neural development occurs at or after birth, altricial rats were ideal subjects for his experiments on brain development. In a letter to Walter Miles, Meyer wrote that rats had advantages over other mammals because they were "ideal to serve for experimentation on the brain of the new-born."[16] In 1897, he completed a study on the impact of cerebellar lesions on the motor coordination of rats. Animals were lesioned at five weeks of age. His results showed several disruptions, particularly on the left side. The animals could climb, but they rotated with difficulty and overbalanced with their right sides, apparently to compensate for deficits on the left. His research notes from 1896-97 also describe plans for a series of experiments on white rats in which he severed the animals' sciatic nerves. The plan lists measures in spinal cord, brain and muscle using several staining methods employed at eight different ages: "1–3–6–12–21–28–40 days, 112 days."[17] Other notes indicate anatomical stains performed on brain tissue from both newborn rats and rat fetuses.

This research is clearly developmental, and the work must have benefited from the animal's slow rate of change. But this is not the whole story. Meyer's interest in development occurred at a time when developmental analyses were steeped in the notion that ontogeny recapitulated phylogeny (Gould, 1977). On this view, developmental was understood in part in terms of evolution. The study of development, therefore, went hand in hand with the study of evolution, and Meyer's rats were useful in this context as well.

A Comparative Approach to Neural Segmentation: The Evolution of Neural Plasticity

Meyer's research included a strong comparative dimension anchored in the concept of evolution. He had been trained as a comparative neurologist at a time when the study of the nervous system was coming of age and when the evolution of brain was closely linked to the evolution of mind (see Lloyd Morgan, this volume). The neuron doctrine put forth by Wilhelm His and Meyer's Zurich mentor August Forel, was hotly debated, as was the question of localization of function in the brain (Finger, 2000). And like many others at the time, Meyer's interest in neural development was matched by a parallel emphasis on evolution. To explain the brain, he believed, one must take "the phylogenetically oldest mechanisms as the starting point" (Meyer, 1898, p. 91). Understanding the human mind and the unity of mind and brain was certainly his goal. But he viewed humans as the product of an evolutionary trend begun much earlier. Uncovering the ontogeny and phylogeny of that trend was central to the promise of his research program. What question guided that program?

The concept of neural segmentation was at the center of Meyer's evolutionary analysis (Meyer, 1898). In fact, his rat research was part of a much larger project on the evolutionary loss of neural segmentation across the vertebrate series. In the course of evolution, independent control by separate segmental ganglia (lower spinal centers in humans) was lost in favor of control by a higher "supra-segmental system," in which Meyer included the vertebrate cerebellum, the midbrain and the forebrain. Phylogenetically, there had been a progressive shift from control by a segmental system, well-illustrated in worms, arthropods and Amphioxus, to control by a centralized "supra-segmental system." In the supra-segmental system, one structure or group of structures could no longer function independently of higher control. Highly specialized afferent-efferent functions, each constrained within a lower body segment and acting relatively independently of the others had evolved into highly inter-dependent functions controlled centrally.[18]

The loss of morphological segmentation, prominent in the mammalian and avian nervous systems, had evolved to serve ever-finer motor coordination. This had reached its culmination in human beings. For Meyer, the functional correlates of the progressive loss of independence to supra-segmental control were complexity and neural plasticity manifest in consciousness. The evolution of a supra-segmental system underlay the great neural plasticity so apparent in human brain and behavior. Meyer's phylogenetic research program was deigned to trace this progressive loss of segmentation in empirical demonstrations of the increasing loss of independence of function from insects, which show a complete segmentation and extreme independence of function, through reptiles and lower mammals, to higher mammals (e.g., dogs). The trend culminated finally in humans, in whom independence was least and plasticity greatest. As 'lower mammals,' rats were somewhere in the middle. The rat cerebellar data illustrated to him how much motor coordination was *still possible* with major "supra-segmental" lesions in a creature that still exhibited strong segmental control. In an 1899 lecture delivered at Brown University, he said:

> From the (reptiles) marsupials upward there is a gradual accumulation of special mechanisms or shunts in the cerebral cortex. The more coordination depends on the cerebral cortex and the pyramidal tract the deeper is the effect of an injury to the cortex and the greater the loss of independence of the segmental mechanism. . . . In a number of rats in which one hemisphere was removed, it became practically impossible to recognize a defect in motion some time after the operation. The coordination of the limbs was not much affected, although one pyramidal tract was destroyed; in the dogs the effects of the same lesion are somewhat more obvious and in man a complete destruction of one pyramid implies the most serious disorders of function, a complete hemiplegia. Now it is evident that man depends as much on his segmental sensory-motor mechanisms as any other animals; but the segments have yielded many arrangements of coordination to the cerebrum, a supra-segmental apparatus, and in a measure as the specialization has relegated certain functions to the hemisphere, the segmental apparatus has lost in independence—certain movements are so complicated that the segmental mechanism alone would not be able to bring about the delicate shades of differentiation while the cortex offers the necessary increase of coordination.[19]

This excerpt clearly illustrates the role that the rats played in Meyer's research program. Meyer was constructing evolutionary phylogenies in brain structure, which, when placed within the context of the extreme developmental plasticity produced by the evolution of the cerebral cortex, led to hypotheses about basis of human neural plasticity. Though he was trained in Switzerland, Meyer studied evolution in London, where he worked both with Thomas Huxley and

John Hughlings Jackson. Meyer seems to have accepted Hughlings Jackson's hierarchical conception of the nervous system, which viewed the cortex as a recent evolutionary achievement that functioned to inhibit lower, more automatic and evolutionarily older functions (see Harrington, 1987). Following Hughlings Jackson, Meyer's question was fundamentally an evolutionary one. The applicability to human psychopathology of research on animals depended both upon heuristic structural homologies in brain processes and on empirical data from humans confirming the limits of animal-based neurological results. He used rats to show that rodents were different from 'higher mammals' and from humans. In fact, his neurological research was completed on a number of animal species. His Worcester research notes contain labeled drawings of the brains of sheep, raccoons, calves, bats, moles, pigeons, lizards, and fish along with those of rats. The presence of so many species and the nature of the research program itself show that Meyer was well aware of the limitations of relying on only one animal. He needed many species so that each could represent a different evolutionary gradation in the historical trend that had given rise to the human brain.

Worcester Rats, Wistar Rats, and Model Systems

Research animals are now placed among the tools that decisively shape the course of the life sciences (see Burian, 1993; Clarke and Fujimura, 1992; Kohler, 1994). Albino rats were probably the first mammal bred expressly for research in physiology and psychology. The animal is, therefore, a major forerunner of the influential animal model tradition that dominates much of American life science today. This tradition has recently come under strong criticism in several fields, including developmental biology and cognitive neuroscience (e.g., Bolker and Raff, 1997; Preuss, 1995, 2000, 2001). The basis of the modern controversy echoes a change in the way in which laboratory animals came to be used in the twentieth century, a change well-illustrated by the fate of albino rats. The early rat scientists sought an animal that could easily be used in experiments; and they clearly wanted a beast that would shed light on questions relevant to humanity. However, though they sought broad generality, rat scientists also had a deep regard for the differences that might distinguish neural and psychological processes in different species (Logan, 1999, 2001).

Lloyd Morgan's canon (1894) shares this regard for diversity. Modern psychology has often used the canon to justify the parsimonious application of the simplest scientific principle derived from animals in an attempt to explain humans. In fact, Lloyd Morgan proposed the canon to do just the reverse: to infer the mental attributes of animals from those of humans. Further, Morgan, like Meyer, justified his principle from an evolutionary perspective that presumed diversity. Morgan saw the canon as a necessary methodological principle to be used to draw inferences about the animal mind from evidence anchored in human introspection. Just because there is so much potential diversity in animal cognition, one must use caution in carrying the analogy with human cognition too far—other species after all might *not* be so highly evolved. The "divergently increasing complexity of their organic structure" (Lloyd Morgan, 1894, p. 55) suggested correlated diversity in mental aptitude, and the canon placed constraints on the extent to which other species' mental attributes were seen as similar to those of human beings. Evolution suggests that there should be important differences, and the canon was an attempt to highlight those differences.

Adolf Meyer was a part of this tradition. His rat research was part of a comparative neurology that would shed light on differences in the ontogeny and phylogeny of the human brain. Moreover, his approach was quite different from the program that underlay Henry Donaldson's use of the Wistar rat. And in suggesting the value of the animal to Donaldson, Meyer fed into a disregard for diversity that he would have considered inappropriate. Donaldson was influenced by the move toward standardization broadly associated with the growth of the experimental method and specifically reflected in the institutional goals of the Wistar Institute (Clause, 1993). By 1915, Donaldson was reluctantly using rats as a 'standardized' animal model of human brain development, which *de-emphasized* the animal's value as representative of a phylogenetic group, a point in a comparative array of diversity on which biological generality depended (Logan, 1999, 2001).

But Meyer and Donaldson agreed on one thing: whether or not rats could aid them in reaching their respective goals was an empirical question. The empirical data they produced would indicate the utility of the animal for the research questions posed. Gradually, however, as more and more rats were used by more and more scientists, those scientists began to assume that the use of a standardized animal virtually assured that their results would be generally applicable. That is, they treated generality as an assumption rather than as an empirical conclusion (Logan, 2002). Meyer's phylogenetic approach to differences in brain disappeared as rats became generic test animals that, before the fact, insured a kind of 'one size fits all' approach to experimentation. By 1933, in his introduction to perhaps the first psychological handbook devoted almost entirely to the white rat, Norman Munn stated: "The present treatise demonstrates that it is possible to write an essentially complete outline of the science of animal behavior without going beyond the available data on the rat" (1933, p.v). Paradoxically, Meyer's involvement with Donaldson and his later support of John Watson had led directly to some of the trends that would make the animal into something he never intended it to be: a generic animal model defining a 'one size fits all' approach to test animals.[20] By Munn's time, animal psychology no longer required the comparative perspective brought to animals by Lloyd Morgan and to humanity by Meyer. Generalizations could instead be based *a priori* on the rodent 'standard,' without regard for differences.

A Priori Generality in Contemporary Animal Models

Many of the model systems used in contemporary neuroscience similarly carry *a priori* the presumption that results obtained from one 'model' animal will generalize to others and to humans. Preuss (1995, 2000, 2001) has addressed these issues in primate neurobiology, noting that the brains of rhesus monkeys and rats are often taken as representative models of the presumably similar human brain. Twentieth century neuroscientists simply assumed that during evolution the mammalian brain increased in size without fundamental evolutionary change in structure-function relationships. Representing a view that he rejects, Preuss says "Brains may become improved, added to and enlarged, but they do not diverge" (1995, p. 1230)[21]. That is, they do not differ. There is just more of the same.

But evolution produces differences as well as continuities. Preuss' (1995, 2000) approach recognizes that common ancestry can certainly result in important shared characteristics, but earlier organizations can also provide preadaptations for the divergence of functional specializations in brain structure that reflect important species differences. Whether differences or continuity apply in a given case is an empirical question.[22]

Preuss is advocating an approach that would be quite familiar to Adolf Meyer. Though the rat's slow development aided experimental studies of brain development, their status as 'lower mammals' made very specific generalizations from rats to humans quite suspect. Taking, as he did, the entire psychobiological system into account, Meyer would be quite comfortable with the principles of equifinality and multifinality, which render general statements from animal research useful, but also may make very specific ones quite misleading (Gottlieb, 2003, this volume). Unlike many contemporary neuroscientists, Meyer presumed that "physical and mental variation is a biological phenomenon."[23] This meant that there were problems that he could *not* solve using rats. Adolf Meyer's albino rats were not just a model of slowly-developing mammals. Indeed, they were not an animal model at all. They were representatives of 'lower' mammals, especially suited to studies of brain ontogeny. They were *rats*, one species among the many that were needed to trace the phylogeny of human neural plasticity and mind.

Notes

1. Previously published in *From Past to Future, Vol. 4 (1), Animal models in human psychology: The uses of comparative methodologies*, pp. 23-36. © 2003 Frances L. Hiatt School of Psychology, Clark University. Author: Cheryl A. Logan, Ph.D., Departments of Psychology and Biology, P. O. Box 26170, University of North Carolina at Greensboro, Greensboro, NC.
2. The author is grateful for permission to quote from the Adolf Meyer papers, which was granted by The Alan M. Chesney Medical Archives at The Johns Hopkins Medical Institutions.

3. The Chicago rats were probably used in laboratory demonstrations for teaching, rather than in programmatic research.
4. See Worcester Research Notes. Adolf Meyer Papers, The Alan M. Chesney Medical Archives. The Johns Hopkins Medical Institutions, Baltimore, MD. It is not clear who first used the albinos. In a 1928 letter to Meyer, Stewart stated that he bought some of his white rats from animal stores in Worcester. He could not recall whether he also obtained rats from Meyer's colony, though he considered it quite possible. Colin Stewart to Adolf Meyer, 7 October 1928, Adolf Meyer Correspondence. The Alan M. Chesney Medical Archives. The Johns Hopkins Medical Institutions, Baltimore, MD.
5. Adolf Meyer to G. S. Hall, 3 December 1896. AM papers, The Alan M. Chesney Archives of the Johns Hopkins Medical Institutions.
6. Clark Teaching Materials, Lecture. Adolf Meyer Papers, The Alan M. Chesney Medical Archives. The Johns Hopkins Medical Institutions, Baltimore, MD.
7. Clark Teaching Materials. Lecture on "the pathology of nervous and mental phenomena". Adolf Meyer Papers. The Alan M. Chesney Medical Archives. The Johns Hopkins Medical Institutions, Baltimore, MD. The Lebenskraft was a hypothetical life force, which was thought by some to distinguish the unique qualities of living systems from those of nonliving systems. Though dominant in the early nineteenth century, by 1900 the concept was hotly debated as reductionists who refuted vitalism attempted to explain life exclusively in terms of the forces operating in physics and chemistry (see Lenoir, 1989). Meyer disagreed, believing that something else must be involved in life, yet he could not accept the early nineteenth century concept. Hence, his new Lebenskraft.
8. In humans, Meyer termed this biological unity 'the person'.
9. Worcester Research Notes. Adolf Meyer Papers, The Alan M. Chesney Medical Archives. The Johns Hopkins Medical Institutions, Baltimore, MD.
10. E. G. Boring (1950) points out that Sanford's laboratory manual, *Course in Experimental Psychology,* was the first methodological manual available in the new science, predating E. B. Titchener's more widely known handbook by as much as ten years. Hall and Hodge's stimulus may well have influenced the Clark rat association studies of Willard Stanton Small begun in 1899 under Sanford's direction. Small's animal research employed the maze, which he invented (Boakes, 1984). Quote from the Adolf Meyer Papers, The Alan M. Chesney Medical Archives. The Johns Hopkins Medical Institutions, Baltimore, MD. See also Meyer (1912).
11. Worcester Teaching Materials. Adolf Meyer Papers, The Alan M. Chesney Medical Archives. The Johns Hopkins Medical Institutions, Baltimore, MD.
12. Ibid.
13. Worcester working notes, August 1897. Adolf Meyer Papers. The Alan Mason Chesney Medical Archives. The Johns Hopkins Medical Institutions, Baltimore, MD. See also Lidz (1966).
14. Worcester Teaching Materials. Adolf Meyer Papers. The Alan M. Chesney Medical Archives. The Johns Hopkins Medical Institutions, Baltimore, MD.
15. Ibid.
16. Meyer to Walter Miles, 17 February 1928. Adolf Meyer papers. The Alan M. Chesney Medical Archives. The Johns Hopkins Medical Institutions, Baltimore, MD.
17. Worcester Scientific Notes. Adolf Meyer Papers. The Alan M. Chesney Medical Archives. The Johns Hopkins Medical Institutions, Baltimore, MD.
18. The supra-segmental concept is the neural instantiation of the synthetic and functional interdependence that is so clear in Meyer's psychiatry. Plasticity, after all,

might entail vulnerability to induced pathology as well as to a potential for positive change and growth. Understanding the mechanisms of neural plasticity would be central to appreciating how influences on human development both produced pathology and led to effective treatments.
19. Worcester Research Notes. Adolf Meyer Papers. The Alan M. Chesney Medical Archives. The Johns Hopkins Medical Institutions, Baltimore, MD.
20. Donaldson later stated that he took some Chicago rats with him when he moved to the Wistar Institute. So, Meyer's Worcester rats may also have been among the forebears of the founding stock of the Wistar breeding colony (see Logan, 1999; Donaldson, 1925). Moreover, even after he became Director of the Phipps Psychiatric Clinic at Johns Hopkins, Meyer saw to it that Watson's rat laboratory was housed at the Clinic. So, though he was no longer engaged in animal research and was very critical of behaviorism, Meyer still saw the comparative perspective as essential to a complete understanding of mind and pathology (Leys, 1984).
21. Reprinted with permission of the MIT Press.
22. Preuss et al. (1999) report numerous empirical examples of specialized neural organizations that differentiate even closely related primate species such as humans and chimpanzees.
23. Lecture on "the pathology of nervous and mental phenomena" (p. 11). Clark Teaching Materials. Adolf Meyer Papers. The Alan M. Chesney Medical Archives. The Johns Hopkins Medical Institutions, Baltimore, MD.

References

Boakes, R. (1984). *From Darwin to behaviourism*. Cambridge: Cambridge University Press.
Bolker, J. A., and Raff, R. A. (1997). Beyond worms, flies and mice: It's time to widen the scope of developmental biology. *The Journal of NIH Research,* 9, 35-39.
Boring, E. G. (1950). *A History of experimental psychology*. Englewood Cliffs, NJ: Prentice Hall.
Burian, R. M. (1993). How the choice of experimental organism matters: Epistemological reflections on an aspect of biological practice. *Journal of the History of Biology,* 26(2), 351-367.
Clarke, A. E., and Fujimura, J. H. (Eds.). (1992). *The right tools for the job*. Princeton, NJ: Princeton University Press.
Clause, B. T. (1993). The Wistar rat as a right choice: establishing mammalian standards and the ideal of a standardized mammal. *Journal of the History of Biology,* 26(2), 329-349.
Cohen, D. (1979). *J. B. Watson: The Founder of Behaviorism*. London: Routledge and Kegan Paul.
Gottlieb, G. (2003). Animal models of human development. *From Past to Future: Clark Papers on the History of Psychology, 4(1)*. Worcester, MA: Clark University Press.
Gould, S. J. (1977). *Ontogeny and phylogeny*. Cambridge, MA: Harvard University Press.
Grob, G. (1963). Adolf Meyer on American psychiatry in 1895. *American Journal of Psychiatry, 119*, 135-142.
Grob, G. (1966). *The State and the Mentally Ill*. Chapel Hill, NC: University of North Carolina Press.
Klerman, G. L. (1979). The psychobiology of affective states: The legacy of Adolf Meyer. In E. I. Meyer and J. V. Brady (Eds.), *Research in the psychobiology of human behavior*. Baltimore, MD: Johns Hopkins University Press.

Kohler, R. E. (1994). *Lords of the Fly: Drosophila Genetics and the Experimental Life*. Chicago, IL: University of Chicago Press.

Leys, R. (1984). Meyer, Watson and the dangers of behaviorism. *Journal of the History of the Behavioral Sciences, 20*, 128-151.

Leys, R. (1990). The correspondence between Adolf Meyer and Edward Bradford Titchener. In R. Leys and R. B. Evans (Eds.) *Defining American Psychology*. Baltimore, MD: Johns Hopkins Press. Pp. 58-114.

Lief, A. (Ed.). (1948). *The Commonsense Psychiatry of Dr. Adolf Meyer: Fifty-two selected Papers, Edited, with Biographical Narrative*. Reprint of A. Meyer (1903). *American Journal of Psychology, 14*(90). New York: McGraw-Hill.

Lindsey, J. R. (1979). Historical foundations. In H. J. Baker, J. R. Lindsay and S. H. Weisbroth (Eds.), *The laboratory rat, Volume 1: Biology and diseases*. New York: Academic Press.

Lidz, T. (1966). Adolf Meyer and the development of American Psychiatry. *American Journal of Psychiatry, 123*, 320-332.

Lloyd Morgan, C. (1894/2003). Other Minds than Ours. Chapter III, from *An Introduction to Comparative Psychology*. Reprinted in *From Past to Future: Clark Papers on the History of Psychology 4(1)*. Worcester, MA: Clark University Press.

Logan, C. A. (1999). The comparative rationale behind the choice of a standard animal in psychological research: Henry H. Donaldson, Adolf Meyer and "the Albino Rat." *History of Psychology, 2*(1), 3-24.

Logan, C. A. (2001). "[A]re Norway rats . . . things?": Diversity versus generality in the use of albino rats in experiments on development and sexuality. *Journal of the History of Biology, 34*, 287-314.

Logan, C. A. (2002). Before there were standards: The role of test animals in the production of empirical generality in physiology. *Journal of the History of Biology, 35*, 329-363.

Maienschein, J. (1988). Whitman at Chicago: Establishing a Chicago style of Biology? In R. Rainger, K. Benson and J. Maienschein (Eds.), *The American Development of Biology*. Philadelphia, PA: University of Pennsylvania Press.

Meyer, A. (1898). Critical review of the data and general methods and deductions of modern neurology. *Journal of Comparative Neurology*, VIII, 113-148. Reprinted in E. Winters (Ed.), (1950). *The Collected papers of Adolf Meyer, Volume I*. Baltimore, MD: Johns Hopkins Press.

Meyer, A. (1912). Remarks on habit disorganizations in the essential deteriorations and in the relation of deterioration to the psychasthenic, neurasthenic, hysterical and other constitutions. *Studies in Psychiatry*, V. I., Nervous and Mental Disease Monograph Series No. 9. Reprinted in E. Winters (Ed.), (1950). *The Collected papers of Adolf Meyer, Volume I* (pp. 421-431). Baltimore, MD: Johns Hopkins Press.

Meyer, A. (1926). Genetic-dynamical psychology versus nosology. Festschrift celebrating Emil Kraepelin's seventieth birthday. Reprinted in E. Winters (Ed.), (1950). *The Collected papers of Adolf Meyer, Volume I*. Baltimore, MD: Johns Hopkins Press. Pp. 57-73.

Meyer, A. (1948). The psychobiological point of view. In A. Lief (Ed.). *The Commonsense Psychiatry of Dr. Adolf Meyer*. New York: McGraw Hill.

Munn, N. (1933). *An introduction to animal psychology: The behavior of the rat*. Boston, MA: Houghton-Mifflin.

Pauly, P. (1987). *Controlling life: Jacques Loeb and the engineering ideal in biology*. Berkeley, CA: University of California Press.

Preuss, T. M. (1995). The argument from animals to human cognitive neuroscience. In M. Gazzaniga (Ed.), *The cognitive neurosciences* (pp. 1227-1241). Cambridge, MA: MIT Press.

Preuss, T. M. (2000). Taking the measure of diversity: Comparative alternatives for the model-animal paradigm in cortical neuroscience. *Brain, Behavior and Evolution*, 55, 287-299.

Preuss, T. (2001). The discovery of cerebral diversity: An unwelcome scientific revolution. In D. Falk and K. Gibson (Eds.), *Evolutionary anatomy of the primate cerebral cortex*. Cambridge: Cambridge University Press.

Preuss, T. M., Huixin, Qi, and Kaas, J. H. (1999) Distinctive compartmental organization of human primary visual cortex. *Proceedings of the National Academy of Sciences*, 96, 11601-11606.

Querner, H. (1974). Beobachtung oder Experiment? Die Methodenfrage in der Biologie um 1900. *Verhandlungen der deutschen zoologischen Gesellschaft, 68,* 4-12.

Ross, D. E. (1972). *G. Stanley Hall, The psychologist as prophet*. Chicago, IL: The University of Chicago Press.

Shorter, E. (1997). *A History of psychiatry*. New York: John Wiley.

15

Zing-Yang Kuo: Personal Recollections and Intimations of Developmental Science[1,2]

Gilbert Gottlieb

This article is a mixture of personal recollections, remarks about Zing-Yang Kuo's theoretical and empirical work, and the bearing of his metatheoretical considerations on the contemporary notion of developmental science.

I first met Zing-Yang Kuo in August of 1963 in Washington, DC. By chance, both the International Congress of Psychology and the International Congress of Zoology were meeting in August in Washington. News that Kuo would be on the East Coast at that time resulted in his being invited to speak at both meetings, his first public appearance in the states since 1939.

ZYK was a person of medium stature with a commanding air about him. Minutes after we met he told me that he was hosting a dinner for a number of European ethologists and American animal behaviorists, and he would like me to join them (I was quite a junior scientist at the time and relished the opportunity), and would I please arrange for a professional photographer to record the occasion. Kuo wanted to register his gratitude to the ethologists in particular for keeping his name alive in the literature. I was amused by this gesture because at least one of the attending ethologists had been highly critical of Kuo for his anti-nativistic point of view, and some of the others probably shared that animus although they refrained from expressing their sentiments in print. The dinner went off without a hitch at a Chinese restaurant (figure 15.1), and I was pleased to have made the acquaintance of Nikolaas ("Niko") Tinbergen, among the others at the dinner.

Although not much science was discussed, I was introduced to a concept of intellectual lineage that was new to me. Before we began the meal, Tinbergen introduced me to G. P. Baerends and J. P. Kruijt, whom he described, respectively, as his intellectual son and grandson. Baerends had been Tinbergen's doctoral student and Kruijt had been Baerend's doctoral student, so that is how they came to be designated in a way that was new to me, as members of an intellectual family. I had recently been claimed as a "student" by someone that I did not regard as an intellectual mentor, so I rather stupidly, right then and there, asked Baerends and Kruijt how they felt about their designations, such behavior marking me as junior in more ways than one. Both Baerends and Kruijt said they were quite happy to be considered descendents of the intellectual tradition of ethology fostered by Tinbergen. After all, he and Konrad Lorenz were considered the co-founders of the modern school of ethology, so Baerends and Kruijt were at the source of what was already becoming a very influential movement in academic zoology (Tinbergen and Lorenz shared a Nobel Prize in 1973).

I first became acquainted with Kuo's writings through theoretical reviews written by T. C. Schneirla and D. S. Lehrman in the late 1950s as I was doing my doctoral dissertation. Among other things, Kuo had done a very extensive series of studies of the behavioral embryology of chickens, in which he had pioneered a technique for making observation windows in the egg shell so as to be able to observe the behavioral development of the chick embryo throughout the entire course of the incubation period (twenty days). Previous behavioral-embryological studies had involved removing the embryo from the shell, which of course severely disrupted the physiological integrity of the embryo. Kuo's procedure not only preserved the integrity of the embryo, it also allowed him to observe how the embryo's behavior was affected by its environment, principally the amniotic sac, in which the embryo was enclosed, and the yolk sac, a near neighbor of the embryo.

I had done my doctoral dissertation on imprinting in newly-hatched ducklings and continued the research after taking a clinical position at Dorothea Dix Hospital, a psychiatric facility in Raleigh, North Carolina. For reasons of which I am only dimly aware, I had always believed as a student that prenatal experiences were important and had consequences for the adaptation, for good or ill, of the newborn. I wanted to pursue my postnatal research findings with ducklings back into the egg but I did not know how to do that. Therefore, in 1961 or 1962, when I learned that Zing-Yang Kuo was still alive and living in Hong Kong, and, that he sought contact with animal behaviorists, I wrote him to ask if he would be willing to come to my laboratory to teach me the techniques of avian behavioral embryology. In essence, I sorely needed someone to hold my hand as I made acquaintance with the duck embryo. I had no biology in my academic background. Kuo later told me that he was disinclined to accept the invitation to work in my laboratory. He didn't add the obvious that I was such a junior person and had not yet secured much of a scientific reputation, while he was all but legendary in the annals of animal behavior and behavioral embryology.

Kuo had left China for Hong Kong in 1946 to avoid whatever misfortunes he foresaw for himself and his family when the communists took over the country, as happened in 1949. Kuo was a well-known academic in China (see figure 15.2), so long before leaving, he had discussed with Chou En-Lai (Zhou Enlai), one of the communist leaders, his plans for helping to bring China into the twentieth century in the areas of science and medical education. That meeting and subsequent events did not sufficiently reassure Kuo about the role he and his wife (a physician) might play in the future of a communist China, so they left China for Hong Kong. Portia Sheen, Kuo's wife, eventually managed to secure a satisfactory position in the British hospital (Queen Elizabeth Hospital), located in Kowloon, Hong Kong, and Kuo himself retired from academic life. (He had been invited to be on the board of directors of the Chinese University of Hong Kong but declined.) He maintained a small menagerie on the porch of the apartment that he and Portia shared in Kowloon, and he also pursued a study of the change in Chinese national character under communism by interviewing new arrivals from China, work that was supported by the Human Ecology Fund, based in New York City.

At the time he received my letter of inquiry in 1961 or 1962, in addition to his manuscript on the "Anatomy of Chinese National Character," he was working on his autobiography, *Confessions of a Chinese Scientist*, and thinking about a book featuring his epigenetic approach to the scientific study of behavioral development. His wife encouraged ZYK to respond in a positive way to my inquiry, and we agreed on a project to make a color and sound 16-mm. film of the development of behavior in the duck embryo. In this way: 1) I could learn the techniques of avian behavioral embryology, 2) we would produce an educational film for use in classrooms around the world, and 3) we would write a research paper based on our observations of the development of behavior in the Peking duck embryo, a domesticated form of the mallard species. I secured a grant from the National Science Foundation to fund our film and research, including a monthly stipend for Dr. Kuo for late summer and fall of 1963. That is how we came to meet in Washington in August of 1963.

Once I let it be known to colleagues that Kuo was coming to the States, he was invited to come to Washington by the Animal Behavior Society to speak at a symposium at the International Congress of Zoology on the Ontogeny of Basic Response Patterns. Kuo gave a talk in which he criticized the adequacy of unconditioned and conditioned reflexes (animal learning theory was still in its heyday and the basic unit of analysis was the reflex), and proposed instead a more developmental notion of "gradients of response" as the basic analytic unit. (This was to become an important part of his 1967 book, *The Dynamics of Behavior Development: An Epigenetic View*.) I had been invited to be a discussant of Kuo's paper, and I endorsed his criticism and made a big plug for the developmental approach to the study of animal behavior, the approach that Kuo had steadfastly adhered to in his research in avian behavioral embryology and mammalian behavioral adaptations. (He had worked with cats, dogs, and mice, among other species). Taking a cue from the writings of T. C. Schneirla, who had kept Kuo's point of view and his research findings alive for thirty years, I tried to show how Kuo's ideas could be helpful when it came my turn to discuss his paper:

> As developmental biologists and developmental psychologists, we must take time to contemplate a state of affairs wherein we are relatively long on facts and relatively short on systematic formulation. I would like to suggest that our relative lack of predictive theory is *not* due to our ignorance or to the fact that we don't work hard enough—I would like to suggest that our general lack of *developmental* theory stems largely from our lack of an adequate basic unit of analysis--a basic unit which somehow allows us to coordinate organic growth and environmental stimulative factors. In the course of behavior development, stimulative and growth factors are inextricably fused and we are in critical need of a unit (or units) which allow us to deal with this fusion [Fusion was Schneirla's term for an idea that Kuo and I endorsed with different language].

I closed with a plug for the probable importance of prenatal experience:

> The contemporary methodological context involves the tendency of modern-day . . . developmental psychologists to begin their studies at the event of birth or hatching. By way of broadening our observational baseline, as well as remaining true to the definition of our discipline, it seems imperative that we make a genuine and open-minded attempt to examine the bearing of embryonic experience on early post-natal behavior.

For my own scientific development, it was very fortunate that I struck up a correspondence and subsequent friendship with another senior scientist, T. C. Schneirla, at the time I began writing to Kuo. Ted Schneirla was then working on a massive manuscript in which he was trying to put the findings of imprinting studies with young birds in the context of his developmental approach/withdrawal (A/W) theory. That theory called for the postnatal perceptual preferences for rhythmic stimuli in the auditory and visual modalities in young birds (and, by extension, mammals) to be ascribed to their experience of "smooth-running rhythms," muscular and otherwise, in the prenatal period. It was a brilliant tour de force which eventually appeared as the first chapter in the first volume of *Advances in the Study of Behavior* (Schneirla, 1965), running to more than seventy pages. While I was never able to do a useful experiment to document the specifics of Schneirla's theory, it was wonderful to have another well-known voice subscribing to the importance of embryonic experience for an understanding of early postnatal behavior. As I have already mentioned, Schneirla took Kuo's implications from his observations on the behavior of the chick embryo very seriously over virtually his entire career, beginning with the Maier and Schneirla textbook, *Principles of Animal Psychology*, published in 1935, to his application of A/W theory to imprinting in 1965.

During the course of our joint research on the duck embryo at Dorothea Dix Hospital, Kuo proved to be an energetic collaborator. I had arranged for a room for him on the grounds of the hospital that made it easy for him to get to and from the laboratory. We often ate lunch together in the hospital cafeteria and when it was necessary to work in the evening, we dined at a Chinese restaurant in downtown Raleigh. One evening he tried unsuccessfully to teach me how to pronounce his name correctly (more like *Gua* than *Quo*). Friends at the local state university gave a party in his honor and faculty from Duke in nearby Durham came to meet the revered Dr. Kuo. Near the end of his stay, my wife and I gave him a farewell party at our farm in the country. We could not afford any help so Zing-Yang pitched in by tidying the living room and showing my wife, Nora, the proper way to cook rice before the guests arrived. (She uses ZYK's technique to the present day.)

Colleagues were eager to have Kuo come to speak on their campuses so I arranged a lecture tour to punctuate our work in Raleigh. One of the more amusing moments came when my newly-employed research assistant, Jo Ann Winfrey, chauffeured Kuo to Durham where he was to speak at Duke. She lost her way briefly and to reassure Kuo that she would eventually find the university, Jo Ann said that she would let her instincts guide her, to which Kuo replied, ever so quietly, "I hope not." I later explained to Jo Ann the significance of ZYK's otherwise enigmatic remark.

Early in the course of our research, I had occasion to visit the Poultry Science Department at North Carolina State University in Raleigh, to borrow some equipment. During a tour of the labs, I noticed a technician making windows in chicken eggs in order to be able to observe the experimental growth of viruses. This was actually a better window than Kuo's for filming and observing the embryo's behavior, so I asked the technician to show me how to make that window. I went back to my lab and rather gingerly told Kuo of my discovery. It didn't take him aback at all and we used that technique as well as his in our research and in our film. Kuo's technique involved cutting the shell off the top (large end) of the egg and coating the inner shell membrane of the air space below with liquefied Vaseline to render it transparent. The other technique, which allowed windows to be made at other places and did not necessitate the Vaseline coating, gave an even clearer view of the embryo and its environment (see figures 17.3, 17.4, 17.5). In our film, *Development of Behavior in the Duck Embryo*, Dr. Kuo is shown making both types of observation window.[3]

The research project was completed in November of 1963, at which time Kuo was scheduled to return to Hong Kong via New York, where I had scheduled two talks for him, one at the Institute of Animal Behavior at Rutgers and the other at the Department of Animal Behavior of the American Museum of Natural History. Daniel Lehrman, head of the Institute of Animal Behavior at Rutgers, was eager to meet Kuo, as was Ted Schneirla and his colleagues at the Museum.

With the assistance of Anne W. Smith and Gus Martin, I continued to work on the film after Zing-Yang departed. Zing-Yang began working on our research manuscript before he left Raleigh and it wasn't long after his departure that I received a draft. I was delighted but somewhat ambivalent that he had me first author. When I protested mildly, he said the project was my idea, I had gotten the funding, we did the work in my laboratory, and so on, so I accepted his position but have always felt mildly uncomfortable about it. Kuo had done a fine job on the Method and Results sections of the manuscript. I took it on myself to rewrite the Introduction and Discussion sections. In the Discussion section I put forward the idea that, based on our observations, embryonic self-stimulation would appear to be an important experiential source that contributed to "the establishment of action (motor) patterns and, possibly, certain perceptual preferences" (Gottlieb and Kuo, 1965, p. 188). Our observations had really excited me and I went on and on about self-stimulation:

> Musculo-skeletal as well as kinesthetic and proprioceptive self-stimulation may be essential to the normal development of action patterns and "sequential ordering" of the embryo's behavior may be due to the developmental dynamics of the growing embryo *and* the changing mechanisms of the amnion-yolk sac-embryo relationship.

Via correspondence, Kuo told me that he didn't want to share the credit for the self-stimulation concept and that I should save that part of the Discussion for an article in which I was the sole author. Somewhat chagrined (embryonic self-stimulation was not my idea), I went back into the literature a bit more scrupulously than before and changed the above sentence to read, "We would like to stress, with Holt (1931), Lehrman (1953), and Schneirla (1956), the concept of *self-stimulation* as a factor which may contribute to (facilitate) the establishment of action (motor) patterns . . ." Kuo accepted this change and I was glad he saved me some considerable scholarly embarrassment had I (we) trotted out the idea as if it were original with us. Kuo never said anything about what I did later in the Discussion section in which I accused one of our dining companions with having ideas that

> may unintentionally impede both the analysis of prenatal behavior and the progress of developmental theory: "What is happening inside the egg when we detect movements of the embryo is, mainly if not entirely, a process of maturation of the innate behavior patterns (Thorpe, 1956, p. 311)" (Gottlieb and Kuo, 1965, p. 188).

Several years later I was actually able to experimentally demonstrate that auditory self-stimulation in the mallard duck embryo (the embryo hearing its own self-produced vocalizations) in the final days of the incubation period was essential to the normal development of its selective response to the maternal call of its species after hatching (Gottlieb, chapter 10, 1971). Sadly, Dr. Kuo had died in 1970, so I had to change the wording of the dedication of my monograph to reflect that unhappy fact: "To the memory of Zing-Yang-Kuo, 1898-1970."

The Dynamics of Behavior Development

After Dr. Kuo's return to Hong Kong in 1963, his writing priorities changed. He set to work in earnest on what was to be his only book in the English language (he had published a number of books in Chinese). By 1964, Schneirla in New York and I in North Carolina started getting chapters to critique for what became *The Dynamics of Behavior Development: An Epigenetic View*, published in 1967 in paperback by Random House. Joseph Stone, a professor of psychology at Vassar, was an editor at Random House, and he encouraged Kuo in the task of writing this small volume, also adding his constructive criticisms to those of Schneirla and mine.

In 1965, I was invited for the first time to speak at the International Ethological Congress in Switzerland. During conversations I told the European ethologists of my work with Kuo and that he was writing a book, and the younger ethologists, in particular, were quite eager to read the book. I duly reported this information to Kuo and he passed my letter along to Joe Stone.

Dr. Kuo did not write well in the English language and Stone suggested that his (Stone's) sister might be just the person to help him on this account, which, I gather, she did. The finished product reads very well. Kuo was quite impatient about getting the book out but he continued to solicit comments from Stone, Schneirla, and myself. The book was being written in a very sprightly way and some of Kuo's remarks sometimes sounded outlandish. He was taking on the animal learning types as well as the nativism (instincts) of the classical ethologists, and he didn't mince words in his criticisms of these points of view as well as what he saw as the entirely hypothetical devotion to the brain as an explanatory mechanism. He believed these approaches were detrimental to the experimental analysis of behavioral development and the advancement of developmental theory at the organismic or holistic level of analysis, although he did not use the latter terminology.

The *Dynamics* finally appeared in 1967. Random House was lax in not sending review copies to pertinent journals and had to be prodded by me to do so. Eventually, reviews appeared in *Science*, *Contemporary Psychology*, and *Animal Behaviour*. The first two were quite negative and did not appreciate Kuo's statement of a radical new program for the analysis of behavioral development. Kuo wrote a letter to *Science* about the misdirection of that review (Hansen, 1968). Robert B. Cairns, then at Indiana University, also wrote a letter rebutting Hansen point by point. *Science* decided to publish Cairns' (1968) letter rather than Kuo's, which was satisfactory to ZYK. Given that Cairns came out of one of the traditions (social learning theory) that Kuo had criticized so roundly, it was even more meaningful that he should try to get Kuo's true message—beyond the polemics—out to the readership of *Science*.

Figure 15.1
Kuo hosted a dinner at the Peking Restaurant in Washington, D.C., in August of 1963. Conceptual friends and foes alike were invited. Clockwise from the far left, N. Tinbergen (Oxford University), author, J. P. Kruijt (University of Groningen), D. E. Davis (Pennsylvania State University), Dr. Sherman (American Psychological Association), J. T. Emlen (University of Wisconsin at Madison), G. P. Baerends (Groningen), Kuo, E. Fabricius (University of Stockholm), M. W. Schein (Pennsylvania State University), J. P. Scott (Bowling Green State University), W. H. Thorpe (Cambridge University), and our hostess, a friend of Dr. Kuo's, whose name I no longer recall.

Cairns' own approach was becoming more friendly to a holistic consideration of behavioral development, and he, himself, was moving toward the establishment of a research program involving developmental behavior genetics with mice. The *Contemporary Psychology* review focused on Kuo's critiques and simply found them out of date (Klinghammer, 1969), akin to the more gently expressed observations by Tinbergen in his letter to Kuo (below). The *Animal Behaviour* piece was appreciative (Jacobs, 1968). Certainly this was a polemical book, a fact that may have gotten in the way of some readers' receptiveness to the positive aspects of the program that Kuo was advocating. In the thirty or so years since its initial publication, it seems easier to assess, in a balanced way, the strengths as well as the weaknesses of the *Dynamics* (see the retrospective review by Rodkin, 1996).[4]

Figure 15.2
Kuo as an academic in China in his younger years.

Figure 15.3
To make an observation window in the side of the egg, it is necessary to make a puncture in the shell over the air space and another in the side of the egg, and then gently draw air through the latter by applying suction to the hole over the air space. That pulls the shell membranes down away from the shell, allowing a window to be cut in the shell without damaging the inner shell membrane which is part of the embryo's blood circulatory system. The egg on the left in the third panel is a duck egg; the egg on the right is a chicken egg.

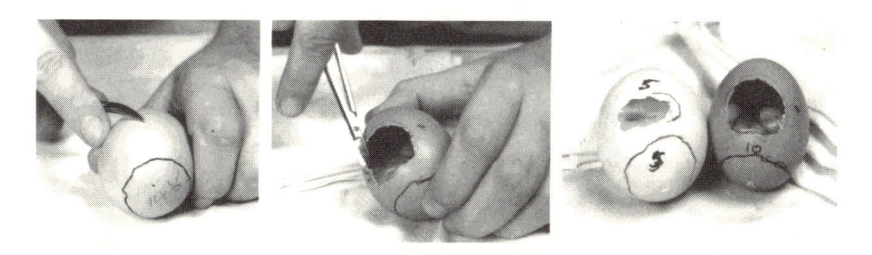

308   Thinking in Psychological Science

Figure 15.4
To make a Kuo observation window, one cuts away the shell and outer shell membrane over the air space of the egg and paints the underlying inner shell membrane with liquefied Vaseline to render the membrane transparent. (Also shown here, Dr. Kuo applied the Vaseline with a Chinese writing brush.) The extent of the air space is determined by "candling" the egg (placing the large end of the egg against an egg candler that emits a light).

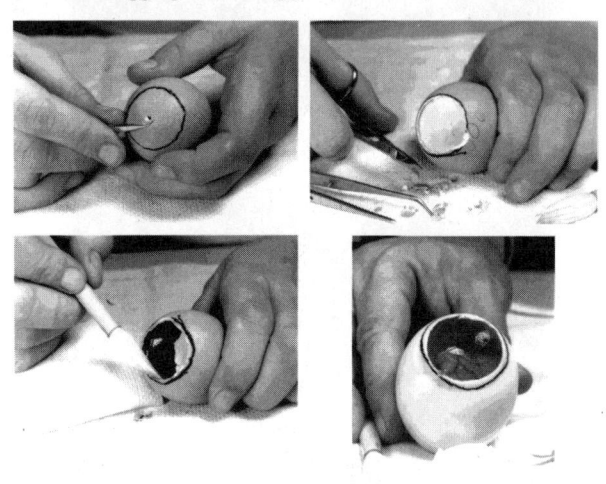

Figure 15.5
Two types of embryonic observation windows. On the right, the Kuo window made in the air space at the large end of the egg. The tip of the embryo's bill is at 7 o'clock, resting on its wing. On the left, the other window technique on the side of the egg. Both of that embryo's legs are between 7 and 9 o'clock. The embryo's head and right eye are at about 2 o'clock. The embryo is surrounded by yolk. The spidery-looking filaments in both windows are veins in the inner shell membrane.

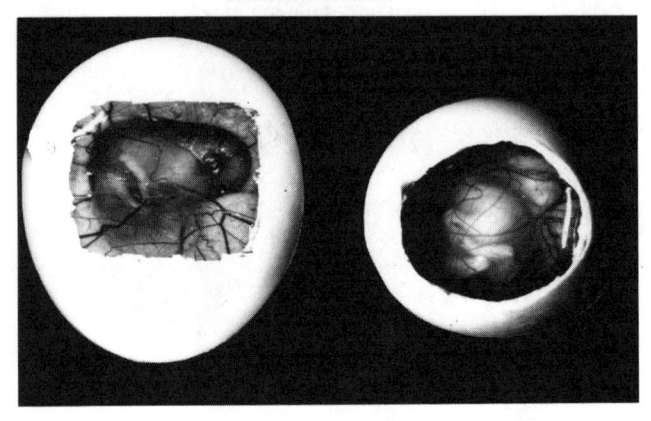

Figure 15.6
Kuo in Hong Kong in the late 1960s.

Shortly after the book was published, Kuo had arranged for a copy to be sent to one of our dining companions, N. Tinbergen, at Oxford. Tinbergen wrote Kuo a friendly letter of thanks for the book, mentioning how the American and European camps were getting closer together, even though there were still differences in emphasis on the validity of the sheerly internal regulation of behavior. In a letter to Kuo dated September 4, 1967, Tinbergen wrote:

> Things have moved a great deal since your and our earlier work! As you will have noticed, we ethologists have learnt, and are learning, a great deal under the influence of our American colleagues (if I may count you one of them). I am myself so disgusted with our earlier simplicisms that I have insisted with the Oxford University Press that my old book "The Study of Instinct" be not reprinted any more. While we are still interested in discovering how much in an animal's behavior is "internally programmed," we are equally fascinated by the interactions with the outside world—or rather with experience in general—that in practice our investigations on behavioral ontogeny now follow very much the same lines as those of many "epigeneticists." I have had a busy correspondence with my very good friend Konrad Lorenz, and have had occasional personal discussions with him, on this very issue; it is the one issue

on which I feel I cannot agree with his approach. But the long interaction between behavior students of different origin is gradually moving us all more together . . .

Tinbergen had previously expressed the same sentiments to T. C. Schneirla, so Kuo was a bit cautious in his acceptance of these kindly remarks, because neither he nor Schneirla felt there had actually been a noticeable change in the theory or research program of ethology. In fact, development (ontogeny) was seen by Tinbergen (1963) as only one of four research questions to be addressed by behavioral analysis, whereas development was central to any and every question raised by the epigenetic approach. I was in closer touch with the younger members of the ethological group and I sensed a greater appreciation of the epigenetic view even if theory and research practices were not being changed in any grand way.

Although Random House did little by way of promoting Kuo's book, it eventually sold out[5] and, in my experience, was appreciated (not uncritically) by the graduate students that I met at home and abroad. Thus, I thought Kuo's book should be expanded and reissued. With the help of Joseph Stone and Ethel Tobach, Seymour Weingarten, of Plenum Press, became enthusiastic about republishing an enlarged version of the *Dynamics*. In my travels I had discovered that young readers of the book were tantalized by the few personal details that ZYK had included in the Preface and they hungered for more. So we secured permission to republish as an introduction to the *Dynamics* my longish biographical essay that had appeared after ZYK's death in the *Journal of Comparative and Physiological Psychology* in 1972. In addition, we added at the end of the book a chapter by ZYK that had appeared in the *Festschrift* for T.C. Schneirla, *Development and Evolution of Behavior*. In that chapter ZYK called for the establishment of a multidisciplinary developmental research center that would focus on particular behavioral topics that could be studied at all levels of analysis (biochemical, structural, behavioral, and environmental), as called for in the new developmental program of behavioral analysis put forth in the *Dynamics*.

Seymour Weingarten got so enthused about the republication that he changed the contract with Portia Sheen, Kuo's wife, to read that the book would appear as a hardback rather than a paperback. In 1976, the enlarged edition was published by Plenum Press.

I like to think that the multidisciplinary group that I belong to at the University of North Carolina's Center for Developmental Science, co-founded by the late Robert B. Cairns and five others of us, received some inspiration from Kuo's proposal, as it originally appeared in his chapter for *Development and Evolution of Behavior* (Aronson, Tobach, Lehrman, and Rosenblatt, 1970). In his review of that book for *Science*, in 1971, Cairns wrote:

> With the recent "independent" discovery by researchers in child development of some common basic concepts (among them reciprocal stimulation, behavioral synchrony, bidirectionality of psychobiological influences), the way may be open for a more

systematic treatment. Both human and animal studies stand to gain. For theorists in child development to continue to use animal studies only for heuristic purposes is about as absurd as not using them at all. Partly for this reason, Z.Y. Kuo's proposal for the establishment of a National Research Center in Developmental Studies seems worth of serious attention (compare the AAAS 1970 symposium on the developmental sciences). Kuo ... points to the need for the explicit integration of the developmental disciplines on common problems. Anything less simply "will not reach the root of the problem of ontogenesis" (p. 271).

Kuo's (1970, p. 191) recommendation for a National Research Center in Developmental Studies reflected ". . . the view that I have maintained for a good many years: that the key to the thorough knowledge of the ontogeny of behavior in breadth and in depth is a concerted research program participated in by psychologists, endocrinologists, neurophysiologists and sensory physiologists, experimental embryologists, zoologists, ecologists, and . . . cultural anthropologists and psychiatrists." I believe this view is becoming more widely shared at the level of individual researchers, universities, and public and private funding agencies. Just in the last few years we have witnessed the birth of two new journals (*Developmental Science* and *Applied Developmental Science*) that seem to fit in with the spirit of Kuo's ideal of integrating developmental studies at all levels of analysis.

Notes

1. Previously published in *From Past to Future, Vol. 2(2), From Instinct to Epigenesis: Lessons from Zing-Yang Kuo,* pp. 1-12. © 2000 Frances L. Hiatt School of Psychology, Clark University. Author: Gilbert Gottlieb late of Center for Developmental Science, University of North Carolina at Chapel Hill, CB# 8115, Chapel Hill, NC.
2. I have previously written several scholarly articles on the life and work of Z.-Y. Kuo (Gottlieb, 1972, 1998). In the present instance, the editor of the Clark Papers on the History of Psychology, Jaan Valsiner, has asked me to write in a more personal way about ZYK. In this undertaking I am frustrated that I have had to rely entirely on my memory for events prior to January of 1964, because I cannot find any remnants of our correspondence prior to that time. The correspondence file from 1964 to 1970, the year of ZYK's death, is almost complete. In addition, I have the extensive correspondence between Joseph Stone and ZYK from 1963 to 1970, and the transcripts of Joseph Stone's interviews of ZYK's wife, Dr. Portia Y. L. Sheen, on my behalf when she was living in Hong Kong (Kowloon) in April of 1971. (I was planning a biography of Kuo at that time, a project that I reluctantly gave up and have now happily relinquished to a professional historian of science, one with a special interest in science in China.)
3. The 16-mm. film is still available for rental or purchase through the Media and Technology Support Services of Pennsylvania State University [mtssmed@psulias.psu.edu or telephone (800) 826-0132)]. A video is available from the author.
4. In a letter to Kuo, dated August 13, 1968, Joe Stone wrote: "I am glad to see your book is still arousing fervent controversy even though Hansen's position on it is ridiculous. I hope the unsolicited comments from Professor Cairns will rouse Random House to further promotion. There is no doubt in my mind that I did the profession a great service into [sic] pushing you to write this book!"

5. In a letter to Joseph Stone and me, dated July 22, 1975, Ethel Tobach says she received a call from one Paul Schensa, of Random House, in answer to a query from her, in which Schensa says that they sold about 10,000 copies of Kuo's book. This is a remarkable figure, especially considering the lack of promotion by Random House and the extreme negativity of two of the book reviews.

References

Aronson, L. R., Tobach, E., Lehrman, D. S., and Rosenblatt, J. S. (Eds.). (1970). *Development and evolution of behavior: Essays in memory of T. C. Schneirla.* San Francisco, CA: Freeman.

Cairns, R. B. (1968). Behavior: A question of influence. *Science, 161*, 522-523.

Cairns, R. B. (1971). Ontogeny and phylogeny: A behavioral integration. *Science, 171*, 270-271.

Gottlieb, G. (1971). *Development of species identification in birds: An inquiry into the prenatal determinants of perception.* Chicago, IL: University of Chicago Press.

Gottlieb, G. (1972). Zing-Yang Kuo: Radical scientific philosopher and innovative experimentalist (1898-1990). *Journal of Comparative and Physiological Psychology, 80*, 1-10.

Gottlieb, G. (1998). Zing-Yang Kuo: Radical scientific philosopher and innovative experimentalist. In G. A. Kimble and M. Wertheimer (Eds.), *Portraits of pioneers in psychology, Vol. 3*, (pp. 197-208). Mahwah, NJ: Erlbaum.

Gottlieb, G., and Kuo, Z.-Y. (1965). Development of behavior in the duck embryo. *Journal of Comparative and Physiological Psychology, 59*, 183-188.

Hansen, E. (1968). Behavior as a continuous process. *Science, 160*, 58-59.

Holt, E. B. (1931). *Animal drive and the learning process, Vol. 1.* New York, NY: Holt.

Jacobs, D. W. (1968). [Review of the book *The dynamics of behavior development: An epigenetic view.*] *Animal Behaviour, 16*, 590-592.

Klinghammer, E. (1969). Epigenetics—An ethological perspective. *Contemporary Psychology, 14*, 342-343.

Kuo, Z.-Y. (1967). *The dynamics of behavior development: An epigenetic view.* New York, NY: Plenum.

Kuo, Z.-Y. (1970). The need for coordinated efforts in developmental studies. In L.R. Aronson, E. Tobach, D. S. Lehrman, and J.S. Rosenblatt (Eds.), *Development and evolution of behavior: Essays in memory of T. C. Schneirla*, (pp. 181-193). San Francisco, CA: Freeman.

Kuo, Z.-Y. (1976). *The dynamics of behavior development: An epigenetic view*, enlarged ed. New York, NY: Plenum.

Lehrman, D. S. (1953). A critique of Konrad Lorenz's theory of instinctive behavior. *Quarterly Review of Biology, 28*, 337-363.

Maier, N. R. F., and Schneirla, T. C. (1935). *Principles of animal psychology.* New York, NY: McGraw-Hill.

Rodkin, P. C. (1996). A developmental, holistic, future-oriented behaviorism: Kuo's *The dynamics of behavior development* revisited. *Contemporary Psychology, 41*, 1085-1088.

Schneirla, T. C. (1956). Interrelationships of the "innate" and the "acquired" in instinctive behavior. In P.-P. Grassé (Ed.), *L'Instinct dans le comportement des animaux et de l'homme*, (pp. 387-432). Paris: Masson.

Schneirla, T. C. (1965). Aspects of stimulation and organization in approach/withdrawal processes underlying vertebrate behavioral development. *Advances in the Study of Behavior, 1*, 1-74.

Thorpe, W. H. (1956). *Learning and instinct in animals.* Cambridge, MA: Harvard University Press.
Tinbergen, N. (1963). On aims and methods of ethology. *Zeitschrift für Tierpsychologie, 20*, 410-433.

16

Kuo's Epigenetic Vision for Psychological Sciences: Dynamic Developmental Systems Theory

Robert Lickliter[1]

Over the course of nearly fifty years of work, Zing-Yang Kuo developed and honed a conceptual framework for a systems analysis of the development of behavior. In this effort, he served both as a critic of his own intellectual times and as a visionary for the future, providing a foundation and agenda for a developmental approach to the study of behavior. In this article I briefly review how Kuo's epigenetic view of behavior, summarized in his 1967 monograph *The Dynamics of Behavior Development*, continues to contribute to psychological sciences as we move into the twenty-first century. I argue that Kuo's writings, while somewhat peculiar and iconoclastic in style, provide a useful organizing framework for guiding our attempts to understand the emergence, maintenance, and modification of behavioral traits and characteristics.

The important test of Kuo's dynamic, epigenetic view of behavior development is, of course, its continued usefulness and ability to provide innovation in psychological theory and research. While Kuo is all but forgotten as a developmental theorist, it is important to ask whether his dynamic perspective has contributed to substantive change in the way we think about behavior development or influenced the way we conduct research in the study of behavior. Can his epigenetic approach continue to pay dividends in the years ahead in terms of better understanding and characterization of the complex processes contributing to behavior? I think the answer to these questions is a resounding "yes." Kuo's remarkable vision for the study of behavior, drawn from work begun nearly eighty years ago (Kuo, 1921), seems to me to continue to have a great deal of relevance to the present and future of psychological research.

Contemporary Status of the Study of Behavior

One of the most profound insights achieved by psychological sciences in this century is that behavior is not represented in a genetic or neurological template prior to its emergence. This hard-won insight of *probabilistic epigenesis* replaced the longstanding notion of predeterminism, in which behavioral development was seen to progress in an orderly and preordained sequence under the control of genetic substrates (see Gottlieb, 1976, 1992, 1997 for historical overviews). From this view, genes were seen as deterministic, guiding the nervous system to mature in a predetermined fashion, and giving rise to "innate" or "instinctive" behavior. Thanks in large part to nearly a half century of comparative and developmental research (see Michel and Moore, 1995 for a review), most psychologists now appreciate that behavior does not unfold from some predetermined template or blueprint.

Over the last several decades, behavior has been increasingly viewed as a system property, an emergent phenomenon resulting from transactions between the organism and its specific environments over the course of individual ontogeny (Gottlieb, 1991a, 1996, Oyama, 1985; Thelen and Smith, 1994). Conventional assumptions of innate or hard-wired behavior (see Eibl-Eibesfeldt, 1989; Mayr, 1974) have gradually given way to the realization that genes cannot, in and of themselves, directly produce behavioral traits or characteristics (Gottlieb, Wahlsten, and Lickliter, 1998). As a result, psychological sciences now generally recognize the value of grounding the study of behavioral development in a system of multiple influences, rather than continuing to rely on simple dichotomies such as genes and environment, instinct and learning, or maturation and experience. As discussed in the companion articles of this issue, this conceptual shift in how behavior is viewed and studied has much of its roots in the pioneering empirical and theoretical work of Zing-Yang Kuo.

Developmental Systems Approaches in Contemporary Psychological Sciences

The view that behavioral development depends on the coaction of features of both the organism and its environment, including such factors as genes, hormones, diet, sensory experience, and social interactions, has come to be known as a *developmental systems* approach (Ford and Lerner, 1992; Gottlieb, 1991a; Lickliter and Berry, 1990; Oyama, 1985). In this view of behavioral development, the various changes, improvements, and reorganizations in an organism's behavior over ontogeny do not represent the unfolding of a fixed or predetermined substrate, independent of the activity, experience, or context of the organism. Rather, the determining factors of behavior are seen in terms of reciprocal, bidirectional interactions among organismic and contextual factors occurring over the course of individual development (Gottlieb, 1996; Lickliter, 2000).

Kuo's thinking on behavior anticipated many of the conceptual advances in comparative and developmental psychology achieved in the last several decades, including dynamic (Fisher and Bidell, 1998; Thelen and Smith, 1994), probabilistic (Gottlieb, 1976; 1991a,b), and systems (Ford and Lerner, 1992; Gottlieb, Wahlsten, and Lickliter, 1998; Oyama, 1985) approaches to behavior development. In particular, Kuo recognized and articulated a key feature of these contemporary frameworks, that the *experience* of the organism is a critical component of the developmental process. As discussed by Gottlieb (1991a, 1996), experience can be construed to be synonymous with function or activity, and includes the activity of the genes, the activity of nerve cells and their processes, neurochemical and endocrine secretion, the use and exercise of muscles and sensory systems, and the overt behavior of the organism itself. Kuo recognized that specifying the contributions to development of the effects of such stimulation from both internal and external sources was a key task of scientific psychology.

This insight, derived from Kuo's empirical and theoretical efforts (culminating in his 1967 monograph), continues to significantly influence and direct the course of contemporary psychological sciences. Kuo argued for and in many cases anticipated the conceptual and methodological advances in perceptual, motor, cognitive, and social development research in the last decades of the twentieth century (see Lerner, 1998 for multiple examples). However, despite their increasingly prevalent use, Kuo's perspectives and insights on the epigenesis of behavior have remained "behind the scenes" and largely uncredited in most of contemporary psychological literature, making his prediction in the preface of his 1967 monograph that "the book will be out of circulation and its name forgotten after a few years" prophetically accurate. His message of the importance of a developmental systems view of behavior is, however, neither out of circulation nor forgotten and Kuo's views continue to offer a useful conceptual framework for the study of behavior .

Kuo's Insights and Vision for the Study of Behavior

As discussed by Senchuk (1991), Kuo's epigenetic view of behavior development is less a fully articulated, formal theory of behavior than an organizing theme for placing empirical findings into a coherent conceptual framework. This framework was built around Kuo's original notions of "behavioral gradients" and "behavioral potentials," which were not well understood or received by most of Kuo's readers in the 1960s and 1970s (see Hansen, 1969; Hogan, 1978) and which continue to be misunderstood or underappreciated in contemporary psychology. While it is beyond the focus of this article to review in detail the background and significance of these concepts to Kuo's view of behavior a brief overview serves to highlight how important the ideas that contributed to these original concepts remain for contemporary psychology.

For Kuo, the term *behavioral gradients* represented the fact that any given response of the organism to its environment, whether it be internal or external in origin, always involved the whole organism. Kuo's concept of behavioral gradients attempts to express the ever-shifting differences (i.e., gradients) in the involvement of the different internal and external parts and organs of the whole animal, as well as their feedbacks and interactions, in the flow of real-time events. For Kuo, behavior cannot be characterized as merely motor movement or glandular secretions. Rather, it includes activities of all the various parts and organs of the organism. Kuo emphasized that an organism's responses to its specific physical, biological, and social environments are dynamic, multileveled, graded in intensity, and sensitive to changing patterns of stimulation and context.

Kuo's notion of *behavioral potentials* represented the enormous possibilities of behavior patterns that each neonate possesses within the limits or range of the normal morphological structure of its species. Kuo realized that all infants are born with far more behavioral potentialities than can be actualized into real behavior during their lifetime. Over the course of development, each individual encounters its own unique array of experiences, opportunities, and constraints, thereby making some behavioral outcomes more likely to be supported and maintained and others prevented or eliminated. For Kuo, the enormous range of the "possible" becomes the "actual" behavior we observe as a result of the organism's real-time activity, its developmental history, and the nature of its environmental context. As a result, each organism is unique in the particulars of its responses to its environment.

While the dynamic, systems-based principles of behavioral gradients and behavioral potentials (discussed at length in Kuo, 1967) have had little direct or observable influence on contemporary psychological theory, it seems to me that several of Kuo's primary insights regarding behavior that underlie these challenging notions have proven more influential and have become more appreciated over the last thirty years (albeit in often unacknowledged ways). For example: a) Kuo recognized and championed the importance of the prenatal period to subsequent behavioral organization, b) Kuo recognized and attempted to sketch out the multi-determined nature of behavior, and c) Kuo recognized and provided evidence for the dynamic, probabilistic nature of development. Kuo is rarely credited for his contribution to the development and application of these key ideas, but they have and continue to inform how we approach the study behavior development. A brief overview of these insights sets the stage for a discussion of how his visionary conceptual efforts continue to provide direction for psychological sciences.

The Importance of Prenatal Experience

As pointed out by Gottlieb (1997), Kuo was among the first to raise the possibility that features of the so-called "instinctive" behavior of neonates may be a consequence of experience that occurred prenatally. Throughout his unusual and often interrupted career, Kuo argued that behavior does not begin at birth or hatching and that prenatal experience cannot be overlooked in attempts to account for the nature and path of behavior development. As a result, he devoted a large part of his career to documenting the nature and effects of prenatal experience in the avian embryo. Similar efforts at tracing developmental trajectories into the prenatal period (see Smotherman and Robinson, 1995) have received increasing empirical attention in contemporary comparative and psychobiological work (e.g., Gottlieb, 1971, 1997; Lecanuet, Fifer, Krasnegor, and Smotherman, 1995; Lickliter and Banker, 1994; Robinson and Smotherman, 1992; Smotherman and Robinson, 1988, 1990), and have demonstrated the importance of prenatal experience to a variety of postnatal behaviors, including perceptual learning and species identification. For example, studies examining the prenatal origins of cerebral lateralization and behavioral asymmetries in precocial birds highlight the dividends of including the prenatal period in the developmental analysis of behavior and underscore the significance of prenatal events to later behavioral development (Casey and Lickliter, 1998; Rogers, 1982, 1986; Zappia and Rogers, 1983). In these studies, the direction of lateralization in the avian forebrain was found to be determined, at least in large part, by the asymmetrical prenatal visual experience of the developing embryo. In the later stages of prenatal development, the precocial avian embryo is oriented in the egg such that its left eye is occluded by the body and yolk sac, while the right eye is exposed to light passing through the egg shell. The differential prenatal visual experience resulting from this postural orientation prior to hatching appears to facilitate the development of the left hemisphere in advance of the right and to significantly influence the direction of hemispheric specialization for a variety of postnatal behaviors, including visual discrimination, spatial orientation, and various motor asymmetries. Similar patterns of prenatal influence on postnatal cerebral dominance have also been proposed for mammals, including humans (Previc, 1991).

A growing interest in the psychobiological development of the human fetus has also emerged in the last several decades. This interest has capitalized on advances and innovations in medical technology, particularly untrasonography, and has allowed detailed description of the fetus and its behavior in real time (James, Pillai, and Smoleniec, 1995; Nijhuis, Martin, and Prechtl, 1984). As a result, insights are being made into the various regulatory processes thought to underlie the emergence of fetal capacities during the prenatal period and their possible consequences for early postnatal organization and development (Gagnon, 1995; Robertson and Bacher, 1995). The old view that the behavioral characteristics infants display at birth are attributable to genetics and those that develop postnatally are attributable to experience is finally giving way to the view long promoted by Kuo, namely that birth is not an adequate starting point for analyses or explanations of behavioral development.

The Multidetermined Nature of Behavior

Kuo was also among the first psychologists to consistently champion the notion that the determining factors of behavior include features internal *and* external to the organism. He argued that behavior is always the result of a complex of morphological factors, biophysical, and biochemical factors, the organism's developmental history, specific stimuli or stimulating objects, and the broader environmental context, and that these varied factors are interwoven, interrelated, and act in unison. Kuo's view, that behavior is always the complex product of many interacting internal and external factors (i.e., hormonal activity, arousal level, sensory experience, diet, social interactions), has become increasingly evident in psychological sciences in recent years. Investigators working in a number of areas, particularly comparative and developmental psychology, are more sensitive to the fact that the functional significance of genes, neural structures, hormonal levels, or any external influence on behavior can be understood only in relation to the larger developmental system of which they are a part. At each level of the system, the effect of any source of influence on behavior is potentially dependent on the activities and influences of the rest of the system, making all factors inherently interdependent and mutually constraining (Gottlieb, 1991a; Oyama, 1993).

For example, the movements of an infant (or an adult) are the product of the activity of the individual's nervous system, the biomechanical properties of the body, the features of available environmental support, and the specific demands of the task in question (Thelen, 1995). The distributed relation between these internal and external factors highlights a core feature of Kuo's vision of behavior, namely, that it is an emergent property resulting from the integration of nervous system activity, other internal physiological and endocrine variables, and specific features of stimulation present in the organism's immediate physical and social context. Simple models of genetic predeterminism or neural templates common in the behavioral sciences until recent years fail to capture this multiply determined, developmentally-based nature of behavior.

In keeping with this insight, Kuo argued for the need for coordinated efforts in the study of behavior development (Kuo, 1967, 1970). He realized that the study of behavior must be a synthetic science, including and integrating research findings drawn from anatomy, embryology, physiology, neurology, psychology, sociology, and anthropology. Kuo argued that since behavioral development is such a complex process, no single branch of psychology or biology can adequately address its study on an appropriately comprehensive scale. In this perspective, Kuo anticipated the development of interdisciplinary graduate training programs now common in many universities, and the emergence of so-called "collaboratories," in which labs working at different levels of analysis join forces to address issues of common interest (see Lickliter and Bahrick, 2000). For example, converging evidence from studies of early perceptual development utilizing neural, physiological, and behavioral levels of analysis and employing animal and human subjects has consistently demonstrated that young infants attend to different stimulus properties when a given object or event is perceived unimodally (information presented to one sensory causes of behavior, still common throughout much of the neurosciences (but see Edelman, 1989), overlooks the fact long championed by Kuo that no single element or factor in the system necessarily has causal primacy or privilege. The functional significance of genes, neural structures, or physiological substrates on behavior development can be understood only in relation to the larger developmental system of which they are a part. This system is comprised of both the structures and activities of the organism and the specific (and changing) set of physical, biological, and social factors with which it interacts over ontogeny.

This dynamic view of behavior, which can be seen throughout the empirical and theoretical efforts of Kuo, makes the organism-environment transaction process the explicit object of study for psychological sciences. For example, to study perceptual development, the researcher needs to be explicitly concerned not only with the organism's neural and sensory systems, but also with the structure of the stimulative environment, of how the organism moves about in it, and of what sorts of perceptual information the environment provides the perceiving organism. From this approach, perception depends upon the kinds of experiences that come from having a body with various sensory and motor capacities, which are themselves embedded in a more encompassing physical, psychological, and social context (see Gibson, 1979; Reed, 1996; Varela, Thompson, and Rosch, 1991).

This more holistic view of the determinants of behavior acknowledges that there is no top-down or bottom-up explanation of behavior that can be adequate to the task. A strict emphasis on any single domain or level in the developmental system, be it genes, physiology, neuroanatomy, or neurochemistry, social interactions, or culture will necessarily be too limited to successfully address the emergence and maintenance of behavior. This realization calls for the broadening and redefining of the traditional scope of psychological inquiry and in so doing directs research attention to the important but often overlooked question of *how* behavioral potentials and capacities emerge in developmental process.

Kuo offered a framework for this challenging task, one in which: a) the initial structure of the organism, b) the activities that structure allows, and c) the typical environment in which they occur are all viewed as causal and coacting to direct the course of individual development. This organizing framework for the study of behavior was built on several key insights achieved by Kuo over half a century of work, including the importance of the prenatal period, the multidetermined nature of behavior, and the dynamic, probabilistic nature of development. These ideas and their implications for research design are only now being meaningfully incorporated into psychological sciences and I believe will continue to positively influence the nature of psychological inquiry in the next several decades.

Conclusions

I have argued that Kuo's profound understanding of development as a "real-time" phenomena, guided and constrained by the specific experiences provided contributors. As a case in point, findings drawn from the study of a variety of avian species have demonstrated that social experience with conspecifics both before and after hatching can have a significant effect on young organisms' emerging perceptual discrimination and perceptual preferences (Gottlieb, 1971, 1997; Lickliter and Gottlieb, 1985; Miller, 1981, 1997; West and King, 1996). For example, prenatal or postnatal auditory stimulation from broodmates can affect subsequent visual responsiveness in avian hatchlings (McBride and Lickliter, 1994; Sleigh and Lickliter, 1996) and prenatal and postnatal tactile stimulation from broodmates can likewise affect chicks' emerging auditory and visual responsiveness (Gottlieb, 1993; Lickliter and Lewkowicz, 1995). Such findings punctuate a key component of Kuo's view of the developmental analysis of behavior, namely that investigators cannot assume that they need only to manipulate the most obvious forms of context or experience to identify causal variables associated with specific behavior development. Kuo repeatedly emphasized that seemingly subtle features of experience can often have a significant effect on the emergence and subsequent organization of behavior.

The study of perception and attention provides rich examples of the variety and complexity of the parameters involved in the development of behavior and the ways in which environmental and organismic factors need to be viewed within a dynamic, interactive framework (Lickliter and Bahrick, 2000; Ruff and Rothbart, 1996). Recent results from the study of the development of perception have demonstrated that nonspecific sensory stimulation such as intensity and amount of stimulation can interact with specific organismic characteristics such as the state of arousal of the infant and the context of the infant to contribute to the infant's emerging capacity for perceptual differentiation and perceptual learning (Gardner and Karmel, 1995; Gottlieb, 1993; Lewkowicz and Turkewitz, 1981; Lickliter and Lewkowicz, 1995). For example, young infants have been shown to visually orient toward less intense sights or sounds when more aroused and to orient toward more intense sensory stimuli when less aroused. This arousal-modulated attention is seen both when infants are endogenously more aroused (such as before feeding) or less aroused (after feeding) as well as when they are exogenously more or less aroused due to the presence of increased or decreased amounts of concurrent sensory stimulation. Such evidence underscores what I consider to be Kuo's fundamental insight regarding the study of behavior, namely, that the organism does not come into the world with ready-made response systems; rather, these systems emerge and are maintained through the convergence of inner and outer conditions over the course of the organism's real-time activity and experience.

The application of the insight that development is fundamentally "activity-dependent" has only recently become more commonplace in psychological sciences. Many psychologists continue to assume that behavior is determined by more "primary" or "hard-wired" processes which occur at the genetic or neurological level. This type of linear, unidirectional, bottom-up view of the as an example of preprogrammed neural growth directing behavioral change, illustrates the scientific value of Kuo's insight that behavior is complex, variable, and takes place in a changing internal and external environment.

Kuo's Ecological Vision: The Need for a Theory of Environment

As highlighted by the above example, one of the challenges facing a contemporary developmental systems approach to behavior is to interpret the concept of the environment in such a way that it incorporates an appropriately dynamic view of the changing relations between the developing organism and its context over time. Empirical findings from developmental science have repeatedly highlighted that as an organism develops, its relation to the external world changes, such that its effective environment, the actual physical, biological, and social factors with which it interacts, also changes (Bronfenbrenner and Morris, 1998; Eppler, 1995; Johnston, 1985). Kuo realized this important insight early in his career and continued to argue the point that the specific and dynamic nature of the organism's developmental context and its role in behavior development cannot be known or specified in advance, it must be empirically discovered.

This empirical concern with the developmentally relevant features of an organism's physical, biological, and social context constitutes a major shift in research emphasis, in that the science of psychology has often reduced animals' habitats or contexts to "stimuli," thereby overlooking the importance of the detailed empirical examination of the complex places, events, and encounters within which behavioral development takes place. In contrast, Kuo repeatedly stressed the fundamental connectedness of the organism to its surroundings and argued for the importance of both the structure of the organism and the structure of its environment to the achievement of behavioral phenotypes. While few contemporary biologists or psychologists would argue against this view, many investigators continue to characterize the young organism's environment as essentially "supportive" or "disruptive" in nature and therefore less than equal partners with genetic factors involved in phenotypic development (e.g., Smith-Gill, 1983). Kuo provides an alternative perspective, one in which not only the genes but also the specific features of the organism's stimulative developmental context are seen to provide the necessary and sufficient resources for behavioral development. Kuo points out that "we must take quantitative measures of stimulative effects of every sensory modality, and make qualitative analyses of the interactions of the component parts of the environmental context or complex" (Kuo, 1970, p. 190).

In keeping with this insight, detailed studies from comparative and developmental psychology have demonstrated that investigators must often consider the developmental consequences of an organism's varied encounters with its environment that have no intuitive or straightforward relation to the behavior pattern under study. Experiential factors that are not necessarily apparent or obvious precursors to a particular behavior may nonetheless prove to be critical modality) versus multimodally (information presented redundantly to two or more sensory modalities). Findings from several different labs, working with different species and at different levels of analysis, indicate that infant attention is more likely to be focused on redundant, amodal stimulus properties such as synchrony, intensity, or rhythm under condition of redundant multimodal stimulation and more focused on modality-specific properties such as color or pitch under conditions of unimodal stimulation (Bahrick and Lickliter, 2000; Lewkowicz, 1992; Richards, 2000; Stein and Meredith, 1993). This type of convergent-operations approach, championed by Kuo in his last published article (Kuo, 1970), holds much promise for future investigations of the development of behavior (see Lickliter and Bahrick, 2000).

The Dynamic, Probabilistic Nature of Development

Kuo deeply appreciated the probabilistic nature of behavioral development, often pointing out that specific behavioral outcomes were not always predictable in any simple, linear way from their antecedents. As discussed above, he realized that inputs from external factors always combined with internal factors, and this put the organism under the stimulation of a very complicated and interwoven process of "dynamic energy exchange" of both intraorganismic and extraorganismic origin. At the time of the publication of his monograph (1967), Kuo viewed the complete analysis of this complex as "beyond the reach of our current studies."

In the ensuing decades, psychological sciences have made some headway in this challenge, with a number of investigators attempting to move away from simple, antecedent-consequence linkages and turning their attention to the discovery and mapping of dynamic, bidirectional relations between levels of organization in the organism-environment system (Fischer and Biddel, 1998; Gottlieb, 1991a, b; Magnusson, 1996; Thelen and Smith, 1994). These efforts have tended to focus on examining the underlying relations among internal and external processes that give rise to orderly patterns of variability *and* stability of behavior, themes prevalent across the various writings of Kuo. For example, Thelen and her colleagues have described the rich interplay between task and intrinsic motor states in the development of infants' reaching behavior (Corebetta and Thelen, 1996; Thelen, Corbetta, and Spencer, 1996). Body architecture, limb coordination, postural and motor experience, motivation, and the properties of the target itself were all found to be involved in the emergence and refinement of reaching. No one part of the system was found to be causally privileged; rather, reaching was found to emerge from the coaction of multiple components over the real-time dynamics of the specific task and goal and the developmental dynamics of the infant's history of moving and reaching (see Thelen and Smith, 1994, 1998 for detailed discussion). This dynamic characterization of the development of infant motor behavior, a phenomenon historically touted and denied the organism over its ontogeny, continues to push the frontiers of theory and research in developmental biology and psychology. Kuo was a developmentalist ahead of his time, demonstrated in part by the harsh reviews of his critics during his lifetime and in part by the continuing application (even if unacknowledged) of his approach to behavior development some thirty years after his death. His unusual anti-authoritarian style and his keen integrative mind allowed him to forge an approach to behavior that appreciated its dynamic, reciprocally determined, and activity-dependent nature during a time when S-R psychology still dominated our field. His writings provided an outline for what the next step in the study of behavior might look like, repeatedly highlighting that the relation between the organism and its environment, rather than the nature of the organism itself, is the appropriate object of study of psychology.

Kuo called attention to the fact that all animals' functional environments are structured, organized, and specific to the organism, and he emphasized that defining the developmentally relevant features of an organism's context was an empirical problem, requiring systematic description and analysis from "coordinated efforts" across levels and domains. These examples make Kuo's own words again sound prophetic: "it [the book, *Dynamics of Behavior Development*] proposes a new prospectus to reorient the study of behavior in the future." To the extent that more dynamic, non-linear, and probabilistic theories of behavior are replacing more predeterministic, bottom-up, or finalistic frameworks in the pages of our journals and texts, Kuo's contribution to psychological sciences can be said to continue to pay dividends in our ongoing quest to better understand and explain behavior and its development.

Notes

1. Previously published in *From Past to Future, Vol. 2(2), From instinct to epigenesis: Lessons from Zing-Yang Kuo* (pp. 39-51). © 2000 Frances L. Hiatt School of Psychology, Clark University. Author: Robert Lickliter, Department of Psychology, Florida International University, Boca Raton, FL.
2. The writing of this article was supported by grant KO2-MH01210 from the National Institute of Mental Health. I thank Jaan Valsiner for his constructive comments on the manuscript.

References

Bahrick, L. E., and Lickliter, R. (2000). Intersensory redundancy guides attentional selectivity and perceptual learning in infancy. *Developmental Psychology, 36*, 190-201.

Bronfenbrenner, U. and Morris, P. A. (1998). The ecology of developmental processes. In: R. Lerner (Ed.), *Handbook of Child Psychology, Vol. 1: Theoretical Models of Human Development* (pp. 993-1028). New York, NY: John Wiley.

Casey, M. B., and Lickliter, R. (1998). Prenatal visual experience influences the development of turning bias in bobwhite quail chicks. *Developmental Psychobiology, 32*, 327-338.

Corbetta, D., and Thelen, E. (1996). The developmental origins of bimanual coordination: A dynamic perspective. *Journal of Experimental Psychology: Human Perception and Performance, 22*, 502-522.

Edelman, G. (1989). *The remembered present: A biological theory of consciousness.* New York: Basic Books.

Eibl-Eibesfeldt, I. (1989). *Human ethology.* New York: Adine de Gruyter.

Eppler, M. A. (1995). Development of manipulatory skills and the deployment of attention. *Infant Behavior and Development, 18,* 391-405.

Fischer, K. W., and Bidell, T. R. (1998). Dynamic development of psychological structures in action and thought. In R. Lerner (Ed.), *Handbook of child psychology, Vol. 1: Theoretical models of Human Development* (pp. 467-561). New York, NY: John Wiley.

Ford, D. H., and Lerner, R. M. (1992). *Developmental systems theory: An integrative approach.* Newbury Park, CA: Sage Publications.

Gagnon, R. (1995). Developmental aspects of alterations in fetal behavioral states. In J. P. Lecanuet, W. P. Fifer, N. A. Krasnegor, and W. P. Smotherman (Eds.), *Fetal development: A psychobiological perspective* (pp. 129-148). Hillsdale, NJ: Erlbaum.

Gardner, J. and Karmel, B. (1995). Development of arousal-modulated visual preferences in early infancy. *Developmental Psychology, 31,* 473-482.

Gibson, J.J. (1979). *The ecological approach to visual perception.* Boston, MA: Houghton-Mifflin.

Gottlieb, G. (1971). *Development of species identification in birds.* Chicago, IL: University of Chicago.

Gottlieb, G. (1976). Conceptions of prenatal development: Behavioral embryology. *Psychological Review, 83,* 215-234.

Gottlieb, G. (1991a). Experiential canalization of behavioral development: Theory. *Developmental Psychology, 27,* 4-13.

Gottlieb, G. (1991b). Experiential canalization of behavioral development: Results. *Developmental Psychology, 27,* 13-16.

Gottlieb, G. (1992). *Individual development and evolution.* New York, NY: Oxford University Press.

Gottlieb, G. (1993). Social induction of malleability in ducklings: Sensory basis and psychological mechanism. *Animal Behaviour, 45,* 707-719.

Gottlieb, G. (1996). A systems view of psychobiological development. In D. Magnusson (Ed.), *The lifespan development of individuals* (pp. 76-103). New York, NY: Cambridge University Press.

Gottlieb, G. (1997). *Synthesizing nature-nurture: Prenatal origins of instinctive behavior.* Mahwah, NJ: Erlbaum.

Gottlieb, G., Wahlsten, D., and Lickliter, R. (1998). The significance of biology for human development: A developmental psychobiological systems view. In R. Lerner (Ed.), *Handbook of child psychology, Vol. 1: Theoretical models of human development* (pp. 233-273). New York, NY: John Wiley.

Hansen, E. W. (1969). Behavior as a continuous process. *Science, 160,* 58-59.

Hogan, J. A. (1978). An eccentric view of development. *Contemporary Psychology, 23,* 690-691.

James, D., Pillai, M. and Smoleniec, J. (1995). Neurobehavioral development in the human fetus. In J. P. Lecanuet, W. P. Fifer, N. A. Krasnegor, and W. P. Smotherman (Eds.), *Fetal development: A psychobiological perspective* (pp. 101-128). Hillsdale, NJ: Erlbaum.

Johnston, T. D. (1985). Environmental constraints and the natural context of behavior: Grounds for an ecological approach to the study of infant perception. In: G. Gottlieb and N. A. Krasnegor (Eds.), *Measurement of audition and vision in the first year of postnatal life* (pp. 91-108). Norwood, NJ: Ablex Publishing.

Kuo, Z.-Y. (1921). Giving up instincts in psychology. *Journal of Philosophy, 18,* 645-664.

Kuo, Z.-Y. (1967). *The dynamics of behavior development: An epigenetic view.* New York, NY: Random House.

Kuo, Z.-Y. (1970). The need for coordinated efforts in developmental studies. In Aronson, L. R., Tobach, E., Lehrman, D. S., and Rosenblatt, J.S. (Eds.), *Development and evolution of behavior* (pp. 181-193). San Francisco, CA: W. Freeman.

Lecaneut, J.-P., Fifer, W. P., Krasnegor, N. A., and Smotherman, W. P. (1995). *Fetal development: A psychobiological perspective.* Hillsdale, NJ: Erlbaum.

Lerner, R. M. (1998). Theories of human development: Contemporary perspectives. In R. Lerner (Ed.), *Handbook of child psychology, vol. 1: Theoretical models of Human Development* (pp. 1-24). New York: John Wiley.

Lewkowicz, D. J. (1992). Responsiveness to auditory and visual components of a sounding/moving compound stimulus in human infants. *Perception and Psychophysics, 52,* 519-528.

Lewkowicz, D.J., and Turkewitz, G. (1981). Intersensory interaction in newborns: Modification of visual preferences following exposure to sound. *Child Development, 52,* 827-832.

Lickliter, R. (2006). Developmental systems and psychological science. In B. D. Midgley and E.K. Morris (Eds.), *Modern perspectives on J.R. Kantor and interbehaviorism.* Reno, NV: Context Press.

Lickliter, R. and Bahrick, L. E. (2000). The development of infant intersensory perception: The value of comparative, convergent operations approach. *Psychological Bulletin, 126,* 260-280.

Lickliter, R., and Banker, H. (1994). Prenatal components of intersensory development in precocial birds. In D. J. Lewkowicz and R. Lickliter (Eds.), *The development of intersensory perception: Comparative perspectives* (pp. 59-80). Hillsdale, NJ: Erlbaum.

Lickliter, R., and Berry, T. D. (1990). The phylogeny fallacy: Developmental psychology's misapplication of evolutionary theory. *Developmental Review, 10,* 322-338.

Lickliter, R., and Gottlieb, G. (1985). Social interaction with siblings is necessary for the visual imprinting of species-specific maternal preference in ducklings. *Journal of Comparative Psychology, 99,* 371-378.

Lickliter, R., and Lewkowicz, D. J. (1995). Intersensory experience and early perceptual development: Attenuated prenatal sensory stimulation affects postnatal auditory and visual responsiveness in bobwhite quail chicks. *Developmental Psychology, 31,* 609-618.

Magnusson, D. (1996). *The lifespan development of individuals: Behavioral, neurobiological, and psychosocial perspectives.* New York, NY: Cambridge University Press.

Mayr, E. (1974). Behavior programs and evolutionary strategies. *American Scientist, 63,* 650-659.

McBride, T., and Lickliter, R. (1994). Specific postnatal auditory stimulation interferes with species-typical visual responsiveness in bobwhite quail chicks. *Developmental Psychobiology, 27,* 169-183.

Michel, G.F., and Moore, C.L. (1995*). Developmental psychobiology: An interdisciplinary science.* Cambridge, MA: MIT Press.

Miller, D.B. (1981). Conceptual strategies in behavioral development: Normal development and plasticity. In K. Immelmann, G. Barlow, L. Petrinovich, and M. Main (Eds.), *Behavioral development* (pp. 58-82). New York: Cambridge University Press.

Miller, D.B. (1997). The effects of nonobvious forms of experience on the development of instinctive behavior. In C. Dent-Reed and P. Zukow-Goldring (Eds.), *Evolving explanations of development* (pp. 457-507). Washington, DC: American Psychological Association.

Nijhuis, J. G., Martin, C. B., and Prechtl, H. F. R. (1984). Behavioral states of the human fetus. In H. F. R. Prechtl (Ed.), *Continuity of neural functions from prenatal to postnatal life.* (Clinics in developmental medicine, 94) Oxford: Blackwell.

Oyama, S. (1985). *The ontogeny of information: Developmental systems and evolution.* New York: Cambridge University Press.

Oyama, S. (1993). Constraints and development. *Netherlands Journal of Zoology, 43,* 6-16.

Previc, F. H. (1991). A general theory concerning the prenatal origins of cerebral lateralization in humans. *Psychological Review, 98,* 299-334.

Reed, E. S. (1996). *Encountering the world: Towards an ecological psychology.* New York, NY: Oxford University Press.

Richards, J. E. (2000). Development of multimodal attention in young infants: Modification of the startle reflex by attention. *Psychophysiology, 37,* 1-11.

Robertson, S. S., and Bacher, L. F. (1995). Oscillation and chaos in fetal motor activity. In J. P. Lecanuet, W. P. Fifer, N.A. Krasnegor, and W. P. Smotherman (Eds.), *Fetal development: A psychobiological perspective* (pp. 168-189). Hillsdale, NJ: Erlbaum.

Robinson, S. R., and Smotherman, W. P. (1992). The emergence of behavioral regulation during fetal development. *Annals of the New York Academy of Science, 662,* 53-83.

Rogers, L. J. (1982). Light experience and asymmetry of brain function in chickens. *Nature, 297,* 223-225.

Rogers, L. J. (1986). Lateralization of learning in chicks. *Advances in the Study of Behavior, 16,* 147-189.

Ruff, H. A., and Rothbart, M. K. (1996). *Attention in early development: Themes and variations.* New York: Oxford University Press.

Senchuk, D. M. (1991). *Against instinct: From biology to philosophical psychology.* Philadelphia, PA: Temple University Press.

Sleigh, M. J., and Lickliter, R. (1996). Type and amount of prenatal stimulation alters perceptual responsiveness in bobwhite quail chicks. *Infant Behavior and Development, 19,* 325-338.

Smith-Gill, S. J. (1983). Developmental plasticity: Developmental conversion vs. phenotypic modulation. *American Zoologist, 23,* 47-55.

Smotherman, W. P., and Robinson, S. R. (1988). The uterus as environment: The ecology of fetal behavior. In E. M. Blass (Ed.), *Handbook of behavioral neurobiology,* (Vol. 9., pp. 149-196). New York: Plenum.

Smotherman, W. P., and Robinson, S. R. (1990). The prenatal origins of behavioral organization. *Psychological Science, 1,* 97-106.

Smotherman, W. P., and Robinson, S. R. (1995). Tracing developmental trajectories into the prenatal period. In J. P. Lecanuet, W. P. Fifer, N. A. Krasnegor, and W. P. Smotherman (Eds.), *Fetal development: A psychobiological perspective* (pp. 15-32). Hillsdale, NJ: Erlbaum

Stein, B. E., and Meredith, M. A. (1993). *The merging of the senses.* Cambridge, MA: MIT Press.

Thelen, E. (1995). Motor development. *American Psychologist, 50,* 79-95.

Thelen, E., Corbetta, D., and Spencer, J. P. (1996). The development of reaching during the first year: The role of movement speed. *Journal of Experimental Psychology: Human Perception and Performance, 22,* 1059-1076.

Thelen, E. and Smith, L. B. (1994). *A dynamic systems approach to the development of cognition and action.* Cambridge, MA: MIT Press.

Thelen, E., and Smith, L. B. (1998). Dynamic systems theories. In: R. Lerner (Ed.), *Handbook of Child Psychology, Vol. 1: Theoretical Models of Human Development* (pp. 563-634). New York, NY: John Wiley.

Varela, F. J., Thompson, E., and Rosch, E. (1991). *The embodied mind.* Cambridge, MA: MIT Press.

West, M. J., and King, A. P (1996). Eco-gen-actics: A systems approach to the ontogeny of avian communication. In D. Kroodsma and E. H. Miller (Eds.), *The evolution and ecology of acoustic communication in birds* (pp. 20-38). Ithaca, NY: Cornell University Press.

Zappia, J. V., and Rogers, L. J. (1983). Light experience during development affects asymmetry of forebrain function in chickens. *Developmental Brain Research, 11*, 93-106.

Index

Abstractive generalization (Bühler), 86-87
Activity contexts, 187-188, 190
Anger, 215-219
Anthropology, 163-165 (see also Boas, Franz), 180-182

Bartlett, Frederick, 187
Berlin, 213-215
Boaz, Franz, 165-168, 181, 203,
Bühler, Charlotte, 78-79
Bühler, Karl, 69-95, his speech theory, 81-82, 97-98, 101-103, 107-114, 116-119
Buytendijk, F. J. J., 220-224

Case study, 185,
Cerebral palsy, 245-248
Chamberlain, Alexander F. 163-178, 179-209
China, 301
Child study, 168-172, 182-183, 185-186
Clark University: intellectual climate, 97-100, 228-229, 235, 243-245, 283-284
Coghill, George, 144-149
Cognitive: activity, 49-52 revolution, 4-6
cognitive linguistics, 116-120
Communication, 88-89, 120
Crisis in psychology, 79-81
Csikszentmihalyi, Mihaly, 53
Cultural psychology, 204

Darstellungsfeld (representational field, Bühler), 89
Dembo, Tamara, 213-233
Development, 141-144, 154-159, 321-322
Devil, 195

Disability, 268-272
Distancing, 97, 107-114
Drawings, 196-198
Duncker, Karl, 3-16, 17-38, 41-42, 59-66
Dyad (as unit of analysis), 274-277

Education, 191-192
Embryology, 144-151
Environment, 322-325
Epigenesis, 288-289, 315-317
Ethical relativity, 46-48
Evolution 294

Fear, 173
Freud, Sigmund, xiii
Gesell, Arnold, 135-162
Gestalt, 8, 19
Gottlieb, Gilbert, 142, 300-306, 318-320

Hall, G. Stanley, 137, 165, 168, 179-180, 182-183, 194, 201-202
History: of science, xi-xii, of German psychology 9-13, 19-26
Hunter, Walter S., 32

Information processing, 6-8
Invention by child, 188-190, 194-195
Jealousy, 138-141

Koffka, Kurt, 73
Kootenay, 196-198
Köhler, Wolfgang, 21-22, 29-31
Külpe, Oswald, 72-76
Kuo, Zing-Yang, 299-311

Language, 193-195
Lewin, Kurt, 214-216, 236-240, 267
Maturation, 149-150
Meaning, 187

Men (and women), 195
Methodology, 253-256, 286-287, 292-293
Meyer, Adolf, 283-298
Modesty, 174-176
McGraw, Myrtle, 149-159
Microdevelopment, 59
Murchison, Carl, 32

Organon model, 69, 74, 80, 84-85

Paedology, 182
Phylogeny, 290-292
Play, 172-173
Poetry, 193
Prague Linguistic Circle, 70
Problem solving, 6, 10-12, 33-34, 39-57, 59-66
Process vs. outcome, 75
Productive thinking, 42-46

Rats, 283-285, 289-290, 292-294
Rehabilitation psychology, 243-244
Russia, 213-214

Selz, Otto, 7, 12-15, 42-46

Sematology, 69
Sigel, Irving, 101-106
Situation: and person, 52-53, 190
Socialization, 125-128
Socio-emotional relationships, 266, 272-274, 277-279
Speech, 186-187
Structure (and process), 256-258
Stumpf, Carl, 20-21,
Subject (participant), 250-253
Symbolic development, 121-124

Thought: flexibility and non-flexibility, 5
Tobacco, 199-200
Tools, cultural, 192-193
Topology, 218

Van Waters, Miriam, 200-202
Vienna: intellectual climate, 77, 82-83, psychology in, 78-79
Vygotsky, Lev, 70-71

Werner, Heinz 60, 106-107, 122
Wundt, Wilhelm, 72
Würzburg School, 71-76, 87